International Arms Control

The Stanford Arms Control Group

John H. Barton, Law

✓ Richard Brody, Political Science

✓ Gordon A. Craig, History

✓ Alexander Dallin, History

Sidney D. Drell, Stanford Linear Accelerator Center

Donald Dunn, Engineering- Economic Systems

Thomas Ehrlich, Law

✓ Alexander L. George, Political Science

Joshua Lederberg, Genetics

John W. Lewis, Political Science

∨ Robert C. North, Political Science

Wolfgang Panofsky, Stanford Linear Accelerator Center

Peter Paret, History

Henry Rowen, Graduate School of Business

✓ Jan Triska, Political Science

✓ Lawrence D. Weiler, Political Science

Franklin B. Weinstein, Political Science

Invited Participants in the Review Conference at Stanford, August 1974

Anne Cahn, Center for International Studies, Massachusetts Institute of Technology

Steven Canby, The Rand Corporation

Albert Carnesale, North Carolina State University

Harold Feiveson, Woodrow Wilson School, Princeton University

Leslie Fishbone, University of Utah

Ralph Goldman, San Francisco State University

James Gustin, University of Wisconsin at Milwaukee

Roman Kolkowicz, University of California at Los Angeles

Joseph Kruzel, Harvard University

George Quester, Cornell University

Eric Stein, University of Michigan

Samuel Williamson, University of North Carolina

International Arms Control

ISSUES AND AGREEMENTS

By the Stanford Arms Control Group

Edited by John H. Barton and Lawrence D. Weiler

Stanford University Press, Stanford, California   1976

Stanford University Press
Stanford, California
© 1976 by the Board of Trustees of the
Leland Stanford Junior University
Printed in the United States of America
Cloth ISBN 0-8047-0921-1
Paper ISBN 0-8047-0934-3
LC 76-14270

Preface

THIS TEXT was written to fill a need perceived by the Stanford Arms Control Group, an interdisciplinary group of nearly twenty faculty who have been jointly teaching an undergraduate arms control course under John Lewis's leadership at Stanford University since about 1970. We have suggested readings for each chapter, some of which can be used along with the text in a one-quarter or a one-semester course. We also hope that the text will be useful to those who wish to include an arms control segment in courses such as international relations, diplomatic history, foreign policy, or national security policy. For example, Chapters 4, 6, 9, and 10 form a package on strategic doctrine, whereas Chapters 2, 3, 5, 12, and 14 would be useful in intensifying the treatment of arms control in a diplomatic history or international relations course.

This text is the result of a group effort. The first major draft, which I edited with the assistance of Steven Moloney, was based on lectures given by the entire Stanford Arms Control Group and by visitors including James Leonard. This draft was used in 1973 and 1974. Lawrence Weiler, drawing on his immense experience in arms control negotiations, prepared a second major draft in 1974, with the assistance of Constance Smith. This draft was reviewed and criticized by a group of arms control teachers and theorists at a conference held at Stanford in August 1974. All of them were extremely helpful and contributed substantially to the text.

Many specific credits are also deserved. Chapter 2 relies partly upon the work of Kurt Lauk. Chapter 3 is adapted in part from a paper prepared by Joseph Kruzel and an outline prepared by Samuel Williamson, both provided at the 1974 Stanford Conference, as well as from an article by Gordon Craig and Peter Paret, first appearing in the *Stanford Journal of International Studies*. Chapter 6 draws upon articles by

Joshua Lederberg, Herbert Scoville, Jr., and Jonathan Medalia in the same issue. Part of Chapter 8 relies upon a talk given by Ambassador James Leonard at Stanford in 1970. Though they were not directly drawn upon, papers prepared by Anne Cahn and Samuel Williamson were invaluable in the writing of Chapter 8. Part of Chapter 10 draws upon Bernard Feld's article in the *Stanford Journal of International Studies*. Ruth Sivard wrote an initial version of Chapter 11. Material contributed by Steven Canby was extremely helpful in preparing Chapters 12 and 13. Chapter 13 also draws heavily upon the report of the Arms Control and Disarmament Agency (ACDA) on arms transfer, and ideas from Ralph Goldman were important inputs to Chapter 15. Lawrence Weiler's contribution was particularly great and included many helpful detailed comments as well as the first draft of much of the material. This book is in many ways his book.

The task of integrating and editing the final draft fell to me. I have not hesitated to revise the individual contributions, and the final version reflects my biases. Responsibility for matters of emphasis, for opinions, and for factual errors is mine.

We would like to thank all those who participated in the review conference; Geraldine Bowman, who organized the conference and helped with the typing; and Louisa Clemens, Patricia Tusch, and Michele Kremen, who all helped with the typing. We would also like to thank the Stanford University Progress Fund and the Ford Foundation, which have supported the preparation of the text.

J.H.B. for the Stanford
Arms Control Group

Contents

1. Introduction   1

   Contemporary arms control and disarmament, 1. Why study arms
   control? 4. The approach of this text, 5.

2. Arms Control: Cultural Context and Motivations   9

   Ethics of war, 9. International law—the law of war, 15. International
   organization and law against war, 18. Motivations for arms control, 22.

3. Modern Disarmament Efforts Before World War II   31

   A special case—attempts to control the Anglo-German arms race
   before World War I, 34. The League and the interwar period, 37.
   Naval arms control in the interwar period, 40. Possible lessons, 44.

4. The Changing Nature of Strategic Weapons   46

   The nuclear weapon, 47. The effect of nuclear weapons, 48. Results of
   a large-scale nuclear attack, 51. Delivery systems, 54. Defensive
   systems, 58. The acquisition of the new weapons, 61. Implications, 65.

5. An Overview of the Negotiations Since World War II   66

   The initial failure to control nuclear weapons, 1945–46, 66. Toward
   comprehensive negotiations, 1947–54, 72. Comprehensive negotiations:
   near-miss, 1955–57, 74. The rise of collateral agreements, 1953–62,
   and decline of comprehensive negotiations, 1957–63, 81. The proliferation of agreements, 1963–74, and of forums, 1969–74, 86.
   Conclusion, 92.

6. Agreements and Treaties Other than SALT and the NPT   94

   Crisis communication agreements, 94. The regime-oriented treaties, 96.
   The limited nuclear test ban treaties, 101. Biological and chemical
   warfare convention, 116.

- 7. Strategic Doctrine   123

Collective security and containment, 123. Massive retaliation, 124.
Nuclear deterrence, 126. Critiques of deterrence: political and ethical,
129. Effects of new weapons developments on deterrence: ABMs, 132.
Effects of new weapons developments on deterrence: MIRVs, 136.
Deterrence versus damage limitation and flexible targeting, 141.
China's strategic doctrines, 144.

- 8. The Institutions of Arms Control   151

Bureaucratic influences on negotiating positions, 152. Congress and
the public, 157. International negotiation, 161. Verification, 163.
Conclusion, 171.

- 9. The Negotiation of SALT I   172

SALT I negotiations, 1969–72, 179. The SALT I agreements, 197.
ABM treaty, 198. Interim offensive agreement and protocol, 200.
Significance of the SALT I agreements, 202.

10. SALT, 1972–1975   208

Ratification of SALT I—The Jackson amendment, 208. The issues for
SALT II, 210. SALT II—The Nixon phase, 216. SALT II—The Ford
phase and Vladivostok, 219. The future of SALT, 223. Conclusion—
The SALT process, 225.

11. The Economics of Arms and Arms Control   228

Dimensions of arms procurement, 229. Domestic economic processes,
237. Economic consequences of military spending, 240. The international arms economy, 242. Economic consequences of arms control, 243.
Budget limitations as arms control measures, 247.

12. Regional Arms Control: The European Example   249

The European background, 250. Toward negotiations: West European
unification, détente, and *Ostpolitik*, 260. Conference on Security and
Cooperation in Europe, 262. Mutual Force Reduction, 264.
Conclusion, 269.

- 13. Control of Conventional Arms   271

Conventional arms in the 1970's, 271. The effects of the growth and
spread of conventional arms, 279. Limitations on conventional
forces, 281. Conclusion, 286.

14. Control of Nuclear Proliferation   288

The agreements of the 1960's, 292. Nuclear proliferation and its
control after the Non-Proliferation Treaty, 301.

· 15. Toward an Evaluation of Arms Control:
  Unanswered Questions   310

  Can negotiable arms control help prevent war? 311. Arms control in
  its political context—the U.S.-U.S.S.R. case, 315. Arms control and
  change in the international order, 318.

Appendixes   323

  A. Glossary of abbreviations   323
  B. The Disarmament Forums, 1945–1975   325
  C. Texts of Major Arms Control Agreements   329

Discussion Questions   419

Suggested Further Readings   425

Index   435

International Arms Control

CHAPTER ONE

Introduction

THE ASPIRATIONS of man to turn his talents and resources from the accumulation of arms to more productive endeavors are ancient as well as modern. The words of Isaiah come from the eighth century B.C.: "And they shall beat their swords into plowshares, and their spears into pruning hooks; nation shall not lift up sword against nation, neither shall they learn war anymore." In 546 B.C., a fourteen-state conference on the cessation of armaments was held in Honan, China, and closed a seventy-year period of wars. Similar aspirations and efforts are reflected in the literature of nearly every civilization.

But although hopes of limiting armies and armament have been a continuous thread in the fabric of political thought, the failure and sporadic nature of most actual efforts to limit arms have often created a sense of disillusionment. Governments and their publics alike have often come to regard the aspirations of the philosophers, religious leaders, and some statesmen as rhetorical, or at best desirable but unrealistic goals. Fear, suspicion, and the memory of bitter experiences with adversaries bent on the use of arms have instead prevailed. The accumulation and the use of arms, rather than their limitation or reduction, have been the dominant theme of history.

Contemporary Arms Control and Disarmament

On July 16, 1945, the first nuclear bomb was secretly tested in a barren spot at Alamogordo, New Mexico. The secrecy was lifted less than a month later when the first nuclear weapon used in war was dropped on Hiroshima, Japan. Three days later, the second—and so far the last— nuclear weapon used in war fell on Nagasaki.

That the world had changed and that the consequences of success or failure of the ancient aspirations had taken on a new meaning were not lost on statesmen. When Bernard Baruch, representing the United States, addressed the newly created United Nations Atomic Energy Commission on June 14, 1946, he began with the following words: "We are here to make a choice between the quick and the dead. That is our business. Behind the black portent of the new atomic age lies a hope which, seized upon with faith, can work our salvation. If we fail, then we have damned every man to be the slave of Fear."

Success was not achieved in the initial efforts to control the new force born to man at Alamogordo, and seven years later, U.S. Secretary of State John Foster Dulles reiterated Baruch's concern in a speech to the U.N. General Assembly: "Physical scientists have now found means which, if they are developed, can wipe life off the surface of this planet. These words that I speak are words that can be taken literally." From this he concluded that the

. . . destructive power inherent in matter must be controlled by the idealism of the spirit and the wisdom of the mind. They alone stand between us and a lifeless planet. There are plenty of problems in the world, many of them interconnected. But there is no problem which compares with this central, universal problem of saving the human race from extinction.

The initial years of the nuclear age, however, were also the years of the cold war, with the tensions, fears, suspicions, and antagonisms that resulted from worldwide confrontation between the Communist forces, led by the Union of Soviet Socialist Republics, and the Western forces, led by the United States. In this climate, efforts to control arms foundered, while modern science created a continuing revolution in the nature of weapons. Nuclear weapons were succeeded by thermonuclear weapons, aircraft were succeeded by intercontinental missiles, and the electronics industry offered a staggering array of new materiel.

In a sense man became, as Baruch predicted, the captive of fear, and that fear was one of the catalysts of the ensuing arms construction. Over the years general publics, if not governments, often tended to push the threats of the nuclear age into the back of their minds as too oppressive to live with or too complicated to influence. But, in addition, men and nations also sought ways to live with and rationalize nuclear weapons. Elaborate, sometimes arcane, theories of strategic and tactical nuclear warfare were developed, discarded, or refined. The cold war itself was affected by increasing awareness of the likely consequences of nuclear war and of the dangers of great-power confrontation in a nuclear world. The increasing sense of shared fate and responsibility for survival produced, particularly between the superpowers, a continuing effort to find more rational and secure paths to security. Soviet leaders, after some pulling and hauling in the mid-1950's, officially changed the Leninist doctrine of the inevitability of war between Communism and capitalism, declaring it to have become outmoded as the result of modern technology. From President Eisenhower's time through the present, American presidents expressed the view that, at least among the major powers, there was no alternative to peace. On both sides, there began to appear over the years official expressions of the view that increasing expenditures on arms had brought decreasing security to both sides, that increased security and prevention of nuclear war required cooperative rather than competitive efforts.

Against this background, the United States and the Soviet Union—often supported or pressured by other nations—reached a series of arms control[1] agreements. These started in the late 1950's, although the first agreement of real significance was the Limited Test Ban Treaty of 1963 (restricting the testing of nuclear weapons), and continued through the Strategic Arms Limitation Talks (SALT) agreements of 1972 and 1974 (restricting U.S. and U.S.S.R. strategic weapons systems). Some, such as the SALT agreements, were bilateral—between just two nations; others, such as the Limited Test Ban Treaty, were multilateral—accepted by many nations. Some of the most important arrangements did not become formal treaties and were instead accepted by tacit mutual consent. Thus, for many years certain intelligence collection activities were tolerated without formal agreement because both sides recognized their value in preventing war.

The negotiation of this new body of arms control agreements has come to draw major attention from statesmen, who more and more view the arms control area as crucial. Thus, there is now reason to believe that the arms control effort will continue in the future.

But the successes of this effort are quite limited. Although complying with treaty obligations, the Americans and the Soviets both continued researching and building strategic nuclear weapons right through

---

[1] During the latter part of the post–World War II years, particularly in the Western world, the words "arms control" and "disarmament" acquired technical meanings. Though the two terms are used rather loosely in both official and private writings (including this text), it is helpful to clarify their technical meanings. "Disarmament" involves the reduction or the elimination of armaments or armed forces. "Arms control" or "arms limitation" involves limitations on the number or types of armaments or armed forces, on their deployment or disposition, or on the use of particular types of armaments; "arms control" also encompasses measures designed to reduce the danger of accidental war or to reduce concern about surprise attack. Although the terms are generally thought of in connection with internationally agreed undertakings, they can also be applied to unilateral actions of states. Postwar negotiations have involved efforts at both arms control and disarmament, but most agreements actually achieved have technically been measures of arms control.

the SALT negotiations, and the 1974 Vladivostok accord on strategic arms was a disappointment to most observers. While these two nations were negotiating about their own strategic arms, China and France were expanding their nuclear forces and India exploded its first nuclear device. Outside the nuclear field, the world was seeing one of history's largest proliferations of conventional arms. In dollar value, the United States—and it was not the only supplier—sold about as many weapons to foreign nations in the 1973–74 period as it had in the preceding decades since World War II. The world's annual military budget was still more than $200 billion in 1974—more than the amount spent on education. And the chances that terrorist groups might obtain access to nuclear or chemical weapons appeared to be increasing each year.

Why Study Arms Control?

The preceding discussion presents the strongest possible argument for studying arms control. In the quarter-century following World War II, the impact of armaments on international politics changed radically. The old ideal of arms control rose up with surprisingly great political force, perhaps in response to, but perhaps also as part of, a broader political context. The phenomenon deserves the attention of anyone who would understand today's international world.

Study of arms control can illuminate other areas as well. Contemporary arms control may have evolved in response to an international danger, but it also evolved in response to technology, and in particular political cultures. It was shaped by bureaucratic forces within governments and by the success and failure of international institutions. Hence anyone who wants to understand technology or political culture or political institutions will find arms control a useful case study. Perhaps most of all, arms control is an example of the intersection of scientific, political, and human interests. There are many other such examples— energy policy, the environment, world food supply—but an important part of anyone's education is to learn the way different perspectives intersect when brought to bear on a single real problem.

Finally, arms control is important to the citizen, and the citizen is important to it. Arms control sometimes appears complex and technical, so that the public, except when touched by specific concerns, tends to "leave it to the experts." Yet it is doubtful that there are any real experts. The key ideas—which are remarkably simple—were developed by arms control amateurs who happened also to be professional scientists, soldiers, diplomats, or politicians. These "experts" have not succeeded: the national and international systems are clearly not yet adapted to the new weapons. Often, the role of common sense is more important than the role of expertise. Thus, citizens should not hesitate to act upon well-thought-out opinions. It has also become increasingly evident that the basic arms control and disarmament decisions are political decisions and that politicians will be unable to move much further toward arms control without the support and pressure of public opinion. Intelligent "common sense" opinions, whether supporting or opposing arms control, could, in the aggregate, have as much effect on future policy as do the day-to-day debates of "experts."

The Approach of This Text

This text attempts to help the reader obtain a balanced understanding of the recent phenomenon of arms control. This phenomenon and the armaments phenomenon to which it is responding are much more complex than any single explanation. At least five kinds of explanation are often needed.

Personal Attitudes and Bias

Arms control is an emotional subject. A person's attitudes toward arms and arms control are likely to depend on his general attitudes toward those who may threaten him. One person may be biased to respond with a counterthreat, another to attempt to accommodate and understand. Thus, the most common, but only partly accurate, statement made about arms control is that it depends on mutual understanding.

Attitudes also depend upon judgments about whether the world can best meet its problems by minor change or by radical reform—judgments that are likely to depend as heavily on the person's mental set as on the state of the world system. The sense of responsibility for having drastically changed the world, for example, has led many of the scientists who developed nuclear weapons to become leading supporters of arms control, in both the United States and the Soviet Union.

International Politics

International politics is central to arms control. It is to knowledge of international politics that one might look for answers to classic dilemmas such as: do arms cause war, or do wars cause arms? At so general a level, such questions are usually unanswerable—the answer is typically sometimes one and sometimes the other. Thus, immediately after World War I statesmen thought the cause of that war was in major part an arms race, and gave relatively serious attention to disarmament. Statesmen after World War II thought the cause of that war was in major part the military weakness of the nations allied against Germany. Immediately after the war they gave little serious attention to disarmament except for the nuclear area, which seemed to be a special case.

For most contemporary arms control agreements, the general questions need not be answered. The issues are typically posed only for a specific weapon in a specific context, i.e. would particular ballistic missile defense deployments by the United States and the Soviet Union make war more or less likely? On such specific questions, experts in international politics are often in relatively strong agreement.

International politics also interacts with arms and arms control in many other ways. For example, the U.S. opening to China may have helped influence the Soviet Union to accept the SALT agreements. And as an example of a possible reverse effect, some argue that the SALT agreements may have encouraged certain other nations to develop or expand their nuclear capabilities.

Domestic and Bureaucratic Politics

Discussions of international politics often assume that each nation is a single rational actor pursuing its own national interest. That assumption that would make it impossible to obtain Congressional support ways false: nations' actions are the outcome of internal politics. Thus, some have said that the United States and the Soviet Union arms and arms control decisions are controlled by military-industrial complexes; others fear that arms control would produce a popular attitude of relaxation that would make it impossible to obtain Congressional support for even the weapons programs they view as essential.

Whether or not one accepts positions such as these, it is clear that the internal forces do affect arms control. Some of the internal forces depend on electoral politics—President Nixon probably wanted to time the SALT I agreements in a way that would help his 1972 political campaign. Other forces are economic—many nations have accepted the idea of paying for oil imports by providing large quantities of arms in return. Still others are internal to the government—at the time of the mid-1974 Summit, the Secretary of State and the Secretary of Defense apparently disagreed on the desirability of particular arms control arrangements, and the President was in too weak a political position to resolve the conflict.

Culture, Ideology, and Doctrine

Each of the actors operates within a particular intellectual perspective. Examples include the traditional English concept of supporting a balance of power on the European continent and the more contemporary concept of defending Western Europe by making it appear likely that a major Soviet attack would lead to nuclear war. Different nations and different groups within a nation have different perspectives. It would be a grievous error to assume that the Soviet view of the military role of strategic nuclear weapons is the same as the U.S. view.

The importance of these cultures and doctrines is impossible to overestimate. They are used in deciding which forces to procure and which forces can be given up. They become frameworks for evaluating political developments. They have their own internal logic and they often last much longer than the factual situation for which they were designed. Many of those who design defenses for Europe use concepts that derive from World War II and are probably irrelevant today. Practically every war has produced surprises in the form of unanticipated tactics.

It is usually relatively easy to evaluate a particular weapon or a particular arms control agreement against a well-understood doctrine or theory. What is much more difficult and much more controversial is determining whether that doctrine or theory sets forth accurately the likelihood or character of the conflict the situation risks, or the events tending to set off the conflict.

Technology

Technology has created the weapons that are the subject of contemporary arms control. Beyond that obvious point, its role is controversial. Some argue that, at least between the United States and the Soviet Union, there is an arms race in the sense that each nation feels threatened by the other's military developments and conducts its own research and development programs in response to the other. Others argue that the technology of each side is developing according to its own dynamic, so that technology is the real driver of arms development. Again, it may be impossible or unnecessary to choose between the two viewpoints. Technology does change and does continuously influence what decision-makers can do and what they believe they should do.

Even this influence is not as direct as commonly believed. Arms control decisions do sometimes depend on technological issues—e.g. can Soviet testing of a high-accuracy strategic missile be detected by intelligence systems? But the way a scientist or engineer will answer such a question often depends on his personal biases. Moreover, the definition of the problem usually has doctrinal components—in the example, one has to decide what sort of test program the Soviets would require. What risk would they choose to run of deploying an insufficiently tested system? The question calls for a reevaluation of both the Soviet weapons development process and Soviet doctrine. Obviously, such an inquiry confronts massive uncertainties. There are some arms control issues appropriate to hard scientific evaluation, but they are fewer than commonly believed.

this is a Q.
research

Factors at all five of these levels have combined to make arms control possible during the 1960's and 1970's. The factors operating at each level have changed, and will continue to change during the coming decades. The arms control agreements could thus have happened only at certain times in history.

This text attempts to show how factors at the five levels affected the development of arms control. Certain of the explanation levels will be discussed systematically in separate chapters. The example of SALT, which is heavily emphasized in this text, will be presented in enough detail to permit an integration and test of the judgments that the reader has developed at that point. Finally, unresolved arms control issues will be discussed. The authors hope that the reader will be able to apply what he or she has learned to form intelligent opinions on these new issues as they arise in a changing world.

CHAPTER TWO

Arms Control: Cultural Context and Motivations

Arms control is often said to have three goals: (1) to make war less likely, (2) to make war less destructive if it does occur, and (3) to reduce the economic cost of armaments. These are not, however, the only reasons nations have entered arms control agreements.

Moreover, arms control is not the only approach that has evolved to help achieve these goals. Other approaches, such as ethics, international law, and international organization, often influence arms control and share political support with it. Since these three approaches form the cultural context from which arms control emerged, they deserve brief discussion before the contemporary motivations for arms control are considered.

Different approaches appeal to different constituencies. For some of the U.S. public, international law, the United Nations, and arms control are all lumped together as "good things" or as dangerously idealistic. Some people will draw distinctions; many, for example, support most arms control proposals but doubt the value of the United Nations. Similarly, a specific arms control proposal may be rejected by some who believe that it would not actually limit war or be supported by others for reasons having little to do with war. Thus, much support for the 1963 Limited Test Ban Treaty was based less on the treaty's expected effect on war than on its effect in protecting the environment by limiting nuclear fallout. Others criticized the same agreement because it probably had very little effect on nuclear testing (which moved underground), but may have absorbed the political support that might have led to a more far-reaching nuclear test ban.

Ethics of War

Practically everyone who has examined the conditions of war has been shocked by the suffering and tragedy it causes and by its frequent irrationality. A few seize upon this irrationality itself as explaining war. To support this judgment, they need only point to the occasional leader who seems to have undertaken deliberate aggression and the the popular support that such a leader seems often to obtain. Thus, man may be biologically and innately aggressive. If so, for these thinkers the task is either to change man genetically or to find harmless ways in which man can discharge his aggressiveness. If men differ in innate aggressiveness, they might be screened psychologically before being allowed to hold public office. If the aggressiveness is learned, men might be educated in ways that discourage aggressiveness.

But most of the thinkers who concentrate on man as the cause of war assume that man is able to control some of his actions. It is therefore useful to try to persuade leaders and citizens that they should not start or participate in particular wars. This thinking underlies the action of anyone who sends a letter to the President urging or condemning a particular action. It also underlies the idea that ethical arguments are relevant to war control.

There is an ethical tradition of absolute pacificism—that all war or violence is wrong, and that the only correct response to an attack is to accept it with passive dignity. This tradition has long been held most firmly by several small Christian groups, such as the Quakers, and by some Indian thinkers. It has broadened its support to include many humanists and is probably stronger today than it ever was. The thinking of Gandhi, the experience of the U.S. integration movements and of Vietnam, the fear that almost any war could become nuclear war and end civilization, and the example of Japan as a nation that has been successful with a low military budget have all contributed to the relative strength of the tradition.

But the pacifist tradition in the United States is strong only in comparison with its past. It is still very weak in comparison with the just-war tradition, a tradition that compares the evils of war with those of submission to oppressive governments and holds that *some* wars are ethically acceptable, going on to propose rules to distinguish just wars from unjust wars. This position has been that of the establishment branch of Christian thinking since the time of Constantine and has generally been the Catholic position. But the position is also found much more widely in contemporary thought. Anyone, for example, who argues that U.S. participation in World War II was moral but that participation in the Vietnam war was immoral is in effect taking a just-war position. Likewise, the Leninist doctrines distinguishing wars that advance the cause of the world revolution from those that hurt this cause are essentially just-war doctrines.

There is some, but only some, agreement on the criteria for distinguishing a just from an unjust war. Very few philosophers make a distinction between defensive and offensive war, at least not in the armchair morality terms of asking who fired the first shot. The philosophers recognize that the first shot might have been fired in response to an aggressive provocation. The first criterion for most is a just cause or goal. It is, for example, presumably a just cause to defend one's own homeland and not a just cause to subjugate another's. If Y is about to attack X, most just-war philosophers would allow X to invade Y to prevent the attack. The second criterion is that the war be fought justly. Although more will be said about this criterion below, the rule is fundamentally one that unnecessary destruction is to be avoided and that noncombatants are to be protected as far as possible. These two criteria are the most widely accepted, although there are great differences of viewpoint about their exact meaning. A Marxist theoretician thinking of the world revolution, a Western just-war philosopher thinking of people defending their nation, and a third-world theorist thinking of the exploitation of the developing nations by the developed nations will have radically different views of a "just cause." Similarly, the interpretation of "just means" ranges from rather narrow limitations on the action that can be taken against noncombatants or prisoners of war to broad doubt that nuclear weapons can ever be used justly.

Other criteria suggested by just-war theorists are less uniformly held. The traditional Catholic tenet adds a requirement of "proportionality" —that the goal of the war be in some way proportional to the likely level of destruction. It is relatively easy to apply this doctrine to tactics within a war; for example, whether it would be ethical to bomb a village that included both civilians and enemy troops would depend on the tactical need to destroy the troops. It is harder to apply the criteria to an entire war—it perhaps suggests that a nation should choose defeat instead of a bloody war that it is bound to lose. Others, such as Augustine and Aquinas, added a criterion that the war be commanded by legitimate authority. This criterion may have been a reaction to undisciplined pillage; it may have been simply acceptance of the social system of the time.

Although it may sometimes be effective in restraining combatants during war, the just-war theory is typically ineffective in preventing war. Both sides will argue that they are fighting justly, and moral and religious authorities will often support their own nation. The theory also tends to shade over into a justification of war. It is easy to make the transition from "it is ethically *permissible* for me to fight this war" to "it is ethically *required* for me to fight this war." This happened historically. Thus, the Crusades became "holy wars" justified by their moral goal. The goal readily justified the means, including any cruelty committed in the name of or to the higher glory of God. It left no room for any compromise with the enemies of the Lord. The same phenomenon— depriving the opponent of any ethical right because of the morality of the underlying objectives of the war—marked the wars of the Reformation. It can be seen today in the arguments made to support wars against colonialism or against racial discrimination: certain injustices are so great, it is argued, that a war to redress them is justified or required and, the argument goes on, the opponents are so bad and the cause so good that ordinary rules of morality do not apply.

For some, these ethical judgments shift over into a glorification of war as the best way to die or the highest way to live. They have argued that combat is one of the few situations in life in which man is expected to be disciplined and unselfish, or that much of man's progress, whether technological innovation or development of nations and cultures, derives from war.

It is partly in response to this perversion of ethics that many thinkers have held that there are *no* ethical issues in war or statecraft. This tradition is often traced back to Machiavelli's description of the amoral behavior of Renaissance princes, although it is not clear that Machiavelli thought that princes *should* behave amorally. The fear of ethical enthusiasm was expressed more recently by an eminent American foreign policy thinker: "I see the most serious fault of our past policy formulation to lie in . . . the carrying-over into the affairs of states of the concepts of right and wrong, the assumption that state behavior is a fit subject for moral judgment."[1] The amoral tradition also rests on deeper philosophical grounds. In the wake of Descartes and Hobbes, it proved easier to reconstruct a philosophical notion of the state than to reconstruct one of the international community. Kant, for example, has often been identified as an early apologist for international government because of his book *Eternal Peace* describing such government. Yet one careful commentator described Kant's view as follows:

States . . . are like individuals in the state of nature. They are neither perfectly good nor are they controlled by law. Consequently, conflict and violence among them are inevitable.

[Kant] has . . . an appreciation of politics as struggle, an idea of possible equilibrium not as simple and automatic harmony, but always as something perilously achieved out of conflict.

---

[1] G. Kennan, *American Diplomacy, 1900–1950* (Chicago, 1951), pp. 95–100.

He was not engaged in the puerile task of telling men of affairs to stop behaving badly.[2]

This tradition, with its implications that wars can be started for "reasons of state," dominates the philosophical statements of today's governments and of many of today's political scientists.

Nevertheless, ethical considerations are applied to war both by the public and by leaders. How this happens is best explained by considering different applications separately: an individual's decision whether to fight in a war; a commander's decision how to conduct a war; and a government's decision whether to initiate a war.

The individual's decision whether or not to fight in a war is normally viewed as an ethical decision. Some persons decide that they cannot morally participate in a war and refuse to accept the draft. The U.S. legal tradition permits this, provided their position rests on pacifist grounds. This legal permission, probably deriving from the high regard given to freedom of religion, does not, however, extend to the selective conscientious objector. The claim of a person who rests his objection to a war on the just-war theory, arguing that a particular war is unjust, is rejected: legal recognition of selective pacifism could " 'open the doors to a general theory of selective disobedience to law,' and jeopardize the binding quality of democratic decisions."[3] The decision of the society to accept the philosophical argument of pacifism and not that of the just-war theory is quite clear. Equally clear is that the number of war resisters is so small as not to affect the ability of states to conduct war.

A theory like that required by the just war has been accepted as governing the conduct of combat. For most theorists, to be just, a war has to be conducted justly, and it would be immoral for a soldier to participate in unjust acts in connection with the war. Efforts to distinguish moral from immoral acts have generally related to the killing of noncombatants and have focused on situations like the treatment of prisoners of war, the siege of fortified cities, blockades of a civilian population's food supply, submarine attack on merchant vessels, and bombing of cities. A closely related line of analysis centers on weapons that cause unnecessary suffering—once dumdum bullets (hollow-nosed projectiles that tear apart human tissues), today napalm and fléchettes.

The idea of distinguishing combatants from noncombatants and the

[2] K. Waltz, "Kant, Liberalism, and War," *American Political Science Review*, 56 (1962): 331, 337, 339, 340.
[3] *Gillette v. United States*, 401 U.S. 437, 459 (1971), quoting Report of the National Advisory Commission on Selective Service, *In Pursuit of Equity: Who Serves When Not All Serve?* (Washington, D.C., 1967).

moral force of that idea certainly derive from this ethical tradition, and from human reactions to suffering. Most within this ethical tradition would permit "accidental" killing of noncombatants, so long as only military targets are actually attacked. Thus, they would not prohibit an air raid on a military headquarters built next door to a hospital, which would almost certainly be destroyed in the attack, but would prohibit an intentional attack on the hospital. With this extension, the idea of morality within war permits great carnage; it is still broadly enough accepted that public opinion and some military tactics seek to limit needless destruction.

The most important contemporary political rejection of this thinking is strategic bombing. The definition of combatants can reasonably be extended to include many civilians who participate in the war effort. Few just-war thinkers would prohibit attack on an arms factory. However, those who supported strategic bombing went much further and urged successfully in World War II that cities be bombed to destroy the morale of the population, to break its will to resist, and to put indirect pressure on the government to surrender. This was the military logic behind the V-2 attacks on London and the firebomb raids on Dresden and Tokyo. Similar logic was used to support the blockade against Germany in World War I and the German submarine campaign against the British. The strategy has been widely expanded, in spite of serious doubt about its military efficiency expressed in the post–World War II Strategic Bombing Survey and in spite of the fact that for most just-war thinkers the strategy is immoral.

It is not only philosophers who have made this ethical argument. For example, practically all the scientists who worked in the U.S. nuclear weapons program during World War II believed their work to be an ethical response to Germany, which was thought also to be developing nuclear weapons. When they realized how destructive the weapon was and that it would be used against Japan, whose defeat already seemed assured, some developed serious doubts. They urged unsuccessfully that the weapon be demonstrated in an uninhabited place rather than used against a city.[4] For many, in *retrospect* the decision to bomb Hiroshima was at least questionable, but the decision to drop a second bomb on Nagasaki was clearly wrong.

With respect to the third type of decision—whether to start a war— the just-war theory has dominated public rhetoric, whereas the real-politik (amoral) theory has dominated in political science rhetoric and

---

[4] A. Smith, *A Peril and a Hope: The Scientists' Movement in America, 1945–1947* (Chicago, 1965).

maybe in practice. There are exceptional situations: the fall of the Eden government after the 1956 Israeli-French-English Suez war, and President Johnson's decision not to seek reelection during the Vietnam war, in which it can be argued that a public's judgment of the immorality of a war affected government action after the fact. The United Nations Charter distinguishes aggressive war from war in self-defense, reflective of a kind of just-war theory. The Japanese constitution prohibits engaging in war. The U.S. requirement that Congress declare war could encourage Congress to debate the ethical merits of a particular war.

But the pattern of practice has been claimed to be realpolitik. Governments make the decision whether or not to go to war according to their goals and the threats they perceive. They use moral arguments to justify the wars to their populations. This second step, exemplified by President Wilson's "war to end all wars," tends to make the war more intense. As already pointed out, it is the fear of these forces that constitutes one of the strongest arguments for realpolitik today. Realpolitik views diplomacy as a subtle game, too complicated to be played by the people or by diplomats with moralistic biases. Yet it would be hard to deny that diplomats often do respond to their own ethical views. Moreover, the pragmatic implications of realpolitik—make sure your wars are necessary, can be justified to your people, and are timed for minimum cost—are not often very different from those of a just-war theory.

Although realpolitik may have been successful in the early and mid-nineteenth century, it is clear that it did not usually prevent war even in the eighteenth and early twentieth centuries. It is doubtful that it will work in the future as the substance of international politics shifts from a strategic chessboard to politically charged economic disputes, and as broader moral doubts are raised about the social status quo, a status quo that realpolitik is adapted to protect.

International Law—The Law of War

The application of ethical principles has failed to prevent war (as it has failed to prevent sin). Many have sought to accomplish the same end legally.

The Western international law tradition, like that of realpolitik, goes back to the Renaissance. There was international law before that time, but law and ethics were not intellectually distinguished as sharply as they are today. The law made by kings and courts was viewed as an expression of the natural law, which was the foundation of ethics. This pattern was understandable in a society that was generally homogenous in religion—a similar pattern can be found quite recently within Muslim culture.[5] With the religious wars and especially with their settlement in the Treaty of Westphalia (1648), law had to be distinguished from ethics. The Treaty of Westphalia was essentially an agreement among different nations to disagree about religion, but religion had been the upholder of the king's authority. The result was that the source of law and authority had to become the king, not the international religious order. The way for this emphasis on the king had been prepared by such thinkers as Jean Bodin, who formulated a theory of sovereignty in 1576. It was completed by Hobbes, who argued in 1651 that the sovereign is not limited by the law; rather, he makes the law.

But once the way was cleared for a law separate from ethics, the possibility of international law seemed undercut. If the different sovereigns were the makers of law, how could they be subject to any form of law? This problem has troubled international lawyers on both the practical and the theoretical levels ever since. Because of this problem, international law is quite limited, but there are enough situations in which nations need some rules to deal with one another (e.g. "let's not kill each other's ambassadors") so that some effective international law does exist.

In relation to war, law has come closest to success in the law of war, a legal analogue to the ethical rules on how to conduct war. There was a pre-Renaissance tradition: for example, Mohammedan law prohibiting poisoning of wells. The contemporary Western tradition, however, goes back to a 1625 book by the Dutchman Hugo Grotius who, appalled by the brutality of the religious wars, formulated legal rules on the conduct of war. In doing so, he rejected the concept of a legal distinction between just and unjust war, which would be too likely to be ineffective. International law has followed this judgment until the time of the League of Nations, and has often been criticized for doing so. To many people, there is a conflict between the idea of law and that of war, and a fear that the possibility of making war less brutal might encourage more wars. Grotius concentrated instead on rules that might make war more tolerable.

These rules have been developed as formal legal doctrines, both by international law writers and by governments. The most influential of the more recent formulators was Francis Lieber, a Columbia University professor who drafted *Instructions for the Government of Armies of the United States in the Field*, rules that were applied in the U.S. Civil War. They also became the basis of the Hague Regulations—treaties negoti-

[5] A. Bozeman, *The Future of Law in a Multicultural World* (Princeton, N.J., 1971), pp. 62–64.

ated at the turn of the century, embodying some of the laws of war. Related treaties were negotiated in Geneva in the 1920's and following World War II.

Each of the treaties normally concentrates on a particular area of warfare. Among the practices that have been prohibited are use of gas, use of dumdum bullets, and use of free-floating naval mines (which, because they drift, could not be deactivated after the war). Negotiations to deal with "inhumane weapons," such as napalm and fléchettes, were in progress in the 1970's. In addition, treatment of prisoners of war has been regulated.

The examples show the possibilities and the limitations of making international law through treaties. Nations will accept only those limitations that appear to benefit them, but there are benefits to everyone in prohibiting some practices such as maltreatment of prisoners of war. Some of these treaties can be self-enforcing. Thus, each side avoids maltreating the prisoners it has taken if it knows that its opponent could respond by maltreating the prisoners it has taken. The system works fairly well, but only as long as there is some symmetry in the numbers of prisoners of war. But the coverage of the rules is sparse; realistic agreements have never been achieved on such important issues as guerilla warfare, aerial bombing, submarine warfare, or even fixed ocean mines. Many of the rules are obsolete, and some are frequently ignored in combat. The resulting pattern of law is less than rational.

This narrow body of law made by treaty, a process that fully respects the theoretical sovereignty of each nation, is supplemented by law made independently of the state's consent. Some of the international law of war derives from customs and some even from domestic courts. A classical example was the law of neutrality, the elaborate doctrines, familiar to anyone who has studied the background of the War of 1812 between the United States and Great Britain, describing what a neutral nation's merchants could and could not ship to a belligerent. This law was developed by courts set up to decide whether a privateer was entitled to keep the merchant vessel it had seized. The courts considered precedents set by foreign courts and sometimes decided against their own nations' desires. The doctrine, however, did not survive the growing totalization of war and the development of the submarine.

The laws of individual states also often reflect principles of international law that have not yet been accepted by treaty. Thus, some nations have laws or policies against supplying weapons to belligerents. Similarly, the national rules sometimes enforced by court-martials such as that of Lieutenant Calley in the Vietnam war may be more strict than those required by treaty. Moreover, the individual soldier is required by U.S. law to disobey an order contrary to international law, meaning in practice that if he is court-martialed for an action contrary to U.S. law, the fact that he was obeying a superior order is not a legal defense. The laws of war are also enforced by public opinion, which has had some effect in situations as diverse as Vietnam and the 1914 German violation of Belgium's neutrality.

A new enforcement mechanism was developed at the end of World War II: the Nuremberg and Tokyo trials. The victors of the war established courts to try the leaders of the losing nations for various offenses against international law. The offenses were carefully defined and reasonable ways were found to allocate responsibility within a military hierarchy. Although the proceedings were fairly conducted and were imitated in a nongovernmental "International War Crimes Tribunal" during the Vietnam war, their value as a pattern has also been questioned. There was some sense that the law had been made after the offense; not that the actions condemned were not known to be wrong and against international law, but that the application of international law to individuals was novel. Previously, states, not individuals, had been considered to be the subjects of international laws. More seriously for the future, the victor's violations of international law were never prosecuted. And the critical issue of strategic bombing was carefully avoided; the victors were too vulnerable. One can fear "victor's justice," and one can also fear that leaders of nations facing defeat will encourage more savage fighting in order to avoid such justice.

International Organization and Law Against War

Finally, nations have begun to question the idea that international law should not judge the morality of a war, but should instead accept war as given and seek only to mitigate it. This change in outlook, although based on many ideas and worldwide trends, is in many respects an American contribution.

For centuries there had been arbitration commissions set up to decide particular international controversies, sometimes on legal grounds, sometimes on explicitly political grounds. The United States and England had a treaty of this character during the nineteenth century, and their relations were marked by growing friendship. It is seldom, however, that nations will allow third parties to decide important disputes. Therefore, one seeks a less ambitious role for third parties: they might help the nations to talk out their disputes and avoid war. This mediation technique had also been used in European diplomacy, formally and informally, particularly during the nineteenth century. These concepts were formalized by the Hague Conventions for the Pacific Settlement of International Disputes of 1899 and 1907, which created the predecessor of the present International Court of Justice. Just before World War I, the United States made a series of proposals for agreements by which some disputes would be automatically submitted to arbitration. These ideas reflected a different theoretical conception of preventing war. It was assumed that men and nations would have problems and disputes, but that they would be able to settle them rationally if they could have time to cool down and talk out their differences, or if decisions tending toward the common good could be reached.

The concepts of arbitration and peaceful settlement of disputes were also at the heart of the League of Nations, established after World War I. The covenant of the League provided several ways to settle conflict that threatened war: adjudication in a court, arbitration, or resolution by one of the political organizations (the Council or the Assembly). Each member further bound itself not to go to war except in certain conditions in which the League machinery failed (the famous loopholes). Thus, the central concept was that these peaceful dispute-settlement procedures would replace war, and the system was used rather skillfully to settle several disputes in the 1920's. At what was expected to be a secondary level, there was an obligation on members to act militarily against a nation that resorted to war "in violation of its covenants."

Extensive efforts were made in the mid-1920's to reinforce this system. The first effort was the Geneva Protocol, an arrangement designed to close the loopholes to war by creating new obligations to arbitrate if those situations should arise. The Protocol was nearly adopted in 1924, but collapsed when the Labor government of Great Britain fell and its successor rejected the Protocol. A second effort was made in the Treaties of Locarno of 1925, an elaborate package that adopted the opposite approach of maintaining peace by threatening military intervention. Current major disputes were settled diplomatically, Germany entered the League, and, crucially, various nations guaranteed that certain German boundaries would be maintained. Thus, for example, England promised France that it would intervene militarily if Germany violated the Franco-German border. From one viewpoint, England would be helping to enforce an international agreement; from another viewpoint, England and France were in an alliance against Germany. (Germany was analogously guaranteed against invasion by France.) The guarantee side of the Covenant, hitherto subordinate, became dominant. The guarantee concept risks war but reflects still another idea of war prevention—a nation will not act aggressively if it finds everyone lined up against it.

But the loopholes to war remained. They were closed dramatically by the Kellogg-Briand Pact of 1928, which prohibited war as "an instrument of national policy." The leaders of the negotiation of this treaty were French Foreign Minister Aristide Briand and U.S. Secretary of State Frank Kellogg, who received the 1929 Nobel Peace Prize for his effort. The treaty was accepted by practically all nations and later became one of the legal underpinnings of the Nuremberg trials. Comments on the treaty ranged from detailed legal analysis of how to integrate it into the League framework to criticism that it was a dangerous illusion.

This structure, which was supplemented by arms control agreements (to be discussed in Chapter 3), collapsed completely in the 1930's. The international court and arbitration systems were never particularly successful. The League, which had been effective in the 1920's, temporized before Japanese actions in Manchuria in 1931. The guarantees given at Locarno were ignored when Germany, also violating its Locarno promise, occupied the Rhineland in 1936. The same year, the League abandoned sanctions against Italy for its invasion of Ethiopia. Munich and World War II were not long in coming.

Planning for a new League, the United Nations, went on during World War II, and was influenced by the failure of the previous system. As the central concept of the League had been arbitration, the central concept of the United Nations was enforcement and guarantee; the five permanent members of the Security Council, who were the five chief allies of World War II against Germany and Japan, were to act together to protect others against aggression. Mediatory and conflict-resolution procedures were maintained, but the core concept was collective enforcement. Under the U.N. Charter, there was even to be an international military staff analogous to the joint commands of World War II, but U.S.-U.S.S.R. rivalries kept the structure from being implemented.

The United Nations did work formally as planned during the Korean war, which began in 1950. The U.S.S.R. delegate had walked out in an argument over the United Nation's refusal to seat the People's Republic of China, so it was possible to obtain a Security Council decision charging North Korea with aggression. The United States was then the dominant foreign participant in a U.N. force that intervened on behalf of South Korea. When the U.S.S.R. delegate came back to the Security Council to be able to exercise his veto to protect Soviet interests, the United States looked to the General Assembly for further power to intervene, supporting its position by the General Assembly's "Uniting for Peace" resolution. This resolution sought to give the General Assembly, a body that had been designed to have broader membership and less power, the right to recommend national action in a crisis when the Security Council was paralyzed by the veto.

The United Nations was never again able to function as an enforcement body as designed. It therefore shifted, especially during the early 1960's, to peacekeeping, a pattern based more on the original design of the League. The idea, as exemplified in the Congo, in the Mideast several times, and in Cyprus several times, was that U.N. forces, supplied by neutral nations, would be positioned to help enforce a truce and decrease the number of incidents between opposing military forces. Thus, the United Nations would not decide who was the aggressor and intervene against that side. Instead, it would help the parties end military conflict; in doing so, it would favor the status quo at the time the peacekeeping forces were sent. The emphasis was not on legalism or on protecting boundaries. It was, rather, on stopping the fighting, and the technique was available only when the five permanent members of the Security Council agreed that the fighting should be stopped. Even this technique has been used only infrequently since a major U.S.-U.S.S.R. dispute over the financing and the constitutionality under the U.N. Charter of the peacekeeping force in the Congo in the early 1960's.

The U.N. Charter also includes a formal war prohibition: "All members shall refrain in their international relations from the threat or use of force against the territorial integrity or political independence of any state, or in any other manner inconsistent with the Purposes of the United Nations." This prohibition does not apply to U.N. enforcement actions, nor does it apply to action taken in self-defense or to certain actions taken by regional organizations. Hence, it leaves room for defending almost any war as being in accord with the Charter; it also leaves room, in contrast, for some legal theorists to develop arguments, for example, that the U.N. Charter prohibits nuclear war. Thus, the U.N. Charter formally continues the tradition of the Kellogg-Briand Pact; the activity of the United Nations in fact, however, is to try pragmatically to halt individual wars.

A further step, suggested by some private individuals but never yet seriously considered by governments, is to disarm to try to make war impossible. Most disarmament proposals, including the draft treaties for general and complete disarmament put forward in the early 1960's by the United States and the Soviet Union, probably for propaganda purposes, recognize that nations might attempt to rearm, and therefore they provide for international police or enforcement bodies, operating as the United Nations was designed to operate. Even in the early phases of U.N. design, some thought was given to complementing it with a disarmament agreement, with force levels chosen so that the permanent members of the Security Council would be able to intervene together anywhere in the world if a nation were rearming and threatening its neighbors. Few of the proposals, however, have seriously faced the questions of controlling the international military force or of deciding what legislative powers would have to be given to the international organization to help it alleviate the injustices that might lead to war.

Motivations for Arms Control

Arms control became a major concern of statesmen only after World War I dramatized the ineffectiveness of ethics and international law in the face of total war, but it builds on some of the same traditions. This chapter shows how the motivations for arms control relate to motivations for the other institutions to control war; the next chapter will trace the historical development of arms control. As one moves from the domain of philosophy toward that of politics, motivations become more and more complex and decisions rest on more and more debatable factual judgments. These tendencies should be clear from the previous discussion; indeed, they are crucial in examining the motivations for arms control.

Although all the motivations of the past are reflected, the danger and absolute destructiveness of nuclear war also underlie the contemporary motivation for arms control. The urgency of war prevention has increased: it is hard to visualize the cause for which one is willing to end civilization. At the same time, the history of failure in comprehensive war-prevention efforts and the impossibility of obtaining agreements on a world level have led statesmen toward narrower and narrower agreements, concentrating on specific weapons. Statesmen hope that these agreements will prevent or limit war. In the process, by compromise, they have obtained the support of many who seek goals other than war prevention. They have also had to choose between conflicting motivations and have had to act without fully understanding the implications of their actions.

The contemporary motivations for arms control tend to overlap, so any listing is arbitrary. Motivations also differ, both in kind and importance, among individual arms control measures. Even for one particular measure, different nations and individuals may be motivated by different considerations. Furthermore, the public debate and official statements may not always reflect some of the more important considerations that move nations, groups, and individuals, sometimes almost subconsciously.

Just as arms control itself includes many arrangements short of formal treaties, some of the motivations support arrangements short of formal treaties. Thus, some of the motivations can be satisfied by one nation's restraint in its unilateral decisions whether or not to build particular weapons systems. Some motivations can be satisfied by tacit arrangements in which, without formal agreement, several nations refrain from building or testing a weapon but are prepared to go ahead if one of the others does so first. A few of the motivations can be satisfied only by a full formal international agreement.

One of the oldest motivations stems from ethical or religious beliefs, reflected in the "swords into plowshares" passage, that it is morally preferable to use man's talents and resources for peaceful purposes, rather than for military purposes. Except for some regimes that have glorified war as a higher form of human endeavor, most societies, at least in principle, accept the concept that peace is preferable to war and peaceful production preferable to military production. The burden of proof, therefore, is often placed on advocates of increased arms; it is sometimes hard to obtain Parliamentary or Congressional approval for arms budget increases. This arms control motivation is often weak, however, when placed in competition with motivations (many also ethically based) to obtain arms.

Closely related to the above motivation is that of some members of society who hold with the pacifist tradition in rejecting violence—or at least indiscriminate violence—in international relations. Rejecting the basic premise that it may be proper to use arms, such groups naturally support almost all arms control or disarmament efforts. They are also likely to support efforts to ban the use, and, if possible, the deployment, of weapons of mass destruction. This motivation is strong for its adherents; it has not, however, exercised any great influence.

The previous motivations of general mistrust of arms and the military and of rejection of arms because of a belief that they cannot be used ethically shade over into the much more broadly held motivations of rejecting arms because their continued procurement might lead to war. This antiwar motivation derives from the same roots as do the ethical and legal traditions already discussed. But opposition to war does not necessarily imply opposition to arms; it depends on the empirical question: do arms cause wars? Some arms control supporters take it as an article of faith that arms cause war, or at least that those arms reductions that are small enough to be politically obtainable would reduce the risk of war.

But a wider group of arms control supporters and opponents believe that the causal connection between arms and war is much more subtle. For example, some wars have occurred in spite of low arms levels, reflecting the folk wisdom that men will fight with sticks and stones if they do not have tanks and airplanes. A dramatic example is the U.S. Civil War, one of the bloodiest of all wars, fought in a nation that had only about 15,000 men under arms at the outbreak of the war. And it is easy to make the next step: sometimes arms can prevent wars. *Si vis pacem, para bellum* (If you wish peace, prepare for war). The most commonly cited example is World War II, where it is argued that greater military preparedness and firmness on the part of France and England would have deterred Germany.

The counterargument has force as well. It is possible that an arms race between England and Germany was a major cause of World War I. It is hard to imagine that governments that have superior weapons will not threaten to use them to improve their bargaining position in the international disputes that are bound to arise. Usually, as in the Cuban missile crisis of 1962, or the generation of incidents preceding World War I, the conflict will be peacefully resolved after the threat. Sometimes, however, a mistake will be made, as in 1914. One would expect the probability of such mistakes to grow with arms levels, with the number of nations having major military forces, and with the complexity and fluidity of international society.

The arms procurement process does not necessarily distinguish arms likely to prevent war from arms likely to lead to war. There are too many different motivations for arms procurement. Suspicion and fear of another nation lend support to arms procurement. Territorial, nationalistic, and ideological ambitions of a nation contribute to fear and suspicion in countries that wish to preserve the status quo, while motivating the acquisition of arms by those who seek a change in the existing order. The suspicion and fear can easily become mutual, particularly in an intense ideological conflict such as that witnessed during the cold war. Each side accumulates obligations through alliances and the desire to protect perceived vital interests throughout the world, adding to its arms requirements. Judgments that armed strength adds to diplomatic strength make their contribution to the competition. Weapons are often viewed as bringing prestige, as a mystical symbol of the importance of the nation. Vested domestic interests, both bureaucratic and economic, that profit from arms procurement are an important factor. Newly independent nations of the post–World War II period have often viewed the acquisition of military establishments as a technique of nation building and developing internal cohesion. And in recent times the rapid technological change in weaponry has produced fears that existing arsenals will become obsolete and has thus stimulated a continuous series of new weapons programs to meet possible future threats. Finally, some believe that "bargaining from strength" in arms control negotiations requires ongoing weapons programs to be used as "bargaining chips."

This background explains the typical character of a political debate on whether to obtain more arms. Those in favor argue that the arms are needed to prevent war and that those who oppose are misguided or traitorous. Those who oppose argue that the arms are likely to encourage war and that those in favor are misguided or aggressive or want the arms for irrelevant reasons. Debate over an arms control proposal will take the same form; the opponents of the proposal will try to show that the arms are needed or that the proposal is dangerously unbalanced, while the supporters will seek to explain why this particular arms reduction is good. There are many such motivations or reasons.

Some persons, following the international organization tradition described in the previous section, think that the system of international politics has to be changed. The way to prevent war is through gradual development of world order and a more international society. The international system's heavy dependence on violence could then be reduced. For these people each arms control measure has a value as a building block, a value that extends beyond whatever ability the individual measure itself might have in preventing war. Even when they cannot describe the goal of a future world system, they see the process of establishing building blocks as important in itself for its effects in creating a world community. Those, for example, who support the strengthening of the United Nations and related international organizations are usually supportive of progress on arms control and disarmament. They regard such progress, together with the development of international peacekeeping machinery and the strengthening of international law and arrangements for peaceful settlement of disputes, as important elements in the construction of an improved international order. Thus, one diplomat described the Latin American Nuclear Free Zone Treaty as a "contribution to the military denuclearization of a zone of the planet" and "a model for the establishment of other similar zones."[6]

Others look specifically at arms procurements such as those by the United States and the Soviet Union, arguing that such nations are in an arms race, and that arms races create a momentum of their own that

[6] H. Gros Espiell, *En Torno al Tratado de Tlatelolco y la Proscripcion de las Armas Nucleares en la América Latina* (Mexico City, 1973), p. 12.

either surely or probably ends in war. Those who hold this view are likely to support arms control measures generally rather than because of the specific military concern that the individual measures seek to resolve. This motivation was once confined to academic circles; with the advent of the nuclear age it has drawn wider support, largely because of the view that survival itself is at stake so that even a small probability that an arms race will lead to war creates too large a risk to accept.

There is a larger body of people who do not accept the proposition that arms races by themselves create a momentum that leads to war, but who, nevertheless, believe that arms competition creates tensions that tend to hinder diplomacy. Insofar as arms control agreements help to reduce tensions and increase a sense of security, they will contribute to the prospects of peace and improve the climate for the settlement of outstanding political disputes. President Nixon was appealing to this motivation when he said of the agreements deriving from the Strategic Arms Limitation Talks (SALT): "these agreements open the opportunity for a new and more constructive U.S.-Soviet relationship, characterized by negotiated settlement of differences, rather than by the hostility and confrontation of decades past."[7] This motivation is one that especially concerns some of the Western opponents of arms control. They fear that an era of détente would produce a political climate in which the Western nations would allow their forces to decline dangerously in comparison with those of the Soviet Union.

Motivations deriving from a desire for a new international order or from fear of an arms race are not the only ones. Many doubt the possibility or desirability of more powerful international agencies. Many doubt that an arms race is likely to create war; some even doubt that the United States and the Soviet Union are, in any real sense, engaged in an arms race; they would say that these countries are building arms for parallel but independent reasons. Even for those who share all these doubts, there are often specific military reasons for arms control, and these reasons are the most broadly accepted ones.

The motivations that have dominated expert discussions in recent years relate to the special nature of nuclear weapons and their modern delivery systems. As these weapons increased in ability to inflict widespread destruction within a matter of minutes on an adversary's cities and on his retaliatory military forces, concern developed about the "strategic stability" of the nuclear relationship between the superpowers

---

[7] The President's Message to the Senate Transmitting the ABM Treaty and the Interim Agreement on Strategic Offensive Arms, June 13, 1972, *Weekly Compilation of Presidential Documents*, June 19, 1972 (Washington, D.C.), p. 1026.

in time of crisis. The concern was that either side might perceive a grave danger in not striking first, thus making a crisis more likely to eventuate in nuclear war. These concerns led to efforts on both sides to develop strategic systems that can survive a first strike, but there has been a growing belief that strategic stability must be supported by agreements that limit certain strategic arms or encourage the exchange of one type of strategic weapon for another. The U.S. interest in SALT was motivated in part by these considerations, as was the U.S-U.S.S.R. arrangement, at first tacit but later formalized in SALT, not to interfere with certain of each other's intelligence systems. Other arms control agreements derived from the closely related desire to minimize the danger of nuclear war resulting from accident or miscalculation. The 1963 agreement to establish a "Hot Line" communications link between Washington and Moscow is an example of this series of measures. While individuals and nations differ on which particular arms control arrangements are best suited to achieve the objective of increased strategic stability, this motivation for arms control probably spans a wider spectrum, from "hawks" to "doves," than any other.

There are other broadly shared motivations similarly relating to other highly specific weapons and war possibilities. For example, there is some danger that nuclear materials might fall into the hands of revolutionary terrorists or criminal organizations and be used for extortion. This danger has become one of the major motivations for international and national arrangements to control nuclear weapons and nuclear reactors. Similarly, many fear the widespread proliferation of nuclear weapons. Other examples can be found in the tactical area, where agreements could be designed to prevent two forces from beginning war through misunderstanding each other's actions. Thus, a 1975 agreement in Europe placed a duty on each side to notify the other of planned military maneuvers.

When political limitations preclude a broader agreement that would appeal directly to an individual's arms control motivations, the individual might accept a narrower agreement for tactical reasons. For example, if it is impossible to make things any better, one can try to keep them from getting worse, in the hope that more positive action will become possible later. Thus, many supporters of the Non-Proliferation Treaty recognized that it did not solve the problem of nuclear proliferation, but thought that it would slow the process and gain time. Many of those who sought unsuccessfully to stop the development of multiple, independently targetable reentry vehicles (MIRVs) were motivated in large part by the fear that such development would make SALT negotiations more difficult. These tactical motivations can lead to agreements to prevent the development of new armaments; such measures are sometimes referred to as nonarmament or preventive arms control. Examples of successful efforts of this form include treaties prohibiting deployment of nuclear weapons in and on the seabed. A second tactic rests on the belief that each successful effort makes it somewhat easier to make progress on "next steps." Many of the supporters of the 1963 Limited Test Ban Treaty, the first major arms limitation agreement of the post–World War II period, viewed its central benefit as the beginning of a generation of negotiations. It is particularly these agreements, reached for tactical reasons, that have been criticized as creating an illusion of arms control progress while having little effect on actual arms construction.

War prevention is not the only international political goal of arms control. For example, a basic Soviet goal in the negotiation of the Non-Proliferation Treaty was to strengthen the legal and political barriers to Germany's acquisition of nuclear weapons, a goal the U.S.S.R. had pursued in a variety of arms control proposals over the years. Some believe that one of the Soviet motivations in SALT is to develop the concept that the United States and the Soviet Union have a special responsibility and role in political disputes in the rest of the world. One of the reasons that Western Europe is participating in negotiations over tactical force levels in Europe is to discourage the United States from withdrawing troops from Europe without obtaining compensatory Soviet troop reductions.

Other motivations operate within society. Of these, the most commonly considered is the economic one, the desire to divert resources from the military sector to meet other needs of societies, and to give tax relief from the "burden of armaments." During the height of the cold war these motivations were intellectually recognized, but did not figure heavily in national debates. As the cold war subsided, as weapons costs increased, and as publics supported larger domestic expenditures, this motivation became more powerful politically. Arms control became part of a public debate about national priorities. So far, except for the part of SALT restricting ballistic missile defenses, arms control agreements have not significantly reduced defense expenditures, but the motivation seems likely to grow in strength and to provide further support for arms control measures. Many, for example, doubt the wisdom of spending enormous sums on new strategic arms to gain "advantages" that may be meaningless in an age when both superpowers can destroy each other. Until recently, however, the economic motivation has not been as important to the professional arms control community, which has tended to respond to strategic motivation, as it has been to political officials.

Analogous motivations derive from political and sociological concerns. Some people see a large, politically and economically powerful military establishment as having an adverse or dangerous effect on the health of a democratic society. Although this motivation will support unilateral actions to reduce the size and importance of the military establishment, arms control measures can often be viewed as politically easier ways to accomplish the same end. Arms control may be supported as a way to express opposition to particular wars such as the Vietnam war. At a more local level, it was discovered during the late 1960's that many people did not want an antiballistic missile based in their vicinity.

Another broader motivation for certain arms control measures is environmental protection. Concern about radioactive fallout resulting from atmospheric testing, for example, created one of the strongest of the political pressures that led to the Limited Test Ban Treaty of 1963. In the 1970's, some of the support for chemical and biological warfare restrictions and for a comprehensive test ban also derived from environmental concerns.

Peace has become popular and is therefore good politics. From World War II to about 1970, publics of Western democracies generally supported political leaderships in their decisions to procure armament; in the 1970's, they became less concerned about Soviet threats and tended to support arms control and arms reductions. Leaders like to have foreign policy accomplishments to point to, and arms control agreements have often become especially useful for this purpose, as SALT was for President Nixon in 1972. This motivation has recently contributed an element of high-level support for arms control efforts and has helped overcome bureaucratic inertia.

Finally, national leaders particularly are responding to a concern quite similar to that of those who broadly fear and reject the technological world. They suspect that, somehow, the arms system has become self-generating and no longer productive of security. There is something absurd about a system in which national leaders carry strategic nuclear communication systems around with them and must invest enormous sums to have a few extra seconds of decision time available. In a world in which one failure could mean the end of civilization, nations must seek security through cooperative measures of arms control lest the system and the machines become the masters of man's fate. It is remarkable how many world leaders have spoken this way, especially when they reflect after leaving power—Dwight Eisenhower, Dean Rusk, Nikita Khrushchev. Some flavor of this motivation is conveyed by a passage from Soviet Foreign Minister Andrei Gromyko's 1969 statement to the Supreme Soviet:*

> One of the most basic questions that has arisen is that of so-called strategic weapons. What is involved here is above all the question of whether the major powers are to reach an agreement on checking the race for the creation of increasingly destructive means of attack and counterattack, or whether each power will seek to pull ahead in one area or another in order to achieve military superiority over its rival, which would compel the latter to mobilize still more national resources for the arms race. And so on, *ad infinitum*.
>
> There is another aspect of the matter that must not be overlooked in the long-range policies of states. This is largely connected with the fact that weapons control and guidance systems are becoming, if one may say so, more and more independent of the people who create them. Human hearing and vision are not capable of reacting accurately at today's velocities, and the human brain is sometimes unable to evaluate the readings of a multitude of instruments quickly enough; the decision made by a human being ultimately depends on the conclusions provided to him by computer devices.
>
> Governments must do everything in their power so as to be able to determine the development of events, not find themselves in the role of captives of these events.

* U.S. Arms Control and Disarmament Agency, *Documents on Disarmament, 1969* (Washington, D.C., 1970), p. 313.

CHAPTER THREE

Modern Disarmament Efforts Before World War II

Historical perspective regarding the arms control and disarmament negotiations of the post–World War II period can be gained by examining several of the attempts made to limit and reduce the levels of armaments prior to World War II. Although most of these attempts were failures, there were major developments in the naval area; these developments will be emphasized in this chapter.

Almost every advance in weaponry, from the crossbow to the bomber, has been accompanied by calls for its abolition. Attempts to abolish particular weapons played a not unimportant role at the end of the Middle Ages, but they were abandoned, until very recent times, as unproductive. There was, for example, fairly widespread revulsion against the introduction of firearms. Throughout Europe, laws were issued against their employment, and in some cases gunners when taken by the enemy were not treated as prisoners of war, but were executed as outlaws. Not surprisingly, these prohibitions failed; the problem of balancing force levels among different nations proved as difficult in the early modern period as today, and the prohibitions were soon renounced.

In the seventeenth and eighteenth centuries several European treaties contained specific proposals for disarmament. For example, one of the treaties of the 1648 Peace of Westphalia stipulated that all of the existing fortifications were to be demolished and that no new fortifications were to be erected. This provision was, however, never observed, let alone enforced.

In 1766 Prince Kaunitz, the Austrian Chancellor, offered Frederick the Great of Prussia a proposal for the limitation of national armaments. Kaunitz proposed a three-fourth reduction of the forces of both Austria and Prussia, but this offer was rejected by the Prussians. Joseph II's renewal of the suggestion in 1769 was also refused.

A similar initiative was taken in 1816 by Tsar Alexander I of Russia, a mystical and aristocratic figure who addressed a note to his fellow sovereigns proposing the negotiation of a reduction in the level of military forces. The first reaction in London was deep suspicion, based on the fact that Russia, alone of the members of the victorious coalition against Napoleon, had as yet taken no steps to reduce its forces. After reflection, the Foreign Secretary, Lord Castlereagh, ordered his minister in Petersburg to inform the Russians that he believed every nation was the best judge of its own military needs, and that, although the British government was always willing to let friendly powers know the extent of British armaments, it was not prepared to make them dependent upon international agreement. The continental powers were not even as accommodating as the British. Speaking for Austria, Prince Metternich showed no interest in the arms reduction proposal at all, arguing that the size of a nation's forces must necessarily be determined by its geographic situation, its resources, its domestic situation, and other parochial factors. Metternich would not even agree to furnish information concerning Austrian armaments to other governments, least of all to Russia.

The outstandingly successful disarmament effort of the nineteenth century was the American-British attempt to reduce naval forces on the Great Lakes. The War of 1812, with its spectacular naval battles on the Great Lakes, had clearly demonstrated the importance of naval control of the Lakes, and there was concern in both Britain and the United States that a costly and dangerous naval arms race could begin between the two countries on the Great Lakes, increasing the chance of another U.S.-British confrontation similar to the War of 1812. The U.S. concern increased in August 1815 when Britain announced its intention to increase its armed forces on the Lakes, and in November John Quincy Adams, the U.S. Minister to London, was authorized to begin negotiations with the British on limiting armaments on the Lakes. These negotiations continued intermittently until April 1817, when a formal agreement was enacted by an exchange of notes. The Rush-Bagot Agreement, which is still in force, limited the naval forces of the United States and Britain on the Great Lakes and Lake Champlain and required a substantial act of disarmament, since those vessels that exceeded the agreed-upon limits were too large to be sailed down the St. Lawrence River and therefore had to be dismantled. In entering the agreement, the British overrode Canadian objections but avoided an arms race that would have been costly and would not have contributed to overall security.

Later in the nineteenth century, reduction of arms was usually proposed by governments when they were feeling at a disadvantage. Self-reliant or ambitious powers never seemed to be moved by any desire to have limits set to their armed forces. Thus, for example, in 1859 Lord Palmerston suggested disarmament to Napoleon III, but the Emperor (already contemplating a war against Austria in Italy) simply looked the other way. Ten years later, however, when Napoleon III was having financial difficulties and could not match the military expenditures of his fast-growing rival Prussia, he was of a different mind and asked the British government whether it would suggest a general arms reduction to the Prussians. The British agreed and the Foreign Secretary, Lord Clarendon, instructed his minister in Berlin to approach Prince Bismarck on the subject. Bismarck, knowing perfectly well that French financial difficulties lay behind the proposal for force reductions, refused even to lay the British proposal before his sovereign, explaining that the King would regard this as an attempt to weaken the striking power of Prussia at a critical time. Not long thereafter, France and Prussia were at war.

In the last decade of the nineteenth century, as relative military advantage grew in importance in the minds of military planners and a sort of "arms race" psychosis began to emerge, there was a revival of interest in arms limitation and war prevention.

The most famous instance of this was the proposal that eventuated in the Peace Conference at The Hague in June 1899. The initiative, as in 1816, came from Russia. In August 1898, without preliminary consultations with other governments, the Russian government issued and published a circular note, calling upon other governments to join it in a general conference to discuss the reduction of armaments. The foreign reaction to the Tsar's proposals was generally unfavorable. Some governments doubted the Tsar's sincerity; others felt that any reduction of armaments would tend to freeze the status quo to their disadvantage. In any event, all governments stalled, and no arms control limitations were reached at the Hague conference. The conference did, however, succeed in some of the areas discussed in the previous chapter that are less directly related to arms control. An international court was established, arbitration was discussed, and the law of war was amended to provide for better treatment of prisoners. Declarations were developed prohibiting the use of expanding bullets and asphyxiating gases and the dropping of explosives from balloons.

Provision was made at this first Hague conference for a second one, which was to meet in 1907. When it did so, the atmosphere was more intense than in 1899, for the balance-of-power system that had worked reasonably well since 1815 had more clearly broken down and Europe was divided into two opposing coalitions, all members of which were heavily armed. Even so, when invitations went out, limitation of armaments was not mentioned among the subjects to be discussed, and when the conference convened, the limitations issue was bypassed. Again, however, the law of war was expanded, with prohibitions of arms "calculated to cause unnecessary suffering" and of poison or poisoned weapons. Moreover, the rules for blockades were tightened and the requirement of a declaration of war was laid down.

A Special Case: Attempts to Control the Anglo-German Arms Race Before World War I

During this era, England and Germany were locked in an expensive naval arms race. Although negotiations to control the race were unsuccessful, the example deserves attention. It weighed heavily on the minds of negotiators after World War I and contributed to success in concluding naval arms control agreements at that time. Moreover, this arms competition is one of history's closest analogues to today's U.S.-U.S.S.R. arms competition. The weapons involved were major technological systems that had never been tested. They were based on a doctrine very close to today's strategic theory. Their construction was supported by military-industrial complexes on each side. And the naval race may have been one of the substantial causes of World War I.

An influential doctrine for sea power had been put forward in 1890 by Captain Alfred T. Mahan, a U.S. naval officer, in the book *The Influence of Sea Power upon History, 1660–1783* (Boston). His argument, based on the simultaneous rise of the British Navy and the British Empire, was that international trade, especially with imperial possessions, was essential to national greatness and that protection of both trade and possessions required a strong navy. Otherwise, the nation would be cut off and vulnerable to blockade. But it would be impractical to control all oceans. The navy, therefore, would have to be designed to destroy other navies in line-of-battle, fleet-against-fleet combat. Mahan's argument was also being made by others such as Alfred von Tirpitz, who was then a captain, appointed to the German naval staff in 1892. It gained strength from the interest of the major European nations in expanding and protecting their own imperial possessions. Naval leagues were created in both England and Germany to lobby for larger fleets.

At the same time, the technology of naval forces was changing rapidly. Wooden construction was being replaced by metal construction; sails by steam, and smooth-bore cannon firing solid shot by torpedoes and rifled cannon firing explosive projectiles. Maintenance of a navy required construction of fleets of new battleships optimized for line-of-battle action, cruisers for speed, and torpedo boats and destroyers for delivery of and protection from torpedoes.

Enormous construction programs were then necessary. Because it had an existing empire and was an island, Britain had long relied heavily on the navy for defense. In 1889, it authorized construction of 70 ships, including 10 battleships, over the next decade, affirming the principle that its fleet should be at least equal to those of its next two competitors combined (then France and Russia).

Germany felt insecure, remembering that England had destroyed the Danish fleet at Copenhagen by surprise in 1807. It moved in 1898, with plans for 19 new battleships and many lesser ships to be built over six years. A new law in 1900 raised the goal to 38 by 1920. These laws were supported by Tirpitz and Emperor Wilhelm II, and by the iron and naval construction industries. The laws passed the Reichstag through the use of all sorts of maneuvering. In 1908, Tirpitz even secretly allotted the construction contracts for two ships which were not to be authorized until 1909. The strategic mission of the fleet was unclear, even to the German Admiralty. Tirpitz's original argument was a deterrence argument: the fleet could be used for diplomatic bargaining, though smaller than the British fleet. The British would not risk an attack on it, because their losses, even after victory, would leave them too weak compared to Russia and France. This rationale failed when Russia and France became aligned with England; no substitute was developed and the German construction can be explained only by inertia and the political position of the pro-naval forces.

England responded to German construction by diplomacy to allow it to concentrate its forces at home where it could face the German fleet. Thus, it signed an Anglo-Japanese alliance in 1902, giving Japan its first equal treaty with a Western nation and permitting England to bring home its Far East Squadron. Similarly, as the entente patterns were built up before World War I, and France became more closely associated with England, defense of the Mediterranean was assigned to the French fleet.

England also sought technological improvement, laying down the *Dreadnought*, the first of a new, more advanced battleship, in 1905. The technological advance was important, because the victor in a line-of-battle action was expected to be the side whose armor and guns permitted it to choose a range at which it could harm the opposing fleet but not be harmed. Tirpitz responded in 1907 with a program for many dreadnought-class battleships. There were further escalations: by the outbreak of war in 1914, Britain had 20 dreadnoughts to Germany's 13 and 40 older battleships to Germany's 20. Britain maintained superiority, but in 1911 it had had to reduce its two-power standard to a standard of 60 percent superiority over the German fleet in dreadnoughts.

Many efforts were made to stop the race, but all failed. Naval arms control came up at the Hague Conferences of 1899 and 1907. Even the weak proposal of agreeing to state a budget level and not exceed it for three years failed at the first conference, whereas the still weaker proposal of exchanging information on construction plans failed at the second conference. When Edward VII of England visited Wilhelm in 1908, the British proposed that Germany voluntarily slow its rate of building. The answer was no, although there were hints that Germany might do so in return for unstated British concessions. The incident was used by British officials to obtain political support for the naval program.

New efforts were made in 1909, following the revelation of the advance allocation of German construction contracts, an action that frightened the British public because of its suggestion of secret German construction. The British proposed neutral inspection of dockyards, but got nowhere. At a broader level, the Germans offered to restrain their construction in return for a political accord that would amount to an alliance. The British rejected this as destructive of its Entente with France and Russia. Bernhard von Bülow, the German Chancellor, dared not offend Wilhelm or the Reichstag by offering more. He made a last unsuccessful effort to obtain concessions from Tirpitz shortly before being defeated in the Reichstag.

By 1912, the new chancellor, Bethmann Hollweg, was practically begging the British to make concessions so he could resist Tirpitz's plans for new construction before they were presented to the Reichstag. Lord Haldane visited Germany, offering political and colonial concessions in return for a German commitment not to increase its naval program. Tirpitz insisted on British neutrality and on including its yet unpublished naval expansion program in defining the baseline. Bethmann Hollweg wanted a weaker position. He and Tirpitz both threatened to resign; Wilhelm sided with Tirpitz. The German expansion program was published and negotiations faded away. In 1913, Churchill twice offered a one-year naval holiday, but his offers were ignored.

Ironically, the elaborate fleets were hardly used in the war. Nearly all the German ships were tied down in their ports by British ʻ.ips, which were equally tied down by this task. The net effect was t ̄.at Germany could not employ surface raiders. There was only one large-scale surface-ship battle during the war: the submarine combat and land combat proved much more significant.

Nevertheless, the arms race did contribute to the outbreak of war. Both Germany and England were paranoid about the other's fleet. Tirpitz clearly wanted naval war with England. Others on the German side may have hoped that its fleet would deter England from entering the war. This hope was dashed by the German violation of Belgium's neutrality, which swayed a wavering British public opinion. The arms race background may also have contributed to that opinion change. It certainly helped provoke public tensions during the years before the war and helped lead England to an alliance against Germany.

The League and the Interwar Period

Long before World War I ended, there was in every country touched by the conflict a strong sentiment that nothing of the kind should ever be permitted to happen again, and the allied governments began to draft plans and proposals for the time when war was over. These had to do with the territorial reorganization of Europe that would follow the war, with the establishment of an international organization that would regulate relations and obviate friction among the powers, and with the question of armed force.

The security arrangements, including the creation of the League of Nations, discussed in the previous chapter, were quite creative. The Covenant of the new League showed the extent to which that organization was to be oriented toward disarmament:

The Members of the League recognize that the maintenance of peace requires the reduction of national armaments to the lowest point consistent with national safety and the enforcement by common action of international obligations.

The Council, taking account of the geographical situation and circumstances of each State, shall formulate plans for such reduction for the consideration and action of the several governments.

Such plans shall be subject to reconsideration and revision at least every ten years.

After these plans shall have been adopted by the several governments, the limitations of armaments therein fixed shall not be exceeded without the concurrence of the Council.

The Members of the League agree that the manufacture by private enterprise of munitions and implements of war is open to grave objections. The Council shall advise how the evil effects attendant upon such manufacture can be prevented, due regard being had to the necessities of those Members of the League which are not able to manufacture the munitions and implements of war necessary for their safety.

The Members of the League undertake to interchange full and frank information as to the scale of their armaments, their military, naval and air programmes and the condition of such of their industries as are adaptable to warlike purposes.

The major effects of this covenant provision were the World Disarmament Conference of 1932 (to be discussed below) and a continuing, but unsuccessful, series of efforts to restrict trade in arms and munitions.

But assigning disarmament responsibility to the League was partly a way to put off hard issues, perhaps until they could be forgotten. Among the victorious powers that met in Paris in 1919, there was no desire for a radical agreed reduction of their own armed forces. Despite the feelings of the public on this score, the statesmen and soldiers who made up the allied delegations believed this to be unrealistic. The armed might of the central powers had been destroyed, but peace had not descended on the world. There was civil war in Russia and Communist armies were fighting in Finland, the Baltic states, and the Caucasus; there were small wars on the frontiers of Poland; and the Middle East, the Arab lands, and the Far East were in turmoil. The allied powers had no way to assess their future military needs in the face of these problems, and were unwilling to bind themselves to any specific provision for control of their armaments. Moreover, there were major differences in viewpoint between England and France. The former rapidly demobilized its land army. The latter was deeply concerned about defense against Germany and wished both guarantees and a favorable balance of military force.

The allies were, of course, perfectly ready to be specific with respect to their enemies, and the most drastic provisions of the peace treaties signed with the former enemy states in 1919 were the so-called arms clauses, which provided for the disarmament of those states. The Treaty of Versailles, for example, prescribed that the Germany army of the future should be limited to 100,000 officers and men, denied Germany the possession of armor and military aircraft, placed severe limitations on its naval armaments, and ordered destruction of the industry that had supported the German war effort. (Germany later built "pocket battleships" designed around the treaty restrictions and devised an army readily expanded to a much larger force.) In the Treaty of Saint Germain, similar provisions were made binding on the Austrian army; and the armies of other enemy states—Hungary, Bulgaria, and Turkey— were treated the same way (although the restrictions on Turkey were lifted in the 1923 Treaty of Lausanne).

In addition to the naval accords to be discussed below, the 1920's saw several less far-reaching agreements. In 1923, for example, the Central

American Disarmament Convention resulted in an agreement by Guatemala, Honduras, El Salvador, Nicaragua, and Costa Rica to limit their armed forces, military aircraft, and war vessels.

A more important and still relevant agreement prohibiting the use of poisonous gas and also the use of chemical and biological weapons, the Geneva Protocol (different from the Geneva Protocol discussed in Chapter 2), was signed by 46 countries in 1925. The protocol successfully passed a major test during World War II, which saw no significant use of chemical or biological weapons, despite the fact that neither Japan nor the United States was a party to the treaty. Questions exist, however, on whether the belligerents were restrained by the force of the protocol or, instead, by the mutual fear of retaliation and the unpredictable tactical consequences of unleashing chemical and biological warfare on a large scale. Many weightier and equally solemn agreements, e.g. those relating to the protection of noncombatants, were systematically violated.

In February 1932 the League of Nations members and the United States and the Soviet Union assembled in Geneva for the World Disarmament Conference. During this conference it became immediately apparent that the key to the situation was France. A disarmament scheme that meant anything would be possible only if the French were willing to scale down their armaments, sacrificing the military superiority over Germany that they had won at Versailles. The French insisted that they could make such concessions only if other nations, particularly Great Britain, would give them guarantees of aid in case war should come again. The commitments of Locarno were not strong enough for France. In the conditions of 1932, the British did not feel that they could take on commitments stronger than the ones already made. At the same time, the British were afraid that the fragile democratic government in Germany would be ousted by its extremist opponents unless its leaders were given a diplomatic victory to show to the electorate. The best diplomatic victory would be an arms agreement to end the inferior armaments position that so many Germans felt to be unjust and humiliating. The British wanted to give the Germans arms equality—that is, equality of status—and then to have each nation scale down its armaments and military budget.

The British used every kind of pressure they could think of, and the French stalled, finally accepting equality for Germany. At the same time, however, events were moving swiftly in Germany. During 1932 three German governments fell, and in January 1933 Adolf Hitler became chancellor of Germany. In May 1933 Hitler unexpectedly announced his support of the British proposals, but this was largely a tactical move to give him time to consolidate his position on the home front. He had no intention of allowing himself to be bound by an international agreement on arms. In October, he announced that Germany was withdrawing from both the Disarmament Conference and the League of Nations, to which it had belonged since 1926.

This was the end of any hope of land disarmament in the interwar period. It is barely possible that *if* the conference had met sooner and *if* the French had not been so stubborn and *if* an agreement had been found to satisfy German feelings on the equality issue, a general agreement on reduction of land armaments might have been worked out that no one would have dared to refuse to sign. After October 1933 no such agreement would become possible until Hitler had been met militarily and defeated.

Naval Arms Control in the Interwar Period

The exception to the dismal picture just described is the effort to control naval arms. This effort began at the Washington Conference of 1921–22, a major diplomatic event that for better or worse put temporary limitations on what might otherwise have been a costly and dangerous arms race. In the years immediately preceding the conference, the United States, Great Britain, and Japan had all announced major new naval construction programs. The three major powers seemed to be on the verge of bitter and unnecessary competition in naval armaments.

In the United States, Woodrow Wilson had argued forcefully for naval preparedness during his administration, calling for a navy that would be "second to none." The Naval Appropriation Act of 1916 had approved the largest construction program ever proposed at one time by any nation. By the end of the war Wilson was calling for further naval building which by 1925 would have given the United States a navy more powerful than that of all the other great nations combined.

Just how serious Wilson was about all of this shipbuilding is debatable. He publicly recommended the "uninterrupted pursuit" of the building program because "it would clearly be unwise for us to attempt to adjust our program to a future world policy as yet undetermined." With the Paris Peace Conference in session and the League of Nations looming large in his image of the postwar world, Wilson's motives may legitimately be questioned. He may have been the first American president to use the construction of military weapons as a bargaining chip for negotiations.

Warren G. Harding was elected in 1920, and said shortly before his inauguration that he saw "no reason to look for a cessation of American naval increase." While not exactly a ringing endorsement of Wilson's navy second to none, this did put Harding down on the side of Big Navy enthusiasts.

Shortly before Harding's inauguration, Congress began debate on a new naval appropriation bill. Public pressure was growing in the United States for curtailment of naval construction, and for some form of disarmament as an alternative to further expenditures for ships. Senator William Borah of Idaho proposed an amendment to the naval bill requesting the President to convene a meeting of the United States, Great Britain, and Japan to consider ways of reducing the naval construction programs of the three governments. Harding opposed the amendment, considering it an infringement on his Executive prerogatives. But public sentiment was so overwhelmingly in support that Harding had no choice but to go along with it. The result was a compromise: the Borah resolution was approved, and in return Congress granted the Administration's full request for naval construction.

The British were concerned over Harding's apparent commitment to naval preeminence. Prime Minister Lloyd George had engineered a dramatic reduction in British naval strength since the end of World War I, and hoped to maintain the navy on this peacetime footing. The Royal Navy, however, had expressed serious concern about the impact of the American construction program. By 1921 the pro-navy forces in the British government had grown in number and strength, and were finally able to force the Prime Minister's hand. In March 1921, Lloyd George proposed a plan for construction of four new capital ships. Many British naval authorities had serious doubts about the future of capital ships in general, believing that the submarine and airplane had virtually negated the effectiveness of ships as weapons of war. Moreover, in the early 1920's, Britain was in the midst of an economic recession. Unemployment was rising, personal income was falling, and there was widespread support for a reduction in income tax. England was also saddled with a tremendous war debt, much of it payable to the United States. The government hoped this debt would either be reduced or eliminated, but care had to be taken to avoid antagonizing the United States. Any British naval buildup also ran the risk of stimulating American naval construction, the result of which might be to leave Britain worse off than before.

Japan had not stood idly by during the years of Anglo-American naval competition. It, too, had begun a process of naval expansion. In 1920 the Japanese Diet approved a program calling for the construction of two new capital ships per year for eight years. By 1927 the Imperial Navy was to have a force of 25 modern capital ships.

Domestic pressures similar to those in England were beginning to build up in Japan. A serious recession had gripped the country by the end of 1920, and in those pre-Keynesian days recessions were thought to be cured by cutting back government spending rather than by increasing it. The naval building program was a likely candidate for the fiscal scalpel. Naval construction was the largest item in the defense budget, and the defense budget itself was over half of total government expenditures. This was an enormous investment in naval might for a relatively small nation. Japan's population was only half that of the United States and Japanese per capita income was only one-tenth of the American. In spite of this disparity, Japan was planning to spend as much on its navy as the United States spent.

It was in this context that President Harding made his call for a conference to consider the limitation of naval armaments. It seemed a perfect case for arms control—three countries, each embarking on a course of naval expansion, two in direct and reluctant response to the naval construction of the third. It appeared to be a classic example of an arms race that could be halted by joint agreement.

The Washington Conference convened in November 1921 for what most observers thought would be a protracted negotiation. Secretary of State Charles Evans Hughes, however, dramatically announced specific figures for reductions of the U.S. battleship fleet as well as those of England and Japan—an announcement that stunned the other delegations and, because of the support it evoked from public opinion, left them no way of refusing. Within a month, all the essential points were agreed upon. Under the final terms of the Five-Power Treaty, all signatories agreed to stop construction of capital ships for ten years, and to limit their total tonnage in capital ships. For the United States and Great Britain the limitation was 500,000 tons; for Japan, 300,000 tons. France and Italy were limited to 175,000 tons each. The three major powers were reasonably satisfied with the outcome, although the Japanese Delegation was heard to grumble that the 5:5:3 ratio sounded a bit like Rolls-Royce, Rolls-Royce, Ford. In order to comply with the terms of the treaty, the leading powers had initially to scrap 68 ships already built or under construction (28 for the United States, 24 for Great Britain, and 16 for Japan).

For Great Britain, the agreement confirmed a new reality—parity with the United States. The argument made in England at the time was that the famous two-power standard had never been applied against the United States; it instead applied only against European powers. And, although neither the United States nor England wanted a naval arms race, the British held to a position that they ought to maintain parity with the United States. This led to restriction of the Washington Agreement to capital ships and aircraft carriers. England wanted a large number of small cruisers for commerce protection; the United States wanted fewer large cruisers, because it had fewer distant bases. A trade-off was not possible, because the cruisers the United States wanted could have outfought the small cruisers in a theoretical battleline engagement, violating the parity concept. Similarly, control of submarines effectively failed. England sought to ban submarines, viewing them useful only as commerce raiders. To the lesser naval powers, especially France, submarines appeared as a cheap counterbalance to large fleets. England had to content itself with a treaty that never went into force. This treaty would have required a submarine to warn a merchant vessel and make provisions for the safety of its crew before torpedoing it.

For Japan, the Washington agreement was far more than an arms control treaty. It was also a replacement of the Anglo-Japanese alliance of 1902 and a guarantee of Japan's predominance in the northwest Pacific. With the new European balance of power, the alliance was no longer so useful to England, and the United States objected to it, fearing that England and Japan might combine against it in the Pacific. There were war scares between the United States and Japan at the time, based on the possible naval arms race and on conflicts over China policy. Japan naturally opposed a combination of changes that would deprive it of its alliance and keep its fleet inferior as well. Part of the response was a four-power treaty of general and mutual respect for Pacific possessions among Britain, America, Japan, and France. This treaty replaced the alliance by a commitment to talk in the event of difficulty. The other part of the response was commitments by the United States and England not to fortify certain Pacific outposts. Japan would then be geographically protected, because the United States and England would be unable to bring their forces to bear on Japan without bases. The immediate effect of the conference was a relaxation of U.S.-Japanese tensions.

The first effort to extend the treaty framework to cruisers and auxiliary vessels—which were being laid down in large numbers—failed at Geneva in 1927. The problems were both those between the United States and England and those between England and the continental European powers, particularly France, which hoped to obtain additional security guarantees in return for its commitment not to build ships.

The U.S.-England difficulty was finally worked out by negotiation of a "yardstick" by which one U.S. 8-inch-gun cruiser would be considered the equivalent of nearly two British 6-inch-gun cruisers. Following this side negotiation, limited success was reached at a new five-power conference held in London in 1930. France and Italy refused to adhere fully, so an "escalator" clause was included, effectively ending the treaty if a nonparty should build enough to threaten a party. The ratios were also adjusted slightly in favor of Japan.

After London, the situation rapidly worsened. No agreements were possible at the 1932 World Disarmament Conference at Geneva. Late in 1934, Japan, facing serious domestic backlash at the inferior position assigned to it by the agreement, formally abrogated the 1922 agreement, effective two years later. A second London Naval Conference in 1935, in which Japan did not participate, produced a treaty whose primary effect was to dismantle much of the elaborate limitation structure of the previous treaties. Great Britain entered several side agreements with Germany and Russia during this era. By 1938, both Great Britain and the United States were embarked on major naval construction programs, and the obligations of the side agreements were denounced by Germany and "indefinitely suspended" by Great Britain during 1939.

Possible Lessons

Although lessons drawn from history are always arguable, several speculations based on the 1890–1940 period seem warranted. The first is the role of individuals—much hung on the individual judgments and actions of men such as Tirpitz and Hughes.

The second is that military-industrial complexes have existed and have been influential as they were in Germany before World War I, where the Chancellor's hands were effectively tied. Pressures for economy, working in the opposite direction, were clearly influential at the Washington Naval Conference. A good case can be made that that conference was merely an agreement not to build ships that would not have been built anyway.

Third, arms races have in some cases contributed to the outbreak of war, as did the pre–World War I Anglo-German race. And the Washington naval treaty, whether or not it prevented an arms race, did bring an era of good feeling between the United States, England, and Japan. Again, however, the point must be balanced; resentment at the inferior position imposed on Japan by the naval agreements was later one of the factors contributing to the rise of Japanese militarism in the 1930's. Similarly, resentment at the one-sided disarmament provisions of Versailles contributed to Hitler's domestic support in much the same way. Any treaty that establishes several classes of nations is likely to provoke difficulty.

Fourth, the naval example makes one doubt the step-by-step theory of arms control. All the easy areas of naval agreement were found at Washington in 1922. What was left for Geneva and London were the hard problems; it is not surprising that they were not easily solved.

Finally, and most important, one must be struck by a sense of the irrelevance of the doctrines that moved both force planners and arms controllers. The battle fleets so expensively accumulated before World War I were barely used in that war, although their existence did limit use of surface commerce raiders. Yet control of battle fleets was the goal of arms controllers during the 1920's. In spite of the agreement to control aircraft carriers and the abortive efforts to control submarines, the negotiators concentrated their attention on subtle battleship vs. battleship calculations. These calculations were irrelevant to the next war, whose naval actions were to be fought in large part with submarines and aircraft carriers. And, as a final paradox, the arms races and agreements on weapons that proved useless may have been illusions, but they were illusions that helped bring good feelings in the 1920's and perhaps contributed to war in the eras immediately preceding World Wars I and II.

CHAPTER FOUR

The Changing Nature of Strategic Weapons

I N THE PERIOD since 1945 there have been revolutionary developments in weapons technology. Some of the changes in conventional weapon technology will be briefly reviewed in Chapter 13. The most dramatic increases in destructive power, range, speed, accuracy, and cost, however, are those of strategic weapons, weapons that would be used to make, or defend against, a direct nuclear attack on a nation's homeland. The more important of the strategic technological developments will be discussed in this chapter.

The Nuclear Weapon

Probably the single most important weapons development of the last 30 years—and perhaps in all of man's history—has been the vast increase in the destructive power of weapons. This destructive power, or yield, is often measured in terms of the number of tons of TNT that would produce an explosion releasing the same amount of energy. The first major jump in yield came in 1945 with the first successful explosion of an atomic bomb.

Whereas the power for a conventional (chemical) explosion results from the energy that is released when the atoms are rearranged in the molecule, the power of a nuclear explosion results from the tremendous quantity of energy that is released when a nucleus of Plutonium 239 or Uranium 235 breaks into smaller pieces. The nucleus can be made to fission in this way when it is struck by a neutron. When the nucleus fissions, it also releases neutrons which can split other nuclei in a chain reaction. The amount of energy released is enormous; the fission of one nucleus releases about five million times as much energy as the explosion of one molecule of TNT. Once the nuclear material is available, construction of the weapon is probably not too difficult. The design problem is to assemble a "critical mass," i.e. a shape and quantity of material in which there are so many fissile nuclei near one another that a chain reaction can be maintained. Enough of the neutrons released from each fission must strike other nuclei rather than escape. As the chain reaction proceeds, the bomb will tend to blow itself apart and therefore end the chain reaction; the designer must find a way, usually with conventional explosives, to assemble the critical mass and to keep it assembled long enough to fission a reasonable proportion of the nuclei present.

The development of the atomic bomb made it immediately possible to increase the destructive capability of bombs by a factor of over 1,000. The largest conventional bomb dropped during World War II weighed 10 tons (and, consequently, had a yield of 10 tons, since for conventional explosions yield and weight are approximately equal quantities). In contrast, the atomic bomb dropped on Nagasaki had a yield equivalent to 20,000 tons, or 20 kilotons (KT), of TNT. It weighed, however, only about 5 tons, so it had a yield-to-weight ratio of about 20 KT/5 tons. This ratio was, therefore, about 4,000 times higher for this atomic bomb than for conventional bombs such as those dropped in World War II.

The extent of damage that a "small" nuclear explosion can cause was demonstrated in the bombings of Hiroshima and Nagasaki in August 1945. A 14 KT atomic bomb was dropped on Hiroshima, and a 20 KT atomic bomb was dropped on Nagasaki. In Hiroshima 80 percent of the homes and buildings were destroyed and most of the rest were damaged. A fire broke out, creating a firestorm, in which the heated air rose with such force as to suck in a severe wind, pulling oxygen away from humans and asphyxiating them. In Nagasaki, four square miles of the city were totally destroyed, and another four square miles were essentially destroyed. The effects on humans for Hiroshima and Nagasaki were as follows:

	Hiroshima	Nagasaki
Population before the raid	255,000	195,000
Dead	66,000	39,000
Injured	69,000	25,000
Total casualties	135,000	64,000

The first hydrogen or thermonuclear device, exploded on November 1, 1952, had a yield in the 1,000,000 ton (MT or megaton) range. It was about 1,000 times more powerful than the first atomic bomb exploded only seven years earlier, and about one hundred thousand times more powerful than the largest conventional bombs used in World War II.

Whereas the atomic bomb derives its power from the energy released during nuclear fission, the hydrogen bomb derives its power from nuclear fusion—the fusing of nuclei of heavy isotopes of hydrogen to form helium. Fusion will take place only under conditions of intense heat and pressure, and a nuclear-fission unit is used within the bomb to create these conditions. There has been controversy over the possibility that fusion could be initiated in other ways, as through use of lasers. So far, this is probably not feasible, at least for practical weapons use.

Although the hydrogen bomb is about five times more powerful than the atomic bomb in terms of units of energy released per unit of starting weight, the main reason why fusion bombs are so much larger than fission bombs is that there is no upper size limitation. Fission bombs must be arranged so there is no critical mass until explosion is desired. Otherwise, spontaneous fission could cause explosion. Then the mass must be quickly assembled; the obvious mechanical problems limit the possible yield of fission bombs. For fusion, however, it is necessary to create very high temperatures to get the fusion reaction to proceed, so there is no problem in preventing spontaneous reactions. Consequently, a fusion bomb can be of practically unlimited size and power, and yields up to 60 MT have been tested. Hydrogen bombs can have a yield-to-weight ratio at least 100 times higher than the Nagasaki bomb.

The Effect of Nuclear Weapons

In order to understand the significance of the jump from conventional explosives to nuclear and thermonuclear explosives, it is useful to consider the damage that results from the explosion of a 20 KT bomb and a 1 MT bomb. There are several different ways that nuclear weapons cause injury and damage. Prompt effects include blast, fire, and radiation. Delayed effects include fallout and various postattack problems. Conventional explosives damage primarily through blast and fire.

Most of the immediate physical damage from a nuclear explosion is caused by the blast. A gigantic blast wave is created at the point of the explosion and expands outward with diminishing intensity. This blast wave is a region of high air pressure and strong winds, both of which last at any point for only a few seconds. The principal blast effect on people is from the wind. People are blown around, hit by flying debris, or caught in collapsing buildings. This wind is several hundred miles per hour in the regions in which the air pressure reaches a level 5 pounds per square inch higher than the normal level of 14.7 pounds per square inch. This region is shown in Figure 1 for yields of 20 KT and 1 MT. The

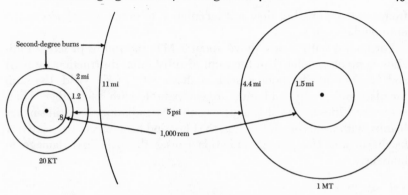

Fig. 1. Damage radii of nuclear explosions.

bombs exploded over Japan had roughly 20 KT yield, while a U.S. Minuteman II warhead has about a 1 MT yield.

Fire

The nuclear materials in the bomb are heated in the explosion to a temperature of several tens of millions of degrees, comparable to the temperature at the center of the sun. A fireball is created. It expands and cools quickly, but for a few seconds it radiates as intense heat about one-third of the energy released in the nuclear explosion. People caught in the open can be burned at great distances, as shown in Figure 1. These flash burns were an important cause of death and injury in Japan. The intense heat can ignite fires, and the blast can start fires by upsetting stoves and furnaces, shorting electrical circuits, and breaking gas lines.

Prompt Radiation

Each uranium or plutonium nucleus that undergoes fission divides roughly into two pieces. Many of these fission products are very unstable and quickly decay, releasing intense gamma rays for a small fraction of a second. A person receiving a dose of 1,000 rem (roentgen equivalent man, a measure of the dose of radiation in terms of its estimated biological effect) over his entire body would certainly die within two weeks. The range at which this dose is likely to be received is shown on the figure. A smaller dose, about 200 rem, is sufficient to cause acute radiation sickness with a chance of death. Shielding against this prompt radiation is difficult, requiring much mass; about eight inches of concrete is necessary to reduce the dose to one-tenth the dose outside. Many persons in Hiroshima were inside buildings that shielded them from blast and fire, but they still succumbed to radiation sickness in the ensuing days and weeks.

For bombs with yields above about 1 MT, the radius of lethal radiation is much smaller than the radii of substantial destruction by blast and fire. For smaller bombs, such as those with 20 KT yield, the radii for blast and prompt radiation are comparable with each other. Thus, many casualties at Hiroshima were caused by radiation. For still smaller bombs, with yields of 1 KT or less, the blast and heat effects are relatively localized, and the prompt radiation causes the principal damage to humans.

Fallout

Fallout results from radioactive fission products, which decay on longer time scales: hours, days, or years. If the explosion is very high above ground, as with the bombs over Japan, the early fallout is negligible. The reason is that immediately after the explosion the bomb materials are vaporized into hot gases, which rise quickly. As the materials cool, they begin to recoalesce into tiny particles, which take months and years to fall to the surface. In this time much of the radioactivity has decayed, and the balance is spread over the globe.

If the explosion takes place on or near the ground, an enormous amount of dirt and debris is swept up. The fission products tend to solidify on the surfaces of these particles, which then drop back to the surface. Fallout begins almost immediately near the explosion and continues for a day or so as the cloud of debris is carried downwind. The fallout distribution varies with the construction of the bomb and wind conditions near the explosion, as well as with the altitude of the explosion, but a 20 KT explosion would cover roughly 10 square miles with lethal fallout, and a 1 MT explosion roughly 1,000 square miles.

Since the radiation from fallout is not instantaneous but is spread over a longer time, it is more feasible to defend against it through a shelter. The length of time that one must remain in the shelter depends on the accumulated fallout outside. A typical period would be two weeks, after which the dose rate would be 1/1,000 of the rate one hour after the explosion.

All the fission products from an airburst and about a third of those from a surface burst are so small that they may take months or years to descend to the surface. During this time they become widely distributed over the globe, and much of the activity decays. Two long-lived isotopes, however—strontium 90 and cesium 137—have half-lives of 30 years.[1] These isotopes accumulate on the earth's surface and are dangerous when eaten in food. Strontium 90, in particular, is a problem because it is chemically similar to calcium; hence, it gets into milk and accumulates in bones to become a long-term hazard.

Results of a Large-Scale Nuclear Attack

Attempts to calculate the consequences of nuclear war have been made by governments and scholars. Some facts can be measured; some cannot. For illustrative purposes, such a calculation, usually made by computer, will be examined. The approach is outlined here.

Census reports give the population, typical housing, and fallout shelter capacity of each census tract. The number of industrial plants, the number of employees, and the value added by manufacture are available for each industry in each small region. A certain level of warning can be assumed; for example, enough time to reach a fallout shelter. Then the attack itself is described: military and civilian targets are chosen, and appropriate-size weapons and burst heights are selected. With the type of information used earlier to draw damage radii, estimates can be made of the number of casualties and deaths in each census tract. The total casualties in all census tracts can then be added up. The destruction of industry can similarly be estimated. The casualties from blast, prompt radiation, and fallout are usually allowed for in the calculations. Even though it is important, the effect of fire is usually not included, for lack of a suitable theory of ignition and spread of large fires.

Estimates of the number of deaths from a nuclear attack against cities are remarkably consistent. Three examples based primarily on blast and fallout are shown in Figure 2. The solid line shows the fraction of the population of the Soviet Union killed as a function of the number of megaton warheads; the figure is taken from an article by Rathjens and Kistiakowsky in *Scientific American*.[2] The dotted curve is a nominal curve of U.S. casualties used for civil defense planning purposes.[3] The X points are from civil defense calculations of U.S. casualties.[4] The prin-

---

[1] This means that over 30 years the radiation level would decay to one-half the initial level, over 60 years to one-quarter the initial level, and so on.

[2] G. W. Rathjens and G. B. Kistiakowsky, "The Limitation of Strategic Arms," *Scientific American*, 222 (Jan. 1970).

[3] R. Rodden, "A Statistical Information System for Estimating the Magnitude and Scope of Nuclear Attacks" (Stanford Research Institute, Menlo Park, Calif., 1968).

[4] J. Green, "The Case for Civil Defense as Developed Through Systems Analysis" (Office of Civil Defense, Washington, D.C., 1971).

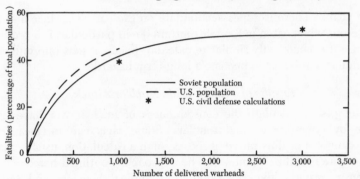

Fig. 2. Effects of a nuclear attack upon cities. (Adapted with permission from G. W. Rathjens and G. B. Kistiakowsky, "The Limitations of Strategic Arms," *Scientific American*, 222 [Jan. 1970], 24. © 1970 by Scientific American, Inc.)

cipal feature of these curves is that approximately half the population of either the Soviet Union or the United States is killed by 1,000 one-megaton-range explosions. The next few thousand explosions do not initially kill a very much larger fraction of the population, because all of the large urban targets have already been struck. Since the military forces of both the Soviet Union and the United States can each easily deliver the equivalent of 1,000 one-megaton warheads on the other, one could expect half the population of each to be killed promptly in a nuclear war in which cities are targeted. The outlook for the other half would be uncertain but not promising.

The immediate outcome of an attack of this magnitude is specified more completely in a nominal attack considered by a National Academy of Sciences symposium on the subject.[5] The attack consisted of 800 warheads, 400 on military and 400 on civilian targets. The average yield was 4.5 MT, and most of the warheads were burst on the ground. Fifty percent of the population was killed in this hypothetical attack, and 15 percent injured, mainly with burns and radiation sickness. Only 30 percent of the industrial capacity was undamaged, and because of fallout much of it was not immediately usable. After ten days, two-thirds of the undamaged 30 percent was usable. Another 30 percent of the industrial capacity was repairable, and 40 percent was destroyed.

The ultimate consequences of a nuclear attack cannot be calculated with the same precision as can the prompt effects, and they are now largely a matter of speculation. There has been a tendency in much

[5] National Academy of Sciences, *Proceedings of the Symposium on Postattack Recovery from Nuclear War* (Washington, D.C., 1967).

debate about strategic capabilities to limit the discussion to consequences that can be calculated with the use of computers. In a sense this is like analyzing only the consequences of the first few hours of nuclear war. Yet the "postattack problems" are almost beyond comprehension.

One problem would be medical care. At Hiroshima and Nagasaki, 90 percent of the doctors were casualties. Presumably this is a likely result of nuclear attack; doctors and hospitals are concentrated in the urban areas, which are likely to be targeted. This great decline in the availability of medical care would come at a time of great increase in demand.

Disease would be a problem. Crowded conditions, poor sanitation, little fresh water, and no refrigeration characterize the likely postattack situation. People would be susceptible to all the diseases common before the advent of sewers and clean water supplies. Widespread epidemics could be expected.

Large amounts of food would survive in warehouses, processing plants, storage bins, and on fields, but much of the food would be contaminated by fallout, and there would be tremendous problems of transportation, distribution, and hoarding. The mainstays of commerce —money, credit, and confidence—might all disappear, making food distribution vastly more difficult than a simple estimate of physical destruction would imply. The importance of these economic factors was shown in the Great Depression, when the gross national product declined by 50 percent even though there was no physical destruction.

Before reconstruction must come reorganization, which might be more difficult. The present social structure is characterized by many interconnections, each part depending on many others. Even if factories that produced one-third of the GNP survived and one-half the workers were alive, it is by no means obvious that they could function as before, because of their dependence on other parts of the economy for raw materials and spare parts.

A possibility generally ignored in calculations (but not in novels) is the breakdown of the social structure. The people might turn against the government that brought on the disaster. Violent competition might break out over food or other scarce resources.

Even areas that did not receive a lethal dose of fallout would still receive a large dose. The effect on the environment of long exposure to moderate doses of radiation is poorly understood. There are possibilities of pest outbreaks, concentration of radiation in the food chain, and huge fires and floods.

Delivery Systems

If the first revolutionary development in strategic systems in the post-war period was in the destructive power of bombs, the second was in the systems for delivering them. In the decade from 1945 to 1955, the destructive power of nuclear weapons increased by a factor of 1,000, but there were no dramatic improvements in the capabilities of delivery systems. In the decade from 1955 to 1965, however, the most revolutionary changes were in the field of delivery systems. The speed of delivery systems increased by a factor of about 20, because of the development of the intercontinental ballistic missile. An ICBM takes 30 minutes to travel from the United States to the Soviet Union, whereas a B-52 bomber takes 11 hours. And since the ICBM was developed, its accuracy has been significantly improved.

A number of missile programs were started in the early and mid-1950's by the United States and the Soviet Union. On both sides, these led to deployment of intermediate-range (about 1,500 miles) ballistic missiles (IRBMs). The United States deployed the Thor missile in England in 1960, and the Jupiter, an Army missile, in Turkey and Italy. During the same period, the Soviet Union deployed a substantial number of missiles of comparable range aimed at Western Europe.

In August 1957, the Soviet Union launched a test ICBM on a trajectory that took it the length of Siberia. The first U.S. ICBM, the liquid-fueled Atlas missile, was tested in August 1958 and became operational in 1960. The performance goals of the Atlas, which were largely met, included a 1 MT warhead, a 6,000-mile range, and an accuracy, or circular error probable (CEP: the distance from the target within which, on the average, half of the warheads will fall), of 5 miles or better. Although the Atlas used technology derived from the German V-2 rockets used in World War II, it was dramatically superior in terms of yield, range, and accuracy. The V-2s carried about 1 ton of chemical explosives, had a range of about 200 miles, and a CEP of from 3 to 5 miles at their much shorter range. The Atlas obtained its accuracy by means of an inertial guidance system—one that measures all accelerations undergone by the missile and then calculates the course adjustments necessary to arrive on target.

The development of the second U.S. ICBM, the liquid-fueled Titan missile, was begun in 1955, and the first Titan was placed in service in 1962. The first Titans and the Atlases were eventually replaced by an improved and somewhat larger Titan II missile. Because second-generation missiles were shortly ready for deployment, few of the first-generation missiles were deployed; there are currently 54 Titan II missiles in the U.S. inventory.

The United States wanted its more advanced missiles to be solid-fueled rather than liquid-fueled, since solid-fueled missiles could be launched more quickly. A liquid-fueled missile would have to be filled before launch, unless a storable liquid fuel could be developed. The first ICBM program using solid, rather than liquid, fuel was begun in 1957 and resulted in the development of the Minuteman missile. The first Minuteman was fired from an operational-type underground silo in late 1961, and deployment began in late 1962. These Minutemen had a yield of about 1 MT and a range of about 6,500 miles. The most recently designed Minuteman warheads probably have an accuracy of about 1/10 mile. The United States currently has 1,000 Minutemen, roughly half of which are the most modern Minuteman III and all of which are in hardened silos to increase their chances of surviving the blast effects of a nearby nuclear burst.

The United States also began the development of submarine-launched ballistic missiles (SLBMs) in the 1950's. This resulted in the development of the Polaris A-1 missile, a solid-fuel missile with a warhead of 1 MT and a range of about 1,000 miles. The first 16 operational Polaris missiles were deployed on the nuclear-powered submarine *George Washington* in November 1960. The second and third models of the Polaris missile, the A-2 and A-3, had ranges of about 2,000 miles and 3,000 miles, respectively. In addition to having increased range, the A-3 also carried three separate warheads on each missile. These multiple reentry vehicles (MRVs) were *not* separately targetable, but rather were designed to land in a tight pattern around the same target. The object of the triple warheads was to increase the area covered by a moderately high level of shock intensity.[6] The first submarine outfitted with the A-3 missile became operational in the fall of 1964. By the end of 1966, the United States had 28 nuclear submarines armed with A-3 missiles and 13 armed with A-2 missiles.

The concept of carrying multiple warheads on a single missile was

[6] At any one distance, the intensity of the shock wave resulting from a large explosion increases with yield only as the cube root. The area covered by shock waves of any given intensity therefore varies with the two-thirds power of the yield. Hence, a greater area of city can be destroyed with a particular weight of payload if the payload is broken into a number of appropriately separated smaller nuclear weapons, so long as these smaller weapons have a yield-to-weight ratio close to that of a large single warhead.

further refined in the late 1960's with the development of multiple, independently targetable reentry vehicles (MIRVs). Whereas the MRVs on a missile hit the same tarket in "shotgun" fashion, individual MIRVs can be specifically aimed at different targets. Thus, a Poseidon missile, which carries 10 MIRVs, can hit 10 different targets some distance apart.

In a MIRVed system, the warheads on the missile are carried on a "bus," which is equipped with its own inertial-guidance system and a set of small rocket motors that can be used to change its velocity and orientation. The bus is launched on a normal missile trajectory. Then, when this trajectory is aimed toward the first target, the bus releases the first warhead. The bus then changes course to a trajectory aimed toward the second target and releases the second warhead toward that target. The bus continues in this fashion until all the warheads are directed at their separate preselected targets. The Minuteman III missiles are designed to carry 3 MIRVs, and the Poseidon C-3 missiles, which are replacing the missiles on 31 Polaris submarines, are designed to carry 10 MIRVs. Each such Poseidon-equipped submarine carries 16 missiles and will have 160 reentry vehicles with nuclear warheads. More advanced missiles are under development.

The Soviet Union had been the first to develop an ICBM, but did not deploy ICBMs and SLBMs as extensively as the United States during the first part of the 1960's. In part because U.S. technical means of surveillance were not as advanced during the 1950's as today, the United States assumed there was or would be an extensive Soviet deployment. This in turn precipitated the "missile gap" issue in the 1960 election and was part of the reason for the large U.S. ICBM and SLBM programs of the first half of the 1960's.

During the latter part of the 1960's, Soviet strategic missile deployments moved forward, first equaling the U.S. number of deployed ICBMs, and by the time of the SALT I agreements in 1972 surpassing the U.S. total in ICBMs and nearing the U.S. total in SLBMs. During this era the Soviet Union sought to increase the number of deployed missiles, while the United States, benefiting from more advanced technology, sought to increase the number of independently targetable reentry vehicles on each missile rather than the number of deployed missiles.

The ICBMs deployed by the Soviet Union are generally larger than those deployed by the United States. Thus the Soviet ICBMs have a much larger carrying capacity, referred to as "throw weight," than U.S. ICBMs. In addition to almost 300 large SS-9s deployed by 1972, the Soviet ICBM force included 220 older, large SS-7s and SS-8s, almost 1,000 SS-11s (comparable in size to the U.S. Minuteman missile), and

TABLE 1
Central Strategic Forces of the Two Superpowers

Force	United States	Soviet Union
ICBMs	1,054	1,618
SLBMs	656	740*
Total missiles	1,710	2,358
Heavy bombers	457	140
Total delivery vehicles	2,167	2,498
Warheads: missiles	3,428	1,970
Warheads: bombers	2,460	250
Total warheads	5,888	2,220

* The 740 number was the figure for Soviet SLBM launchers agreed upon for purposes of the SALT I agreements. The United States, which used different criteria for defining "under construction," had put the Soviet SLBM total at 650. See Chapter 9.

fewer than 100 SS-13s, the only solid-fuel ICBM then in the Soviet arsenal. The Soviet Union is generally considered to trail the United States in missile technology (accuracy, miniaturization, and computer technology). It had not developed a MIRV capability by the time of the SALT I agreements. However, in the period immediately following those agreements, the Soviets tested four new ICBMs, apparently intended as replacements for current ICBMs. Of these four new missiles, one, the SS-18, is bigger than the SS-9. Three of the new missiles, including the SS-18, have been tested with MIRV warheads. The fourth, the SS-16, is a solid-fuel missile. It can be anticipated that in time the Soviet Union will also develop a MIRV technology for its SLBMs.

The central strategic forces of the two superpowers, either operational or under construction, at the time of the SALT I agreements (1972) are set forth in Table 1. In thinking about their implications, numerous considerations must be kept in mind. The Soviet Union has many hundreds of intermediate- and medium-range ballistic missiles that are targeted on U.S. allies but cannot reach the United States. The United States has many hundreds of nuclear armed aircraft abroad, based within range of the Soviet Union. The largest part of the U.S. strategic megatonnage is still carried by the U.S.-based heavy bomber force of B-52s, now equipped with "stand-off missiles" with ranges in the hundreds of miles. And there are many other asymmetries. For example, bases in Europe permit U.S. submarines to spend a greater portion of time on station and within range of their targets, while population and industry are concentrated in fewer targets in the United States than in the Soviet Union.

Numbers concerning nuclear weapons have a way of paralyzing understanding. Some indication of the power of the new strategic weaponry can, perhaps, be gained by considering the capability of *one* Poseidon submarine. One such submarine, equipped with 16 MIRVed missiles, can deliver warheads to a number of targets greater than the total number of German and Japanese cities subjected to strategic bombing in World War II. For bombers carrying conventional high explosives to deliver a total explosive energy equivalent to that of the nuclear warheads of the missiles of the one submarine would require sorties by several hundred thousand B-52s or more than one million World War II B-17 bombers. Yet the megatonnage in the missiles of that one Poseidon submarine is only a small fraction of 1 percent of the megatonnage in the U.S. strategic arsenal.

Thus, since World War II, nations have vastly increased the destructive power of each weapon, the total size of their arsenals, and the number of targets that can be struck. The number of reentry vehicles on the strategic missile forces of the two sides will, in the absence of further agreements on strategic arms limitation, continue to increase, the United States having already over 7,000 such warheads.

Defensive Systems

This explosion in offensive systems led naturally to efforts to build defensive systems. During the 1950's, when strategic weapons were carried in aircraft, both sides deployed air defense systems. These systems generally relied upon radar to track oncoming aircraft, which would then be attacked by an aircraft or missile carrying a nuclear or nonnuclear warhead. The deployment of the Soviet Union was particularly massive, with use of systems similar to those it later placed in North Vietnam.

Both the United States and the Soviets have sought to extend this technology to antiballistic missile (ABM) systems, designed to stop incoming strategic missiles. In an ABM system, a radar would pick up and track incoming warheads. A computer would predict the future paths of those warheads, distinguish some decoys (fake warheads designed to attract interceptor missiles) from real warheads, and calculate a flight path for interceptor missiles to destroy the warheads. The interceptor would be guided, usually through another radar beam that it would follow, and the interceptor warhead, usually nuclear, would be triggered to destroy the incoming warhead vehicle. Such a system would differ from an air defense system in complexity, size, and operating speed, although not in principle. Since the incoming warhead would be smaller than an airplane and moving faster, a higher-power detection and tracking radar would be needed, the intercept missile would have to go faster, and destruction at the point of intercept would probably have to be through nuclear rather than chemical explosion. Since there would likely be many missiles, and events might happen rapidly, the computer for an ABM system would have to handle much more data more quickly than for an air defense system. Moreover, the radars, which must be at least partly above ground, would have to continue to operate in the environment of a nuclear attack.

Both the United States and the Soviet Union began work toward such a system in the late 1950's. On the U.S. side, the program initially created the Army's Nike-Zeus system. By 1962, this program led to a successful test interception at Kwajalein Island in the Pacific of a missile fired from Vandenberg Air Force Base in California. Until 1967, however, successive presidents resisted any decision in favor of an operational deployment of the Nike-Zeus or a follow-on ABM system.

At about the same period, 1960–62, there was evidence of what appeared to be Soviet deployment of an ABM system around Leningrad, and a new Soviet missile, believed to be an ABM missile, was displayed in the 1964 military parade in Moscow. Subsequently, however, the Soviet program made only halting and unsatisfactory progress: the Leningrad system was dismantled and a new system was started around Moscow in 1964. U.S. experts believed the Moscow installation had only limited defense value, if any, since it included few antimissile launchers; at the time of the 1972 ABM Treaty, the Moscow ABM complex contained only 64 such launchers. During the last half of the 1960's, however, the possibility that there would be large-scale Soviet ABM deployments caused much concern in Washington.

During the mid-1960's the U.S. research and development program for ABMs had continued, and the system being considered was given a new name, Sentinel. It was designed for deployment around urban areas to give limited protection against large-scale Soviet attack and more effective protection against a future, smaller Chinese ICBM force.

In 1967, the U.S. government decided to proceed with Sentinel deployment. Great controversy surrounded both the Sentinel program and its successor, renamed Safeguard by the Nixon Administration. In both cases there was much criticism of the program on technical grounds and concern for its effects on the arms race. In the case of Sentinel, opposition also stemmed from public concern at having nuclear-armed ABMs near cities. This source of objection caused considerable Congressional opposition to the program.

Essentially no deployment of the Sentinel system had taken place by the end of the Johnson Administration. The Nixon Administration decided to continue to press for an ABM program, but proposed that the initial deployments be around ICBM fields rather than around cities. However, components of the new Safeguard system would be essentially the same as those that had been planned for the Sentinel system. In August 1969, after extensive debate and three months before the SALT I negotiations began, the Senate, by a bare margin, authorized the initial deployments for the Safeguard system.

The new system combined two significantly different philosophies: area defense and terminal defense. In area defense, the point of interception is at relatively high altitude, using a relatively long-range defensive missile. Such a system, if it works, can cover a large area and is essential for the defense of a soft target such as a city. In terminal defense, the point of interception is at relatively low altitude, using a shorter-range, higher-speed defensive missile. This technique defends a smaller area, but is more suitable for defense of a hard target such as a missile silo. If terminal defense were used to defend a soft target, the defensive burst itself could cause significant destruction to the target it is seeking to protect.

Safeguard and Sentinel combined these two functions, making use of two radars: the Perimeter Acquisition Radar (PAR) and the Missile Site Radar (MSR). Incoming ICBM's would be detected first by the PAR at a range of some 2,000 miles, or about 10 minutes of flight time. Tracking might then be transferred to the shorter-range MSR. Each of the radars was a rectangular pyramid, which could contain radars in any or all of the four "faces." The faces were about 200 feet long in the PAR and about 120 feet long in the MSR. Both radars were hardened to withstand substantial overpressures. Computers within the radars would calculate intercept points and would launch interceptor missiles and guide them to the target. There were also two interceptor missiles: Spartan, a 55-foot, three-stage missile with a warhead of several megatons and a range of several hundred miles; and Sprint, a smaller missile about 27 feet long with a warhead of 2 kilotons and a range of 25 miles. Sprint was a high-acceleration missile fired from its silo by a gas-driven piston. Spartan was used in area defense, and Sprint in terminal defense: either radar could be used in either form of defense.

By the time the ABM Treaty was concluded in 1972, the United States had one ABM complex near completion and a second under construction, with two additional complexes authorized. All but the system near completion were discontinued following the 1972 and 1974 SALT agreements, and the remaining system was to be discontinued in 1976. In spite of the fact that development of this new weapons system was effectively precluded by the ABM Treaty, the potential of the system had profound effects upon the strategic arms race and upon strategic doctrine; these effects are discussed in Chapter 7.

The Acquisition of the New Weapons

Construction of these new weapons requires a process radically different from that used before World War II. The weapons are much more complex, so that their design and construction require many different forms of expertise. A weapons system is often designed on the assumption that new technology can be developed during its construction. Since design goals depend on this technology and on information known about U.S.S.R. systems, the goals are likely to change during system construction. To meet these demands, the military and defense contractors cooperate quite closely in a large-scale procurement process presaged by the Manhattan District of World War II, the organization that developed the fission bomb.

Concepts for new weapons systems can originate anywhere within the defense community—among the military services, defense contractors, or Department of Defense (DOD) itself. Underlying research is conducted by all three; defense contractors are frequently reimbursed for this research, since it often has little application outside the defense area. The new concepts are reviewed by the services and by the DOD, which selects some for funding. The President and his staff make a further review prior to submitting a budget to Congress, which has the right to fund or refuse to fund development programs. The review by Congress, however, usually tended in the past to be pro forma, unless a particular weapon became a political issue, as did the ABM in 1969. Demands of time and expertise worked against detailed review at both the Congressional and the higher Executive levels.

The decisions on which weapons concepts to fund are based on many criteria. Strategic theories imply certain weapons designs, or U.S.S.R. developments may call for particular U.S. weapons improvements. This dependence of U.S. weapons on U.S.S.R. weapons (and vice versa) creates a lead-time problem—each nation has to design its weapons according to its estimates of what the other will have in the period roughly 10 through 30 years in the future when the weapons about to be started will be operational. The strategic calculations are made carefully, using computer estimates like those described earlier in this chapter, but can be no better than their inputs. Since intelligence information is imperfect and there is a strong tendency to be "conservative," i.e. to err on the high side, predictions are often based on what the opponent might have, not on what he will have. This is the concept that one must look to the opponent's capabilities, not to his intentions. Deployments may, thus, like the U.S. ICBM deployments of the early 1960's, be larger than turns out later to have been necessary.

It is clear, however, that the strategic calculations are not necessarily decisive. There is controversy about strategic theory, and proponents of particular weapons will often argue in favor of the strategic theories that would require construction of those weapons. There are economic influences at work—the defense budget is often seen as a noncontroversial way to bring government dollars to various parts of the nation. The need to maintain a healthy defense industry is thought of as an important part of national preparedness. Programs may be supported simply as ways to develop technology that might someday be needed. Bureaucratic pressures have their impact: the Secretary of Defense and the President find it hard to say no too often or to allow spending for one military service to fall far behind that for the others.

By the 1970's, high-level review of procurement decisions had become somewhat less pro forma. Secretary of Defense McNamara had introduced a systems analysis group into his office during the 1960's to provide an independent evaluation of weapons programs. This group, which relied heavily on civilians to develop mathematical models for comparing weapons systems, was criticized by many military officials, who argued that the mathematical models did not reflect the intuitions of experienced officers. Although the group was eventually downgraded, some of its evaluation procedures survived as part of the procurement process. Moreover, Congress and the President both sought to restrain military costs as the federal budget expanded in the late 1960's and early 1970's and as defense spending became unpopular in the wake of the Vietnam war. Thus, the President, advised by the Secretary of Defense; by the Joint Chiefs of Staff, who have direct access to the President; and by the Office of Management and Budget, the President's economic staff, would prepare a military budget that reflected a balance between military, economic, and political factors. Congress typically reduced this budget somewhat, depending on political attitudes at the time.

The review process emphasizes financial considerations so heavily that some have feared that the strategic characteristics of weapons receive inadequate attention. This emphasis is part of the explanation for what has been called the "momentum" of a weapons system. Early in the development of a weapons system, expenditures are relatively small, going mainly to research and development. Being small, they receive little high-level attention. By the time such attention comes, the weapons concept is well-developed, and elements of the bureaucracy and potential contractors are already committed to the weapons. It thus becomes politically harder to decide not to continue the program. This phenomenon may be important in explaining the development of the MIRV and of the cruise missile, weapons systems which, as will be explained in Chapters 9 and 10, significantly affected the SALT I and II negotiations, respectively.

Once the decision is made to go ahead on a program, the program is usually contracted out to private industry. The choice of firms may be made by competitive bidding; sometimes, however, different firms are encouraged to offer different designs, and the government will choose what seems to be the best combination of design and cost. In this latter case and in the case of contracts negotiated with specific firms without competitive bidding, the choice may be influenced by political considerations, as well as by military and price considerations. Contractors are expected to do much of the design and research work. For a big system, most of the work is subcontracted to other firms; the prime contractor may assemble major components, but its chief expertise is in coordinating an extremely technical large-scale development program. The contracts usually place on the government much of the risk of higher-than-expected costs; this is believed to be the only practical way to cope with technological problems that are not yet fully resolved at the time of entering the contract. The result is that the price may rise rapidly during the course of development, sometimes by a factor of 4.

Since the technological advance from system to system is so great, extensive testing is required. Component tests can often be conducted in laboratories and are used for design, for checking the capabilities of prototypes, and for ensuring that production components meet specifications. The entire system is also tested again at both the prototype phase and the production phase. These are the tests that require elaborate missile or nuclear test ranges, and that, since they are usually detectable by other nations, might be prohibited as a way to limit weapons development. No tests, however, can reflect actual combat conditions, particularly since the 1963 Limited Test Ban Treaty, which prohibited nuclear explosions in the atmosphere.

As the weapon is deployed, organizations have to be established to train those who will use it and those who will maintain it. These ongoing costs of operating weapons are often much greater than the original acquisition cost. The initial deployment is also likely to be followed by modification to incorporate new technology: weapons systems may have a lifetime of several decades, and the technological advance between several models of one weapons system is often greater than that between one weapons system and another.

The weapons acquisition process just described has been responsible for the nearly unbelievable increases in weapons capability since World War II. It has also been the target of much criticism. From every viewpoint, there is concern that the technological advances have come at a very high cost. The cost to the United States of developing, procuring, and operating strategic weapons systems is roughly a fifth of the defense budget. It is the rate of increase in cost that is particularly perturbing to defense analysts, including those quite sympathetic to military procurement. The B-52 bombers built in the mid-1950's were seven times more expensive than the B-17s used in World War II; this trend has continued and applies to practically all weapons (although capability does increase at the same time). Each Minuteman III costs about $11 million, and each Poseidon missile about $193 million. The Safeguard ABM system designed to protect the missile site at Grand Forks, North Dakota, cost $5.5 billion. The two major new systems that have been proposed, the supersonic B-1 bomber and the Trident missile submarine, are considerably more expensive than their predecessors. The B-1 was estimated in mid-1974 to cost $46 million per plane, and it was estimated at the same time that each Trident missile submarine would cost about $1.3 billion, but these numbers were also increasing rapidly.

Many also question the desirability of the technological advances, but there are profound differences in how even these people explain the technological advances. Some point to phenomena such as the lead-time problems and suggest that the United States and the Soviet Union are in an arms race in which each side is building in response to the other side. Control could then be achieved by arms control agreements and the exchange of information, so that both sides could stop together. For a few who share the same arms race perception, control is unnecessary; it is possible and desirable for one side to outbuild the other. Others vehemently deny that there is an arms race. One side or both sides, they would argue, are building in response to internal pressures such as a military-industrial complex. Control would then be achieved through decreasing the domestic political power of those who seek to build arms.

The new technology in armaments is not restricted to the United States and the Soviet Union. Nuclear weapons technology is held by at least six nations, five of which have tested thermonuclear devices. Delivery vehicle technology, although much more expensive, is also widespread. Although only the United States and the Soviet Union have deployed ICBMs, at least five nations have deployed SLBMs or IRBMs. These later imitators can often develop technology much more quickly than the first developers. Thus, it took the United States seven to nine years to develop its first thermonuclear bomb after it had developed a nuclear bomb. Comparable times for the Soviet Union were four to six years, for Great Britain five years, for France eight years, and for China three years.

Implications

Over the last 30 years, strategic weapons have increased dramatically in destructive power, number, range, accuracy, and cost. Their potential for destruction is orders of magnitude greater than ever before known in history and is continuing to grow.

There are other, more qualitative aspects of the new weaponry that are seldom noted, but that may have equally great impact on the world. The first aspect is the uncertainty surrounding the new weapons. No one knows how well they would operate in actual nuclear war. No one even knows what a nuclear war would be like—the computer-based models mentioned in this chapter are undoubtedly but a primitive description. The distance between what is known and what is estimated is greater than ever before. It is hard to imagine that this knowledge gap would not greatly affect diplomacy and the way people view war.

Second, the combat that the weapons are designed for is further removed from human emotion than has ever before occurred. One can understand the human rivalry of hand-to-hand combat or a World War I dogfight; one can draw back in horror at the death one is causing in infantry combat. The new strategic technology leaves no room for these emotions, except perhaps on the part of designers. This psychological sterility of the new weapons—which might make their use harder or easier—is particularly sensed by the military. Undoubtedly one of the reasons the Air Force continues to press for aircraft and the Navy for conventional surface ships is that duty in a missile silo or Poseidon submarine is boring.

Third, the weapons are not designed to be used. As will be discussed in Chapter 7, it is generally assumed that each side's possession of strategic weapons will deter the other side from using them. To the extent that this is believed, procurement becomes somewhat artificial and decision-makers' attitudes are likely to become somewhat blasé. Assuming that the weapons are never really used, one cannot imagine the world untouched by the fact that several nations have committed large resources to a venture that is both dangerous and, in a sense, futile.

CHAPTER FIVE

An Overview of the Negotiations Since World War II

SINCE World War II there have been many negotiations on the control and reduction of conventional and nuclear weapons. This chapter discusses the general course of those efforts; even unsuccessful negotiations were important in establishing the intellectual and diplomatic framework for the successes, which began in 1959. The details of the negotiation of SALT I and of the other modern arms control agreements, to be dealt with in this chapter only briefly, will be discussed in detail in following chapters.

It is impossible to describe historical events as a progression of exact chronological phases; events at any one time are rooted in what has gone before. Nevertheless, three approximate phases can be noted. In the first of these phases, the period immediately following World War II, the United States sought unsuccessfully to establish a world-wide control system for the new nuclear weapon. The next era of serious negotiations was during the Eisenhower years as all the great powers of the time narrowly failed to agree on comprehensive disarmament. As these efforts were failing, the United States and the Soviet Union moved toward "collateral measures," less comprehensive arms control negotiations oriented specifically to their own arms competition. The price of this new emphasis on collateral measures was general loss of interest on the part first of France and later of developing nations, and specific loss of U.S. and U.S.S.R. interest in comprehensive proposals that would give a role to the United Nations; the benefit was that during a fluid phase in the 1960's and 1970's, collateral measures prospered in a proliferation of agreements and negotiating forums.

The Initial Failure to Control Nuclear Weapons, 1945–46

The international climate following World War II was not nearly as favorable to arms control as that following World War I. After World

War I, there was deep disillusionment with war. Most members of the League of Nations believed that the maintenance of peace required the reduction of national armaments to the lowest point consistent with national safety. This belief was supported by the belief that World War I was partly caused by a prior arms race between the participants. The League Covenant, as noted in Chapter 3, included provisions strongly supporting disarmament.

Conversely, after World War II, arms were widely regarded as necessary to prevent war. The proponents of this view argued that had the Western powers (France, Britain, and the United States) been strong enough to oppose Hitler early on, he would not have built up his armies, and peace would have been preserved. Force was needed to control force.

Not surprisingly, the U.N. Charter's statement on disarmament was relatively weak: "The General Assembly may consider the general principles of cooperation in the maintenance of international peace and security, including the principles governing disarmament and the regulation of armaments, and may make recommendations with regard to such principles to the Members or to the Security Council or to both." The collective security concept was the keystone of the U.N. Charter, drafted at San Francisco by a group practically none of whose members knew of the impending nuclear weapon: "The Purposes of the United Nations Are: To maintain international peace and security, and to that end: to take effective collective measures for the prevention and removal of threats to the peace, and for the suppression of acts of aggression or other breaches of the peace." This concept assumed that an aggressor, once identified, would be restrained by use of force, and the force would have to be available.

The emphasis on the use of force to prevent aggression was soon intensified by the cold war, as the United States and the Soviet Union found their positions opposed over Eastern Europe, Iran, and the occupation of Germany.

As after World War I, disarmament was readily applied to the losers, Germany and Japan, who were considered to have committed aggression. In the 1945 Potsdam Declaration, the heads of state of the different allied governments similarly agreed that the purposes of the occupation of Germany were

the complete disarmament and demilitarization of Germany and the elimination or control of all German industry that could be used for military production. To these ends: All German land, naval, and air forces, . . . the General Staff, the Officers' Corps, military schools, war veterans' organizations, . . . shall be completely and finally abolished in such manner as permanently to prevent the revival or reorganization of German militarism and Nazism; all arms, ammunition and implements of war and all specialized facilities for their production shall be held at the disposal of the Allies or destroyed. The maintenance and production of all aircraft and all arms, ammunition and implements of war shall be prevented.

The same goal was sought in Japan, but supplemented in a more sophisticated manner through the insertion (at U.S. insistence) into the Japanese Constitution of Article 9:

Aspiring sincerely to an international peace based on justice and order, the Japanese people forever renounce war as a sovereign right of the nation and the threat or use of force as a means of settling international disputes. In order to accomplish the aim of the preceding paragraph, land, sea, and air forces, as well as other war potential, will never be maintained. The right of belligerency of the state'will not be recognized.

The exception for which disarmament of the victors was seriously considered was the nuclear weapon. Its potential danger for the world had been recognized by some scientists even before the weapon was used on Japan. These scientists were not successful in persuading the United States government that any use at the end of the war should be restricted to a demonstration that would encourage "the achievement of an agreement permitting an effective international control of the means of nuclear warfare." The immediate exigencies of the war with Japan prevailed with Truman and nuclear weapons were used on Hiroshima and Nagasaki.

After the war, however, the climate changed and the global significance of the nuclear bomb was more fully recognized. During the latter part of 1945 and the early part of 1946, debate raged over how to control nuclear energy domestically. Responsibility for nuclear energy, including weapons, was finally separated from the military and placed under a civilian Atomic Energy Commission (USAEC). This commission was to have a total monopoly over nuclear materials and nuclear knowledge; such a monopoly was viewed as the only way that the technology could possibly be controlled.

The arguments were equally persuasive for international control of nuclear energy. As early as September 11, 1945, Secretary of War Stimson had written President Truman:

Subject: Proposed Action for Control of Atomic Bombs.
The advent of the atomic bomb has stimulated great military and probably even greater political interest throughout the civilized world. In a world atmosphere already extremely sensitive to power, the introduction of this weapon has profoundly affected political considerations in all sections of the globe. In many quarters it has been interpreted as a substantial offset to the growth

of Russian influence on the continent. We can be certain that the Soviet government has sensed this tendency and the temptation will be strong for the Soviet political and military leaders to acquire this weapon in the shortest possible time. Britain in effect already has the status of a partner with us in the development of this weapon. Accordingly, unless the Soviets are voluntarily invited into the partnership upon a basis of cooperation and trust, we are going to maintain the Anglo-Saxon bloc over against the Soviet in the possession of this weapon. Such a condition will almost certainly stimulate feverish activity on the part of the Soviet toward the development of this bomb in what will in effect be a secret armament race of a rather desperate character. There is evidence to indicate that such activity may have already commenced. . . .

If the atomic bomb were merely another though more devastating military weapon to be assimilated into our pattern of international relations, it would be one thing. We could then follow the old custom of secrecy and nationalistic military superiority relying on international caution to prescribe the future use of the weapon as we did with gas. But I think the bomb instead constitutes merely a first step in a new control by man over the forces of nature too revolutionary and dangerous to fit into the old concepts. I think it really caps the climax of the race between man's growing technical power for destructiveness and his psychological power of self-control and group control—his moral power. If so, our method of approach to the Russians is a question of the most vital importance in the evolution of human progress. . . .

My idea of an approach to the Soviets would be a direct proposal after discussion with the British that we would be prepared in effect to enter an arrangement with the Russians, the general purpose of which would be to control and limit the use of the atomic bomb as an instrument of war and so far as possible to direct and encourage the development of atomic power for peaceful and humanitarian purposes. Such an approach might more specifically lead to the proposal that we would stop work on the further improvement in, or manufacture of, the bomb as a military weapon, provided the Russians and the British would agree to do likewise. It might also provide that we would be willing to impound what bombs we now have in the United States provided the Russians and the British would agree with us that in no event will they or we use a bomb as an instrument of war unless all three Governments agree to that use. We might also consider a covenant with the U.K. and the Soviets providing for the exchange of benefits of future developments whereby atomic energy may be applied on a mutually satisfactory basis for commercial or humanitarian purposes.

I would make such an approach just as soon as our immediate political considerations make it appropriate.[1]

In early November 1945, President Truman, British Prime Minister Attlee, and Canadian Prime Minister King met in Washington and agreed on the need for international action under the auspices of the United Nations to ensure the use of atomic energy for peaceful purposes only, to outlaw atomic weapons and other weapons of mass destruction, and to provide for inspection safeguards. In December 1945, during the

[1] "Development and Control of Atomic Energy," *Foreign Relations of the United States, 1945* (Washington, D.C.), Vol. II, pp. 41–44.

Council of Foreign Ministers conference in Moscow, U.S. Secretary of State Byrnes and British Foreign Secretary Bevin obtained Soviet agreement to co-sponsor a resolution in the coming General Assembly session to establish a U.N. commission on atomic energy. The resolution establishing the U.N. Atomic Energy Commission (UNAEC)[2] was accepted unanimously in January 1946.

During this procedural diplomacy, the United States was also formulating basic substantive positions on the international control of atomic energy. In December 1945 a committee, headed by then Under Secretary of State Dean Acheson, was appointed to study the policies the United States should follow, and in January 1946 a Board of Consultants, headed by David Lilienthal, was created to assist the Acheson Committee.

The "Acheson-Lilienthal Report," made public in March 1946, concluded that the only way to assure that nuclear energy would not be used for weapons purposes was to create an international authority that would hold a monopoly over nuclear research and development. It proposed a supranational International Atomic Development Authority, which was to be entrusted with all phases of the development and use of atomic energy, starting with the raw materials themselves. Such a monopoly, it held, would be the only way to ensure that nuclear materials were not diverted to weapons uses. The Authority would have the power to manage, control, inspect, and license all atomic activities, but would have no specific power to apply sanctions against wrongdoers. The goal of the organization, as Acheson viewed it, was to provide a warning signal in the event of danger.

After the report was completed, Truman chose Bernard Baruch to present the plan to the UNAEC, which was scheduled to meet that summer. It turned out, however, that Baruch disagreed with the plan's lack of sanctions; he wanted deterring penalties clearly and specifically defined if anyone should violate the treaty proposed in the report. Baruch was particularly worried that the United Nations could not adequately deal with violations because the Security Council veto could be used to protect the violator. Acheson's response was that if two great powers are opposed, having a formal sanction procedure would not help anyway. Baruch disagreed, and insisted on provisions for "immediate, swift and sure punishment" of those nations or individuals who violated the agreement, and argued that the permanent members of the Security Council should not be given the power to veto punitive action approved

[2] See Appendix B for a more detailed discussion of past and current negotiating forums.

by a majority vote in the Security Council. Acheson and Baruch met to iron out their differences, and Baruch, being the one selected to present the plan, won. Truman agreed, and provisions for sanctions by a majority vote of the Security Council were included in the Baruch Plan presented to the UNAEC in June 1946.

In the Baruch Plan, therefore, the United States proposed that manufacture of atomic bombs should cease, that existing U.S. bombs should be disposed of, and that the proposed international agency should be given possession of all information relating to the production of atomic energy—but not until sanctions for possible violators had been defined by treaty and an adequate system of control was in effective operation. The control system was to be established in successive stages, with the United States turning over appropriate information and control of nuclear facilities at each stage.

The Soviet Union rejected the Baruch Plan for a number of reasons. The Soviets had insisted on the veto during the negotiations of the U.N. Charter and viewed the plan to punish violators through the elimination of the Security Council veto as a way the United States, if it chose, could use the United Nations to organize military ventures against the Soviet Union. They considered that the proposal for international ownership and management of atomic facilities would subject the Soviet economy, at least insofar as nuclear energy was concerned, to control by a body dominated by Western governments inherently interested in hampering Communist economic development. A U.S. proposal for a quota system for nuclear power production confirmed these suspicions that plans for economic development would be hampered. Equally important was the fact that any effective inspection—let alone managerial control of nuclear facilities—would inevitably imply a massive breach of the Iron Curtain. Stalin looked upon inspection by outside agents as a threat to internal security and a potential method of espionage, which would give the West otherwise unavailable information on the organization and location of Soviet industrial facilities. And the Soviets felt they were being asked to accept these costs of a control system *before* the United States gave up its nuclear monopoly.

The Soviets responded with a proposal whose only purpose seems to have been to oppose the Baruch Plan. This proposal envisioned two treaties. The first would prohibit the production and use of atomic weapons and would require the destruction of all stocks of atomic weapons within a period of three months from its entry into force. The second treaty, to be negotiated within six months from the effective date of the first, would establish penalties for violators of the convention.

These sanctions would be administered by the Security Council and would be subject to the veto rights of the permanent members. The United States rejected the Soviet proposals. Negotiations continued, but agreement was never in sight.

Thus, the first phase of post–World War II negotiations—those seeking international control of nuclear weapons—failed. This failure is often attributed to the control problem: which comes first, control or disarmament? The United States answered "control" and the Soviet Union answered "disarmament." This explanation is probably valid, but it is only part of the full explanation, which also rests on relative force levels. The United States had a nuclear monopoly at the time and also had effective control of the United Nations. It could not conceive of relinquishing its power until it had reshaped the world along lines conducive to its safety. The Soviet Union feared that it would not be safe in any world until it had also acquired nuclear weapons; and it did not want to give up its opportunity to obtain a position of equal power.

Not until a decade later, when both sides had thermonuclear weapons, did they reach even the narrow agreement to set up a much weaker International Atomic Energy Agency (IAEA). Still another decade later the United States and the Soviet Union sought to expand on the IAEA through the Non-Proliferation Treaty (NPT), designed to limit the number of nuclear nations, and found themselves aligned together against some of the potential nuclear powers in a negotiation somewhat parallel to that of 1946.

Toward Comprehensive Negotiations, 1947–54

By 1947 the cold war had clearly begun. Efforts to agree on the major peace treaties for Germany and Japan were at an impasse. The Truman Doctrine to contain Soviet "expansionism" was announced in 1947. The 1948 Communist coup in Czechoslovakia raised new fears in the West about Soviet intentions in Europe. After 1948, Western interests were focused more on strengthening the West's military position in Europe than on disarmament efforts deemed unlikely to produce results. Recurring crises over Berlin and the Korean war (1950–53) made the political climate even more unfavorable to arms control efforts. The immediate U.S. postwar drive to achieve a revolutionary solution to the nuclear problem subsided, and with no fanfare—or even consultation of Congress—the United States decided in 1950 to build the H-bomb. The decision gave it only a few months' lead over the Soviet Union. The United States concentrated on building an alliance structure to prevent the spread of communism, and soon supported the creation of the North Atlantic Treaty Organization (NATO). Arms control discussions on both sides became directed less at negotiation and more toward propaganda to influence international opinion. A Commission for Conventional Armaments was established by the Security Council in 1947, but its meetings resulted in no measurable progress. In January 1950, when the Soviet Union began a boycott of the U.N. meetings in response to the United Nation's refusal to seat the delegates of the Chinese People's Republic, both the UNAEC and the Commission for Conventional Armaments became moribund.

President Truman's address to the 1950 session of the General Assembly marked the beginning of a new U.S. policy on arms control. In this address Truman indicated that the United States would be willing to consider the control of nuclear and conventional armaments together. Although the growth of the cold war left little hope that agreement would be possible, this coupling between nuclear and conventional armaments shaped the negotiating agenda for the next half-decade. Before this time, the United States had refused to focus on conventional arms limitation prior to progress in the nuclear field. The new approach was prompted in part by the Korean war, which demonstrated that conventional military aggression would remain a serious threat even if international controls for nuclear energy were established. It was viewed as unrealistic to eliminate nuclear weapons without regulating conventional forces. Such a course could be a threat to the security of the United States and its allies. The willingness to consider nuclear and conventional weapons together also appeared to open a new approach to agreement, in which, in effect, the United States would trade its nuclear superiority against the Soviet conventional force superiority. Moreover, the force asymmetries were not as great as they had been: the Soviet Union had exploded its first nuclear bomb in 1949, and the United States, which had reduced its conventional forces after World War II, increased them during the Korean war.

In keeping with its new policy, the United States supported a General Assembly resolution in January 1952 to create a single U.N. Disarmament Commission to replace the UNAEC and the Commission for Conventional Armaments. In this new forum, in April 1952, the United States presented a working paper defining a process for verification of the various stages of disarmament through international inspectors operating under a control organ that would "have access to the entire national territory" of each state at all stages. In May, France, Great Britain, and the United States offered a proposal that suggested military manpower ceilings and tied the beginning of conventional arms reduction to the initiation of a process for eliminating nuclear weapons. The Soviet Union refused to consider these Western proposals as a basis for discussions or to elucidate its own proposals, and characterized the first as a blueprint for a massive intelligence operation. The Soviet Union was still concerned with its nuclear inequality, and had supported a propaganda campaign against nuclear weapons, culminating in the Stockholm "ban the bomb" appeal of 1950. The Soviets insisted that there was no point in discussing the details of a disarmament system until the Western powers accepted an immediate prohibition on nuclear weapons and withdrew support for the Baruch Plan. This the Western powers were unwilling to do.

The next two years brought no important negotiations. They did, however, bring important political changes which helped to break the deadlock. The levels of U.S. and U.S.S.R. nuclear forces grew and each side realized the dangers of nuclear weapons more clearly. Stalin died in 1953 and was replaced by a new generation of Soviet leaders willing to consider new political tools. On the U.S. side, after a campaign in which he promised to end the war in Korea, Eisenhower replaced Truman as President. Eisenhower's first major address touching on disarmament policy advanced two new ideas: a proposal that all nations agree to limit the proportion of total production of certain strategic materials to be devoted to military purposes, and the suggestion that national military and security forces might be limited by absolute numbers *or* by an agreed international ratio. Neither proposal generated any interest on the part of other states. Nevertheless, the new President showed heightened interest in arms control. He continued the diplomacy of comprehensive agreements initiated under Truman, and also proved willing to consider "collateral measures"—arms control measures short of more general disarmament.

Disarmament discussions were resumed in the spring of 1954 in the newly established Subcommittee on Disarmament, which met in London. This Subcommittee, established to seek solutions through relatively private negotiations, consisted of Canada, France, Great Britain, the United States, and the Soviet Union.

Comprehensive Negotiations: Near Miss, 1955–57

In the first series of meetings of the Subcommittee, the United States proposed an international control organ like that of the Baruch Plan, but without the requirement that the great powers relinquish their veto in the Security Council with respect to the application of sanctions. Even so, the Soviet Union refused to consider the U.S. paper, arguing that it merely continued the U.S. effort to focus on inspection arrangements aimed at gathering intelligence information.

The British and French sought to bridge the gap in June 1954 with a general outline of a disarmament program. The use of nuclear weapons would be prohibited except for defense against aggression, pending the total prohibition and elimination of nuclear weapons. A control organ would be constituted within a specified time, and disarmament was to proceed in three phases, each phase to be initiated when the control organ reported that it was able to enforce the measures contemplated. In the first phase, all states would limit their military manpower and expenditures to 1953 levels. In the second phase, one-half of agreed reductions in conventional armaments and manpower would be carried out. Afterward, the manufacture of all types of nuclear weapons would cease. In the third phase, the reductions in conventional armaments and armed forces would be completed; then nuclear weapons would be totally prohibited and all stocks of nuclear material would be converted to peaceful purposes.

The United States indicated, somewhat grudgingly, a general endorsement of the proposal. The Soviets initially rejected it, pressing for a one-third reduction in military expenditures, armaments, and armed forces from existing levels, and insisting on their traditional position of an unconditional renunciation of the use of nuclear weapons as a first step toward their elimination. Just months later, however, during the U.N. General Assembly session of 1954, the Soviets appeared to reverse their position, proposing that the General Assembly request negotiators to prepare a draft treaty "on the basis" of the June 1954 Anglo-French Memorandum.

Following up this position, the Soviet Union introduced a comprehensive three-part proposal at the Disarmament Subcommittee on May 10, 1955, covering measures for the relaxation of international tensions, a program for the reduction of armaments and the prohibition of atomic weapons, and an outline for a system of international control. The measures for relaxation of tensions were reiterations of previous U.S.S.R. proposals: liquidation of overseas bases, withdrawal of occupying forces from Germany, and settlement of outstanding questions in the Far East. The disarmament part of the Soviet proposal, however, went further than any previous Soviet proposal to meet the Western positions. The Soviets abandoned their call for one-third reductions from existing levels and adopted the Western approach of ceiling force levels, with figures of 1 million to 1.5 million for the United States, the Soviet Union, and China. And the proposal for international control, although vague on many points, did suggest a control organ with more extensive powers than that of previous Soviet proposals. Moreover, the proposal suggested a willingness to proceed with partial measures prior to agreement on a comprehensive disarmament program. Numerous differences remained, but a closing of many of the gaps appeared to have taken place; the positions of the two sides were closer together than they had ever been in the postwar period.

The Western powers greeted the Soviet proposal with responses that were, in varying degrees, positive. Internal U.S. developments were, however, to dash the expectations of those observers who regarded the Soviet proposals of May 10, 1955, as a "moment of hope."

In March 1955, Eisenhower had appointed Harold Stassen as his Special Assistant for Disarmament and created a special White House disarmament staff. This was an effort to strengthen the governmental apparatus for disarmament. Traditionally, almost all governments had handled the staffing for disarmament matters through small sections in the United Nations division of foreign offices. (In most governments this is where disarmament offices are still located.) These offices were supplemented by interagency committees whose function was to help coordinate policy.

The new organization, intended to bring greater and more sustained effort in disarmament, took over, however, at a time of increased pressure within the U.S. government for a review of disarmament policy. Part of this pressure resulted from the U.S. AEC's desire to abandon the goal of complete nuclear disarmament. Part of it resulted from the fact that the U.S. proposals then on the table were, in effect, carry-overs from the previous administration, and U.S. leaders, including Stassen, wanted to have policies of their own. In addition, few of the new U.S. officials dealing with the problem had been involved in the negotiations of the Subcommittee on Disarmament, so most were oblivious to the potential importance of the Soviet May 10 proposals.

In addition to these internal political factors, there were substantive problems. For nine years, the United States had accepted the elimination of nuclear weapons as the main objective of disarmament negotiations, but this objective no longer seemed technically feasible in 1955. Nuclear weapon stockpiles had increased to the point that it was no longer possible, using the available control systems, to account completely for all past production of nuclear materials. As a result, even if all nations agreed to destroy their nuclear weapons and subjected themselves to control, enough hidden weapons might remain that an aggressor could launch a significant nuclear attack against a nation that had destroyed all its nuclear weapons. Moreover, Secretary of State John Foster Dulles was suspicious of disarmament and feared in particular that the Soviet interest in disarmament was designed to slow the rearmament of Germany, a step that he viewed as the safest road to peace.

A decision was made to "reserve"—in effect to withdraw—all previous U.S. disarmament proposals. Except on certain first-step arms control proposals, Stassen was unable to obtain U.S. governmental decisions in support of new serious disarmament proposals until 1957.

The brief exchange of views among the heads of government at the Geneva summit in 1955 provided the first public indication of the significant change in U.S. disarmament policy. At the summit meeting Eisenhower set forth part of the U.S. conclusion: that it had become impossible to construct an international control system capable of detecting all nuclear weapons and materials. The Soviets had acknowledged the point in their May 10 proposal, but they continued to call for the elimination of nuclear weapons.

At the summit meeting, Eisenhower did offer the "open skies" proposal—reciprocal aerial inspection of the United States and the Soviet Union and exchange of the blueprints of U.S. and Soviet military establishments. This proposal was intended to establish an effective warning system to lessen the fears and dangers of surprise attack. The Soviets responded that aerial surveillance should not be permitted until the last stages of a comprehensive disarmament process, and Soviet leaders presented instead an abbreviated version of the Soviet proposals of May 10. The only new features were a suggestion, obviously aimed against West German rearmament, that levels of armed forces for states other than the big five should not exceed 150,000 to 200,000 men, and a proposal that, pending the conclusion of an international convention prohibiting nuclear weapons, the four powers declare that they would not be the first to use nuclear weapons against any country.

The impasse sharpened. Premier Bulganin wrote President Eisenhower in October 1955 that the Soviets would not accept the U.S. open-skies proposal apart from a general disarmament plan, and repeated a May 10 proposal for the establishment of control posts at large ports, at railway junctions, on main motor highways, and in airports as a means of guarding against surprise attack. The Western powers responded that this approach would not provide adequate security against surprise attack unless it were supplemented by aerial inspection. The Soviets countered that inspection before disarmament was merely a form of espionage and could intensify the fear of surprise attack, since the newly acquired intelligence could be used for aggressive purposes.

At the Subcommittee on Disarmament, which reconvened in the fall of 1955, Harold Stassen made public the U.S. "reservation" upon all its pre-Geneva substantive positions. The United States continued to urge adoption of Eisenhower's open-skies plan, while the Soviet Union continued to adhere to its May 10 proposal. The Subcommittee adjourned amid decreasing hopes for progress. The following year's session was equally unproductive, in part because the United States had not yet developed new proposals for comprehensive programs.

Perhaps in response to the impasse, new ideas began to emerge for subsidiary agreements which would not have to wait for agreement on a complete disarmament program. President Eisenhower wrote Premier Bulganin in March 1956 proposing a mutual cut-off in the production of fissionable materials for nuclear weapons, so as to halt the growth of Soviet and American nuclear arsenals. In conjunction with this proposal, he also suggested that the United States and the Soviet Union reduce their nuclear stockpiles by transferring agreed amounts of fissionable materials from military to peaceful purposes. The Soviets never accepted the U.S. proposal, because of the requirement for on-site inspections and because of the tendency of a cut-off to freeze the U.S.S.R. inferiority in amount of fissionable materials.

The Soviet Union offered its own subsidiary measures which might be adopted independently of any general disarmament agreement. These included the creation of a denuclearized zone in both East and West Germany, the reduction of military budgets by up to 15 percent, and the cessation of nuclear weapons tests, all of which were rejected by the United States. The Soviets also agreed for the first time to consider aerial photography, but restricted it to a zone 800 kilometers deep on both sides of the line between NATO and Warsaw Pact forces in Europe. The United States welcomed Soviet willingness to consider aerial photography, but called on the Soviets to accept the open-skies proposals for aerial survey and the exchange of military blueprints, as well as the cut-off of fissionable material production for military purposes. This exchange took place at the end of 1956 in the political climate following Soviet suppression of the Hungarian uprising, and may therefore have been foredoomed to failure.

Nuclear test explosions also gained attention as an arms control issue, primarily because of growing public concern about fallout. The U.N. General Assembly established a scientific committee in 1957 to examine the effects of nuclear radiation. In the United States, the issue became a subject of political debate, as the 1956 Democratic Presidential candidate, Adlai Stevenson, called for a test ban. The U.S. government, however, refused to consider a test ban as a separable item; a test ban would have to be accompanied by a cut-off on the production of fissionable materials for military purposes.

When the Disarmament Subcommittee reconvened in London in

March 1957, the opening proposals of the parties included some of the new ideas that had come forward since 1955. For example, the United States offered a package including its cut-off proposal, nuclear test limitations after the installation of an inspection system to verify the cut-off agreement, progressive installation of inspection systems against surprise attack, and a 10 percent first-stage reduction in military budgets and armaments. On April 30, 1957, the Soviets dropped their previous demands for the total elimination of all foreign bases, and instead called for negotiation on the elimination of certain foreign military bases. They accepted Western proposals for first-stage reductions of force levels, but insisted that the first-stage reduction must be followed by second-stage reductions to stated levels. In response to U.S. proposals for aerial inspection in specific areas of Europe and the Far East, the Soviets accepted aerial inspection zones in the first stage and proposed smaller zones that would include a part of the Soviet Union. The Soviets again called for a prohibition on the use of nuclear weapons in the first stage, but no longer insisted that the manufacture of nuclear weapons be prohibited and stockpiles be eliminated in the first stage.

The agenda was very different from that of 1955; it now included much more specific detailed measures. It was clear that a serious arms control negotiation was in process, with flexibility being exhibited on both sides. The formal negotiations in the subcommittee were supplemented by lengthy bilateral meetings, particularly between the U.S. and Soviet delegations. And in Washington, Moscow, and the capitals of the major NATO countries, debates took place between those who wished to press forward and those who had reservations about making particular concessions or about the wisdom of entering any agreement before settling outstanding political issues.

Among the issues debated were whether a test ban or other individual measures might be negotiable as separable measures, what measures should be a part of any first-stage general disarmament program, and whether such a program should proceed to a second stage without political settlements. While the West argued that the establishment of a control system and the cessation of the production of fissionable materials for military purposes should precede any agreement to limit nuclear testing, the Soviets argued that a test ban was of such importance that it should be implemented immediately, independent of any other disarmament measure and without control. This Western position was particularly important to France, which had not yet tested nuclear weapons and believed that a test ban alone would freeze the superiority of the three nuclear powers.

In May, during a subcommittee recess, Stassen returned to Washington and argued for positions that would reduce the differences between the United States and the Soviet Union. Secretary of State Dulles and others were, however, reluctant to agree to more than minor first-stage reductions prior to progress on German reunification, and were concerned that inspection zones limited to the central part of Europe might lead to "neutralization" of West Germany. Stassen's position was also complicated by the fact that he retained ambitions for the Presidency, leading some to be suspicious of his motives or fearful of his success. Nevertheless, he obtained new and more flexible instructions from Eisenhower and returned to London on May 27 for the resumption of negotiations.

On May 30, fearing a reversal of his instructions because of military and allied opposition, Stassen gave an informal U.S. delegation memorandum to the Soviet delegation at the same time that he transmitted its contents to the major NATO allies. The memorandum reduced many of the differences between the U.S. and U.S.S.R. positions and stimulated an early Soviet response which brought the two positions even closer together. However, it also resulted in immediate high-level protests to Eisenhower from U.S. NATO allies, who were concerned both with its substance and with what they charged was lack of consultation. Stassen was temporarily recalled to Washington for "consultations," and the United States privately repudiated the memorandum. When negotiations resumed, a senior State Department official was assigned to the delegation as Stassen's "political adviser."

The May 30 U.S. delegation memorandum had proposed that a test ban be preceded by a ten-month moratorium on testing and take effect in the first stage prior to the cut-off on production of fissionable material. It had also suggested zones of inspection in Europe that "split the difference" between the previous proposals of the two sides, suggested a formula for limiting use of nuclear weapons, contained a provision prohibiting the transfer of controls of nuclear weapons to other states, and proposed force-level figures for the United States, the Soviet Union, and China. It did not require political settlements as a prerequisite to second-stage reductions. The Soviets' response accepted a suggestion in the memorandum for the exchange of lists of arms to be reduced. The Soviets also modified their position somewhat on the reduction of foreign bases and, finally, indicated they would accept the establishment of control posts to verify a test ban.

But with the effective repudiation of the U.S. delegation memorandum, the major attention of the Western delegates was consumed by efforts to formulate a proposal acceptable to NATO. Western agreement was finally achieved, and on August 29 a new paper was presented on behalf of all NATO governments. Some of the points of the May 30 memorandum were retained: the idea of an initial, short, test moratorium preceding establishment of controls for a test ban, the concept of a test ban preceding a cut-off, the non-proliferation proposal, and the force-level figures. On other positions, however, the joint proposal drew back from the May 30 memorandum. Second-stage reductions could not take place until after progress on solution of political issues. The new NATO proposal would enlarge the inspection zones in Europe, thus broadening the differences between the two sides. On the use of nuclear weapons, the NATO proposal also drew back from the U.S. delegation memorandum, permitting their use if an armed attack placed a country in a situation of individual or collective self-defense. The United States' European allies were clearly concerned that the unity of NATO would be split if different parts of Western Europe were treated differently. They also believed that the United States had to maintain the right to use nuclear weapons to deter the Soviet Union from making a conventional attack against NATO.

On August 27, anticipating the NATO proposal, the Soviet representative violently attacked the United States, the NATO countries, and what he called the "fruitless disarmament talks." The Soviets regarded the Western states' proposal of August 29, which was submitted as an "inseparable" package, as a retreat from earlier U.S. submissions, and rejected it the day it was submitted. On September 6 the subcommittee ended its sessions and the Soviet Union refused to agree to its resumption. The Soviets felt that negotiations had reached an impasse, and they were unwilling to continue further in a general disarmament forum in which they were outnumbered four to one by Western states. One effect of this failure was the loss of what was probably the last chance to restrict nuclear weapons to three nations.

The Rise of Collateral Agreements, 1953–62, and Decline of Comprehensive Negotiations, 1957–63

Shortly after the end of the Disarmament Subcommittee, Stassen resigned and the White House disarmament staff was abolished. There was to be no further serious exploration of staged-disarmament programs except for a short period in 1962. Arms control efforts would be directed primarily at individual measures rather than staged packages. From the subjects discussed in the subcommittee as parts of a package, however, there emerged such later measures as the Limited Test Ban, the Non-Proliferation Treaty, and the Outer Space Treaty.

There are many reasons for the shift in attention. The Soviet Sputnik was launched in 1957 and ushered in the age of missiles. It undoubtedly altered security perceptions on both sides, and perhaps contributed to the failure to pursue comprehensive negotiations. In the United States, arms control was dealt with by a series of ad hoc groups brought together for particular negotiations and then usually disbanded. Not until the creation of the Arms Control and Disarmament Agency (ACDA) late in 1961 were U.S. efforts centralized and placed on a permanent basis. Moreover, the negotiations themselves had focused attention on collateral issues. What was discussed in 1957 was quite different from what had been discussed in 1955, and the new ideas were ideas that could become first steps.

Some of the collateral measures were older. For example, in December 1953, in his "Atoms for Peace" address to the U.N. General Assembly, Eisenhower had proposed the establishment of an international agency to which nations would make contributions from their stockpiles of fissionable materials. The agency would be responsible for allocating these nuclear materials "to serve the peaceful pursuits of mankind," so they would become unavailable for military uses. The Soviet Union had initially refused to consider the proposal apart from the general issues of atomic energy control and prohibition of atomic weapons. It subsequently reversed its position, but only after the United States had made it clear that it would proceed to establish the agency, with or without Soviet cooperation. The resulting International Atomic Energy Agency (IAEA) was set up in July 1957 with headquarters in Vienna, and the United States immediately offered to contribute a substantial amount of fissionable material. The agency distributes the nuclear materials contributed to it, and operates an elaborate control or safeguard scheme for peaceful nuclear activities. Thus, the IAEA is one of several parallel ways to transmit nuclear materials from countries that have them to the countries that do not. And IAEA safeguards do provide some control over nuclear materials; however, in recipient nations they cover only the nuclear materials supplied through the IAEA and those placed under control by agreement. They do not cover the materials that the United States and the Soviet Union reserve for their own military purposes.

Another early collateral agreement, in a sense, "just happened"; it was never part of the arms control negotiations. This was the Antarctic treaty, which, in effect, made the Antarctic a demilitarized zone and became a model for several later arms control agreements. In the 1957 International Geophysical Year, scientists of many nations had cooperated in studies of the earth, including the Antarctic. This experience awakened a desire on their part to keep the Antarctic open for further research, a desire that could be frustrated by military development of the area or by a number of outstanding territorial claims. Following U.S. initiative, a conference was held which produced a 1959 treaty protecting the area from military activity and holding territorial claims in suspense for a number of years. (This agreement is discussed in more detail in the following chapter.)

The measure from the 1957 package that most affected future negotiations was the nuclear test ban. Ever increasing world-wide concern over fallout forced the United States to change its policy and to accept the test ban as a separable measure. A Conference of Experts to study verification questions was successful, and was followed by a tripartite U.S.-U.S.S.R.-U.K. "Geneva Conference on the Discontinuance of Nuclear Weapons Tests," which began in late 1958 and led ultimately to the 1963 Limited Test Ban Treaty. France, not yet a nuclear power and unwilling to accept a separable test ban, was not represented.

An analogous conference of experts to study measures that might be helpful in preventing surprise attack also began in Geneva in November 1958. This conference of NATO and Warsaw Pact powers lasted only six weeks, however, and was adjourned *sine die* in December 1958. The parties failed to agree on even an agenda. Both conferences, however, simply by assembling a large number of experts, had the important long-term effect of interesting many U.S. individuals in arms control.

It would, however, be some years before these new ideas could be converted into agreements. In August 1959 the U.S., U.S.S.R., British, and French foreign ministers did agree to establish a new international negotiating forum, the Ten-Nation Disarmament Committee. This committee, which would replace the London Subcommittee on Disarmament, included five members from NATO and five from the Warsaw Pact, in order to satisfy the Soviet desire for parity. After fruitless discussions of general and complete disarmament (GCD), the conference recessed in April 1960, only a few weeks after it opened. During the recess an American U-2 reconnaissance aircraft was shot down over the Soviet Union. Soviet recriminations were bitter and a planned summit conference between Khrushchev and Eisenhower collapsed. The Soviet delegation returned briefly to the Ten-Nation conference to present a new proposal for GCD, but the Warsaw Pact countries walked out of the conference on June 27, before the presentation of new Western proposals. The Ten-Nation Committee was never reconvened.

Negotiations were clearly never serious during the brief Ten-Nation conference. The United States feared a Soviet lead in ICBM development and was interested less in arms control than in redressing this perceived developing strategic imbalance. Propaganda exchanges were the order of the day, not negotiations, as the West sought to blunt the international impact of Khrushchev's GCD campaign, which extended to the General Assembly as well as to the conference. Moreover, the United States was unprepared for disarmament negotiations, and its limited organizational resources were largely devoted to the test ban negotiations. Finally, the summit collapse implied that any new effort would have to await the advent of a new administration in Washington.

When President Kennedy took office in 1961, he decided to begin a massive missile deployment program to counterbalance what was then believed, erroneously, to be a large-scale Soviet ICBM deployment effort. At the same time, he wished to strengthen the government's resources for dealing with arms control, and appointed John McCloy as his adviser on disarmament. Largely through the efforts of McCloy, of his deputy, Adrian Fisher, of Senator Hubert Humphrey, and of the President's Science Advisory Committee, Congress established the Arms Control and Disarmament Agency (ACDA) in September 1961. ACDA was assigned the following primary duties: "(a) the conduct, support, and coordination of research for arms control and disarmament policy formulation; (b) the preparation for and management of United States participation in international negotiations in the arms control and disarmament field; (c) the dissemination and coordination of public information concerning arms control and disarmament; and (d) the preparation for, operation of, or, as appropriate, direction of United States participation in such control systems as may become part of United States arms control and disarmament activities." The Director of ACDA was designated principal adviser to the Secretary of State and to the President on arms control and disarmament and, under the direction of the Secretary of State, was assigned primary responsibility within the government for the subject. During the following years ACDA, with a staff of around 250 and a budget of around $9 million, played a central role in U.S. disarmament efforts. William Foster was appointed Director and Adrian Fisher became Deputy Director.

Bilateral discussions between the United States and the Soviet Union also took place during 1961 and led in the latter part of the year to a Joint Statement of Agreed Principles for Disarmament Negotiations and to agreement to establish the Eighteen-Nation Disarmament Committee (ENDC).

The Joint Statement declared that the goal of negotiations was to achieve a program for GCD that would include elimination from national arsenals of all stockpiles of nuclear and other weapons of mass destruction and essential abolition of national military establishments. Various general principles were set forth as criteria for developing the GCD plan. In particular, GCD was to be accompanied by a strengthening of the United Nations. The Statement also endorsed the concept of partial measures, calling on states to achieve "the widest possible agreement at the earliest possible date." In later arms control discussions, both sides have used the rhetoric of the Joint Statement to support their positions, but translating the principles into mutually agreed programs has proved difficult.

The new ENDC began its sessions in Geneva on March 14, 1962, and became the continuing forum for multilateral disarmament negotiations in the following years. The new forum included the nations that had been members of the Ten-Nation Committee and eight additional neutral states designed to give the body a broader geographical representation. The test ban negotiations were transferred from the Trilateral Test Ban Conference to a subcommittee of the ENDC. The United States and the Soviet Union were the permanent co-chairmen of the conference, which used U.N. facilities but was technically separate from the United Nations. In 1969, the ENDC was enlarged to twenty-six members and its name was changed to the Conference of the Committee on Disarmament (CCD). Although France was assigned a seat at both the ENDC and the CCD, it has not participated in the work of either. A few discussions of general and complete disarmament were held at the ENDC, but after the early part of 1963, the test ban negotiations and other collateral measures dominated the discussions.

The years of nearly fruitless negotiations of the 1950's may appear to have been wasted, and possible opportunities were certainly lost. Nevertheless, the era saw fundamental developments that made later agreements possible. Relations between the United States and the Soviet Union had been so dominated by cold war attitudes early in the era that comprehensive agreements would have been almost unthinkable. The strategies and the force levels of the two sides were so different that it would have been hard for even a disinterested party to design agreements in the interests of both sides. By the early 1960's recognition of the need for arms control was increasing and an agenda of feasible partial measures was available. And the machinery for negotiation had been built in both Geneva and Washington.

But there was a price to be paid for the shift to collateral measures. The new agenda was dominated by U.S. and Soviet interests and risked slighting the interests of others. This domination was reflected by the U.S.-Soviet co-chairmanship of the ENDC and the separation of the

ENDC from the United Nations. The domination and the emphasis on partial measures led early to the alienation of France. Later, as will be seen, it led to the alienation of some of the developing nations.

The Proliferation of Agreements, 1963–74, and of Forums, 1969–74

Starting in 1963, the ENDC led to a series of agreements, negotiated essentially one at a time. Whereas the earlier discussions of GCD concerned general concepts, the negotiation of specific agreements required time-consuming effort to agree upon and negotiate specific detailed provisions. Governments found it difficult to engage in more than one detailed arms control negotiation at a time, particularly when internal controversy had to be resolved. Thus, each "active" negotiation dominated the agenda in its turn. Other matters were debated, but attention was focused on the measure that had become "ripe for agreement."

The Cuban missile crisis of October 1962, in which nuclear war appeared close, changed the climate for arms control. Decision-makers on both sides realized the danger of war. They also discovered the difficulty of communication in time of crisis. In December 1962 the United States submitted a working paper to the ENDC on the Reduction of the Risk of War Through Accident, Miscalculation, or Failure of Communication. This paper proposed a series of measures, including the establishment of a direct communications link between major capitals. In April the Soviets agreed to consider the proposal. Bilateral U.S.-U.S.S.R. negotiations began immediately, and the "Hot Line" agreement was signed in Geneva on June 20, 1963. (All these agreements are discussed in more detail in the following chapter.)

The nuclear test ban negotiations were similarly ripening, and on June 10 President Kennedy announced that special trilateral (U.S.-U.S.S.R.-U.K.) test ban talks would be held in Moscow. After intensive negotiations, the Limited Test Ban Treaty was initialed on July 25, 1963. This agreement prohibited the testing of nuclear weapons under water, in the atmosphere, and in outer space. Senate ratification required a large-scale campaign by President Kennedy and rested partly on the argument that the treaty would decrease fallout; arms control was slow to become politically popular. This agreement did permit underground testing and therefore permitted the continued development of nuclear weapons. It also eliminated all hope of a Sino-Soviet reconciliation; China saw Soviet acceptance of the agreement as a betrayal of Communist doctrine. Nevertheless, the agreement was, and was looked upon as, the first real attempt at limiting the arms race. As such, it raised new hopes for further progress.

At the General Assembly session in September, Foreign Minister Gromyko accepted the idea of banning the placement of nuclear weapons in orbit. This idea had been put forward by the United States in 1960 and discussed bilaterally in 1962 and 1963. In October 1963 the two nations supported a successful General Assembly resolution on the subject. Later negotiations led to the Outer Space Treaty of 1967.

The immediate momentum ended with that agreement. The two leaders, Kennedy and Khrushchev, who had taken a personal hand in pressing for the 1963 agreements after the Cuban missile crisis, were removed from office by assassination and purge. New leadership required time to reflect and decide before taking the initiative in arms control negotiations. And one of the causes of Khrushchev's removal was opposition to his regime by Soviet military leaders.

The issue of on-site inspection, demanded by the United States and opposed by the Soviet Union, continued to stand as a barrier to a comprehensive test ban. The Soviets argued for a 10 to 15 percent military budget reduction, but the United States responded that the best way to reduce budgets was through agreed arms reductions. The United States and the Soviet Union attempted to achieve a less formal "mutual example" reduction of their military budgets, but this effort evaporated by 1965 with the expansion of U.S. military expenditures for Vietnam. The United States proposed a "bomber bonfire" of U.S. B-47s and Russian TU-16s, which were to be taken from operational inventories and destroyed at a rate of 20 per month over a two-year period, but the Soviets recognized that the U.S. B-47s were already being phased out of active inventory. They proposed the elimination of all bomber aircraft, but this was unacceptable to the United States, which had considerably more bombers than the Soviets. The United States continued to suggest variations of its proposal for a cut-off in fissionable materials production for weapons purposes, but the Soviets exhibited no interest. It appeared that the asymmetry in fissionable material stockpiles of the two sides was too great for any common ground to be achieved.

New agenda items, however, were being developed. In January 1964 President Johnson proposed a verified freeze on the numbers and characteristics of offensive and defensive strategic nuclear delivery vehicles. Although the official Soviet reason for rejecting the freeze was that it would constitute "control without disarmament," the Soviets at the time had only about one-fourth as many ICBMs and SLBMs as the United States. A freeze would have frozen them into strategic inferiority. The Soviets became willing to discuss strategic freezes only in the late 1960's, when they began to reach strategic parity with the United States.

There was a second Soviet objection: the Soviets did not want a strategic freeze until after a non-proliferation treaty (NPT), to relieve them of the fear that Germany would develop nuclear weapons. Since the United States was also interested in preventing proliferation, negotiation of the NPT came to the forefront of the disarmament agenda and dominated arms control discussions in the ENDC, the eight-week session of the U.N. Disarmament Commission, and the U.N. General Assembly by 1965. Strategic arms questions were postponed: the strain on U.S.-Soviet relations imposed by the Vietnam conflict was burden enough for the one ongoing negotiation, the NPT effort. In 1967, in the longest session in the ENDC's history, the U.S. and U.S.S.R. negotiators and their governments produced an agreed NPT text (minus one article). The non-nuclear nations still had objections, which they expressed in the ENDC and then in the General Assembly. These nations were the ones who would be controlled by the treaty and whom it would subject to IAEA inspection of nuclear facilities. Finally, on July 1, 1968, the treaty was signed in Washington, Moscow, and London, after U.S. and Soviet compromises to meet the demands of the non-nuclear nations.

During this long negotiation, two other agreements were successfully concluded in other forums. On January 27, 1967, the Outer Space Treaty was signed in Washington, London, and Moscow. Although it prohibited the orbiting of weapons of mass destruction, it had many non–arms control features relating to issues such as astronaut rescue and the making of territorial claims in outer space. Less than a month later, on February 14, the Latin American Nuclear Free Zone Treaty (or Treaty of Tlatelolco) was signed in Mexico City, after negotiation by the Latin American nations themselves.

One of the concessions the nuclear nations had to make to obtain non-nuclear nation support of the NPT was a commitment to seek an end to the nuclear arms race as well as to pursue other measures of disarmament. These pressures from the international community for further progress were strongly reflected in General Assembly debates and in a Conference of Non-Nuclear States held in September following the NPT signing. The non-nuclear nations argued that they were being asked to give up the right to build nuclear weapons. In return, the superpowers ought to control their own "vertical proliferation" of weapons.

The United States and the Soviet Union reacted in two ways: first, by starting strategic arms limitation talks (eventually called SALT), and second, by moving forward in the ENDC to less controversial "next steps." The conclusion of the NPT itself resolved one of the Soviet concerns with strategic arms negotiations. On the day of its signing, President Johnson announced that agreement had been reached with the

Soviet Union to enter into such discussions. Although international pressures played a part in moving the United States and the Soviet Union into serious negotiations in SALT, the dominant forces were the dangers and costs of the strategic competition itself. Strategic offensive arms deployments or developments were proceeding in both countries. A small Soviet ABM deployment around Moscow earlier in the decade was followed by a 1967 U.S. decision to proceed with an ABM system. Both sides seemed to recognize that a crossroads had been reached, but the Soviet military intervention in Czechoslovakia in August 1968 changed the international atmosphere after President Johnson's announcement and prevented the beginning of SALT during that year. The Nixon Administration took office in January 1969 and wanted time to reevaluate the strategic situation. SALT was not to start until November 17, 1969, in Helsinki. Two and a half years later, at the May 1972 summit meeting in Moscow, these critical negotiations were brought to a conclusion. These negotiations dominated arms control discussions—and much of U.S.-Soviet relations—during the 1969–75 period. Four agreements resulted from SALT I. The most important—probably the most important arms control agreement of the postwar period—was a treaty placing substantial limitations on ABMs. Accompanying this treaty was a five-year interim agreement temporarily restricting the construction of offensive strategic missile systems. During SALT I, agreement was also reached on an up-grading of the "Hot Line" through use of satellite communications and on measures to reduce the danger of accidental war.

Negotiations in what became known as SALT II followed, although they were hampered by the Watergate crisis. In July 1974, a protocol to the ABM Treaty was signed to reduce the number of permitted ABM sites for each nation. During their bilateral discussions, the two superpowers also negotiated a proposed weak bilateral extension of the Limited Test Ban Treaty, which would limit underground tests to those below a threshold of 150 KT. Efforts to achieve limitations on offensive strategic systems, however, proved more difficult. A general outline of a SALT II agreement was agreed to at the November 1974 Vladivostok summit meeting, but negotiations to reach final agreement based on this accord were not successfully completed during the following year.

The superpowers also sought to respond to non-nuclear nation pressures through further agreements at the ENDC. The subject that seemed to offer the best prospect for early and relatively painless agreement was an arms control arrangement for the seabed. Discussions had already taken place in a U.N. Ad Hoc Committee, and the United States had proposed the subject to the ENDC. The Soviets concurred. Both countries submitted draft treaties in 1969, and reached agreement on a common approach in October. Extensive and complicated negotiations were still required because of issues raised by other states concerning verification procedures and the relationship of the seabed treaty to law-of-the-sea questions. The treaty was finally signed on February 11, 1971.

During the negotiations of the Seabed Treaty, most other members of the Geneva Forum, now enlarged again and called the Conference of the Committee on Disarmament (CCD), sought to prod the United States and the Soviet Union toward progress on more significant arms control questions. These nations welcomed SALT I, though they were not pleased with its secret bilateral nature, and they were generally pleased to see progress being made in the CCD on a "next step." Still, they argued, a seabed agreement was not a significant measure. Most of their attention was devoted to a comprehensive test ban. They argued that improvements in seismic verification capabilities had reduced the need for on-site inspection. Sweden, for example, submitted a draft treaty banning underground tests. But the United States continued to insist on on-site inspection, and the Soviet Union seemed uninterested in a full test ban unless all nuclear nations, including China, would also be bound.

In 1969 the United States amended its proposed cut-off on fissionable material production by narrowing the inspection requirement to IAEA verification of peaceful nuclear activities. The United States had decided it could rely on its national technical means of verification to detect possible clandestine facilities. The Soviets rejected the offer, arguing that the proposal showed that the United States was overproducing fission-able materials; the Soviets were, however, placed in the uncomfortable position of rejecting a form of verification they were asking non-nuclear states to accept under the NPT.

An effort to achieve arms control on chemical and bacteriological weapons followed closely behind the negotiation of the Seabed Treaty. The U.S. government was under strong domestic and international pres-sure to control these weapons after an accident at a Utah test range and after the extent of the use of certain types of chemical weapons in Viet-nam was revealed. In November 1969, President Nixon unilaterally re-nounced the use of biological as well as lethal and incapacitating chem-ical weapons, and indicated that the United States would dispose of existing stocks of biological weapons. He also associated the United States with a draft treaty banning biological warfare that the British had tabled in the Conference of the Committee on Disarmament in August. By the end of the year, the Soviet Union submitted its own draft treaty, but sought to cover chemical weapons along with biological weapons. The Western nations opposed the Soviet draft because chemical weapons raised complicated definition and verification problems. Almost a year and a half later, the Soviets unexpectedly accepted the more limited Western app. oach. Negotiations moved fairly rapidly, and a convention banning development, production, and stockpiling of biological and toxic weapons and requiring destruction of existing stockpiles was signed on April 10, 1972. This was the first postwar arms control agreement to require actual disarmament.

After the biological warfare convention, the CCD turned its attention to the more difficult problem of chemical weapons, but had not reached agreement in this area at the end of 1975. During 1973, 1974, and 1975, morale was low in the CCD because of the feeling that the measures being discussed were not significant enough. The 1974 agreement between Nixon and Brezhnev for a threshold test ban treaty did not alleviate this sense. The agreement was negotiated bilaterally, it permitted continued underground testing at yields of interest to the superpowers, and it was not to become effective until 1976. Many nations viewed it as worse than nothing. To these doubts about U.S. and U.S.S.R. intentions, there were added beliefs that the CCD forum would not be useful until China was included and that China would not enter unless the forum was restructured.

Other new forums arose during the early 1970's to supplement SALT and the CCD. In Europe, two new negotiations began in 1973: the Conference on Security and Cooperation in Europe (CSCE) and the talks on Mutual Force Reduction (MFR). The first of these had long been supported by the Soviet Union as a way to obtain Western recognition of the Eastern bloc's position within Europe. The West responded for a number of years with a proposal for talks on force reductions in Europe. In May 1971, Brezhnev accepted this proposal and the two parallel conferences were established. When the planning sessions were held, the West succeeded in placing freedom of communications in Eastern Europe on the CSCE agenda, but had difficulty defining a position for the MFR negotiation it had sought for so long. The CSCE came to a somewhat unsatisfactory conclusion in mid-1975, but the MFR talks seemed still stalled at the time.

Other new strands were emerging at the United Nations in the 1970's. A U.N. subcommittee was established to examine an Indian Ocean Zone of Peace, a proposal to limit great-power naval activity in the Indian Ocean. A meeting of experts on nuclear free zones was held in 1975. Several nations were also working for a World Disarmament Conference

(WDC) as a way to increase the attention being given to arms control and to bring China into the negotiations. This effort and a series of initiatives for a conference of the (then) five nuclear nations became occasions of bitter Sino-Soviet acrimony. Under a carefully worked out diplomatic formula, however, China was associated with the preparatory work for the WDC.

Conclusion

Even though—with the exception of the ABM Treaty—none of the agreements of the era since 1963 placed severe restrictions on either of the superpowers, the arms control record of that era is impressive when compared with the previous two decades or with the 1920's. One reason is the negotiating background accumulated during the 1950's, which developed an agenda and must have assisted the United States and the Soviet Union toward a common understanding of some of the issues. Another reason was the decision to concentrate on small steps. Probably the most important reason was the change in political climate. Negotiations in the 1950's had suffered from the handicap that any serious negotiation carried a political aura of "treating with the enemy." Cold war attitudes in the United States almost prevented ratification of the partial test ban in 1963. By 1972, President Nixon judged that arms reduction was so favored by the public that he timed agreements for favorable impact on elections. Among the U.S.S.R. leadership, economic needs appeared to contribute to support for arms control.

The cost of choosing partial measures was also paid. France and China had not really entered the negotiations by 1975; nations such as Brazil and India were antagonized by the Non-Proliferation Treaty and rejected it, criticizing the United States and the Soviet Union for inadequate progress in controlling their own arms. Whether the United States and the Soviets would proceed far enough in SALT to satisfy other nations appeared unlikely at the end of 1975. And it was unclear whether any of the many new forums would bring the disaffected nations into helpful negotiations.

Even this brief review of the era shows some of the negotiating problems and techniques. The availability of staffs to examine and develop proposals was clearly crucial; negotiations sometimes failed because of their absence. The Soviets clearly preferred to deal with negotiators who had strong political positions at home; they were quite sensitive to Stassen's weakness after his "fall" in 1957, and they seemed willing to make more concessions to President Ford in November 1974 than to his predecessor, who negotiated under the shadow of Watergate a few months earlier. The Soviets also insisted on changes in the negotiating forum before resuming negotiations that had been broken off; the Chinese are similarly likely to find current forums unacceptable.

The United States and the Soviet Union both used the technique of linkage many times, coupling one proposal with another not expected to be acceptable to the other side. They used the technique for propaganda purposes, to satisfy allies, and to stall for time while working out positions. One U.S. negotiator, not altogether facetiously, suggested that the United States and the Soviet Union often had similar proposals, but either at different times or linked to unacceptable demands.

Any observer must, however, be somewhat disturbed by comparing the negotiation history of this chapter with the armaments history of the preceding chapter. Most of the negotiations failed to come to grips with the issues posed by the armaments that were being built. The critical armaments decisions, such as the H-bomb decision of 1950, the missile programs of the 1950's, and the MIRV programs of the late 1960's, were hardly even discussed at the arms control negotiations of the time. And many of the proposals seemed unlikely to accomplish the goals of a more peaceful, less heavily armed world. The Acheson-Lilienthal plan wears better than any plan in the entire history; the fact that it was not followed can help explain the nuclear proliferation of the 1960's and 1970's. It was chiefly in SALT that arms control began again to deal carefully with the issues being faced in current arms procurement decisions.

CHAPTER SIX

Agreements and Treaties
Other than SALT and the NPT

THE PREVIOUS chapter discussed the general course of negotiations, leaving to this and later chapters the more detailed discussion of specific agreements. The SALT strategic accords will be discussed in Chapters 9 and 10, and the agreements designed to control
proliferation in Chapter 14. Those agreements discussed in this chapter
are the "Hot Line" Agreements (signed in 1963 and 1971); the Antarctic
Treaty (1959); the Outer Space Treaty (1967); the Seabed Treaty
(1971); the Limited Test Ban Treaties (1963 and 1974); and the Biological Weapons Convention (1972).[1] Contemporary negotiations in
closely related areas are discussed together with the agreements.

Crisis Communication Agreements

During the Cuban missile crisis in the fall of 1962, as the two superpowers teetered on the brink of nuclear war, their leaders in Washington and Moscow experienced serious difficulties in communicating rapidly with each other, difficulties so serious that bargaining strategies were
affected. Two months after the crisis, in an ENDC working paper on
Measures to Reduce the Risk of War Through Accident, Miscalculation,
or Failure of Communication, the United States proposed the establishment of direct communication links between major capitals as one of
several collateral measures. Although the Soviets had previously refused
to consider such measures outside the framework of a broader disarmament agreement, they modified their position and agreed in April 1963
to negotiate a separate agreement on the direct communications link.
By June 20, 1963, the Memorandum of Understanding Between the
United States of America and the Union of Soviet Socialist Republics

---

[1] The texts of all these agreements are reproduced in Appendix C.

Regarding the Establishment of a Direct Communications Link was signed and entered into force.

This agreement, commonly known as the "Hot Line" agreement, is designed to permit rapid Soviet-American communications "in time of emergency," in order to clarify intentions and prevent accident, miscalculation, or misunderstanding from leading to unintended war. The communication link is not by telephone but by teletype. It was decided that telephone communication would lead to too heavy a reliance on rapid translation. Printed messages would provide greater clarity and give time for reflection before replying. The Memorandum of Understanding, together with its Annex, therefore provides for the establishment of telegraph-teleprinter equipment at the terminal stations in each capital, a full-time duplex wire telegraph circuit between Washington and Moscow, routed through London, Copenhagen, Stockholm, and Helsinki, and a second circuit for backup and service purposes, consisting of a full-time duplex radio telegraph circuit routed through Tangier.

The agreement specifies that any message, other than servicing messages, must be transmitted promptly to the head of government. Messages can be transmitted in English or Russian. To assure privacy, messages are encoded; under the agreement the United States provides the encoding equipment to the Soviet Union, which reimburses the United States.

The Hot Line was used during the Middle East June 1967 war and the Middle East crisis of September–October 1970, and may have been used at other times; the extent of its use is classified.

During the early part of SALT I, the two countries agreed to improve the communication link by adding satellite communication circuits; this was the Agreement Between the United States of America and the Union of Soviet Socialist Republics on Measures to Improve the U.S.-U.S.S.R. Direct Communications Link with Annex, Supplementing and Modifying the Memorandum of Understanding with Annex, of June 20, 1963, which was signed and entered into force on September 30, 1971.

Although there are strong incentives to use the Hot Line during crisis, neither of the two agreements actually requires its use. In an additional agreement, the Agreement on Measures to Reduce the Risk of Outbreak of Nuclear War Between the United States of America and the Union of Soviet Socialist Republics, also deriving from the SALT negotiations and signed and entering into force on September 30, 1971, the two nations agreed to notify each other in certain situations presenting a risk of nuclear war. These include accidental or unauthorized launch of a nuclear weapon and the detection of unidentified objects by missile warning systems. The nations also undertook to maintain and improve their organizational and technical arrangements to guard against accidental or unauthorized use of nuclear weapons, and to notify each other beforehand of any planned missile launches beyond national territory in the direction of the other nation, and, generally, in any situation involving unexplained nuclear incidents, to act so as to reduce the possibility of misinterpretation. For transmitting urgent information and requests, the nations were to make primary use of the Hot Line.

The Regime-Oriented Treaties

Several of the postwar arms control nonarmament measures were designed to prevent the nuclearization or militarization of an area on the theory that it is much easier to do so than to remove nuclear or other weapons already deployed. There is mutual benefit in keeping the arms race out of specific areas such as Antarctica; the military costs to either side are not high so long as there are no arms yet deployed in the area. These nonarmament measures, designed to prevent the development of an arms control problem, include treaties that ban military activity in Antarctica and ban nuclear weapons from outer space and the seabeds.

The Antarctic Treaty

Since Antarctica's discovery in 1821, many overlapping territorial claims have been made on various sectors of it. In 1948 the United States took the initiative in urging international jurisdiction over the continent, but its proposal was unsuccessful, in part because the Soviet Union was not invited to participate. The next substantial step was the quasi-official 1957 International Geophysical Year (IGY). An international group of scientists (including both U.S. and U.S.S.R. scientists) jointly studied the earth, correlating their measurements and findings. This cooperation was encouraged by the spirit of Geneva, where Eisenhower and Khrushchev had met two years earlier. In spite of the arms control failures of the Geneva summit, the meeting left a spirit of good feeling and a hope of achieving international friendship through technical cooperation. To avoid political overtones, the IGY was carefully kept unofficial. There was no treaty; everything was done through scientific organizations acting unofficially. As the IGY drew to a close, the participating scientists and others exerted pressure to keep the Antarctic open for continued scientific explorations and investigation. The United States proposed an international conference, to be held in 1958, and the following year, after many months of preparation, the Antarctic Treaty was signed by 12 countries: Argentina, Australia, Belgium, Chile, France, Japan,

New Zealand, Norway, South Africa, the Soviet Union, the United Kingdom, and the United States. This first post–World War II arms control agreement entered into force on June 23, 1961.

The treaty sought to serve both arms control and scientific goals. It makes Antarctica freely available for scientific investigation, but prohibits using such investigation as a basis for any territorial claims. The treaty states that Antarctica is to be used for peaceful purposes only, and prohibits the establishment of fortifications or military bases, with reasonable exceptions for the fact that military personnel frequently staff research facilities in such remote areas. The treaty also prohibits the testing of any type of weapon and, in particular, prohibits the explosion of nuclear weapons and the disposal of radioactive waste material in Antartica. Because of the uninhabited nature of the area and the absence of military installations there, it proved possible to achieve agreement to an inspection system, giving each party the right to visit and overfly others' research facilities. To keep these procedures alive rather than because of any concern about violations, the United States conducted such on-site inspections in 1964, 1967, and 1971.

The Outer Space Treaty

The prohibition of weapons in space was proposed as early as 1957, when the four Western members of the London disarmament talks proposed the establishment of a technical committee to design an inspection system to ensure that objects would be sent through outer space only for peaceful and scientific purposes. The Soviet Union, which had just tested the first ICBM, rejected this proposal. President Eisenhower raised the issue again in his January 1958 letter to Premier Bulganin, proposing that outer space be used for peaceful purposes only. In reply, Bulganin did not deny the importance of the issue, but stated that it should be considered only within the context of general nuclear disarmament. The Soviet Union continued this link between a ban on nuclear weapons in outer space and general and complete disarmament into the early 1960's.

After agreement was reached on the test ban, however, the Soviet Union changed its position. In September 1963, Soviet Foreign Minister Gromyko announced that the Soviet Union was willing to take steps to prevent the spread of the arms race to outer space and desired an agreement with the United States to ban the placing of nuclear weapons in orbit. The United States agreed to begin negotiations and stated that it would refrain from stationing weapons of mass destruction in outer space.

On October 17, 1963, the General Assembly of the United Nations unanimously adopted a resolution stating that outer space should be used for peaceful purposes only, and urged all states to refrain from placing weapons of mass destruction in orbit, on the moon, or on other celestial bodies. This resolution formed the basis for the Treaty on Principles Governing the Activities of States in the Exploration and Use of Outer Space, Including the Moon and Other Celestial Bodies, which was signed in 1967 and entered into force the same year.

The Outer Space Treaty provides, *inter alia*, that there is to be freedom of scientific investigation in outer space and that outer space, including the moon and other celestial bodies, is like the high seas, not subject to national appropriation by claim of sovereignty: parties to the treaty undertake not to place in orbit around the earth any objects carrying nuclear weapons, to install such weapons on celestial bodies, or to station such weapons in outer space in any manner. The establishment of military bases or installations and the testing of any type of weapon on celestial bodies are prohibited. The parties to the treaty are to regard astronauts as envoys of mankind in outer space and to render to them all possible assistance in the event of accident or distress. The treaty also provides that all stations, installations, equipment, and space vehicles on the moon or other celestial bodies are to be open to representatives of other parties on a basis of reciprocity.

The Outer Space Treaty showed a combination of arms control and scientific objectives analogous to that of the Antarctic Treaty. There was the desire to prevent territorial claims, coupled with the judgment that outer space is of limited military utility except for surveillance, which is not prohibited by the treaty. Outer space was believed to be less satisfactory for basing nuclear weapons than silos or submarines, where the weapons can be maintained better, launched with a higher degree of accuracy, and controlled with more assurance. At one time the orbital bombardment satellite was considered a threat, but in actuality such a weapon was judged less accurate than one launched from the surface of the earth. An added factor supporting the treaty is that surveillance systems can provide accurate information on what is in orbit, and a large number of satellites would be needed for a militarily useful bombardment system. Hence, there is doubt whether maintaining weapons in orbit has any military value except the psychological one of making forces more visible to the public. That value is one the United States and the Soviet Union were willing to give up to avoid the costs of an arms race in space. The agreement exemplified a trend away from formal inspection toward reliance on intelligence—early thought of inspecting space vehicles on their launch pads was rejected in favor of reliance on the minimal military value of bombs in orbit, the need to have many such bombs to gain any military utility, and the high visibility of a system of many satellites in orbit at once.

There has been concern that the Soviet Union has violated the spirit of the treaty with a fractional orbital bombardment system (FOBS). Such a system would be launched into orbit and be brought down from orbit before going all the way around the earth. Although there might be some loss in accuracy, the warhead would approach its target from an unexpected direction and at a lower elevation than an ICBM. Thus, it could be useful against an ABM system. In testing such a system, the Soviet Union is not technically violating the Outer Space Treaty unless it uses a nuclear warhead in the test; the United States has not publicly raised the issue.

The Seabed Arms Control Treaty

The Seabed Arms Control Treaty, which prohibits the stationing of weapons of mass destruction on the ocean floor, is the third regime-oriented or nonarmament treaty. For the United States and the Soviet Union, the incentives to enter the treaty were familiar; there was little current military value in such weapons, so they might as well be prohibited while possible. In addition, a ban on nuclear weapons on the ocean floor was expected to show U.S. and Soviet good faith in fulfilling their Non-Proliferation Treaty promise to seek further steps in nuclear arms control.

In 1967 Arvid Pardo, the Maltese Ambassador to the U.N. General Assembly, called attention to the danger that the seabed and ocean floor might be used for the emplacement of military installations. He proposed a treaty to reserve the seabed and ocean floor beyond the limits of national jurisdiction exclusively for peaceful purposes. The General Assembly established an Ad Hoc Committee to Study the Peaceful Uses of the Seabed and the Ocean Floor Beyond the Limits of National Jurisdiction. After working sessions of the Ad Hoc Committee in 1968, the question of preventing an arms race on the seabed was placed on the provisional agenda for the 1969 ENDC session.

At the ENDC in March 1969, the Soviet Union submitted a draft treaty that would have banned all military uses of the seabed beyond a 12-mile coastal maritime zone. The United States found the Soviet draft unacceptable. Believing that complete demilitarization was impractical because of the difficulty of defining the meaning of "military uses" and because of the need for defensive military and detection warning devices, the United States submitted its own draft treaty in May 1969. This draft would prohibit only the emplacement of nuclear weapons and other weapons of mass destruction on the seabed beyond a three-mile coastal maritime zone.

After private negotiations with the United States, the Soviets, who were eager to achieve a follow-up arms control agreement to contribute to the viability of the NPT, agreed to accept the more limited U.S. approach. Between early August and early October 1969, the two delegations worked out a text that was acceptable to both governments, and formally tabled it in the CCD on October 7.

The draft received a cold reception from most of the CCD. A number of nonaligned countries felt that negotiations on a seabed treaty were an unimportant diversion from more significant arms control and disarmament measures. Moreover, they felt that the U.S.-U.S.S.R. draft treaty ignored their interests, particularly in its verification procedures and its definitions of territorial waters used to specify the parts of the seabed to which the treaty would apply.

The article on verification of the October draft was extremely simple. Both the Soviets and the United States had felt that there was no verification problem. For nuclear missiles on the seabed to be militarily important, there must be many missiles. Their emplacement in violation of the treaty would have to take place in the high seas, an area where by long tradition any nation can place its naval forces. Presumably it could use those forces to examine a suspicious activity. Therefore, it was argued, there was no verification problem, and the U.S.-U.S.S.R. draft did not try to establish any new rights or procedures for international verification.

The smaller and less technologically advanced countries argued that these national verification procedures might be practical for large, advanced countries, but not for the smaller nations. If they were to be parties to this treaty, they needed assistance in verification. If the treaty were to be used in its present form, it should be only a bilateral treaty between the United States and the Soviet Union.

As a result of these and later criticisms, the United States and the Soviet Union made several changes in the original draft. The final verification article gives each party the right to verify the agreement through observation by itself, with other parties, or through the United Nations, provided that the observation does not interfere with legitimate seabed activities. If reasonable doubts remain after observation, then the party having such doubts and the party whose activities are causing the doubts are to consult, and if necessary, cooperate in the inspection of the suspicious objects or structures. Finally, the controversy may be referred to the Security Council.

Other criticisms of considerable intensity centered on the legal definition of territorial waters to be used in the treaty. The developed and developing countries disagreed over the definition of territorial waters and the law of the sea in general, particularly as they affect fishing rights and the ownership of undersea minerals. As a result, no nation wanted to accept a definition of territorial waters that would prejudice its position in any future discussions on the law of the sea. After extensive and complicated negotiations, a compromise was reached. The treaty was to cover the seabeds outside of a 12-mile coastal "seabed zone." However, this zone was not defined as each country's territorial waters, and the text specifically stated that nothing in the Seabed Treaty was to be interpreted as supporting or prejudicing the position of any party with respect to the recognition or nonrecognition of rights or claims, asserted by other parties, related to the waters off its coast.

The final text of the Treaty on the Prohibition of the Emplacement of Nuclear Weapons and Other Weapons of Mass Destruction on the Seabed and the Ocean Floor and in the Subsoil Thereof was signed on February 11, 1971, and the treaty entered into force in May 1972. The treaty prohibits the placement of nuclear weapons, "other weapons of mass destruction," as well as structures and launching installations designed for storing, testing, or using such weapons on the seabed and the ocean floor beyond the parties' 12-mile coastal "seabed zone." "Other weapons of mass destruction" are not defined in the treaty, but the U.S. negotiator, Ambassador James Leonard, defined them in the Senate hearings on the treaty as including chemical and biological weapons and possible new kinds of weapons. The treaty prohibits vehicles that move along the seabed if they are specially designed for weapons of mass destruction, but does not affect submarines even if they are resting on or anchored to the seabed.

The Limited Nuclear Test Ban Treaties

The nuclear test ban negotiations were the most prolonged of all arms control efforts. Although the concern originated earlier, the 1954 Bikini explosions carried out by the United States intensified worldwide concern about nuclear testing: by an unforeseen chain of events, fallout from the explosion of a 15-megaton hydrogen bomb contaminated the Japanese fishing boat *The Lucky Dragon*. Prime Minister Nehru of India and the British Parliament petitioned the United States to cease testing. The United Nations established a committee on fallout. Scientists reported that increasing amounts of strontium 90 were being detected in the bones of children, and the test ban question became a political issue in the 1956 United States Presidential election. By 1957, international pressure to halt atmospheric radioactive pollution reached a crescendo. Japanese, German, and other scientists made declarations, and the British Labor Party, the Pope, and the German Bundestag, among others, appealed to the superpowers.

The 1957 sessions of the U.N. Disarmament Subcommittee in London ended in disagreement on the test ban (as on other issues), but the Soviet Union agreed to the principle of a control system on its own soil and the Western powers suggested a technical committee to look at the substantive issues. However, the critical disagreement, as discussed in the previous chapter, was that the Soviets wanted a separate test ban, while the West "coupled" the test ban to broader measures of arms control.

But the pressures remained. President Eisenhower wrote Bulganin in January 1958, proposing technical studies of various disarmament issues, including the test ban, "without commitment as to ultimate acceptance, or as to the interdependence, of the propositions involved." The Soviet Union then brought matters to a head by declaring, at the end of a long and intense series of nuclear tests, that it was discontinuing testing unilaterally. Eisenhower rejected a Soviet appeal to discontinue testing also, but after more letters, the leaders agreed that spring to convene a Conference of Experts to study the purely technical problems of verifying a test ban. The conference began in July, with experts from four Western and four Eastern nations.

The conference arrived at an agreed report, although the Soviets pushed the U.S. delegates to an optimistic evaluation of the ability of seismic devices to detect explosions. The delegates defined a compromise control system, including 170 to 180 control posts worldwide and some on-site inspection, and assessed the system as able to identify correctly about 90 percent of the natural seismic events of magnitude corresponding to a 5 KT explosion. Nevertheless, the conference contained the seeds of disaster—the Soviet and the Western delegates differed fundamentally in their understanding of their roles as experts. The Soviet Union did not see a distinction between "technical" and "political"; the West felt the distinction so sharply that the delegates were not even given negotiating instructions by Secretary of State Dulles.

In accepting the conference report in August, President Eisenhower announced that the United States was willing to negotiate a test ban agreement and would be prepared to suspend testing on a year-by-year basis. However, Eisenhower's announcement again involved "linkage": it made suspension of testing contingent on the effectiveness of the control system and on progress in other arms control negotiations. The Soviets attacked these linkage requirements, but agreed to tripartite negotiations among the United States, the Soviet Union, and Great Britain. While all this was going on, first the United States and then the Soviets started a new test series, presumably to beat the expected cutoff. Yet the tripartite conference started in Geneva in November 1958, and no testing took place from November 7, 1958, until 1961. This moratorium, and the political concern when it broke down in 1961, were important steps toward a test ban.

January 1959 saw two significant Western actions. On January 19, the United States and Great Britain dropped the linkage that made a test ban contingent on progress toward disarmament. This shift helped make a test ban possible, but, as noted in the previous chapter, it also antagonized France, which had reaffirmed its position in the previous fall's General Assembly debate.

The other Western step appeared to the Soviets to be a deliberate step backward. On January 5, 1959, the U.S. delegation introduced "new data" implying that there were many more earthquakes equivalent to a given size of nuclear explosion than the Conference of Experts had estimated. This made the problem of distinguishing between natural earthquakes and nuclear test explosions much more difficult. The United States also introduced the requirement of detecting nuclear tests in space, a region not considered by the Conference of Experts. The Soviets objected to this development, saying that they considered the experts' report to be the "agreed base" for political negotiation. The U.S. decision to drop the linkage of the test ban agreement to other arms control measures did little to soften the blow of the U.S. move, which the Soviets interpreted as simply a bid for a much larger number of control posts and inspections.

What had changed the U.S. technical position? First, the 1958 test series had included two high-altitude shots, one at 50 miles and one at 27 miles, and revealed many hitherto unknown phenomena of nuclear explosions at high altitude. Eight underground tests had also been made in Nevada, so the data base on underground detection was a great deal richer than that available earlier to the experts. Second, scientists at the Rand Corporation and the Lawrence Radiation Laboratory made a concentrated effort to study the technical possibility of evasion. Several ways emerged by which a cheater could decrease the seismic signal produced by an underground explosion. For example, it was suggested that by exploding a nuclear weapon in a very large cavity, one could "decouple" the explosion from the earth, and thereby make it much more difficult to detect the seismic signals from the explosion.

Against the background of this reappraisal at home and the technical impasse at Geneva, Eisenhower proposed that, as an alternative to a complete nuclear test ban, he would be willing to consider a partial ban involving only atmospheric tests producing fallout. Khrushchev agreed to consider at least the high-altitude test problem, thereby retreating from the Soviets' rigid adherence to the Conference of Experts' report as the only technical base for negotiation. The parties set up Technical Working Group I on the detection of high-altitude explosions, following the pattern set by the Conference of Experts. The technical group agreed rather rapidly on the design of a control system that included satellites to detect radiation from nuclear explosions in space, ground-based equipment to detect light flashes from nuclear explosions, and radio devices to observe the ionospheric effects of nuclear explosions in space. A further satellite system orbiting the sun was included as an optional item.

In spite of the success of this Technical Working Group I, the basic issue concerning underground detection remained at an impasse at Geneva. The fall meeting of the U.N. General Assembly increased the pressure for progress, and the Soviets made a further concession permitting the establishment of Technical Working Group II to consider the "new data" that the Americans had introduced and to discuss criteria for dispatching inspectors to the site of a suspicious seismic event. "On-site inspection" raises fundamental difficulties. If an international organization or a foreign party has the authority to conduct on-site inspection of suspected violations and the host party has no control over where and how this inspection is to be carried out, the host party, with some justification, fears that such an arrangement would be abused for espionage. On the other hand, if the host country exercises a veto power over inspection, then the foreign party reasonably fears that this veto can be used to hide a violation. Exercise of the veto would be regarded as tantamount to a violation and would be likely to lead to a grave international crisis. Therefore, Technical Working Group II was to search for a substitute way to regulate on-site inspection: scientifically "objective" criteria, acceptable to all sides, to define the locations of suspicious events where inspection could take place.

This second technical working group was a very painful undertaking. For the American negotiators became acutely aware that the so-called new data introduced by the United States at the beginning of the year, although representing additional technical information, did not actually change the thrust of the findings of the Conference of Experts. The change in the possibility of detection implied by the "new data" was smaller than the general uncertainty of seismological assessments. Therefore, the American delegation found it difficult to justify why the United States had prevented progress in negotiations under the guise of "new data." This unfortunate situation reflected conflicts at home and in particular the ignorance of the U.S. political leaders about the limitations of science. At home the advent of the "new data" was described in such strong terms as "betrayal by science," or "the experts have sold us down the river." In fact, the question of when earth shocks produced by earthquakes and explosions will be equivalent in magnitude and character is complex, uncertain, and dependent on local conditions; the military value of the tests at issue is equally complex and uncertain. Therefore, much could be said for the Soviet position that the earlier assessment on this subject should have been considered a political basis for decision rather than a technical document to be continuously updated. Thus the cavity-testing concept deepened mutual distrust among the scientific negotiating groups at Geneva. The strictly scientific basis of the calculations was incontrovertible. When the U.S. delegation introduced the concept at Geneva, the Soviets were genuinely surprised and tried to discredit it technically, but were not able to do so. The real problem, though, was not a scientific question but a political and engineering question. How much would it cost to excavate such a cavity, and would the construction be detectable? What confidence would one have that the roof and walls would not collapse and cause disturbances difficult to conceal? Finally, even if the deception were successful, would the gain be worth the effort to a violator?

The United States sought to break the impasse by proposing a phased treaty that would ban all explosions in outer space, in the atmosphere, underwater, and underground, with the experts' control system as the basis of verification. However, the only underground tests banned would be those above a "threshold" or magnitude at which all but the most skeptical U.S. seismologists felt that explosions could be confidently distinguished from earthquakes. A joint research program was proposed to lower this "threshold" and thereby increase the future coverage of the treaty. The proposal ran the risk that a relatively small shift in technical data would cause a continuous reassessment of the treaty provisions and substantial uncertainty about the actual meaning of the treaty. The Soviets agreed in principle to the new proposal, but required that a moratorium cover all explosions below the "threshold"; they did not wish to commit themselves on how the moratorium would be terminated. Impasse was again reached, since the United States correctly interpreted the Soviet condition as creating an unverified test ban for the lower yield explosions. Agreement was reached, however, to start a joint seismic research program.

At this point, the U.S. U-2 reconnaissance airplane was shot down over Soviet territory, effectively delaying negotiations until the end of Eisenhower's Presidency. After a new technological review, President Kennedy offered a phased treaty with the modification that a moratorium would prohibit explosions under the threshold of identifiability during a three-year research program. The Soviets deliberately hardened their conditions, trying to test the strength of the new President. They proposed an unmanageable, three-headed directorate for the control commission and linked the nuclear test ban to a treaty on general and complete disarmament.

In view of this deteriorating situation, pressures increased within both nations to resume nuclear testing. The President appointed a technical panel to examine the question of whether the Soviet Union had in fact tested clandestinely and whether there was urgency for the United States to resume nuclear tests. According to Arthur M. Schlesinger's biography of Kennedy,[2] the panel reported that there was no evidence of Soviet testing, but that technically the Soviet Union could have tested small devices. The panel also stated that there was no urgency to resume. In September 1961 the Soviets did resume testing after giving advance hints that they were under severe pressure from their military to test large bombs to be carried by long-range rockets and after complaining about nuclear testing by France, a U.S. ally. President Kennedy proposed an immediate halt to all tests in the atmosphere without requiring an international control system, thus effectively agreeing that national means would be sufficient to detect atmospheric testing. He also ordered resumption of underground tests—for which the United States was ill-prepared—and six months later ordered atmospheric tests.

Their resumption of testing placed the Soviets in a weak position before public opinion. In November 1961 they withdrew previous proposals and offered a ban on tests in outer space, the atmosphere, and underwater, to be verified entirely by national means, but insisted at the same time on an unverified moratorium on all underground tests. A future GCD treaty would provide the control system for such tests.

[2] A Thousand Days (Boston, 1965), p. 456.

The Soviets thereby abandoned the elaborate international control systems that had been arduously developed in the technical conferences. The trilateral test ban conference ended in January 1962, but discussions were soon resumed at the newly created Eighteen-Nation Disarmament Committee (ENDC).

In the United States, in spite of Congressional reaction against Soviet resumption of testing, public pressure for a test ban increased during 1962 and 1963 as more evidence on the biological effects of fallout became available. Nevertheless, the negotiations in the ENDC failed to make progress during all of 1962, even though the eight nonaligned members of the ENDC proposed several compromises between the U.S. and the U.S.S.R. positions, and the United States and Great Britain offered new proposals.

Then, with October, came the Cuban missile crisis which probably provided the key impetus to the 1963 agreement. In its aftermath, leaders on both sides increased their efforts. Initial efforts emphasized a comprehensive test ban (CTB). The Soviets, building on scientists' suggestions, proposed use within the Soviet Union of a few automatic seismic stations with sealed recording equipment (often referred to as "black boxes"), and added an offer to allow two to three on-site inspections a year. The United States responded with a proposal that included periodic inspection of national stations rather than international supervision of them, ten "black boxes" in each of the territories of the two nations, and a yearly quota of eight on-site inspections. Despite what appeared to be a narrowing of differences in ambassadorial talks in New York and the intensive personal involvement of Kennedy and Khrushchev through exchange of heads-of-government messages, the efforts at first fell short of success. Khrushchev interpreted the ambassadorial exchange differently from Kennedy, claiming that his offer of two to three on-site inspections was made with the impression that it would produce an agreement. Under internal pressure resulting from his Cuban fiasco, Khrushchev withdrew the inspection offer in April.

Both leaders, however, continued their efforts. On June 10, 1963, Kennedy gave a commencement address at American University calling for a reexamination of attitudes toward the cold war and arms competition. He announced that special discussions on the test ban question would soon begin in Moscow, and stated that the United States would not conduct any further atmospheric tests unless the Soviet Union resumed testing. Although U.S. leaders still hoped agreement might be achieved on a CTB, they were prepared to consider a more limited agreement, should the Soviets alter their position. In May, 34 senators had offered a resolution proposing such an agreement. The American University speech was well received in Moscow, and a change in the Soviet position did take place. In a speech in East Berlin, Khrushchev indicated the Soviets were prepared to accept a limited agreement.

At the trilateral talks in Moscow, the U.S. team led by Averell Harriman found, as expected, that efforts to agree on a comprehensive treaty foundered on the inspection issue. The American negotiators knew that the Senate would not consent to a comprehensive test ban treaty that did not provide more on-site inspections on Soviet soil than the Soviets would accept. A partial ban was a different matter, however, and agreement was rapidly reached to ban nuclear tests in the atmosphere, in outer space, and underwater, and also those underground tests that cause fallout outside the territory of the testing state. Verification would be by national means. Each party would have a right to withdraw on three months' notice if it decided that "extraordinary events" had jeopardized its "supreme interests."

The Treaty Banning Nuclear Weapon Tests in the Atmosphere, in Outer Space, and Under Water (the Limited Test Ban Treaty or LTB) was signed in Moscow on August 5, 1963, and entered into force on October 10, 1963. Over 100 nations have signed and ratified it, including India, Great Britain, the United States, and the Soviet Union among the six nuclear powers. France has not signed, arguing that the treaty has "only limited practical importance." Neither has China, which called the treaty a "big fraud to fool the people of the world" and accused the Soviets of "selling out the Communist camp." The treaty thus intensified the Sino-Soviet split.

Even this Limited Test Ban agreement was the occasion of a major battle for ratification in the U.S. Senate. Some opponents who had objected to the earlier treaty proposals on the basis of the danger of Soviet cheating now objected to the agreement on the basis that American military progress needed atmospheric tests. It was argued that such tests were necessary to gather more information on the effects of nuclear explosions, to improve yield-to-weight ratio, and to develop a "pure fusion" weapon, i.e. a nuclear weapon that derives all its energy from a fusion reaction and bypasses the need for a fission trigger. The "effects" tests, it was argued, had to include atmospheric and space tests to evaluate radar blackout and communications effects, X-ray effects, and blast effects for an ABM system. Although yield-to-weight ratios could conceivably be increased and "pure fusion" bombs developed using only underground tests, it was argued that a limited test ban would delay these developments and make them more difficult to attain.

In support of the treaty, Kennedy stressed four points: the treaty would reduce fallout, limit proliferation, lead to détente, and slow the pace of the arms race. The reduction of fallout had been one of the primary reasons given for a test ban throughout the 1950's and early 1960's. Although everyone agreed that testing produced fallout and that the treaty would greatly reduce it, there was disagreement whether the health benefits of eliminating fallout were offset by the security risks of eliminating testing. The supporters of the treaty tended to emphasize the biological damage caused by fallout, and the opponents of the treaty tended to minimize the dangers of fallout.

The proliferation issue was far less controversial. How serious nuclear proliferation would be was subject to some debate, but many saw it as a grave danger. Kennedy had told newsmen in March 1963 that he feared that unless a test ban were negotiated, there might be 10 nuclear powers by 1970 and perhaps 15 or 20 by 1975. He went on to say that he regarded the possibility of a U.S. president's having to face a world of 15 or 20 nuclear powers as "the greatest possible danger." The treaty was expected to slow proliferation. Secretary of Defense Robert Mc-Namara said that underground testing was more difficult and time-consuming than atmospheric testing. Therefore, nations ratifying the treaty would be agreeing to an obstacle in their nuclear development programs, and the treaty would increase the political and psychological costs of developing nuclear weaponry.

Proponents of the treaty also claimed that it would be a first step toward détente. It had already provided negotiating experience. It could reduce cold war tensions by demonstrating that the Soviet Union could be trusted, that there were areas of common interest between the United States and the Soviet Union, and that security for both nations could be promoted through negotiations. Even describing the treaty as a first step, as was often done, called attention to the possibility of further steps. Opponents argued that the first step was in a dangerous direction. They feared a Western euphoria, in which the West would lose its suspicion of the Soviet Union, would accept disadvantageous treaties, and would eventually leave itself open to Soviet attack.

The treaty was also argued to limit the arms race through curtailing warhead development. No one knew how much could be learned from underground testing, since there had been relatively few underground tests. Such testing was expected to lead to only some nuclear development. Therefore, ending all other forms of nuclear testing was expected to slow the arms race. Opponents argued that the treaty would provide the Soviets with an opportunity to cheat by conducting tests that the

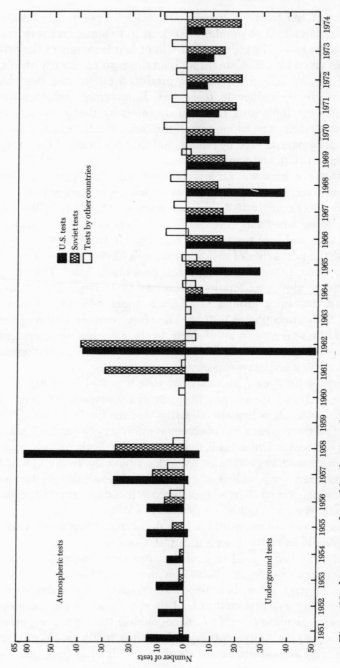

Fig. 3. Nuclear tests conducted by the United States, the Soviet Union, Great Britain, France, and China, 1951–74. Adapted (through 1970) with permission from "World Armaments and Disarmament," *SIPRI Yearbook, 1972,* p. 408.

United States would not be able to detect, while it would prevent the United States from testing. The Soviets might thereby produce weapons that would threaten American security.

Despite considerable opposition, the supporters of the Limited Test Ban prevailed, and in September 1963 the Senate consented to ratification, 80–19. However, Kennedy had to pay a high price for Senate acceptance. He gave assurances to the Joint Chiefs of Staff and to Senate leaders that included promises to maintain an extensive standby capability for atmospheric testing and to pursue a vigorous underground nuclear test program.

As can be seen from Figure 3, these assurances were honored. The intensity of the U.S. nuclear test program increased greatly after signature of the treaty, while that of the Soviet Union remained roughly the same. It turned out that many types of tests previously carried out above ground could be carried out more reliably underground. Nuclear weapons design advanced significantly in the decade following the treaty. Several underground tests, primarily on the U.S.S.R. side, have also "vented"—released small amounts of radioactivity into the atmosphere in technical violation of the treaty, since the radioactive particles went beyond national boundaries—but no major nation raised serious public objections.

Thus, this long effort reached only a limited objective. Fallout, and therefore the health hazard, from radiation was enormously reduced. Though the importance as a precedent of a treaty seeking to limit the evolution of a new technology should not be underestimated, arms competition was not significantly slowed.

As signatories of the 1963 treaty, the United States and the Soviet Union pledged to seek the cessation of all nuclear weapons test explosions, including those underground, and to continue negotiations to this end. This pledge was reiterated in 1968 in the preamble of the Non-Proliferation Treaty. Despite these public declarations of American and Soviet support for a CTB and despite extensive prodding from the non-nuclear weapons nations, no serious negotiations since 1963 have been directed at the achievement of such a ban. Only in 1974 did the two heads of government agree on even a very limited extension of the Limited Test Ban.

Verification difficulties have always been the primary public explanation for failure to reach agreement on a CTB. As pointed out above, an underground explosion produces seismic signals. The task for a verification system is both to detect these signals and to distinguish them from those produced by earthquakes. Throughout the 1960's many U.S. defense officials and some scientists argued that this task required on-site inspection to make sure that some seismic events were not weapons tests. The Soviet Union, however, generally opposed verification schemes that included on-site inspections within Soviet territory.

In the early 1960's, the seismic criteria available to distinguish earthquakes from explosions were relatively poor. The number of natural seismic events per year is quite large (about 150 events within the Soviet Union larger than magnitude $m_b = 4.0$ on the Richter scale[3]); therefore, there could be many suspicious events which would require on-site or other non-seismic data for identification. This was particularly true at lower magnitudes; as magnitude decreases, the number of natural events increases rapidly and the amplitude of the seismic signal becomes small in comparison with natural background noise. However, research programs improved the quality of the instrumentation. By careful placement of the instruments and by computer processing, smaller signals could be detected in spite of the background noise. In the late 1960's, more effective criteria were developed to distinguish explosions from earthquakes. The most important such criterion is the ratio between the magnitude of the surface wave and that of the body wave. The surface wave propagates along the surface of the earth. It can be distinguished because it arrives shortly after the body wave which goes more directly through the earth. An earthquake produces relatively more energy in the surface waves than does an explosion. Using these new criteria and a very extensive network of stations outside the territory of the Soviet Union, it is possible to distinguish the seismic signature of an explosion from that of an earthquake down to a magnitude of approximately $m_b = 4.0$.

The corresponding explosion size depends on the geological medium in which the test is conducted. In hard rock, an explosion with a yield of 4 KT or even less, depending on the rock, would give a seismic wave of magnitude approximately $m_b = 4.0$. A 20 KT explosion would be roughly equivalent to $m_b = 5.0$. In dry porous material, such as alluvium, the energy from the explosion is poorly coupled with the earth, so a 15–40 KT event might yield a magnitude $m_b = 4.0$. But the supporters of a CTB pointed out that for explosions greater than a few KT, it is extremely difficult, if not impossible, to find alluvium at depths sufficiently great to prevent visible surface effects after even a completely

---

[3] The size of a seismic event can be described by a magnitude m_b, determined from the amplitude of the body wave, a short-period seismic wave transmitted through the earth. These magnitudes are expressed on a logarithmic scale; a change in magnitude of one represents a change of a factor of ten in the energy transmitted.

contained explosion. The Nevada test site, for example, is dotted with subsidence craters where the earth has settled a few months after an explosion in uncompacted soil; such craters would be easily visible to reconnaissance.

Moreover, the CTB supporters pointed out, any successful weapons development would require a series of tests, and the evader would have to be confident that none of the series would be discovered. The cavity-testing decoupling concept might be used, but reconnaissance might discover the construction of the cavity. A clever evader might wait until there was a natural earthquake that would provide a confusing background signal. This would require long preparation and its success could not be guaranteed. Thus, most concluded during the late 1960's that a test in the 10–20 KT range ran an appreciable risk of detection and identification, and that a series of even smaller tests might be discovered.

Since such small tests were of doubtful military value, why not sign a CTB? If new warheads could not be tested, it might be easier to stabilize the balance of strategic forces, for new weapons would have to be designed around the warheads that had already been tested. A CTB might also strengthen efforts to control the proliferation of nuclear weapons. The United States and the Soviet Union could argue much more persuasively that non-nuclear states should refrain from developing and testing nuclear test programs. Some of the nuclear-capable powers that had not ratified the Non-Proliferation Treaty might either accept a CTB or be restrained by the existence of a widely accepted CTB. Finally, a CTB would help end whatever adverse environmental effects might be produced by underground nuclear testing.

But there were also arguments against the CTB. On the U.S. side, these arguments were based on a desire to test warheads for new systems, at first the ABM systems and later the MIRVs being fitted to various delivery vehicles. A large portion of the U.S. tests were below 20 KT, suggesting that small tests were of some military value. There were also arguments for testing weapons to help build a more advanced strategic system, for proof-testing to ensure that weapons in the current arsenal had not deteriorated, and for continuing testing to encourage scientists to stay in the weapons laboratories. The Soviet Union presumably had even greater motive to develop new warheads, since it began to test MIRVs on land only in 1973, and at the end of 1975 it had not yet tested them at sea. Moreover, the Soviets appeared to want to continue a program of experiments with "peaceful nuclear explosives" (PNEs) designed for excavation and the like. And the United States had an interest in not complicating its new relations with China, which might regard a CTB as a hostile act because it would create a dilemma between unfavorable world opinion if China continued testing and a permanently unfavorable weapons posture if it stopped. On the other hand, perhaps fearing that China could use a U.S.-U.S.S.R. test ban to catch up, the Soviet Union may—there is some controversy over the point—have insisted that any CTB be accepted by China. The result was continued deadlock.

The issues raised by PNEs deserve special attention. When the Limited Test Ban Treaty was negotiated in 1963, the technology for using nuclear explosives for peaceful purposes was in its relative infancy. The United States suggested that a clause be inserted in the treaty to allow tests for such purposes, but the Soviets demurred, protesting that this was a problem for the future. Since most development work envisaged at that time could be carried out by underground tests, the United States concurred, with the understanding that the subject might be raised at a later date. Since then the United States has undertaken considerable development work, and the Soviet Union in turn has initiated an extensive program of its own. PNEs might be used for excavation of harbors or canals, for release of certain mineral resources, and for some energy generation purposes. There are many problems that must be solved if the technology is to be technically and economically feasible. Many in the United States are skeptical about the economic practicality of such explosions, whereas many in the Soviet Union and in nations such as Brazil and India express greater optimism.

It would be very difficult to verify an agreement that permits PNEs but bans tests for military purposes; weapons development tests could be carried out under the guise of peaceful explosions. Internal inspection of the device might disclose sensitive weapons information. An agreement could prohibit use of some of the sensors that might be needed for military development purposes, but it would then be hard to develop PNEs for new purposes, and additional development work is needed if PNEs are to be economical and safe (assuming that they can ever be economical and safe). Moreover, if some of the proposed missions for PNEs were demonstrated to have economic value, their exploitation might involve hundreds or thousands of explosions per year. It is clear that PNEs could present a large loophole in a comprehensive test ban. The United States had lost much of its interest in PNEs but the Soviet Union seemed to be increasing its interest in PNEs during the early 1970's.

This balance of arguments left many doubtful that either nation was really willing to accept a CTB. Congress became interested after learning of a July 1970 government-sponsored conference at Woods Hole, Massachusetts, which highlighted the advances that had been made in seismology. The government sought to withhold the original conference summary, which was optimistic on seismic discrimination capabilities, but succeeded only in drawing additional attention to the conference report. Hearings of a subcommittee of the Senate Foreign Relations Committee brought the new seismic data into the public domain and revealed the government's desire to continue underground testing to ensure the reliability of nuclear warheads. The Joint Committee on Atomic Energy, a forum more favorable to the opponents of a CTB, held hearings shortly thereafter, and produced the major surprise that the committee chairman, Senator John Pastore, had begun to doubt the Administration's position. In November, the Cannikin test, a large U.S. underground burst at Amchitka Island in the Aleutians, further focused attention on the CTB. During 1972, several senators introduced resolutions calling for a CTB, but election-year politics and political controversies over SALT I intervened; none were brought to a vote.

Not until July 3, 1974, was there any action by the two governments. President Nixon visited Moscow while politically weakened by Watergate. He was unable to obtain significant SALT agreements, but did sign the Treaty Between the United States of America and the Union of Soviet Socialist Republics on the Limitation of Underground Nuclear Weapons Tests. This was a threshold ban, meaning that it prohibited only those underground tests above a particular level, set in the treaty at 150 KT. Although there were no provisions for on-site inspection, the parties agreed in a protocol to specify their test areas, to exchange data on the geological characteristics of each test area, and to exchange details on two shots in each test area so that seismic devices could be calibrated. "Peaceful nuclear explosions," defined as those outside the specified test areas, were explicitly excluded, and the parties agreed to conduct separate negotiations on this subject.

The treaty was so narrow that it avoided all the arguments against a CTB and responded to few of the arguments in favor of a CTB. The agreement brought a storm of criticism from arms control supporters. They argued that the threshold was set so high as to be essentially meaningless. A threshold somewhere between 5 and 30 KT was technically feasible, using verification by national means only; with improving missile accuracies, the important yield range for new warheads would fall below the treaty's 150 KT limit, which would not become effective until March 31, 1976. The acceptance of peaceful explosions was regarded by many as a major loophole that encouraged nuclear proliferation. Moreover, the verification arrangements were restricted to the United States and the Soviet Union, providing no clear way to extend the agreement to other nations. The treaty abated neither national nor international criticism; its chances for ratification appeared questionable and the political decisions required by a proposal for a full CTB had not been faced. Nevertheless, several meetings were held to discuss questions of peaceful nuclear explosives, and agreement on verification of such explosions and on their limitation to 150 KT was reported in April and May 1976.

Biological and Chemical Warfare Convention

Biological weapons (BW) are designed to distribute living organisms, usually bacteria or viruses, to disable or kill an enemy by causing disease. The infecting organisms are expected to multiply in the targeted individual. Crops may be targeted as well as human beings. Research and development of biologicals in the United States were originally impelled by American fears that Nazi Germany's military technology might uncover a weapon for which the United States would be unprepared. Even though the United States, and probably the Soviet Union, continued to invest substantially in BW research after World War II, BW have never become useful militarily during modern times. Their effects are delayed while the organisms incubate. It is difficult to assure that BW will cause reliable damage to a target, and to assure that they will not cause infections that could spread outside the theater of war. At the present state of development, therefore, biological weaponry offers little if any advantage over conventional weapons in planned military operations. These military factors, together with the fact that most people find biological warfare morally revolting, help explain the move to control it.

The control of BW, however, became intertwined with the control of chemical weapons (CW). Chemical weapons use toxic compounds for hostile effect. Very small doses of such compounds as nerve gas can kill within a very few minutes. The chemical does not multiply in the body, nor does it spread progressively in epidemic fashion. Differing in these ways from BW, CW have relatively well-proved tactical applications and are supported by some experience.

Gas warfare had been considered at the Hague conferences, but the startling development of CW technology by all sides in the course of World War I gave impetus to movement for stronger chemical and biological arms control. In 1918, CW munitions composed more than 20 percent of artillery munitions used, and were responsible for 15 percent of the combat casualties but only 1.4 percent of the deaths. Anti-German atrocity propaganda emphasized the fact that the Imperial German Army had taken the first steps in the military use of poison gas. Defeated Germany was forced to renounce CW manufacture in the Versailles Treaty.

Continued characterization of such warfare as a German atrocity fueled persistent diplomatic efforts to ban CW, culminating in the Geneva Protocol of 1925. The 1922 Washington Disarmament Conference had produced a treaty which noted that the use of poison gas had been "justly condemned by the general opinion of the civilized world," and declared such use prohibited among the signatories. Although ratified by the United States, this treaty was rejected by France and never entered into force. The Geneva Protocol itself was drafted at U.S. insistence, at a 1925 conference on the international arms trade. The language of the 1925 protocol stemmed directly from the 1922 disarmament treaty, but the signatories agreed to ban the use of bacteriological weapons as well as of chemical weapons. The U.S. Senate withheld its constitutionally required consent for nearly 50 years, however, and did not approve the treaty until the end of 1974. In the meantime, enough nations did ratify the Geneva Protocol that it entered into effect in 1928.

The text of the protocol is rife with confusion. Its preamble asserts that the use of gases is already "justly condemned" and prohibited by international law. The treaty text, however, binds the parties only among themselves. Furthermore, most parties, following the lead of France, specifically reserved the right to use chemical weapons in retaliation against a foe that resorted to them first. The Geneva Protocol is, therefore, essentially a no-first-use agreement, and in no way prevents the development and stockpiling of chemical weapons as deterrents against possible use by an enemy.

From the signing of the Geneva Protocol in 1925 to the beginning of the Vietnam war in 1962, CW and BW were used rarely, and never contributed particularly to military objectives. Mussolini did use mustard gas in Ethiopia in 1936; his action was widely condemned as an egregious barbarism in a war of naked aggression. Italy admitted the use of gas, but claimed that it was not fighting an international war, and that it had a right of reprisal against decapitations and other atrocities by the Ethiopian tribesmen. There were numerous reports of Japanese experiments with CW in the invasion and occupation of China from 1937 to 1945. However, during World War II there was mutual restraint in the use of CW and BW, prompted in large part by the belligerents' fear of retaliation. Both the United States and the Soviet Union captured large stocks of German nerve gas at the end of World War II. They conducted extensive research and stockpiled large quantities during the cold war, but use in this period was isolated. The Chinese made unsubstantiated allegations of American use of BW (infected insects) in the Korean war. There is fairly persuasive documentation that Egyptian forces used mustard gas during their intervention in Yemen (1963–67).

Sporadic proposals for CW and BW arms control failed. Some viewed any formal restraint on American investment in CW and BW, even one as feeble as the protocol, as disadvantageous in the face of the Soviet Union's secrecy about its stockpiles. Furthermore, it was argued, the protocol would prevent the North Atlantic Treaty Organization (NATO) from developing a policy of possible deployment and use of CW to defend Germany against Soviet attack. Also some in the United States feared that the precedent of a ban on first use of BW and CW would lead to greater pressure for an analogous ban on use of nuclear weapons. But, most of all, there was no stimulus to attract the attention and interest of policy-makers.

The stimulus came with the U.S. use of defoliants and tear gas in Vietnam. CW created major controversy, intensified by bitter domestic conflict over the war itself. In March 1968, an accidental release of nerve gas from a U.S. Army proving ground led to the death of some six thousand sheep at Skull Valley, Utah. Research and testing of CW turned out to be an inadequately monitored health hazard. These CW incidents created opposition to BW as well, for BW seemed even more difficult to control.

The reaction was both international and domestic. The U.N. General Assembly commissioned an international group of experts to study CW and BW. The Conference of the Committee on Disarmament (CCD) was soon urged to give high priority to CW and BW. President Nixon ordered a review of the American position soon after coming into office. On November 25, 1969, he expressed support for the Geneva Protocol, subject to an interpretation that would permit tear gas and chemical herbicides, and announced that he would resubmit the protocol to the Senate for belated ratification. He renounced biological weaponry in any form, even in retaliation, thus going beyond the Geneva Protocol. The President also announced commitments to suspend further development work in BW, to destroy existing BW stockpiles, and to work with Great Britain to negotiate a comprehensive treaty to bind other nations to a similar policy.

Even this dramatic statement left a zone of confusion. Toxins, poisonous chemicals produced by some microorganisms, are extraordinarily potent: a few ten-millionths of an ounce, if inhaled, are lethal. By any precise technical criterion, toxins are chemical compounds, not living biological agents. The Army therefore believed it had an unimpaired mandate to continue toxin research and development. However, toxins are produced as by-products of bacterial growth; the limitation on biologicals would not be credible if secret work on toxins continued. Nixon therefore extended the proscription on February 14, 1970, to include toxins.

The Conference of the Committee on Disarmament began serious consideration of BW and CW during the summer of 1969. The Soviet Union initially insisted on an essentially unverified ban on both CW and BW. Great Britain, supported by the United States after November 1969, responded with a draft treaty that would prohibit BW development and production but would not affect CW. The United States and Britain argued that CW and BW control should not be linked, because the difficulty of verifying CW controls was so great that no CW agreement at all would be possible in the near future. Unlike BW, CW had already proved its significance in warfare. Large stockpiles of nerve gas might be concealed, in the face of agreements that did not provide for verification. Moreover, some products of any developed chemical industry (e.g. agricultural herbicides and pesticides) are quite similar to CW materials, and the production facilities are also quite similar to those needed for CW. Under these conditions, the argument went, a CW treaty would amount to one-sided disarmament by the more open societies of the West.

BW control also offered the hazards of concealed stockpiles; however, BW had never been tested under realistic field conditions. The Western powers were willing to accept the risk of clandestine evasion of a BW treaty in order to forestall a BW technology race that would inevitably lead to the spread of such weapons. Hence the West proposed a minimal form of inspection: any party that feared another's violation could lodge a complaint with the U.N. Security Council, and each party to the treaty would agree to cooperate with any investigation the Security Council might initiate. This procedure might make a violation embarrassing, a risk that might be enough to deter that violation in the first place. The Soviets responded that to ban BW alone would be to legitimize CW and undo the good work of the Geneva Protocol. If the United States refused to ban the stockpiling of nerve gas, it must intend to use such gas, as it had used other agents in violation of the Geneva Protocol. This impasse continued for almost 18 months. On March 30, 1971, however, the Soviet delegation unveiled a separable proposal for BW. The CCD was able to forward an agreed draft convention to the United Nations on September 30. The Convention on the Prohibition of the Development, Production, and Stockpiling of Bacteriological (Biological) and Toxin Weapons and on Their Destruction (the Biological Weapons Convention) was signed on April 10, 1972.

This convention, similar in content to the U.S. unilateral ban of BW, prohibits the development, production, and stockpiling of biological and toxin weapons and requires the destruction or diversion to peaceful purposes of all biological weapons. The convention also contains a commitment by the parties to reach early agreement on effective measures for the prohibition of development, production, and stockpiling of chemical weapons. It contains no provisions for on-site inspection, but includes the Western procedure for investigation by the U.N. Security Council. Thus, it gives the United Nations a greater role than does any previous agreement.

The U.S. Senate did not vote consent to ratification until the end of 1974. This delay resulted from a dispute between the Nixon Administration and the U.S. Senate, particularly with Senator J. William Fulbright's Committee on Foreign Relations, over the interpretation of the scope of the Geneva Protocol. The Administration argued that the protocol did not prohibit herbicides and tear gas; whether this interpretation was accurate was a subject of legal controversy. Because the BW convention makes several approving references to the Geneva Protocol, the Senate was reluctant to proceed on the convention for fear that the action would give support to the Nixon Administration's interpretation of the protocol.

This roadblock was broken in late 1974. On December 10, the Director of the Arms Control and Disarmament Agency (ACDA) told the Senate Foreign Relations Committee that President Ford had decided to renounce the first use of herbicides and riot control agents in war, with certain narrow exceptions. There was criticism that the Administration was simply making a unilateral policy statement rather than accepting the Senate's interpretation of the protocol. Nevertheless, three days later, the committee reported both the 1925 Geneva Protocol and the BW convention for full Senate action, and the Senate unanimously approved both on December 16, 1974. The United States also announced that destruction of all U.S. stockpiles of biologicals and toxins (except for laboratory quantities) had been completed.

The result, therefore, was that production and stockpiling of BW materials were prohibited. Presumably, basic research that would have pharmaceutical benefits could continue. The first use of lethal CW against Geneva Protocol parties was also prohibited. The military use of herbicides and tear gas was prohibited by U.S. unilateral policy, but not by clear international agreement. Research in and stockpiling of CW were not prohibited, though the agreements discouraged such activity.

Although further restrictions on CW are on the agenda of the CCD, it will be quite difficult to achieve significant restrictions. The Geneva Protocol's prohibition of first use demands little verification. It is enforced primarily by the threat of retaliation. A ban on use of CW would probably be resisted on the Western side because of a fear that it would be transformed through domestic politics into a system of unilateral chemical disarmament. The Anglo-American position has been that a weapon useful in battle—like CW and unlike BW—should not be given up unilaterally, since unilateral renunciation would create a weak bargaining position in negotiations for a multilateral renunciation. Moreover, it would be argued, the Soviet Union showed in the 1973 Mideast war that its equipment was designed to operate in a CW environment.

Proposals for a ban on CW production and stockpiling, as pointed out above, have also foundered on the ancient shoals of verification. It may be possible with national technical means to verify that new chemical weapons are not deployed, but it is virtually impossible with such means alone to account for stockpiles that could be hidden and retained in violation of a ban. Intrusive verification procedures, including on-site inspections, might be used to detect production, but there is considerable concern that such procedures would threaten the industrial secrets of competitive private industries. Since many potential CW agents are also articles of peacetime commerce, there is also a serious definitional problem of deciding which chemicals should or should not be prohibited.

The control of CW became more urgent with the development of binary chemical munitions during the 1970's. In binary chemical weapons, two chemicals, themselves nontoxic, are mixed within a weapon to produce a toxic gas only after the weapon has been fired. Because the agents are nontoxic until mixed together, they could be handled by conventional chemical industrial facilities. Binaries could therefore be cheaper to produce because they would not require the heavy investments in elaborate plants and in skilled personnel that conventional CW requires for safety purposes. As a result, nations that have previously shown little interest in chemical weapons might seriously consider the development of a binary CW capability. In addition, civilians and terrorist groups could conceivably buy the components of a binary weapon independently and build their own binary weapon, using a minimal amount of laboratory equipment. And the absence of elaborate safety facilities makes verification harder.

Owing to the problems of verification, it appears likely that the control of binaries will have to be through unilateral restraint or through multilateral arrangements which, like the BW convention, rely on the lodging and investigation of complaints to provide a form of verification. It would appear to be in the interest of every government to adopt national controls to prevent the development and use of binary weapons by unauthorized groups.

CHAPTER SEVEN

Strategic Doctrine

To UNDERSTAND the Strategic Arms Limitations Talks (SALT), one must first understand strategic doctrines, or theories of the role strategic weapons play in warfare and in preventing war. These doctrines are intended to provide guidelines for both the use of existing weapons and the acquisition of new weapons. They tend to change with the military and political environment; new strategic doctrines have evolved during the postwar period in response to developments in nuclear weapons and delivery systems and to the changes in the relative strengths of the two superpowers. However, the shift from doctrine to doctrine is generally evolutionary; sometimes it has even moved in cycles. There probably is a lag between a change in strategic realities and the corresponding change in strategic doctrine; sometimes the relation between strategic doctrine and strategic reality seems slight.

It is important to keep in mind that there are no "experts" on nuclear war; there are only "theoreticians." There is dispute on whether a strategic doctrine accurately describes human behavior or possible nuclear war. Nevertheless, such doctrine has played an important role in public debate and certainly in arguments for and against various weapons systems and arms control agreements.

Collective Security and Containment

Immediately after World War II, the West adopted a modification of the doctrine of collective security. The concept of collective security that underlay the United Nations was the idea that security can be best assured if all nations act together to oppose any act of aggression or threat of aggression. An effective collective security system requires the existence of both a common conception of aggression and a common will to respond to aggression. In particular, several great powers must be willing to act in concert against an aggressor, and there must be no great power willing to oppose such action (or be the aggressor itself). Collective security is unlikely to work effectively in an alliance structure, since no member of an alliance is likely to act in concert with members of the opposing alliance against an ally that is committing aggression.

Although its theoretical concept was one of collective security, the United Nations was basically organized as an alliance of the victors of World War II, to ensure against the resumption of aggression by the Axis powers of Germany, Italy, and Japan. This alliance of victors collapsed under the strain of the cold war.

By 1947, the United States had adopted the policy of containment. This policy, also known as the Truman Doctrine, stipulated that the Soviets were, by the nature of their ideology, aggressive, and must be met and contained at every point of attempted expansion. Whereas the collective security model assumed a multiple world with general common interests, the Truman Doctrine assumed a bipolar world with competing interests. The United States soon supported formation of the North Atlantic Treaty Organization (NATO), an alliance among the United States, Canada, and the nations of Western Europe. The Soviet Union reacted with the Warsaw Pact, an alliance among the socialist nations of Eastern Europe. In later years, the United States attempted, generally less successfully, to spread its alliance pattern through East Asia and the Mideast.

In both East and West, the military assumptions in the immediate postwar period were close to those of World War II. A conventional force engagement would be decisive in any war. The United States sought to build large conventional forces in Western Europe and fought a conventional war in Korea in the early 1950's. The Soviet Union maintained large forces (over 200 divisions, although these are substantially smaller than U.S. divisions) in Eastern Europe. Neither nation's doctrines fully recognized the revolutionary implications of nuclear weapons. For the United States, nuclear weapons were an extension of the strategic bombing capabilities developed during World War II; their task was to punish an opponent and to support conventional force operations. The Soviets did not have nuclear weapons until 1949; Stalin hesitated to accept the importance of a weapon he did not possess. He stifled creative military thought within the Soviet Union, but hedged his position with an ambitious program to develop nuclear weapons and advanced delivery vehicles.

Massive Retaliation

In this bipolar but asymmetrical world, the West developed the doctrine of massive retaliation. Under this doctrine, as enunciated by Secretary of State John Foster Dulles, the United States would retaliate "by means and at places of its own choosing" to any attack. The doctrine carried the implicit threat that the United States would respond to any major Soviet foray by making a major nuclear attack on the Soviet homeland.

This doctrine was economically attractive, since it called for procuring relatively inexpensive nuclear forces rather than relatively expensive conventional forces. It was often described as the policy of "more bang for the buck." The United States built large numbers of strategic aircraft capable of bombing the Soviet Union from U.S. bases and from widespread overseas bases.

Massive retaliation also reflected the asymmetry in the European military balance. The Communist bloc had a large conventional superiority over the Western forces in Europe, whereas the United States had a large nuclear superiority. The West believed that the Soviets could be deterred from launching a conventional attack on Western Europe only by the threat of massive nuclear retaliation on the Soviet homeland. Thus the United States sought to deter a major Soviet *conventional* attack by the threat of a major U.S. *nuclear* reply.

However, even in the early 1950's, deterrence worked both ways. The Soviets saw the Americans as deterred from launching a nuclear attack by the threat of a Soviet conventional attack on Western Europe. Thus the Soviet population was hostage to the U.S. nuclear forces and the European population was hostage to the Soviet conventional forces.

This concept of replying to a U.S. nuclear attack by large-scale "conventional" war was at the heart of the Soviet military doctrine developed during the same era. Stalin's death in 1953 permitted the resumption of serious military thought within the Soviet Union. Soviet military leaders recognized the importance of strategic nuclear weapons and proposed three responses. First, the Soviets would attempt to blunt a U.S. attack through extensive defense against incoming aircraft. Political leaders accepted this recommendation, created an Air Defense Command parallel to the three traditional services, and built an elaborate air defense system. Second, the Soviets would also attempt to blunt the U.S. attack by a policy of striking at the U.S. strategic forces before they were launched. Whether their "first strike" or preemptive attack recommendation was accepted by political leaders is unclear. Third, the Soviets would strengthen their ground forces for action in Western Europe. The political leaders did accept this recommendation, and supported their Eastern European forces with tactical nuclear weapons and intermediate-range missiles based in the western Soviet Union and targeted on Western Europe.

The validity of massive retaliation was increasingly questioned in the West during the mid- and late 1950's in response to the gradual buildup of Soviet nuclear weapons. The doctrine was nearly obsolete at the end of the decade, as the Soviets developed ICBMs. Once the Soviet Union had a nuclear warfare capability, as it did by about 1955, the United States was deterred from using its strategic nuclear weapons except in defense of the most crucial national interests. The threat of massive retaliation was perhaps credible to deter a major Soviet incursion into Europe; it was not credible to deter low-level actions such as Ho Chi Minh's defeat of the French at Dien Bien Phu in 1954, or the Chinese shelling of Quemoy and Matsu in 1958. And doubts of credibility in even the European context played a part in the French decision to build nuclear weapons, discussed in Chapter 12.

Nuclear Deterrence

The doctrine of mutual nuclear deterrence evolved during the late 1950's. As the Soviets achieved a substantial nuclear capability, the West extended its concept of using nuclear weapons. Now the threat of nuclear retaliation would be used not only to deter Soviet conventional attacks; it would also be used to deter Soviet nuclear attacks on the United States. By 1959, Premier Khrushchev had reached a similar conclusion: the United States would not attack the Soviet Union so long as the Soviets were able to reply with nuclear weapons. He therefore upgraded the Soviet Strategic Rocket Forces in the early 1960's as the Air Defense Forces had been upgraded a few years earlier.

Each nation was then deterred from attacking the other. According to the doctrine, Country A would refrain from making a first strike on Country B, provided Country A realized that Country B was likely to reply with second-strike forces that would survive A's first strike and still inflict unacceptable damage on Country A.

As the doctrine was logically developed, at least in the West, there are two main elements of deterrence: survivability and vulnerability. Both sides must have second-strike forces that can survive a first strike, and both sides must be vulnerable to the other's second-strike forces. If a country's second-strike forces are not survivable, then in time of crisis that country could conceivably be tempted to make a preemptive first strike or to launch its forces on warning of an attack in order to make sure the forces are not destroyed before use. On the other hand, if a country is not vulnerable to the second-strike forces of the other, then the other country has no way to deter the first from launching a first strike. Therefore, for a stable deterrent situation, both sides must have survivable second-strike forces and must be vulnerable to each other's second-strike forces.

In the 1950's, the strategic bombers were the major deterrent forces. The West's forces were targeted mainly against the opponent's population and industrial centers in order to ensure unacceptable damage in a second strike. Thus, the targeted regions became hostages to prevent the Soviets from initiating an attack. Soviet targeting doctrine was less clear; it may have reflected the idea of fighting a combined conventional and strategic war instead of or in addition to deterring strategic war. Targeting may thus have been against military and strategic centers as well as against population and industrial centers.

Because the strategic bombers were themselves vulnerable and might be destroyed by a surprise attack on their bases, it was important to have as much warning as possible of an attack. There was a relatively long flight time between the two nations to provide warning of a surprise attack. Moreover, most realistic attacks would probably involve many bombers. But nations were still worried that their bombers could be destroyed. The Americans, for example, built a radar line across northern Canada to provide warning of attack so more bombers could take off in time to avoid destruction. Bomber forces were kept on alert.

In this climate, some efforts were made toward achieving greater stability, if not control. The point of President Eisenhower's "Open Skies" proposal of 1955 was to take advantage of the warning provided by take-off. Each country would allow designated reconnaissance planes from the other country to fly over it and look for these preparatory signs. This would lessen the likelihood of surprise attack by providing early warning. However, as the Soviets argued, the bombers derived some invulnerability from the secrecy of their location. This secrecy would be lost under the aerial inspection envisioned in the "Open Skies" proposal; the United States, the Soviets argued, would obtain targeting information about the Soviet Union.

With the advent of the missile age, heralded by the first U.S.S.R. Sputnik flight in 1957, defense planners realized that a missile could be launched at an air base. The warning time between discovery of the missile and impact—a few minutes—would allow only a few of the planes on the ground to take off. An initial missile could then make a preemptive attack, one that destroys a nation's strategic forces and greatly diminishes that nation's capacity for a second strike. The system's stability was temporarily diminished. In the United States, a portion of the strategic bomber force was put on airborne alert, though this procedure was costly.

The strategic situation became more stable in the 1960's after the development and deployment of less vulnerable second-strike missile forces, particularly submarine-launched ballistic missiles (SLBMs) and hardened land-based missiles. Because submarines can be hidden in the oceans, a submarine-based nuclear force can survive a first strike largely unscathed and retain the capability to strike back. Moreover, because they are less accurate, SLBMs do not appear as effective as ICBMs for counterforce use, i.e. to destroy the opponent's missiles (rather than his cities). As a result, SLBMs do not currently pose the same threat to the survivability of the opponent's second-strike forces.

During the 1960's, both the Americans and the Soviets also began to place land-based missiles in "hardened" silos in order to make them less vulnerable to a first strike. The underground concrete silos were designed to withstand a nearby nuclear blast. Based on the expected accuracy and payload of U.S.S.R. missiles, an estimate can be made that a reasonable proportion of, say, the U.S. Minuteman missiles would survive an attack and be available for a second strike. It would not be necessary to launch missiles while an incoming attack was in flight—the President would have longer than just a few minutes to decide whether to order a counterattack. The first Minutemen were deployed around the end of 1962 and the force grew to 1,000 missiles during the decade.

The doctrine of deterrence was by no means fully trusted during this period. Evidence of this on the U.S. side was the short-lived fallout shelter campaign of 1961–62. It took time to deploy the new missiles, and the posture of the early 1960's was one in which there could still be doubt that the second strike would be big enough to deter the first strike. After the Soviet intermediate-range ballistic missiles (IRBMs) which had been moved to Cuba to be targeted on the United States were returned to the Soviet Union following the missile crisis of 1962, Khrushchev said that the United States was still covered by 80 to 120 missiles. The U.S. figures were not grossly different, because the deployment of Minutemen did not grow rapidly until after 1962.

Many evidently felt that these force levels were not large enough. Moreover, independent of deterrence calculations, some drew the conclusion from the Cuban missile crisis that their arms should be increased. The Cuban outcome was influenced heavily by both bargaining skill and the likely pro-U.S. outcome of any conventional naval actions in the area. Some on both sides, however, concluded that nuclear superiority provides political leverage and that diplomatic bargaining favors the side with more nuclear weapons. There was also a general ignorance about future force plans and current forces of the other side. Satellite reconnaissance and other technical means of intelligence were not as developed as today. Thus, for example, when the Soviets deployed medium-range missiles (MRBMs) targeted against Western Europe, the United States interpreted the deployment as the beginning of a large-scale ICBM deployment. The United States then started a large-scale strategic missile program, which, together with the Cuban missile crisis, caused the Soviets to have doubts about its forces. The United States carried out the decisions made during Kennedy's first year in office to deploy what seemed like an extravagantly large force: 1,000 Minutemen, 656 Polaris launching tubes, 50 Titans, plus aircraft-carried weapons. The Soviets began to deploy what appeared to be a first ballistic missile defense system and laid the groundwork for later deployment of a large number of ICBMs.

After these decisions, the arms race could have been expected to reach an upper limit, which would have been stable against war and have made further production unnecessary. The large force levels would leave little doubt that after any attack an adequate number of missiles would survive to make a retaliatory strike. The Soviet Union and other powers could be expected, sooner or later, to accept the deterrence doctrine; the Soviets moved in this direction after the 1962 Cuban missile crisis. Intelligence errors of even a few hundred missiles would not affect stability against surprise or preemptive attack or even affect bargaining power in diplomatic crisis, so there would be little reason to build additional missiles. Hence it was possible to foresee agreement, tacit or explicit, against construction of further strategic systems. Unfortunately, two new technological developments, the antiballistic missile (ABM) and the multiple independently targetable reentry vehicle (MIRV), conspired with political factors to postpone this denouement.

Critiques of Deterrence: Political and Ethical

The deterrence concept has dominated U.S. defense discussion ever since the late 1950's. It is eminently adaptable to force calculations: there are numerous computer models examining nuclear exchanges to evaluate the effect of varying one or another force component. Deterrence theory is implicit in the SALT I agreements. But the theory has not been without its critics, and it is wise to review the broad criticisms before moving on to apply the theory to ABMs and MIRVs.

One line of criticism focuses on the psychological validity of the theory. A rational national leader will carefully evaluate the effects of a nuclear war before initiating one. If forces are designed in accordance with deterrence theory, the leader will probably never decide to initiate nuclear war. But how many national leaders are rational? What is the chance that a leader, whether acting messianically or masochistically, will initiate nuclear war precisely because retaliation is certain? How will even a normally rational leader behave when he has committed his nation's prestige and his own prestige to a particular position in a crisis with another nuclear nation? Even if two rational leaders are facing each other in a crisis like the Cuban missile crisis, will their signals to each other and their commands to their own forces be interpreted correctly? And how important are the subtle calculations? The specialized language of deterrence theory can be a way to avoid thinking about the human realities, and no one knows what would really happen in a nuclear war. Perhaps just the idea of nuclear war is enough to deter most leaders, but even the most overwhelming imbalance might not deter the irrational leader.

A second line of criticism points to the international political effects of deterrence. The United States and the Soviet Union are locked in a deterrence pattern that has its own demands and dynamics, independent of other issues at stake between the two, and even of whether there are any conflicts between the two. If deterrence fails, it leaves little way that the two might war without holocaust. If it succeeds, it leaves allies feeling vulnerable. They fear that they will not be defended and may, as have England, France, and China, develop their own nuclear weapons. Unaligned nations, such as India, see the two superpowers placing their nuclear relationship above all else, and are tempted to copy the superpowers by also developing nuclear weapons.

The most striking criticism is the ethical one. The concept of deterrence leads to targeting on population centers, which are held as innocent hostages. But one of the most traditional ethical principles of war, reflected in much of the law of war, is a duty to spare the innocent. As Vatican II stated in 1965, "Any act of war aimed indiscriminately at the destruction of entire cities or of extensive areas along with their population is a crime against God and man himself. It merits unequivocal and unhesitating condemnation."[1] Similarly, Protestant thinker Paul Ramsey drew on traditional just-war theory to present two principles for the conduct of war: "(a) the principle of discrimination or the moral immunity of non-combatants from intended direct attack, and (b) the principle of proportion or prudence, or the requirement that costs in destruction accepted and exacted be warranted by benefits there is reasonable expectation of gaining."[2] Dr. Ramsey did not hesitate to

---

[1] Gaudium et Spes. §80 (Vatican City, 1965).
[2] P. Ramsey, "A Political Ethics Context for Strategic Thinking," in M. Kaplan, *Strategic Thinking and Its Moral Implications* (Chicago, 1973), p. 132.

draw the implication that the Vatican Council had left unstated: "To put the point bluntly, if counter-population warfare is murder, then counter-population deterrent threats are murderous."[3] Under traditional standards, nuclear deterrence is unethical.

In contrast with traditional ethics, today's pragmatic ethics often approve deterrence. Its greatest ethical asset (and ethical problem) is that it appears to work. Whether one agrees or not, the Soviet and American populations are held mutual hostage, and this relationship may be unavoidable. An ethical justification lies in the fact that the hostages are still alive and that there seems in practice to be no way to keep them alive except by keeping them hostage at the same time. Moreover, deterrence doctrine offers a theory under which strategic weapons can be limited, a way to say how many weapons are enough. Consequently, many believe that they have an ethical responsibility to help maintain and stabilize deterrence.

The tension between traditional ethics and pragmatic ethics has important consequences. A strategist seeking to preserve deterrence must attempt to explain its counterethical and counterintuitive aspects to an often incredulous public. A leader who launches nuclear weapons at his opponent's cities, even in retaliation, is committing what is traditionally an immoral act. Deterrence may be weakened because of an opponent's doubt whether the leader will commit such an act. This problem is more serious when nuclear weapons are used to deter a non-nuclear attack, such as one on Western Europe. It is difficult enough for most people to accept an argument that it is moral to threaten nuclear attack on innocent people in order to prevent nuclear attack on innocent people. It is harder, even for those who accept an ethical duty to defend Europe, to accept the idea of threatening nuclear attack on innocent people in order to prevent defeat in a non-nuclear war. Deterrence is less effective, precisely because it raises serious ethical difficulties.

Ethical motivations help explain why some strategic thinkers have looked for ways to defend Europe with tactical nuclear weapons rather than with strategic deterrence and why some have sought to reshape strategic forces to place greater emphasis on attacking the opponent's missiles rather than his cities. In response, other strategic thinkers argue that tactical nuclear weapons or counterforce targeting might make nuclear war more likely by making a limited nuclear war seem more possible. It is understandable that strategic thinkers want to avoid the starkness of a strategy in which survival depends on the mutual threat of mass destruction; disarmament might be able to serve this purpose.

[3] *Ibid.*, p. 135.

The opposing approach is to accept nuclear deterrence and to try to make it as stable as possible; the SALT negotiations, as will be seen, reflect this approach.

Effects of New Weapons Developments on Deterrence: ABMs

As noted in Chapter 4, both the United States and the Soviet Union began research on an ABM system in the late 1950's. At the time many were not confident that deterrence was stable; it seemed realistic to look for ways to limit destruction in case of strategic nuclear war. In the early 1970's, both nations effectively rejected ABM systems by agreeing to limit them to a nearly negligible level.

The reasons for this decision are both strategic and technical. If both sides had a large number of ABM systems that worked well and covered the entire nation so that no attack could penetrate, the resulting situation would be stable. There would be no point in launching a missile attack, because the attack would make no difference and would simply be parried. Some analysts have recommended ABMs for precisely this reason. Their argument is that the only way to end the strategic competition is for the defense to become dominant, creating a defensive stability that is not based on deterrence.

Despite the logic of this position, however, such defense dominance is probably not technologically available. Most analysts believe that ABM systems cannot be made effective enough and that the costs of a system even remotely approaching the ideal of an "unpenetrable shield" would be enormous. The ABM systems can at best intercept only some offensive missiles, and the attacker can concentrate his forces against specific targets, leading the defender to have to cover all targets of value.

How the ABM would modify deterrence also depends on how the ABM systems are used. Although it is generally argued that ABMs could not stop a massive attack by either side, they might give some protection to population and industry from some nuclear missile attacks. In this population-protection role, their function would fit into a "damage-limiting" mission. If the Americans began to build such a countrywide system, the Soviets might suspect that the United States was considering launching a first-strike preemptive attack against the Soviet Union and was planning to have its ABMs available to blunt a retaliatory strike. An ABM would probably be more effective against a smaller second strike than against a large first strike. The Soviets would respond to such a U.S. ABM system by an increase in offensive missilry if they wished to preserve confident deterrence against U.S. attack. Similarly, the United States would view the emergence of a U.S.S.R.-wide ABM defense with alarm and would respond with increased offensive armaments. As will be discussed below, these offsetting offensive armaments can probably be built much more cheaply than the defensive system. Thus an effort to build and maintain a country-wide heavy ABM population defense would clearly accelerate the arms race.

An alternative mission of an ABM system is the protection of missile sites. This mission is less escalatory in terms of the arms race than the defense of cities and industry. If ABMs were designed and deployed in a way that defended the U.S. Minuteman silos but did not promise defense of cities, the Soviets should not see it as evidence of a U.S. first-strike intent: if the United States did plan to strike first by launching its missiles against the Soviets, little would be gained by defending empty silos. If, on the other hand, the United States were trying to preserve its ability to retaliate against a Soviet first strike, then an ABM system *dedicated specifically* to defending U.S. missile silos and effectively engineered to do so might make sense: like hardening of silos, such a defense would preserve the ability to deter a first strike.

Thus ABM can have two roles, one fitting a "damage-limiting" strategy which tends to escalate the arms race, and the other fitting a "deterrence" strategy which preserves the present stalemate between the nuclear powers without further escalation. The problem here is that both the stated purposes of the U.S. Safeguard ABM and its actual engineering and deployment plans were ambiguous as presented in the 1969–71 period. The hardware of Safeguard was taken over from the earlier Sentinel system designed for city defense; these same components were to be employed in defense of the Minuteman silos. According to its opponents, the result was the worst of both worlds. The system being built was expensive and relatively ineffective as a defense of Minuteman silos. At the same time Soviet military planners would have to view it as the beginning of a city and industrial defense and conclude that Soviet ability to deter a U.S. strike might be eroded.

The effect of ABM in defense of cities is that it may lead the opponent to take countermeasures, such as producing new missiles. If these countermeasures are relatively cheap, building an ABM would be pointless; if they are relatively expensive, it might be wise to attempt to shift from offense-dominated to defense-dominated stability. A more precise expression of these relative costs is the "exchange ratio," defined by the following calculation. Assume that if Country A attacks first, it could produce a certain level of damage to Country B. Suppose then that Country B increases its defense by a certain increment, and Country A increases its offense to inflict the same damage to Country B as before Country B installed its defense. The exchange ratio is then the ratio between the incremental cost that Country A must bear to penetrate the defense and the incremental cost of the defense that Country B installed.

This definition of the exchange ratio is not the only index of whether an offense-dominated or defense-dominated search for stability is indicated; nevertheless, it is often used as the primary index. Is the exchange ratio large or small for modern nuclear systems? On the offensive side there are airplanes, nuclear missile-carrying submarines, and fixed or mobile land-based missiles. On the defensive side there are ABM, air defense, and civil defense. If the exchange ratio is small compared to one, the response to ABM will be an increase in the opponent's offensive forces; if this ratio is large compared to one, it might be better for both to build ABMs and to try to shift to defense-based stability.

The calculations, although often attempted, are extremely difficult to make reliably. A first problem is the general uncertainty surrounding all nuclear exchange calculations. The blast and radiation effects of single nuclear explosions are well understood, so it is possible to estimate what structures or human beings might be expected to survive the first impact of a single weapon. Fallout is also fairly well understood, but, as pointed out in Chapter 4, little is known about the fire effects, and still less about the total effects on society and ecology that a large-scale attack might bring.

Second, the details of the actual tactical exchange between offense and defense are not readily predictable, and many technical devices are available to affect this exchange. Strategic aircraft can carry jamming or spoofing devices to disrupt defensive radars, or they can carry "stand-off" missiles to fire these weapons at longer distances from the target. Nuclear bursts may perturb radar transmission. Missiles can carry various forms of "penetration aids," such as decoys or devices to counteract the defender's radar. One can make relatively light decoys that to enemy radar are indistinguishable from the real weapon projected by the rocket until they reach the atmosphere; as soon as that occurs, the warheads and the decoys can be distinguished. For penetration aids to continue their deception into the atmosphere is a much more difficult task and requires a heavier decoy. Use of these devices requires the offensive force to dedicate more payload to penetration aids, and less to explosive power or to the fuel needed for range. Alternatively the "decoys" themselves can be given warheads, so that they will destroy targets if not attacked by ABMs. Much may also depend on particular strategies of attack or defense; for example, the offense may concentrate on undefended targets or may attempt to saturate defense capabilities or to exhaust the defensive missiles available in an area. A defense system might be programmed to allow the attacker to waste its missiles on some targets and to defend others at all costs.

In the face of these uncertainties, estimating an exchange ratio is at best a chancy proposition. If it is assumed that the purpose of a defense, be it ABM, air defense, or civil defense, is to hold damage to the population from enemy attack to a relatively small fraction, say no more than 10 percent, then the cost for an attacker to cancel the effect of the defense will always be very much less than that of the defense. The exchange ratio would be much less than one. It is only if the defense is satisfied with much higher casualty levels, somewhere above one-half of the population, that such calculations indicate that offense and defense costs approach equality. However, at such enormous lethality levels these calculations are totally unbelievable. The most serious unknowns, the long-range effects of nuclear war, all act in one direction: to make the actual damage level higher than estimated and therefore to make defense even less cost-effective relative to offense. It is clear that, at current force levels, stability must be sought through offense dominance rather than defense dominance.

But the conclusion forced upon the decision-maker who sets the level of offensive forces is a somewhat different one. Even though he believes himself reasonable in relying upon deterrence-based stability, he tends to be conservative about errors in setting that force level. Thus, he will choose his margins of error so as to underestimate his own ABM system and penetration aids and overestimate the opponent's systems. This is the concept of worst-case analysis. Given the uncertainties of intelligence data and of the technical evaluation of the data, the evaluations of the two sides will differ substantially in an escalatory direction, that is, one that tends to bend each side to increase its offensive force levels.

Two additional considerations intensify this last effect. The first is lead time. The force designer is planning for an anticipated situation some years in the future and must credit his opponent with capabilities that might be developed in the meantime. In the ABM case, this means he must assume that a large number of defensive missiles could be added quickly to the opponent's system; the time needed to deploy such missiles is much shorter than the time needed to deploy the radar. The theoretical capabilities of the radar then dominate the calculations.

The second point is "mirror-imaging." The United States and the Soviet Union do not reveal to each other the exact level of their technical capability. Hence each attributes to the other all the technical capabilities shown by intelligence plus all the technical capabilities that he himself has, unless the opponent's possession of these capabilities is positively excluded by intelligence data. Each side tends to evaluate the other as a mirror image of itself. During the U.S. ABM program, the U.S. ABM designers and the U.S. penetration-aid designers were in effect in an arms race with each other, as were presumably their U.S.S.R. counterparts. These effects, together with the tendency toward conservative or worst-case design in an area as uncertain as ABM technology, help increase the pressure for greater deployments in an arms race that includes ABMs.

The dangers of ABM deployments were ultimately recognized by both nations. On the U.S. side, discussions before SALT had been influenced by the political problems of evaluating a weapon whose procurement was being considered. The weapon was evaluated more coolly in the internal U.S. government discussions during SALT, and the decision was made to accept an agreement limiting ABM deployments to a nearly negligible level. The U.S.S.R. decision came fairly abruptly about 1969. Before that time, Kosygin and leading Soviet strategists had put forward the idea that an ABM is harmless because it is defensive, designed to save lives and not designed for attack. Such statements ended in 1969 and the Soviets soon agreed to SALT's limitation on ABMs. This shift may indicate that the Soviets finally rejected their 1950's notion of fighting a nuclear war and accepted a deterrence doctrine; it could, however, indicate only their decision that because the ABM would encourage counterdeployments, it would be undesirable from either a war-fighting or a deterrence viewpoint.

Effects of New Weapons Developments on Deterrence: MIRVs

Multiple Independently Targetable Reentry Vehicles (MIRVs) are multiple nuclear warheads carried by a single long-range ballistic missile launched from either land or sea, with each warhead aimed at independent targets in the opponent's country. The total explosive power carried by the combined warheads is less than that of a single warhead of the same total weight; however, the destruction produced by a multiple impact of smaller weapons might be larger than that of a single warhead, depending on the nature of the target and the accuracy of the warheads. The United States developed MIRVs during the late 1960's and began deploying them in both the Minuteman and the Poseidon forces. The first Soviet MIRV was tested in 1973.

Although the MIRV was also developed to increase targeting capabilities, a major part of the U.S. justification for developing and deploying MIRVs was to aid in penetration against ABMs. If the MIRVs are aimed at different targets or fly trajectories so that they arrive at one target at different times, separate interceptor missiles may have to be fired at each one. In effect, each MIRV is a "decoy" containing a warhead. By substantially increasing the number of interceptors needed, the attacker may more easily exhaust or saturate the defense.

The actual U.S.S.R. ABM deployment during the 1960's was so small that this argument did not seem to ring true, even when lead times were considered. The Soviets did not have a significant ABM, but U.S. MIRV proponents argued that they might build one so rapidly that the United States could not produce a countermeasure fast enough to maintain an assured deterrent. U.S. Defense Department spokesmen argued that the widely deployed Soviet defenses against airplanes might possibly be clandestinely upgraded in short order into an effective ABM, a possibility discounted by many outside experts.

ABM and air defense systems require the same types of fundamental components: radars for detection and tracking purposes, computers for evaluating targets and directing interception, and missiles for intercepting and destroying the target with nuclear or non-nuclear explosions. Furthermore, since antimissile systems have evolved from antiaircraft systems, it would not be surprising to discover that a collection of technical experts would have some difficulty defining a technical specification that would establish a boundary between antiaircraft and antimissile systems. The sensitivity of the radar depends on the size of the antenna, the strength of the transmitted signal, and the size of the target. A missile is much smaller than an airplane and, because of its higher speed, must be detected at greater distance and in a shorter time interval. Thus the antimissile radar will require higher power and/or larger antennas than the antiaircraft radar. The extent of the difference will depend on the assumed characteristics of the missile and aircraft targets. Technical arguments could easily develop concerning the differing computation and control requirements for ABM and antiaircraft systems; the ABM system must handle many more targets much more quickly. However, even if agreement could be reached concerning differences in computer requirements for the two types of systems, detection of these differences would not be easy. ABM missiles normally would differ in performance characteristics from antiaircraft missiles. These differences, however, are not so great as to completely rule out the use of modified air defense missiles in some ABM roles and particularly in defense of hardened missile sites. Observation of tests involving interception of incoming ICBM warheads would of course provide great assurance that an ABM system was being tested.

Thus there is a continuum between ABM and air defense systems. Design of an arms control agreement to prohibit ABM but permit air defense requires great care, and a force planner must give attention to the possible upgrading of an air defense system. Yet, as will be seen in Chapter 8, the definition problem was solved in SALT I. And the actual estimate of U.S.S.R. capability for purposes of MIRV deployment is probably equally resolvable. If one were to give the Soviets credit for "instant ABM," one would assume them capable of a feat that the United States has been unable to accomplish after protracted research and development effort costing billions of dollars. Moreover, in the unlikely case that the Soviets should attempt to convert their antiairplane defense system into an antimissile defense, there are many options other than MIRVs to defeat such a move.

If the only objective of MIRV were to offset a real or imagined Soviet ABM system, then it was clearly not necessary for such missiles to be highly accurate. They needed only to be on trajectories that pose threats to cities or large military targets. Nevertheless, the United States pursued intensive programs to upgrade the accuracy of its MIRVs. When challenged on this point before the Congress, Dr. John Foster, then Director of Defense, Research, and Engineering, explained that the accuracy was needed to destroy industrial targets such as steel mills. This explanation did not stand up well under criticism. The first nuclear bomb had a destructive power substantially less than that of the smallest MIRV and missed by a distance larger than the present accuracy of the Minutemen, but caused enormous destruction to a steel mill in Hiroshima.

The U.S. decisions to build and deploy MIRVs were undoubtedly somewhat unthinking; high-level decision-makers may have focused on only some of the MIRV's strategic properties. These weapons and increased accuracy seemed to be the next logical step in arms development. Moreover, they were more cost-effective. Nevertheless, there was at least some U.S. interest in a counterforce capability, a capability to destroy opposing military targets and particularly opposing ICBMs. This capability is not needed to support a deterrence strategy, and is clearly a form of "damage limiting" or "war fighting" to shape a nuclear war's outcome as favorably as possible. On the U.S. side, while the SALT I negotiations were in progress, then Secretary of Defense Melvin Laird and other U.S. spokesmen raised the analogous specter of Soviet first-strike intentions by pointing out that the multiple warheads (not yet independently targetable) that the Soviets were testing on their large SS-9 missiles could develop into a threat to the U.S. Minuteman missile.

MIRVs can threaten silos, provided they are accurate. The reason is that high overpressures are needed to destroy a silo and are available only in a relatively small region around the attacking burst. Since the radius of this region increases relatively slowly with yield, as shown in Figures 4 and 5, one will optimize missile-destroying ability by using several smaller, accurate warheads.

If there were no other strategic forces, this threat to silos in a world of accurate MIRVs would create first-strike incentives like those when deterrence was based on aircraft and a few missiles. Without MIRV, a leader has relatively little incentive to order an attack on the opponent's missile force unless he is certain that that force is about to be launched against his own cities. Any missile fired against the opponent's missiles is one less missile available for deterrence—and, depending on reliability and accuracy, it might or might not destroy an opposing missile. For each missile the attacker fires, he would destroy an average of perhaps 0.6 or 0.8 opposing missiles. But with MIRVed systems with, say, three warheads with the same individual effectiveness, the initiator could destroy 1.8 to 2.4 opposing missiles for each missile fired. These destroyed missiles could in turn have destroyed perhaps five of one's own missiles or cities. The incentive to go first in a crisis would be magnified. This incentive is only somewhat magnified, since there are other forces, such as submarine-based systems and aircraft launched on warning, that cannot be destroyed by a first strike. Nevertheless, MIRVs do, to some extent, threaten deterrence.

From the point of view of verification and control, MIRVs also pose a difficult problem. Once a particular missile has been tested with MIRVs, it must be assumed that all launchers that can accommodate that missile contain MIRVed missiles. Even with on-site inspection, multiple warheads might be substituted after the inspector has left. If a missile has not been tested in a MIRVed mode, it can, however, normally be assumed that the launchers capable of accommodating this missile do not contain MIRVed missiles; a nation is unlikely to deploy as complex a device as a MIRVed missile without testing it first. Testing of MIRVs would presumably involve long-range firing of the missile and its multiple warheads; suitably detailed observations during the launch and reentry phases could be sufficient to indicate the presence of a MIRV system. Moreover, accuracy, the crucial parameter, is particularly hard to verify. In observing a test, it is presumably relatively easy to determine whether there are several reentry vehicles and where they land. It is harder to tell where they were aimed in order to estimate

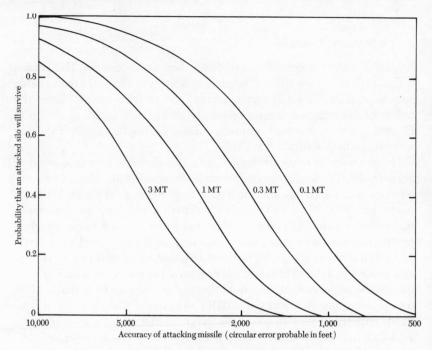

Fig. 4. Probability of survival of a silo hardened to withstand overpressure of 300 pounds per square inch.

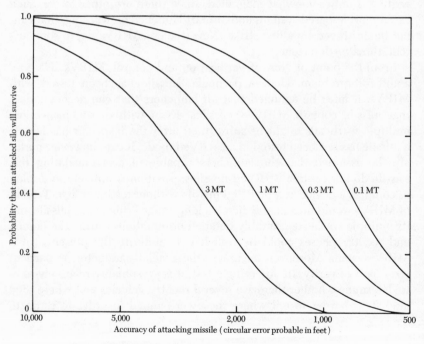

Fig. 5. Probability of survival of a silo hardened to withstand overpressure of 1,000 pounds per square inch.

accuracy. Consequently, each side will assume the worst about the other's MIRVs and may feel forced to increase its offensive forces. MIRV can fuel an arms competition.

The MIRV, unlike the ABM, was not effectively controlled by SALT. The United States, which was leading in MIRV technology, developed and deployed MIRVs for the complex reasons suggested in this section. Some critics, particularly in Congress, suggested that the United States wait to test MIRVs until a limitation had been pursued at SALT. The critics were unsuccessful; the United States continued its testing program. At SALT I, neither side proposed a MIRV ban acceptable to the other. Soon after SALT I, the Soviet Union began a series of MIRV tests. The proposed Vladivostok MIRV levels were set very high and the number of MIRV warheads can be expected to increase during the latter part of the 1970's.

It is important to note that MIRV capabilities will probably not, however, reach the level needed for a first strike on land-based ICBMs before sometime after 1980 (and may not then). This is because of serious technical difficulties in targeting MIRVs for effective simultaneous arrival against an opponent's missile force. The exploding warheads appear likely to interfere with one another in a form of fratricide. Moreover, the attacked nation might launch its missiles on warning of an incoming attack; the first strike then hits empty silos. But continued accuracy improvement can also be expected, to levels on the order of 50 feet by 1980. At these accuracy levels, a relatively small warhead (perhaps eventually a non-nuclear warhead) can destroy almost any stationary target, even a hardened silo. Further changes in doctrine are likely.

Deterrence Versus Damage Limitation and Flexible Targeting

The MIRV history shows that, despite official statements, deterrence has not been the only strategic doctrine followed in making deployment decisions. In addition, doctrines such as "damage limiting" or "war fighting" are also followed. These doctrines imply that some counterforce capability should be acquired and that in the event of nuclear war, U.S. armaments should be able to minimize damage to the United States. These two strategic objectives, namely deterrence and damage limitation, are in direct contradiction in the sense that they effectively countermand each other if adopted by both the Soviet Union and the United States. If the United States were to increase its ability to limit damage from Soviet nuclear attack, Soviet military leaders might conclude that the United States could be harder to deter from striking first and might even be planning such a strike. Conversely, concern that the Soviet Union might put up an extensive "damage-limiting" defense that could blunt U.S. nuclear retaliation led many in the United States to conclude that the Soviet Union would be harder to deter from striking first, and that the United States should be pushed to increase offensive forces accordingly. Mutual deterrence seems to require that the damage to oneself not be limited.

The Soviets have been even more reluctant than the Americans to abandon the policy of damage limitation through the use of defensive weapons. This reluctance may have reflected in large part traditional Soviet emphasis on defense and the Soviet views of the 1950's that the nation should prevent nuclear war by preparing to prevail in nuclear war. Although by about 1965 many Soviet leaders were willing to accept the doctrine of deterrence, some continued to argue that the Soviet Union should hedge against a possible failure of deterrence by creating and maintaining defensive forces, like ABM, which would limit damage if deterrence failed. As pointed out above, it was not until 1969, at the first SALT meeting in Helsinki, that the Soviets made it clear to the United States that their ABM policy had changed. And the Soviet Union has long given substantial attention to civil defense—shelters and evacuation procedures to reduce loss of life during nuclear war.

On the U.S. side, most independent members of the technical community have concluded that deterrence is the only feasible strategy for avoiding nuclear war, and that "damage limitation" has no meaning in the nuclear age. Many military men, however, even in the face of the overwhelming destruction that nuclear weapons can bring to the world, adhere to their traditional mission that, should deterrence fail, they should be able to "fight a war and prevail." Diplomats add that crises might be resolved more favorably if their side could credibly threaten to initiate nuclear war, i.e. could survive nuclear retaliation. Thus, during the 1960's, Secretary of Defense Robert McNamara emphasized that damage limitation was also a strategic objective. In a 1967 speech in San Francisco, he showed sensitivity to the argument that a heavy ABM system would erode the Soviets' confidence in their deterrent, but did announce deployment of a light ABM system which he said was not designed to threaten the Soviet deterrent capability. Some support for damage-limiting continued through the Nixon Administration, intensified by the questioning of some outsiders whether deterrence was moral or could be expected to last stably for long into the future. Moreover, by some time in the 1960's, it became pragmatically necessary to target many warheads against the opponent's missiles and military forces—

there were many more warheads available than there were population and industrial centers worth targeting.

Early in 1973, Secretary of Defense James Schlesinger continued the debate, putting forward a doctrine of "flexible targeting," or "limited strategic options." His argument was that current U.S. targeting procedures (like those of the Soviets) envisioned only large-scale "spasm" use of the deterrence force.[4] He wanted to supplement the current system with new procedures to increase the President's abilities to order more selective attacks. He has never been very explicit about the character of such an attack, but one supposes examples to be attack on just a few cities, on the military supply capabilities to support a particular conventional war, or on a surviving component of the Soviet ICBM force. He also sought improvement of missile accuracy; such improvement would presumably allow selective attacks against hard targets. However, he was very careful to indicate that he did not seek a preemptive first-strike capability and did not think one possible for some years.

The U.S. government put forward several arguments in support of these capabilities. One is the traditional damage-limiting argument. If deterrence fails or nuclear war erupts by mistake, one ought to have the ability to conduct the nuclear war with as little harm to populations as possible. This may require careful targeting against the opponent's military system. A second argument is based on a conceivable specific Soviet attack pattern. Suppose the Soviets were to use part of their force to make a first strike against the U.S. land-based missile force in a way designed to spare U.S. cities. The remaining U.S. forces are presumed not accurate enough to destroy the reserved Soviet missiles. The United States would then be in the position of having to capitulate to Soviet demands or having to initiate an attack against Soviet cities in the face of the threat that the Soviets would reply against U.S. cities, still only somewhat damaged. Third, the new capabilities are argued to be more effective for extended deterrence, for example, the defense of Western Europe. Many doubt the likelihood that the United States would carry out its threat to make a nuclear attack on the Soviet Union in response to a Soviet conventional attack on Western Europe. If the United States were prepared to make lesser strikes, this threat, it is argued, would be more credible. Thus, extended deterrence, and any use of nuclear threats for crisis bargaining, are argued to require selective, high-accuracy strategic capabilities. Finally, the apologists for the new strategic capabili-

---

[4] Actually, the United States already had available an ability to make smaller attacks. Secretary Schlesinger's argument was thus one seeking additional flexibility in strategic doctrine and in the command and control systems.

ties argue that the Soviets are acquiring such capabilities. Some admit that it might be better if no one had them, but they argue that it is better for both to have them than for only the Soviets to have them. Asymmetry would weaken the U.S. position before allies and in crisis bargaining. Therefore, it is necessary to meet the Soviet Union in deploying a full range of flexible options.

The defenders of traditional deterrence theory argue primarily that the proposed innovations make it easier to begin nuclear war and there-fore weaken deterrence. They point out that damage-limiting, under whatever name, can only appear to the opponent as a step toward a first-strike capability and will lead him to intensify his strategic program. In addition, they are dubious about all the above arguments. The critics argue, for example, that the postulated Soviet attack against the U.S. missile force is bound to fail. For at least several years, neither side will be able to make that sort of first strike with high effectiveness. Critics note that the proposed strategy has been coupled with requests for high-accuracy weapons, which could be used against ICBMs. Yet, although the accuracy of these warheads varies, the number of available warheads is already so great that any target list necessarily includes a preponder-ance of counterforce and antimilitary targets, and any effort to attack missile forces alone would kill so many civilians that the initiator of the attack would reasonably fear retaliation. The other arguments appear curiously vague—seeming to rest on generalities such as "it is necessary for the United States or for the Western Alliance to have available op-tions so that the Soviets will not believe that U.S. strategic forces are unavailable for purposes other than the defense of the American cities."[5] None of the Administration spokesmen has yet given a persuasive ex-ample. Any example seems to raise more questions than it answers; e.g. could a single nuclear weapon exploded on even a foreign military base avoid provoking a reaction like that to Pearl Harbor? The critics there-fore wonder if the desire to build more weapons comes first and an empty strategic rationalization follows. It would not be the first time that a weapon comes before the doctrine explaining how to use it.

China's Strategic Doctrines

It is often said, almost disparagingly, that the Chinese want nuclear weapons for political as well as military reasons. This is precisely why any country wants such weapons—to gain the political leverage that can come from advanced military power. Nevertheless, China's nuclear strat-

[5] Interview with Defense Secretary James Schlesinger, BBC Radio 4, "Analysis," October 24, 1974.

egy differs from that of other nations. Its cultural background is different from that of the other nuclear powers. It is not, like the United States and the Soviet Union, locked into a bilateral strategic relationship that dominates other nuclear balances. Neither is it, like Great Britain or France (whose nuclear strategy will be discussed in Chapter 12), aligned with one of the nuclear superpowers so that its strategy must be analyzed in relation to that superpower's nuclear guarantees. Rather, the People's Republic of China seeks to guarantee its security in part by attempting to use the position of one superpower to constrain the other.

In the 1950's, after the Korean war, the Chinese developed a military program that was closely coordinated with the Soviet Union. The Chinese had a treaty of alliance with the Soviets. They adopted the terminology and the general organizational structure of the Soviet Red Army and worked with Soviet advisers to restructure the People's Liberation Army along Soviet lines. The Chinese were especially hopeful that this transformation of their armed forces would protect them through the Soviet nuclear umbrella and through general deterrence derived from close military association with the Soviet Union.

Soviet assistance included direct help to China in building a nuclear industry. The Soviet Union provided a reactor in 1955, and trained a number of Chinese scientists at Dubna, a nuclear research facility in the Soviet Union controlled by an international consortium of Communist states. In 1957, in association with the Soviet Union, the Chinese established an Institute of Atomic Energy, which sponsored a variety of research and training activities and built a series of research reactors and related facilities. In time the Chinese established the large complex needed to develop and deploy nuclear weapons. A key person in this complex was China's best-known weapons expert, Ch'ien Hsüeh-sen, who had been trained in the United States.

In association with this program, the Chinese in 1957 signed an agreement with the Soviet Union to receive advanced information on nuclear weapons. Although this agreement lasted only a few years, the Russians presumably did supply the Chinese with advanced technology, the precise details of which are not known. When the Soviet Union abrogated the agreement in 1959, the Chinese had to continue on their own. They invested substantial resources, some 2–3 percent of their gross national product, in nuclear weaponry. Ch'en Yi, the former Foreign Minister of China, was quoted as describing this investment thus: "It cost us our pants. We were willing to do it because we felt we had to. It was a tremendously costly effort." And what was begun as a cooperative Sino-

Soviet effort soon became a Chinese program to counter a Soviet threat much more than an American one.

China established two types of facilities to produce fissile materials: a gaseous diffusion system built largely near the city of Lanchow, and a plutonium system, using chemical separation, near Peking. The more costly was the gaseous diffusion system at Lanchow; it has been said that the Chinese diverted around one-tenth of their entire electrical power output for the period between about 1959 to 1965 to the Lanchow plant, using virtually all the power from the hydroelectric plants along the Yellow River west and north of Peking. These investments drastically affected the availability of resources for other programs, but were assigned the highest priority. To a large extent the facilities were built, organized, and run with Chinese effort and Chinese equipment. At Lanchow the Chinese, for example, are said to have spent on the order of only $200,000 for imported instruments, bought largely from Europe and Japan. By early 1976 the Chinese had conducted approximately 18 nuclear tests, the first an atomic bomb in October 1964. A hydrogen weapon was exploded in June 1967. Two of these tests were underground, possibly to gain information that could not be gained from atmospheric tests and possibly to keep the Americans and the Soviets from learning too much about the weapon's characteristics. The Chinese are said to have had difficulty in reaching high yield-to-weight ratios, but they have clearly become a nuclear power.

Nuclear weapons require delivery vehicles to have real military significance. As early as 1961, A. R. Hibbs of the Jet Propulsion Laboratory in Pasadena had written that the Chinese then possessed the capability to develop a delivery vehicle for a countercity strike force. Their possession of the industrial plant to build large boilers, gyros, and other components led to this conclusion. This position was ridiculed at the time, but turned out to be correct: the Chinese launched their first guided missile with a nuclear weapon aboard on October 27, 1966. They also conducted static tests of first stages of a very large missile, so it appeared as if they were building a long-range missile capable of striking the United States rather than attempting first to build intermediate-range systems that would reach nearby targets such as India, Japan, or the Soviet Union. Later evidence, however, indicated that the Chinese had not achieved long-range capability by 1976, and they were not expected to do so until the end of the decade. They have launched four space satellites, two in the early 1970's and two in the mid-1970's, but all were lightweight; observers did not believe that the technical systems that launched the satellites were powerful enough for intercontinental missiles. The Chinese were, instead, emphasizing medium- and inter-mediate-range systems capable of reaching Asian targets, including those in the Soviet Union. According to U.S. sources, Chinese missiles and bombing could by 1976 reach "all around the periphery of the PRC, at distances up to 3200 nautical miles." China's missile systems were gradually being hardened and placed under a relatively sophisticated command-and-control network by the mid-1970's.

The impact of China's strategic position was felt acutely in both Moscow and Washington. At hearings before the Senate, the U.S. Secretary of Defense noted in 1974:

Many of the studies of arms control by the arms control community have presupposed a two-man game, as it were. The addition of a third party is a destabilizing element. If, for example, both the United States and the Soviet Union were to desire to have equality with two major opponents, you would have arithmetically, or mathematically, the portents for an astronomical growth in strategic requirements. I think this is an issue that is not disturbing in the short term, because the Chinese capability remains relatively small compared to the capability of the two major states. But in the longer run, it is a subject that is disturbing, and we have not got a method of grappling with it as yet.[6]

Similar concerns are voiced regularly in the Soviet press.

China also upgraded its conventional forces. The whole structure of military discipline had been called into question during the Cultural Revolution from 1966 to 1969. The Chinese had played down the buildup of their professional military forces and concentrated on the role of the army in "serving and educating" the citizenry. In that period their air force consisted of about 2,800 planes, many of which were old and obsolete. Peking then began a major replacement and modernization program especially of its fighter aircraft. This pattern of modernization apparently continued into the 1970's, but at a much reduced rate. The production and procurement of military hardware in the 1972–74 period is believed to have fallen about 25 percent from a 1970–71 peak. Much of the across-the-board upgrading of the military between 1968 and 1971 probably followed from the new domestic emphasis following the Cultural Revolution and from China's great preoccupation with the possibility of a Soviet attack.

Throughout all of these shifts the Chinese position on disarmament and arms control remained amazingly static—very close to the Russian attitude at the time of the Baruch proposal. For the Soviet Union at that

[6] Senate Armed Services Committee, FY 1975, Authorization for Military Procurement (Feb. 5, 1974), p. 256.

time, arms restrictions appeared to offer few if any advantages because any real restrictions would leave the country in a dependent or inferior position. The Chinese similarly dismissed arms control proposals as a way to control them or force them to accept a dependent status. It was consistent with this thinking for them to refuse to sign the Limited Test Ban Treaty and the Non-Proliferation Treaty. Nevertheless, China took no steps that would spread nuclear weapons or increase the dangers of nuclear war. Its actions in this respect have always been cautious.

Here, however, the Chinese strategic dilemma arose. Peking also wanted to have broad political influence during a period when it felt itself to be very vulnerable; a number of famous statements about nuclear weapons reflect this dilemma. The most famous of these was Mao's statement in 1946 belittling nuclear weapons as "paper tigers." The Chinese declared that reliance on nuclear weapons paralyzes the major powers and that this paralysis greatly enhances the political capabilities of those who are not bound up in a deterrence world. For this reason China has attempted to downgrade the military significance of nuclear weapons while at the same time trying to become a nuclear power. This division between theory and practice, as one can imagine, has caused China great difficulty.

Peking insists, for example, that only when China and other "revolutionary" nations acquire nuclear weapons can the American-Soviet duopoly be broken and the potential ended for blackmail against China and the other revolutionary nations. Chinese theorists see a "contradiction" between those who view the world order as given and those who would like to create a world order in which all play a part as equals. In describing this contradiction the Chinese say, as one would expect, that time is on their side and that it is the losers who will resort to violence. Thus violence will increasingly be the tactic used by the opponents of change and equality; that is, by the superpowers who are trying to stop the wave of the future. Going further, the Chinese then argue that the revolutionary countries must be able to respond in a tit-for-tat way to violence directed against them. They do not necessarily advocate or initiate violence but do not wish to surrender in the face of it. Out of the tit-for-tat struggle or the threat of it, the Chinese argue, can come compromise. Mao has consistently talked about compromise as one important outcome of Chinese strategies and, as events since 1971 have shown, has sought to engage in that compromise with the United States.

Without more detailed information on Chinese nuclear programs, it is almost impossible to evaluate whether these ideas are followed in those programs. The ideas are, however, reflected in China's arms control position. The Chinese emphasize that nuclear test bans, especially those devised by the major powers, are deceptive measures designed to camouflage the ongoing arms race rather than to halt it. They have argued, instead, that nations should go all the way toward disarmament—or will, by the logic of the nuclear world, go all the way toward acquiring nuclear weapons—and they have regularly called for measures leading to total nuclear disarmament. China has pledged not to be the first to use nuclear weapons and has frequently called on other nations to make similar pledges. Such pledges might particularly benefit the revolutionary nations. Peking appears to be arguing that the superpowers have a choice. They can enter into a more and more complicated nuclear arms race or they can join in an effort leading toward total disarmament.

Arms control favors only the superpowers, and thus will not do. The speeches by Ambassador Ch'iao Kuan-hua at the United Nations have been highly negative on U.S.-U.S.S.R. arms control agreements and have demanded that the two nations agree not to use nuclear weapons first, not to use nuclear weapons against non-nuclear nations or nuclear free zones, and to remove all nuclear weapons based abroad. At the General Assembly in 1973, Ch'iao repeated China's position:

To put it bluntly, any disarmament must first of all be the disarming of these two super-powers. . . . As to the numerous small and medium-sized countries, the real problem they face is definitely not disarmament, but strengthening of their necessary and independent defence capabilities. . . . The Chinese Government is in favour of convening a world conference on genuine disarmament. But there must be the necessary preconditions and clear aims for the conference. That is, all nuclear countries, and particularly the two nuclear super-powers, the Soviet Union and the United States, must first of all undertake the unequivocal obligation that at no time and in no circumstances will they be the first to use nuclear weapons, particularly against non-nuclear countries and nuclear-weapon-free zones . . . and they must withdraw from abroad all their armed forces, including nuclear missile forces, and dismantle all their military bases, including nuclear bases, on the territories of other countries.

At this same U.N. session, China announced its adherence to Protocol II of the Latin-American Nuclear Free Zone Treaty (which will also be discussed in Chapter 14). Since then, while retaining its support for no-first-use agreements, it seems to have dropped its demand for the dismantling of foreign military bases; it views the U.S. bases in the Far East as a defense against the Soviet Union. China has also, in spite of some maneuvering against the Soviet Union, indicated its qualified willingness to cooperate with a U.N. committee of states preparing for a world disarmament conference.

It is hard to evaluate the relative influence of China's military position and of its ideological view of the world's structure on China's actual strategic doctrines. It is essentially impossible to predict the evolution of that doctrine as China's leadership changes. Nevertheless, although it may well be deterred by the prospect of nuclear war, China appears much less likely than the United States or the Soviet Union to rely upon a theory like deterrence as a way to design its strategic nuclear forces or as a way to devise agreements restricting those forces.

CHAPTER EIGHT

The Institutions of Arms Control

THE HISTORICAL discussions already presented show that arms control negotiations are greatly influenced by their political and institutional context. This context is one of men and organizations seeking security through military preparedness and traditional diplomacy as well as through arms control. The bureaucracies supporting these alternative approaches to security have their own criteria for evaluating arms control proposals and desired weapons postures.

Bureaucratic interests within different nations frequently interact. For example, the U.S. military procurement bureaucracy follows Soviet military developments very closely and often argues from a possible Soviet development to the need for a U.S. counterdevelopment. Worst-case analysis and the long lead times between weapons research and weapons deployment could help turn such interaction into an arms race. Some analysts have suggested that this concept of an arms race does not accurately describe the U.S.-U.S.S.R. arms competition.[1] Either an arms race concept or a concept that arms procurements are driven by internal forces may, however, be necessary to explain why the arms competition continued into the 1970's in spite of a general relaxation of U.S.-U.S.S.R. tension. But whatever model is accurate, the bureaucracies on both sides view themselves as guardians of national security and judge arms control agreements according to their beliefs of how to obtain security.

Thus, arms control is immersed in the policy process it is designed to change. As a result, domestic pre-negotiations precede and accompany any international negotiation; these pre-negotiations within governments shape arms control more than those between governments.

[1] Albert Wohlstetter, "Is There a Strategic Arms Race?" *Foreign Policy*, 15 (Summer 1974): 3.

This chapter analyzes these negotiations systematically; first, those within the Executive bureaucracy and then those in the broader public and Congressional areas. United States processes are used as the example, but somewhat analogous processes take place in most governments. International negotiating structures are then briefly discussed. The chapter concludes with comments on verification.

Bureaucratic Influences on Negotiating Positions

The negotiator does not always enter negotiations with a fixed idea of a specific, concrete goal. He has some idea, but in fact he often develops a position only as he begins to see what some of the issues are or as he begins to obtain information on the opponent's position. He may also revise his position; one of his major functions is to report to his authorities on the opponent's position and to convince his own government of what concessions are needed in his negotiating position or explain where no negotiating position has yet been adequately prepared. Nevertheless, the negotiator has only limited discretion in a contemporary arms control negotiation. He works on the basis of instructions and positions prepared for him back home, although he may have had a hand in their shaping. The instructions are sometimes extremely explicit, even to the point, for example, of directing him not to raise issue X except as a counterargument if the opposing delegate raises issue Y first. The result is that the negotiator is almost as much a negotiator with his own nation as with the opposing nation. This process becomes very complex.

In negotiations with his own nation, the negotiator is forced to recognize diversity within his own government. As Jerome Wiesner, the science adviser to President Kennedy, later told the Subcommittee on Arms Control of the Committee on Foreign Relations:[2]

I have seen more arms limitations proposals destroyed by the compromises that had to be made to get them agreed to by everyone who had to agree to [them] in the Government, and very many times what one does in this process is to make a sort of treaty.

I used to say when I was working in the White House that we were fighting a four-front war when we tried to do something about arms limitations.

We had to deal with the Pentagon, we had to deal with the Congress, we had to deal with the public; and I was never certain which of these groups gave us more problems because we rarely got to deal with the Russians.

He went on to suggest that domestic difficulties were the biggest ones for both him and the Soviet negotiators, and that the negotiators often

---

[2] Hearings on ABM, MIRV, SALT, and the Nuclear Arms Race (May 28, 1970), p. 405.

ended up in what amounted to a conspiracy to negotiate with their respective governments.

One might expect the President or some other senior official to dictate a position to the different groups within the government. In fact, presidents seldom exercise their power this way. There are two reasons for this. The first is that the President has only limited time and energy to comprehend problems. He and his staff are unlikely to be expert on such issues as the detailed properties of specific weapons systems, possible technological advances, or attitudes of allies. Therefore, the President will necessarily rely on senior officials and experts—and the experts are scattered through the bureaucracy including the defense community. Not only does the President feel a need to consult in order to choose carefully thought-out positions; he also feels a need to save his own time for crises and the many issues other than arms control that he must face. Arms control issues are seldom urgent in the sense of requiring decisions within a few hours. Therefore, the President prefers a process by which the bureaucracy normally negotiates within itself at lower levels, presents international negotiators with prepared positions, and refers only the most crucial questions to him.

But it is not just the limitations on the President's time and energy that lead him to rely upon bureaucratic bargaining. The President may be politically vulnerable to some elements of the bureaucracy. Many times, for example, the Defense Department or the Joint Chiefs of Staff have had an effective veto power over any arms control agreement. From about 1960 until at least the early 1970's, there were a number of senators who would not vote for an arms control agreement unless the Joint Chiefs had certified that the agreement was in the national interest. Since the votes of these senators might be needed to approve a treaty, the President had effectively to negotiate with the Joint Chiefs to make sure that proposed agreements would be acceptable. Seldom does any element of a bureaucracy have such a clear veto, and one can argue that the President might have overridden the Joint Chiefs during the 1960's. Nevertheless, the different components of the bureaucracy each have supporters in Congress and some have supporters in the public. If the President antagonizes them, he hurts his position in Congress and before the public; whenever possible, he will negotiate rather than antagonize.

These limitations are not unique to the United States. Every chief ·executive in the world is deluged by more issues than he or she can understand. He must therefore rely on his staff and bureaucracy to resolve as many noncritical issues as possible. In some nations, arms control issues—and often foreign policy generally—are considered unimportant by the chief executive, who is therefore likely to leave decisions to the foreign ministry or the military.

And most executives must, for one reason or another, maintain the support of various parts of their government and therefore negotiate with those parts in making policy. In a cabinet system such as that of England, the cabinet itself is likely to be powerful compared to the bureaucracies, but it is important for the cabinet to maintain a unified position. Thus, each minister has some power over the Prime Minister's policies. Moreover, some decisions will be made by the bureaucracy rather than by the full cabinet, and the cabinet must consider the views of its parliamentary constituency. In the Soviet Union, although the nature of the influence is unknown, the political leadership gives great weight to the views of the military leadership. Perhaps more important, the leadership itself is in part collective. Decisions will then be made only as a consensus or a majority can be achieved within the leadership; the resulting policy, which will be bargained, may reflect special interests and lack cohesion. In many developing nations, military support is essential to the regime; the military's viewpoint on arms control may not, however, be as parochial as often assumed in the developed world.

Each of the various elements of a bureaucracy will evaluate a negotiating proposal from a different viewpoint. Some theorists argue that the ultimate criterion is the budget or the survival of the particular bureaucratic component: the Navy, for example, would always oppose an agreement restricting aircraft carriers. Undoubtedly, most leaders of bureaucratic organizations have a strong bias to increase their organization's size and budget, but this effect can be overstated and there are more subtle factors also at work. Each bureaucratic organization tends to develop its own tradition or culture, and this tradition shapes the organization's evaluation of a proposal. The tradition is partly a psychological rationalization of why the organization should exist, but it is also influenced by persuasion and argument. Organizations do adopt new missions and do respond to political leadership. Nevertheless, a bureaucratic tradition is likely to change more slowly than the world changes. Thus, the U.S. and British navies applied an analysis suitable to the 1890's in evaluating the 1922 Washington Naval Agreements. The U.S. Air Force's culture is not yet reconciled to the idea of ICBMs. It was primarily outside civilian analysts, not military or defense officials, who developed the theory of deterrence.

Because of these cultural influences and because of the importance of

individual personalities, it is dangerous to generalize about the biases
of different bureaucracies. The Joint Chiefs, as representatives of the
individual military services, have generally been dubious about arms
control. Nevertheless, they did support agreements such as the 1963
Limited Test Ban and the 1972 SALT agreements, albeit with conditions
that required continued military expenditures and limited any effect
the arms control agreements might have in slowing the arms race. It is
probably impossible to know whether these conditions were negotiated
deals, by which the White House obtained support, or whether they
were simply considered judgments of what was necessary to maintain
the defense of the nation. The Department of Defense, as a civilian
authority over the military, has a slightly different view of defense requirements. Under Robert McNamara, it sometimes looked at arms control as a way to decrease budgets; under James Schlesinger, it sometimes
opposed arms control out of fear of strategic inferiority. The State Department is not always more supportive of arms control; it is after all
the organization that conducts many diplomatic negotiations and senses
a need to have military power available to support its negotiating position.

The positions of these different agencies—and of the intelligence agencies, whose biases are hardest to characterize—are often reconciled in a
committee before presentation to the President. Eisenhower used the
National Security Council; Kennedy and Johnson used the Committee
of Principals. The membership of such committees includes officers such
as the Secretaries of State and Defense, the Directors of the Arms Control and Disarmament Agency (ACDA) and the Central Intelligence
Agency (CIA), and the Chairman of the Joint Chiefs of Staff. The committee strives to reach a unanimous decision, often working first through
a committee of assistants or deputies to the principals. The benefit is
that necessary studies can be made early and that committee decisions
can save the President's time. The difficulty is that a unanimous position
is often that of the lowest common denominator, and the disagreements
left to the President may not focus his attention on the important choices.
Moreover, many argue, power on the committee may not be balanced.

In a few nations, such as Mexico, the opposing bureaucratic pressures
are weak enough or uninterested enough that an arms control decision-
maker has great freedom. In a few other cases, such as Sweden, these
pressures encourage arms control negotiations. Usually, however, the
dominant effect of bureaucratic pressures is to limit arms control possibilities. Chief executives hope that the bureaucratic negotiations will
protect their nations from disadvantageous arms control agreements.

The process is effective for this purpose, unless all the bureaucratic components use mistaken assumptions or an irrelevant theory. But the process tends to impose a stronger limitation than the national security one. The tendency, as shown in Chapters 5 and 6, is to permit only agreements that are in accordance with a widely accepted strategic doctrine or that restrict relatively unimportant weapons. Therefore, one of the strategies, both of arms controllers in the bureaucracy and of chief executives, has been to restructure bureaucratic negotiations to decrease the limitations they impose on arms control.

Many presidents have met this need through a close adviser who is not beholden to any particular part of the bureaucracy. Thus, Nixon put Henry Kissinger on his staff and relied on him heavily, just as Kennedy relied on Jerome Wiesner and McGeorge Bundy and Eisenhower relied on Harold Stassen. This approach gives the President unfiltered advice; it does not necessarily help obtain bureaucratic assent and cooperation. Conflict between the staff and the bureaucracy, like that between Stassen and Secretary Dulles, may be resolvable only by the President. The President is likely to delay resolving such conflicts until action is forced upon him by an international negotiation, and the adviser is not usually the only person consulted.

The creation of ACDA, described in Chapter 5, is another example of a strategy of bureaucratic restructuring. At the time, there was considerable opposition in Congress, resulting, for example, in very severe security clearance restrictions, designed to be even stronger than those for the Department of Defense, and a provision to prevent the agency from disseminating propaganda to the American public. These restrictions were eliminated in 1975. In spite of a low budget, ACDA's role in arms control has been important. It can present an arms control position in routine bureaucratic bargaining; sometimes no one else except the President is interested in presenting such a position. For SALT I, the Director of ACDA was also the chief negotiator; this was changed in SALT II, reducing ACDA to a less important bureaucratic force in the negotiation.

Both SALT negotiations, however, were substantially controlled by Henry Kissinger, first in the White House and later as Secretary of State. Dr. Kissinger mistrusted the SALT negotiating positions prepared by the bureaucracy under President Johnson, believing that they blurred important issues. Therefore, he developed a Verification Panel framework for SALT I to limit the effect of bureaucratic pressures. The relevant agencies would together define a sequence of possible plans, ranging from hawkish to dovish. This technique would force Defense to cooperate in defining the most favorable dovish position and force

ACDA to help define the most favorable hawkish position. The options would then be presented to Kissinger, and, in theory, there would never be a point at which a Defense plan had to be accepted or rejected in contrast with an ACDA plan. It would then be harder for bureaucratic weight to dominate and for the power imbalances of the various agencies to affect the negotiations. Moreover, all the agencies would have some sense of being consulted. In practice, however, the different agencies did press preferred positions. The scheme also put pressure on the President and Kissinger when it came to choosing among the options; in making the choice and in parts of the negotiations, they acted essentially alone. Their action was resented by much of the bureaucracy; many felt they could have prevented mistakes or better helped the President had they been better informed. The Verification Panel structure still existed at the time of SALT II; whether it was still being used to avoid bureaucratic pressures was not clear.

Finally, the bureaucracy will not enter serious internal negotiations or make substantial internal compromises unless absolutely essential. Hence, one of the strategies of those favoring arms control is to impose a deadline on the internal negotiations. What finally moved the United States to respond to political pressure for a biological warfare convention was the need to prepare a position for the Conference of the Committee on Disarmament. This need focused enough attention on the issue that decision could be reached. Summit meetings can serve the same purpose and can also indicate the President's interest in making a proposal.

These factors explain why the interest of a strong chief executive has been crucial to the development of any U.S. arms control proposal that creates controversy in any major part of the bureaucracy. The bureaucratic structure that most encourages such proposals is likely to depend more on the President's decision-making style than it is on any other factor.

Congress and the Public

The Senate has the constitutional power to advise and consent, by a two-thirds vote, to the ratification of treaties by the United States. This veto power is often extremely important, as suggested by the commitments that President Kennedy had to make to achieve Senate ratification of the Limited Test Ban, and by the Jackson amendment debate, to be discussed in Chapter 10.

The effect of the Senate debate can be to slow momentum and thwart the hope that limited arms control agreements will create the political climate needed to encourage more substantial arms control agreements.

To pass a treaty through the Senate, the President has at times had to tell the Senate how much this treaty strengthens the U.S. position vis-à-vis the Soviets. Like the negotiator, he has had to emphasize at home the exact opposite of what he was attempting to emphasize to the Russians. The ratification requirement may also strengthen the U.S. negotiating position. The U.S. negotiator can tell the Soviet Union that he and the President would be willing to yield a point, but that the resulting agreement would not be approved by Congress. Perhaps the Soviet Union would then yield the point.

Potentially, Congress has other sweeping powers over arms control. Congress approves the military budget as part of its general power of the purse. Sometimes, especially as part of legislation that the President particularly desires and will therefore sign, Congress enacts riders directing or prohibiting particular actions in the foreign policy area. For example, it has prohibited or limited the supply of arms to particular nations; in working in this way, Congress often places major pressures on the President in favor of arms control.

Congress has also acted specifically to protect its role in all arms control agreements. Section 33 of the 1961 act creating ACDA states: "No action shall be taken under this or any other law that will obligate the United States to disarm or to reduce or limit the Armed Forces or armaments of the United States, except pursuant to the treaty making power of the President under the Constitution or unless authorized by further affirmative legislation by the Congress." Representatives of the Executive branch have argued that this provision is an unconstitutional invasion of the foreign policy power of the Executive, but they have generally respected it. There were secret aspects of SALT I that were not submitted to the entire Congress, but President Nixon did submit the interim offensive forces agreement to Congress. As an Executive agreement, this agreement would not legally have had to be submitted to Congress were it not for Section 33.

In spite of these sweeping powers, Congress has generally participated very little in arms control negotiations and has often not even been well briefed. Some of the reasons are continuing features of U.S. foreign policy. In general, few people in the public are very interested in any foreign policy issue, least of all in arms control. Congressmen therefore tend to slight the subject, preferring to concentrate on issues of greater interest to their constituents. Moreover, at least until the time of the Nixon Administration, there were relatively few arms control experts outside the Executive branch. Thus, Congress had few sources of information except the Executive. The Executive agencies had their own Congressional supporters, and arms control issues tended to emerge only on the infrequent occasions when particular agencies disliked the probable outcome of internal negotiations and wanted to gain Congressional support for their positions. Often the Executive was also able to control the flow of information to Congress, using arguments that secrecy was important for negotiations and for the protection of national security. The general trend of American history has therefore been that Congress enters foreign policy negotiations only at ratification time and through occasional choice of a congressman as a member of a negotiating team. Before the Vietnam war, most observers favored this arrangement, arguing that Congress was likely to act less wisely than the President and citing such examples as the rejection of the League of Nations.

The fact that the current generation of arms control efforts emerged during the late 1950's and early 1960's also shaped Congress's approach. At the time, the politics of foreign policy were bipartisan; the cold war was believed so important that foreign policy goals were little debated. Congress, reflecting public attitudes, gave strong support to the military and to military expenditures. Many in Congress feared that the Executive would be insufficiently firm in dealing with the Soviet Union; the provision cited above was inserted into the ACDA act for this reason.

The serious arms controllers of the time were often scientists, who had access to the Executive because of their expertise. They were afraid of Congress and looked to the Executive as their ally against it. As the theory of deterrence was developed, for example, many sought to persuade the Executive that the theory provided a sensible basis for the limitation of strategic arms. Few made comparable efforts to persuade Congress or the public. Arms control took on an aura of expertise. Public movements in the United States were left to those supporting more radical policies, such as drastic disarmament, and to those pointing to such specific issues as radioactive fallout.

The Vietnam war reversed the position of Congress and the Executive. The war ended the old bipartisan foreign policy. Before the war, Congress feared that the Executive would be insufficiently firm; after the war, it feared that the Executive would be overly bellicose. Public opinion turned against military expenditures for the first time since immediately after World War II. Well-informed pressure groups arose outside the government, building, for example, on people's desire not to have antiballistic missiles near their homes. Scientists who had been working with the Executive began to work with Congress. Congress seriously debated the ABM decision in 1969; although it finally supported the ABM, the debate was the first time in decades that a defense program desired by the President came anywhere near rejection.

The public therefore rewarded SALT I in the 1972 elections rather than fearing arms control, as it had a decade earlier. But relatively few people understood the deterrence theory on which the agreement was built. One result was that the SALT I agreement drew criticism that it need not have drawn. What might have been informed discussion about the pros and cons of deterrence theory was often instead uninformed discussion about SALT. A second result was that SALT drew praise that was probably equally undeserved. President Nixon put it forward as a symbol of détente more than as an agreement to begin regulating a phase of the arms race. The symbolism came to dominate so heavily that many argued that agreements—significant or not—were being made simply for domestic political benefit. And the Executive and the Defense Department learned how to bargain with each other and with Congress so that arms control agreements could be designed without reducing military budgets. New weapons programs would be justified as "bargaining chips" to help in negotiations or as ways to provide for national security after treaty ratification.

This situation was probably not stable. By well before the time of Nixon's resignation in 1974, Congress had come to question many of the President's foreign policy initiatives. The military may have lost some of its support in Congress with the House reorganization of early 1975. Knowledge of deterrence theory, staff expertise, and Congressional confidence in challenging military or Presidential judgments were spreading; the Vladivostok accords (to be discussed in Chapter 10) were criticized, as much for not going far enough as for going too far. But the attitudes were ambiguous: at the same time that the intelligence community was under attack in 1975, there were also signs of reaction against détente and agreements with the Soviets.

Congress still finds it difficult to play an active role in arms control. Secrecy in negotiation inhibits Congressional participation. Large bodies such as Congress move cumbersomely and inefficiently. Hearings tend to propagandize more than to inform or educate. Legislation is poorly adapted to directing an unwilling Executive to negotiate; it is better adapted to modifying the defense budget. Finally, Congress's staff is still very small compared with that of the Executive.

The attitudes of the public and of Congress and their change in the wake of the Vietnam war form a pattern unique to the United States. Few nations have a tradition of struggle between Legislative and Executive over the control of foreign policy. Moreover, each nation has a different history, which is likely to lead to deficiencies in public attitudes toward arms control. For example, the 1962 war with China tended to turn India against arms control, and India's 1973 explosion of a nuclear device was probably supported by public opinion. Labor appealed to a disarmament vote and emphasized nuclear issues in the 1964 British election, but reverted to Tory nuclear policies after winning office. Public opinion in Japan opposes things nuclear, but many in that nation are quite ambiguous about ratifying the Non-Proliferation Treaty. These attitudes follow poorly understood patterns; they are clearly important to arms control. Their importance is probably much greater in the West than in the Soviet Union; this is why many fear that détente and arms control can lead the United States to ignore defense and become dangerously weak. Public support, however, has seldom forced agreement upon decision-makers, but public opposition can prevent the conclusion of arms control agreements. Most important, public and Congressional comprehension are essential if negotiations are to be useful. Otherwise, the bureaucratic process can easily produce agreements that are unwise or merely symbolic.

Because of the difficulties of bureaucratic processes and the need for agreements to be airtight to survive ratification, some arms controllers argued in the mid-1970's that unilateral restraint or perhaps tacit or informal agreements should be more heavily emphasized. Tacit agreements on a unilateral decision against building a new weapon could be reversed at any time. They would therefore be less risky than a treaty, which might have to be abrogated. Moreover, the unilateral decision might not arouse as much bureaucratic opposition as would a treaty. The hope would be that their own political processes would encourage other nations to respond by exercising similar restraint.

International Negotiation

As a domestic position is developed, it is tested in international negotiations against the positions held by other nations. Each negotiator tries to obtain the best outcome possible for his nation. Therefore, he will be extremely reluctant to make even those concessions he is authorized to make. Moreover, the interests of the different nations are not always directly opposed. Often, a concession will be much more important to one nation than to another. The negotiator's problem is to find those concessions that permit beneficial agreement.

The process of finding agreement can be suggested by some of the procedures of the Conference of the Committee on Disarmament; many of the working procedures of other forums are closely analogous. The CCD was established by agreement between the United States and the Soviet Union, which furnish its present co-chairmen. It is technically independent of the United Nations, but is endorsed by and reports to the

General Assembly, and its expenses and staff are supplied by the United Nations. The CCD has an open agenda, with no limitation on the subject matter within the general field of disarmament. Any member can raise any topic he wants, and no one is ruled out of order for raising a question, even one rather remote from disarmament.

The committee normally meets two or three times a week, with each meeting lasting for three hours. There are some 30 delegations, each with two people seated at a long table, with other advisers behind them. After the chairman opens the meeting, two or three, sometimes four, of the delegates make speeches. These speeches follow prepared texts, which are read at the meeting, usually in an unemotional manner. After the speeches, there is occasionally discussion, and someone may ask a question or two. Rarely are the questions answered at the time; two or three weeks later, they *may* be answered. In the early years of the conference, questions were answered at once, but this procedure proved "bad for relations among nations and the cause of disarmament." A stenographic record is kept of the meetings, but it is not made public for several weeks.

As soon as the meeting is over, the delegates who have made speeches give copies to the press, which is waiting outside in the halls. No press representatives are actually in the room during the meetings, which are in effect closed but not secret. The absence of the press helps to reduce the compulsion to engage in propaganda and oratory. Thus, the talks have been businesslike and relatively free of propaganda on matters that are extraneous to the negotiations themselves.

The function of the speeches in this situation—it is a clear and useful function—is to record the attitude of a particular delegation on a particular subject at a particular time. The speeches also serve to advance arguments in a coherent, systematic way, perhaps better than could be done in informal conversation. Obviously there is no real bargaining done at the table. The real work is done in the corridors and in the coffee rooms and in the offices—delegates often call on each other in offices around Geneva—as well as at the receptions, lunches, and dinners that the delegates are compelled to tender each other. The most important of these small-group meetings are those between the Soviet delegation and the American delegation. That is where the military power lies, and it is in the meetings between those two groups that agreements are usually first hammered out. The U.S. delegation meets with that of the Soviets some four or five times a week in one way or another—by twos or threes or fours.

Various devices are used to facilitate agreement. Sometimes, third nations are able to suggest acceptable compromises. Often it is useful for the delegations to work with each other through their number-two people. The deputy in the U.S. delegation will go to the number-two man in the Soviet delegation and tell him he might be able to persuade his superior to concede on X if the Soviet could persuade his superior to concede on Y. And the Soviet comes back after a few days, replying that if the U.S. number-one man would frame a specific proposal to the U.S.S.R. number-one man, the latter might accept. The principals then go through the charade in which each says what his deputy has arranged for him to say, and agreement is reached on an issue. Since neither side has been committed until the principals make their statements, the process can be cut off at any point and no one is embarrassed by an inability to proceed along the line that is being proposed.

Draft texts require prior approval from home, often by the very highest authorities. This causes each side to resist minor changes because it is not easy, a short time after obtaining approval for one version, to ask for approval to change a few words. Five or ten pages of explanation have to be written on why these words need changing and why one side should change instead of the other. Occasionally the approval requirements are eased by "agreement ad referendum." This means each delegation says that a text is now acceptable to its members and that the delegation is prepared to recommend the text back to its capital. The capital of course has the freedom to decide whether or not to accept the text.

Governments are unlikely to find a more rapid or expeditious way to negotiate; therefore, arms control measures of a general character, both multilateral and bilateral, require long, hard work. This is true even when one proceeds, as has the CCD, by working on a small part of the problem. Moreover, the review process at home usually controls the negotiators quite effectively. This implies that nations will never enter arms control agreements unless the leaders (and often the bureaucracies as well) of all the participating nations regard the agreement as beneficial. Any agreement will have to benefit all participants. Agreements are therefore unlikely to be unbalanced. There are exceptions, such as the Non-Proliferation Treaty, but the pressures from home are likely to prevent negotiators from accepting a treaty that implies permanent inequality.

Verification

Fundamentally, nations honor arms control agreements because their leaders have already judged the agreements beneficial to the nation.

Intentional violation is most likely only if there is first a major change in the national leadership or in the world. A new leadership might, as did Hitler in Germany, repudiate the ideas behind a treaty. To cope with change in the world, most contemporary treaties provide an escape clause permitting abrogation of the agreement under variously defined circumstances. In all the arms control agreements yet reached, the ultimate judge of these circumstances is the government of the nation considering abrogation.

But verification and control have occupied a prominent position in nearly all the post–World War II negotiations. The whole concept of verification is much more difficult than it appears at first sight. What, actually, is verification and what difference does it make? Simple-sounding answers may frequently appear: inspection is needed to make sure no one cheats, or as a return for rights being given up. On closer analysis the answers turn out to be rather more difficult.

At the outset, several distinctions should be made, the first being ACDA's distinction between verification and inspection. For ACDA as well as for many writers in the area, inspection is action carried out by formal agreement under defined procedures and safeguards. The vision is one of inspectors going around within a country or of black boxes being left in agreed places. Intelligence is information from any other source, including the traditional espionage sources, but relying much more heavily on technical systems and on public data sources. The agency's definition of verification is the combination of these two: inspection plus intelligence. This definition was developed as part of the trend in which arms control relies more on intelligence data than on formal agreed inspection. This trend has developed to its logical conclusion in the SALT I agreement not to interfere with certain of each other's intelligence systems, the national technical means of verification.

A second distinction is that between verification and response. Learning whether or not a party to a treaty has cheated (verification) is only the first step. One needs to know what to do next (response). Any of a number of responses are possible: withdrawing from the treaty, breaking off diplomatic relations with the offender, resuming construction of the relevant weapons, even declaring war. Currently the threat of withdrawing under the treaty clauses mentioned above is the primary sanction or response to enforce the treaty.

An alternative form of response or sanction is a legal penalty. This concept is used in domestic legal systems, and is also at least theoretically available to the European Atomic Energy Community (EURATOM). It has further been proposed for some of the far-reaching plans of General and Complete Disarmament. The concept is spelled out in this description of EURATOM:[3]

The Treaty distinguishes two types of violations of the control provisions: opposition to the carrying out of an inspection and all other infringements. . . . The Commission is . . . empowered to impose penalties on persons or enterprises in the event of any violation by them of their obligations under the Treaty. The sanctions, depending on the gravity of the offense, range from a simple warning, to the withdrawing of special privileges, such as financial or technical assistance, to the placing of the respective enterprise under the administration—for a period not exceeding four months—of a person or board appointed jointly by the Commission and the State having jurisdiction over the firm, [and] to the partial or total withdrawing of source or special fissionable materials.

This reads like a statute and it is enforced like a statute, meaning that before a sanction is imposed it is necessary for an enforcer to meet a specified standard of proof in an administrative procedure similar to a court. The administrator will then decide on the appropriate sanction, such as taking the nuclear materials away. The procedure is closely analogous to that of criminal law.

The criminal law analogy suggests the difficulty of defining a desirable enforcement procedure. Several goals are typically stated for criminal law: it should deter people from committing crimes; the criminal should be incarcerated so that he cannot commit further crimes, and so that attempts at rehabilitation can be made; and society should enforce the law in order to condemn the conduct. These goals may be substantially met without discovery of every offense, or they may be unattainable even with heavy policing. And heavy policing has many social costs. How much enforcement is needed turns out to be an extremely difficult question, even in the traditional criminal law area. The EURATOM directorate has a still more difficult problem, resolvable only by politics and intuition, in deciding how much money to spend and how many inspectors to use in its effort to keep fissionable material from being siphoned off from the various nuclear industries in Europe. There is no clear answer.

It is nearly as difficult to define the verification requirements where the response pattern is a political one such as treaty abrogation. The United States might conduct a verification analysis for SALT in the following manner. Both U.S. and U.S.S.R. force levels are known, presumably through intelligence sources. One would then assume a U.S.S.R.

[3] Stephen Gorove, "The First Multinational Atomic Inspection and Control System at Work: Euratom's Experience," *Stanford Law Review*, 18, no. 1 (1965): 180–81.

evasion, say deployment of a ballistic missile defense system that is made
to look like an air defense system for as long as possible during construction. The technical details of the postulated evasion will then be
worked out as carefully as possible: the timing of various steps of Soviet
production, the points at which the United States could detect the Soviet
action through its intelligence systems, and the points at which there
would be a significant effect on the strategic balance. The analysis then
moves to response time: from the point at which the evasion is detected,
will there be enough time for the United States to make a countermove?
Can the United States respond to the evasion by appropriate forms of
construction? If the United States can detect an evasion in time to
build a response before the evasion takes on operational capability, then
the treaty is verifiable against the evasion. The analysis must consider
many different kinds of evasion, and the difficulties of determining at an
early point of evasion exactly what is happening and what response
should be made. If a treaty is verifiable in this strict sense against all
evasion, security is not jeopardized in any manner by entering into it.

A theoretical difficulty with this concept of minimum-risk verification
is that it is too sensitive to production rates. If, for example, the United
States is able to build countermeasures faster than the violator can build
violating systems, then little lead time is needed, compared with the time
when the deployment begins appearing. If the United States can build
only more slowly than the opponent, all the lead time in the world will
do no good against an opponent determined to evade and to obtain a
strategic lead. For the strategic arms race, results from this analysis will,
then, depend heavily on assumptions made about alternate production
capabilities and willingness to use those capabilities.

The foregoing analysis of minimum-risk verification is often used in
evaluating arms control proposals in the United States. It is a good technique for designing an intelligence system, since it assumes an uncontrolled arms race. If applied to an arms control situation, however, it
effectively assumes that the arms control agreement has no force whatever, and that the other party will cheat if he can. It further assumes
that the only response to such cheating is to counterbuild, and that the
availability of that response is the prime way to encourage the other
party to live up to the treaty. These assumptions may be appropriate
to some crucial agreements, but they seem somewhat paradoxical in
an arms control situation. And only for relatively restricted treaties can
this standard be met without highly intrusive verification.

The response on the part of arms control thinkers has been to look
for other reasons why a nation might honor an arms control treaty. There

are, for example, bureaucratic pressures that encourage a nation to live up to a treaty. Few within the nation think of violation; most strategic planning will be based on the assumption that the treaty will not be violated, and only a minor amount of planning for violation is done. The policy options typically brought to decision-makers therefore seldom involve violation of the treaty. A violation would probably require either a major bureaucratic decision (possibly visible to the opponent) or a new side bureaucracy to plan the violation.

Verification can seek to build on these bureaucratic foundations by giving additional weight to the arguments of those planners who want to honor the treaty. Verification can be effective, under this theory, by creating a risk that the evasion *might* be detected; one does not have to make absolutely certain that it will be detected. One assumes that a bureaucracy will not violate unless it can be highly confident of avoiding detection. The risk factors are turned against violation to achieve effective deterrence to violations with less verification than might be needed for absolute detection. Under this theory, there is a risk for the inspector, but there is one for the violator as well, and the analyst begins to balance risks.

There is a further application of these political factors, which builds on the politics that go on in the "innocent" country. This theory assumes that violation would result from a form of escalation. Thus, if the United States began a program that appeared to be a possible violation of SALT, debate would erupt in the Soviet Union between groups charging that the United States is or is not about to violate the treaty. The former group, expecting U.S. violation, might recommend treaty abrogation or make preparations to violate out of fear of the United States. Some of these actions might be detected in the United States, where the political balance would shift to meet what might be considered a probability of U.S.S.R. treaty violation. The process could escalate until there was a violation. Verification, then, would be designed in part to prevent this process, to give each side enough *assurance* of the other's compliance that suspicions do not escalate. The verification helps both sides obtain the benefits they sought by entering the treaty. Each side would be given increased confidence that the other side is living up to the treaty, and each side would have an incentive to assure the other that it is complying. The informal understanding between the United States and the Soviet Union to permit certain intelligence-gathering techniques fell within this pattern of providing assurance. SALT I thus included an explicit agreement not to interfere with the other's "unilateral means of verification."

Each of these last analyses of verification, unlike the minimum-risk analysis, leads to only intuitive estimates of verification needs. One must weigh the degrees of suspicion on each side and the dangers of a violation in order to define verification requirements. Both theories depend on the assumption that the treaty was entered into for a reason, and that there is a shared value in not going ahead with the arms race. Each side needs to know that the other party continues seeing that value; there is no need to assume that the other will evade the treaty, but some safeguards are desirable to keep the situation stable. One accepts less than foolproof inspection, knowing that the other might be entering the treaty only as a way to catch his opponent off guard, but also knowing that the other's self-interest and the estimates of political goals at the time of treaty entry make this deceptive posture very unlikely. Verification standards will be set according to a highly complex judgment, comparable to that made in domestic law enforcement, that balances a number of risks.

To the extent that such balances are made, the intensity of verification will differ for different treaties. The International Atomic Energy Agency (IAEA), for example, is the inspection agency for the Non-Proliferation Treaty. It has a multilateral system of gathering information through inspectors. But the information, if used at all, would probably be used only for diplomatic purposes. Although the IAEA can terminate the flow of its nuclear materials to a violating nation, the important response in the event of violation is not a formal legal one but a diplomatic one: censure of other parties, abrogation of the treaty, supply of weapons to threatened nations, or, conceivably, inaction. The inspection technique does give the IAEA substantial privileges to examine operating power and research reactors, but gives the IAEA little ability to look for clandestine nuclear facilities. After all, low importance was placed on complete nonproliferation, so that the rest of the signatories were willing to go ahead in spite of both China's and France's nuclear postures. The short-term dangers to the United States or to the Soviets from possible evasions were quite mild. The great powers were willing to accept inspection performance well below conceptual perfection and were not concerned at the absence of formal legal response to violation. They did want an arrangement that would inhibit proliferation politically and provide a reasonable chance of detecting—and therefore deterring—violation. An inspection system could in theory provide pairs of potential nuclear adversaries such as Egypt and Israel with some assurance that the other is not violating, but the existing system may not be strong enough for this purpose.

The earlier nuclear test-ban negotiations represent the other extreme of nearly absolute verification requirements. For nuclear tests there are few indicators of slow buildups, nor are there obvious counterdeployments available as responses. The problem was viewed quite seriously. There was no way of knowing what technical advance might be achieved with a clandestine test. With the knowledge that the other was testing, each side would have some way to estimate the probability that major technical developments had occurred; without this knowledge one side could conceivably gain a serious advantage without warning to the other. Consequently, there was strong pressure in the United States for complete certainty about whether the Soviet Union was living up to the treaty. Contributing to this were many less rational elements—memories of Pearl Harbor and surprise attack, and confusion between the information needed for political responses and that needed for judicial sanctions. The result was the treaty that permitted underground tests precisely because they might not be detectable, and prohibited other tests because they could be detected. From an intelligence viewpoint, the treaty may have increased the probability that one side would make a breakthrough in nuclear weapons development that the other side would not know about, because one can learn more about another's atmospheric tests than about his underground tests; yet this result was reached for quite understandable reasons.

In the mid-1950's, arms control conjured a vision of international disarmament organizations, with inspectors traveling the world. Under most of the actual arms control agreements of the late 1960's and early 1970's, the only effective verification is unilateral, through a nation's own intelligence system. The United States to some extent, and more particularly the Soviet Union, appear generally opposed to other kinds of inspection. The Soviet preference substantially limits the arms control agreements that can be reached. Intelligence systems can do some things well but not others. Ground inspectors have different capabilities; they can detect some evasions well that intelligence systems cannot.

This much is straightforward, but there are also subtleties based on the problem of using intelligence data. Nations are hesitant to reveal too much about their intelligence systems. An example is President Kennedy's action in the 1962 Cuban crisis. That situation was parallel to an arms control agreement, an expectation that certain kinds of weapons would not be introduced into Cuba. In order to call the Soviet "violation," President Kennedy had to reveal substantial information about the U-2 system's capabilities by releasing photographs taken with it. The costs were real. The information released could be valuable in the future to one attempting to conceal a development from the intelligence system. Moreover, Kennedy had to admit that the United States had been over-flying Cuba. These are costs that intelligence agencies and national governments prefer not to accept. A potential violator of an agreement verified only by intelligence might then be tempted toward small violations on the assumption that its opponent will not accept the costs of revealing its intelligence capabilities. There is also a question of whether unilateral intelligence data will be persuasive before public opinion. President Kennedy might not have carried off the U.S. position in 1962 in Cuba so effectively had he not released the U-2 pictures that showed the missile sites, or had the intelligence data been in a form harder to explain to the public.

Other implications of using intelligence rather than formal multi-lateral inspection relate to the rigidity of the standards applied. If the inspection function is delegated to an international body, the inspection standards may be difficult to change. If the United States and the Soviet Union find that they want much stronger verification of developing-nation nuclear programs, they may be unable to make the IAEA change its standards. Vis-à-vis each other, they can unilaterally increase their intelligence efforts. Likewise, with unilateral verification a treaty violation can perhaps be ignored or dealt with through quiet diplomacy. With a multilateral system in which the violation is reported through the IAEA to the General Assembly and the world public, a violation cannot be so readily minimized. The U.S.S.R. nuclear tests that vented by re-leasing a little radioactive gas had no substantial effect on relations be-tween the United States and the Soviet Union. Under a multilateral system this technical violation might have taken on greater importance.

But this effect cuts both ways. Use of intelligence may also decrease the power of the public and of legislatures to review the way the agree-ments are performed and to evaluate whether the treaties have turned out to be consistent with the verification ability. An analogy is suggested by the demilitarization of Laos. This arrangement, made under Ken-nedy, resembled an arms control agreement verified by unilateral means. The United States and the Communists each knew the other was sub-stantially violating the arrangement, but the violations were kept out of public view for a long time. One can wonder whether similar dangers could arise in strategic situations where verification is through covert techniques known only to the national governments involved.

One who criticizes consultations held in privacy must, however, con-sider the example of the Standing Consultative Committee, a joint U.S.-U.S.S.R. body set up to help resolve problems arising under the SALT accords. The body works privately, so SALT problems do not necessarily become known to the public. Yet the privacy is probably the only way to establish a working relationship with the Soviet Union that keeps the meetings from degenerating into propaganda exercises. This body might be the predecessor of an international enforcement operation, but the character of consultations will probably have to change if arms control agreements ever reduce arms substantially.

Conclusion

Arms control reflects the long political tradition of foreign policy: the negotiations are often conducted secretly, Executive branch control has dominated over Legislative or public control, agreements are designed to support the national interest, verification relies heavily upon classified intelligence information. What is special about arms control is that the military developments it is designed to regulate often have powerful supporters within the foreign policy bureaucracy. The result is that arms control agreements are often nearly irrelevant, and Presidential leadership is essential if forces are to be substantially limited or reduced.

At least in the United States, however, many of these institutional premises were in doubt in the mid-1970's. Congress was seeking a coordinate role in foreign policy; it was reforming itself in a way that might well weaken the military's political position; the public began to doubt the Executive's expertise in foreign policy.

The trend was revealed in the SALT negotiations, to be discussed in the following chapters. SALT I (1969–72) was designed at the bureaucratic and Executive level; SALT II (1973–) was relatively more influenced by public and Congressional opinion. If this effect is to be healthy, public and Congressional knowledge will be deeply needed.

The U.S. changes had not yet run their course at the end of 1975. Nor can their future effect be estimated, particularly since the most important negotiating partner, the Soviet Union, is still committed to secrecy and bureaucratic dominance.

CHAPTER NINE

The Negotiation of SALT I

IN JANUARY 1964, in a message to the Eighteen-Nation Disarmament Committee (ENDC), President Johnson proposed a "verified freeze of the number and characteristics of strategic nuclear offensive and defensive vehicles." This proposal, the first for a separable limitation on strategic arms, was the product of a U.S. study of strategic arms control that had started shortly after President Kennedy took office.

The Soviet Union rejected the proposal partly because the United States had called for on-site inspection. However, of perhaps greater importance was the Soviet Union's relative strategic position. In mid-1964, the United States was ahead in bombers and also had 834 ICBMs and 416 SLBMs compared with the Soviets' 200 ICBMs and 120 SLBMs. A freeze in 1964 would have perpetuated Soviet strategic inferiority in both ICBMs and SLBMs. Many have felt that the achievement, or at least the approach to achievement, of approximate strategic equality with the United States was a clear precondition for Soviet willingness to begin serious negotiations on limiting strategic arms. As long as the Soviets were strategically inferior, they would have little incentive to enter negotiations for freezing or limiting strategic arms. Although the Soviet and American forces were not numerically equal when the Strategic Arms Limitation Talks (SALT) did finally begin in 1969, the Soviets were approaching numerical parity in both ICBMs and SLBMs and reached numerical parity in ICBMs a few months later.

Throughout the mid-1960's, U.S. interest in a limitation on strategic arms was heightened by concern about Soviet ABM systems and the fear, explained in Chapter 7, that ABM systems would destabilize deterrence. The Soviets deployed a small ABM system around Leningrad in 1962. This deployment, although subsequently dismantled, together with continuing concerns about Soviet ABM intentions were substantial factors in the U.S. decision to develop MIRVs. Then, in November 1964, the Soviets paraded an ABM missile in Moscow, and subsequently began deploying a limited ABM system around Moscow. This system, called the Galosh, intensified Congressional pressure for the deployment of a U.S. ABM system. The United States had developed ABM system components, but both Kennedy and Johnson had resisted pressures to deploy the system on cost-effectiveness grounds. The Soviet deployment, which many analysts predicted would be expanded into a nationwide ABM system, restricted Johnson's political alternatives to deploying the U.S. ABM system or negotiating a U.S.-U.S.S.R. ban on ABM systems.

Johnson chose to stave off Congressional pressures for a U.S. ABM system by attempting to persuade the Soviet Union to begin negotiations on limiting strategic arms. In December 1965, the United States began a new series of overtures to the Soviets, but there was initially no favorable response. Congressional pressures for a U.S. ABM system mounted. In 1966, Congress approved, against the wishes of the Johnson Administration, more than $160 million for advance preparation to deploy an ABM system. In early 1967, Johnson requested authorization to begin an ABM deployment, and stated that he would use the authorization in 1967 unless the Soviets indicated sincere willingness to begin negotiations on mutual arms limitations. Johnson also wrote Premier Kosygin and again proposed the initiation of private bilateral discussions on strategic arms. Kosygin responded in March 1967 and agreed in principle to bilateral discussions on "means of limiting the arms race in offensive and defensive nuclear missiles." The Soviets did not, however, specify a particular time or place for the talks, and continued to drag their feet.

As noted above, one reason for the Soviet hesitation to begin SALT at this time was that strategic parity with the United States was still not achieved. In mid-1967 the Americans had 1,054 ICBMs and 656 SLBMs, while the Soviets had 460 ICBMs and 130 SLBMs. Another reason was that the Non-Proliferation Treaty (NPT) negotiations were still not completed. From the time of the 1955 Western decision to allow West Germany to rearm, the Soviet leaders had feared and fought against the possibility that West Germany might acquire nuclear weapons. This Soviet determination to keep nuclear weapons out of West German and, to a lesser extent, out of Japanese hands, was the main driving force behind Soviet interest in the negotiation of the NPT. The Soviets made clear that they were not willing to begin SALT negotiations until the NPT negotiations were completed. It would not, therefore, be coincidence that President Johnson later publicly announced upcoming SALT talks on July 1, 1968, the day the NPT was signed by both nations.

A further reason why the Soviets rejected these Western overtures lay in the Soviet attitude toward strategic defense, and particularly toward ABMs. Although U.S. Secretary of Defense McNamara and some Western analysts argued that ABMs fueled the arms race and created instability, many Soviet theorists (along with some Western analysts) refused to acknowledge any link between defensive weapons and the arms race. They argued that it would be irresponsible for the Soviet leaders to refrain from doing everything possible to protect the Soviet people in the event of nuclear war. Premier Kosygin seemed to share these views. As late as February 1967, he stated that a defensive system was not a cause of the arms race but rather a "factor preventing the death of people."

Finally, the Vietnam war contributed significantly to Soviet unwillingness to begin private bilateral talks with the United States in 1967. The Soviets were totally opposed to the U.S. actions in Vietnam. They feared they would lose prestige in the Communist world if they engaged in private bilateral negotiations with the United States while the Americans were escalating the fighting against North Vietnam. (Although the Soviets did negotiate with the United States on the NPT while the United States was still actively involved in Vietnam, these negotiations were in a multilateral forum. When the Soviets and Americans negotiated NPT language, they submitted identical but separate drafts to the ENDC.) The U.S. involvement in Vietnam became a weaker impediment after the United States seemed no longer to be seeking a military solution to the conflict. Thus, the 1968 limitations on U.S. bombing of North Vietnam and the beginning of the Paris peace talks helped Moscow to justify the beginning of secret bilateral negotiations with the United States on arms control. Once the United States began to extricate itself from the conflict and a negotiated settlement seemed possible, the situation in Vietnam no longer prevented formal SALT negotiations.

While all these factors were delaying SALT, at least one factor was evolving to encourage SALT. Revolutionary improvements in "national technical means" of acquiring information about each other's military deployments were proceeding in both nations. The critical means were observation or reconnaissance satellites. After the launch of the first satellite in 1957, both nations began to develop satellites that could carry instruments able to observe and film the territory over which they passed. The United States orbited its first weather satellites in 1960, and during the 1960's both the Americans and the Soviets continually improved their observation satellites until they could resolve objects a few feet across or even smaller. Infrared sensors were developed to detect missile launchings and to make certain observations at night. During the exchanges preliminary to SALT, the United States, although not excluding some possibility of on-site inspection, made clear that its interest was mainly in measures that could be verified by each side's national technical means. This reassurance increased the Soviet's expectation that talks might actually produce agreements.

In June 1967 the United States made another unsuccessful effort to begin strategic negotiations, when Premier Kosygin and President Johnson met at Glassboro, New Jersey. McNamara warned Kosygin that an increase in the Soviet ABM deployment would require the United States to increase its offensive forces. Kosygin remained unwilling or unable to accept the link between defensive and offensive forces.

The Glassboro summit made clear the impossibility of beginning SALT before the next budget message to Congress, and Johnson was unable to postpone further the decision on ABM deployment. On September 18, 1967, in a speech in San Francisco, Secretary of Defense McNamara announced that the U.S. would deploy a limited or "thin" ABM system, later named Sentinel. Sentinel was to be primarily for defense against a future Chinese nuclear threat, but also for defense of Minuteman sites and for protection against an accidental ICBM launch (China had no ICBMs at this time). In his San Francisco speech, McNamara first argued against the deployment of a "thick" ABM system designed to protect U.S. cities against Soviet missiles. Such a system would be very expensive and would only encourage the Soviets to build up their offensive forces to offset the U.S. ABM deployment. Then, after presenting a forcible case for restraint, McNamara concluded by announcing the decision to begin deployment of a thin Chinese-oriented ABM system.

McNamara subsequently argued that the Soviets should not be concerned about deployment of a thin Chinese-oriented ABM system, but the Soviets, as well as many members of the U.S. government, realized that a thin Chinese-oriented ABM system would not be significantly different from a thin Soviet-oriented ABM system, and also that any thin ABM system would have considerable growth potential, particularly after a radar base was established. McNamara's efforts to convince the Soviets that one could distinguish between an anti-Chinese and an anti-Soviet ABM system were hardly facilitated by statements by ABM supporters, such as General Earle Wheeler, the Chairman of the Joint Chiefs of Staff, who assured Congress that the anti-Chinese system had anti-Soviet potential and could be expanded into a thick ABM network.

McNamara's San Francisco speech and subsequent U.S. statements stressed that the deployment of a thin ABM system did not make an agreement on offensive and defensive systems any less urgent, and he continued to call for negotiations on strategic arms. There was logic in this position, for, whatever the rationalizations about the U.S. ABM decision, the basic reason for the decision was political: if the Soviets had an ABM, the Americans must have one also. In the 1968 Congressional debates on ABM, a number of influential congressmen and senior defense officials set forth a bargaining chip rationale for deploying ABM. According to this theory, one must threaten to deploy a system in order to persuade the other side to negotiate seriously. Thus, it was argued that an active U.S. ABM program was necessary to induce the Soviets to begin serious negotiations on strategic offensive and defensive weapons.

It was a series of probes at this time that finally resulted in a Soviet announcement in May 1968 of willingness to negotiate practical steps for limiting strategic delivery vehicles. The 1968 Soviet decision to begin SALT can be attributed to a number of other factors as well. The factors restraining the Soviet Union were changing. Although the United States still had 1,054 ICBMs and 656 SLBMs in mid-1968, the Soviets had 800 ICBMs and 130 SLBMs and were in the process of achieving parity or approximate equality with the United States. The NPT had been signed in July 1968. There was evidence that the Soviets had begun to modify their strategic understanding of ABMs and were viewing them as a potential catalyst of the arms race. The United States was visibly changing its Vietnam objectives.

There were also new strategic, economic, and political incentives for beginning SALT talks with the United States. Many Soviet leaders were increasingly concerned about the dangers of a continued and escalated arms race. Successful SALT talks might release sorely needed material and human resources to meet the rising Soviet demand for consumer goods and to make the investments needed for future economic growth. Bilateral negotiations would further the goal of détente and indicate that the United States accepted the Soviet Union as a strategic and political equal, a long-sought Soviet goal. Secret bilateral negotiations would also further the Soviet goal of seeking the appearance and realization of world condominium with the United States. Such a condominium would benefit Soviet policy in the third world and would reduce the risk of a two-front military conflict if active hostilities were to break out with China.

On July 1, 1968, at the signing of the NPT, Johnson announced that the United States and the Soviet Union had agreed to "enter in the nearest future into discussions on the limitation and the reduction" of both offensive and defensive strategic weapons.

As the Soviet Union was deciding to enter negotiations, the U.S. government was engaged in the final phases of an effort to draft a negotiating plan for the talks. Johnson hoped to initiate the talks at a summit meeting in the Soviet Union, and made it clear that he wanted an opening proposal that would represent a general consensus of both civilian and military views. Basic issues that were to divide the government during SALT had already surfaced; the President's condition that the U.S. opening position represent a consensus constrained the type and specificity of proposals that could be agreed upon within the government. The Arms Control and Disarmament Agency (ACDA), many in the State Department, and some in the Department of Defense (DOD) were concerned about the effects of MIRVs on the arms race and wanted to have them banned. Many of the same organizations wished to ban ABMs or at least to limit them drastically. Proposals to ban MIRVs or ABMs would not, however, have obtained a consensus within the government at that time. Johnson did not want to resolve such politically charged disputes before the talks had even begun or before there was any indication that the talks would be productive. Thus the "arms controllers" within the government did not press these issues. The main task, in their minds, was to start SALT and then to face these questions after there was an indication of Soviet interest. This same line of reasoning caused those who favored a temporary hold on the planned U.S. MIRV-testing program not to press for their position at the time.

The initial negotiating position, on which a consensus was reached in 1968, was therefore a fairly general one. It called for a limit on U.S. and Soviet ABMs at some specific and equivalent number and a limit on the number of SLBMs and ICBMs, with no freedom to mix between the two. No limits on MIRV were proposed, nor were restrictions on strategic bombers proposed.

On August 19, 1968, Soviet Ambassador Anatoly Dobrynin informed Washington that the Soviet government was ready to begin the talks at a summit meeting between Johnson and Kosygin starting on September 30. A joint announcement was to be made on August 21. When the Soviet military moved into Czechoslovakia on August 20, the plans were abruptly canceled and the talks were indefinitely postponed.

Although the Soviet invasion of Czechoslovakia temporarily halted the plans for talks, strategic weapons development continued. The first flight tests of two U.S. MIRVed missiles, the Minuteman III and the Poseidon, were carried out in mid-August as planned. This test program was to have a significant effect on the SALT outcome. It increased commitment within the U.S. government to the production and deployment of MIRV. It created a MIRV technology gap: once the United States had tested MIRVs and begun to perfect MIRV technology, there were strong pressures for the Soviet Union to test its own MIRV systems in order to overcome this technological gap. Thus once MIRVs had been tested, a MIRV ban would become much more difficult to implement.

The Soviets indicated in November 1968 that they were prepared to begin SALT talks at any time, but Johnson was unable to initiate them during the last few months of his Presidency. Johnson sought a lame-duck summit meeting before President-elect Nixon took office in January 1969, but Nixon's incoming Administration indicated to the Soviets that it would not be bound by anything Johnson did. The SALT talks were further postponed. The Soviets raised the subject again after President Nixon's inauguration in January 1969. Nixon, however, insisted on a total review of the U.S. negotiating position on strategic weapons. With Presidential adviser Henry Kissinger, he developed the elaborate Verification Panel arrangement described in the previous chapter.

It was during Nixon's reevaluation of the U.S. SALT position that the Sentinel ABM system was found to draw strong community opposition. Planners in 1968 had feared that the citizens of cities *not covered* by the proposed Sentinel system would demand that their city be covered; it turned out that it was the citizens of some of the cities *covered* by the proposed system who were the most vocal critics of Sentinel. In February 1969, Secretary of Defense Melvin Laird ordered a temporary halt to the deployment of Sentinel pending a one-month review of the system. The next month, President Nixon announced a plan for a new ABM deployment called Safeguard, which would, at least initially, protect ICBM sites rather than cities. This proposal produced a storm of controversy in Congress. The President committed his prestige quite heavily and emphasized the need for a bargaining counter at SALT. He barely won approval for the first phase: the crucial Senate vote was on an amendment that would have held up deployment. The vote was a 50-to-50 tie and the amendment therefore failed. Nevertheless, the domestic politics of the ABM had become radically different from those that had encouraged President Johnson to seek negotiations.

Debate over the MIRV never reached the level of visibility and political controversy that characterized the ABM debate. There were, however, efforts within both the Senate and the bureaucracy to place a moratorium on MIRV testing and deployment pending the result of SALT. In April 1969, for example, Senator Edward Brooke met privately with Nixon and urged him to seek an immediate joint moratorium with the Soviets on MIRV testing and deployment. These and other recommendations for a MIRV moratorium were rejected by the Nixon Admin-

TABLE 2
Approximate Strategic Forces

Year	United States			Soviet Union		
	ICBM*	SLBM	Long-range bombers	ICBM	SLBM	Long-range bombers
1963	424	224	630	100	100	190
1964	834	416	630	200	120	190
1965	854	496	630	270	120	190
1966	904	592	630	300	125	200
1967	1,054	656	600	460	130	210
1968	1,054	656	545	800	130	150
1969	1,054	656	560	1,050	160	150
1970	1,054	656	550	1,300	280	150
1971	1,054	656	505	1,510	440	140
1972	1,054	656	455	1,527	560	140
1973	1,054	656	442	1,527	628	140

SOURCE: *The Military Balance for 1973–1974* (London: International Institute for Strategic Studies).
* This count of ICBMs does not reflect increases in U.S. force capability deriving from installation of MIRVs.

istration. MIRV testing continued and MIRVs were subsequently deployed.

In June Nixon announced that the United States was ready to proceed with SALT, and suggested that talks begin sometime between July 31 and August 15. The Soviets, however, were now concerned lest they appear too eager to begin talks. They did not immediately respond, and it was not until October 25, 1969, that the two nations made a joint announcement that SALT would begin. The talks were set for Helsinki on November 17, 1969. The effect of the various delays was considerable. The United States had become more committed to ABM and MIRV development and deployment programs. The MIRV program was to result in a substantial increase of independently targetable missile warheads in the U.S. inventory. And during the five years from the Glassboro meetings to the completion of SALT I, the Soviets would deploy approximately 1,000 ICBMs and 400 SLBMs, as shown in Table 2.

SALT I Negotiations, 1969–72

The first session of SALT opened in Helsinki on November 17, 1969, and continued until December 22, 1969. The next six sessions were to alternate between Vienna and Helsinki: Vienna in April–August 1970, Helsinki in November–December 1970, Vienna in March–May 1971, Helsinki in July–September 1971, Vienna in November 1971–February 1972, and Helsinki in March–May 1972. The term "SALT I" is generally used to describe the entire set of negotiations from November 1969 to May 1972, when the SALT I agreements were concluded, whereas "SALT II" is used to describe the second phase of the SALT negotiations which began in Geneva on November 21, 1972.

The U.S. SALT I delegation was headed by Gerard Smith, Director of the Arms Control and Disarmament Agency. In addition to Smith, the delegation was composed of representatives from the Departments of State and Defense and the Joint Chiefs of Staff (JCS), together with a senior scientist from the private sector and a number of advisers from various agencies. The Soviet SALT I delegation was headed by Vladimir Semenov, a Deputy Foreign Minister. The rest of the Soviet delegation was roughly a mirror image of the American delegation.

The meetings were secret and the specifics of the negotiations were never made public during SALT I. Even Congressional committees and European allies were briefed only periodically in closed sessions.

Session 1

The first session in Helsinki was largely exploratory, amounting almost to a seminar in strategic theory. Negotiations on specific proposals did not begin until the second session in Vienna the following spring. In spite of its more elaborate preparatory studies, the Nixon Administration had followed the same course as the Johnson Administration by putting off hard decisions until Soviet interest could be tested. Thus, the United States did not enter SALT with firm proposals; instead it put forward strategic concepts and conceptual approaches to arms control. Among the issues discussed with the Soviets in Helsinki were the action-reaction phenomenon, the concept of deterrence, the effects of ABM, and, in general terms, various alternative approaches to limiting strategic arms, including U.S. views on what offensive systems should be limited.

During this first session, it became clear each sought unilateral advantages by defining "strategic system" differently. This difference was to last throughout SALT I and at least until the end of 1975. The Soviets argued that a strategic weapon was any weapon capable of hitting the other side's homeland from where it was deployed. The Soviet definition thus included U.S. Forward-Based Systems (FBSs), since these systems are capable of hitting the Soviet homeland. U.S. FBSs mainly include short-range fighter-bombers deployed in Europe and on aircraft carriers in the Mediterranean, the North Atlantic, and the Northwestern Pacific. There are at least 600 U.S. planes deployed in Europe alone, and most of the forward-based aircraft are capable of carrying both conventional and nuclear weapons. The United States maintained that these FBSs were tactical weapons that served as a counter to Soviet ground forces and to the approximately 600 Soviet IRBMs and MRBMs aimed at U.S. allies in Western Europe. Moreover, the U.S. FBSs were parts of defense arrangements involving U.S. allies and thus could not be dealt with in a bilateral negotiation. The United States further insisted that the negotiations should, in any case, attempt to limit what it called the "central strategic systems" rather than systems that had only a peripheral effect on the strategic balance.

The central issues in SALT concerned ABMs and MIRVs, the two emerging catalysts of strategic arms competition. Yet on neither subject was the exploration in the first session more than limited. The Soviet Union did make clear in this preliminary Helsinki session that it had reversed its previous doctrine on ABMs and that it desired to discuss their limitation or banning, but the United States made no specific proposals for ABM limitations during the session. On MIRVs, there was no exploration of the views of the two sides; the United States decided not to initiate discussion of MIRVs during this session. The omission was obvious and rang loud to the Soviets, who had unsuccessfully attempted various informal explorations of a MIRV test moratorium prior to the beginning of SALT. They waited for the United States to raise the issue; when it did not happen, they decided to open the subject themselves.

The exchanges in the initial session were so general that there were later delays in reaching specifics. The first session did, however, set a healthy atmosphere for future negotiations. Both sides were doubtful at the beginning whether serious and nonpolemical exchanges could take place, but both found useful exchanges possible. Indeed, the Soviets, somewhat to the surprise of the Americans, decided to begin "negotiations" as distinct from "preliminary discussions" only as part of their concluding assessment of the first session. This subtle but important distinction was reflected in Soviet statements, including the joint communiqué at the end of the first session, which ended on December 22, 1969.

Session 2

The second session, which began in Vienna on April 16, 1970, was the longest session and probably the most critical in terms of its effect upon the course of the negotiations and the final SALT I outcome. During the four-month recess between the first session in Helsinki and the second in Vienna, both sides developed their initial proposals.

As part of this process, the United States developed four options; as mentioned in Chapter 8, Nixon and Kissinger asked the bureaucracy to give them alternative options rather than set negotiating positions. The ABM options ranged from one for Zero ABM to one permitting all 12 sites originally planned for Safeguard. Various combinations of limitations on offensive strategic focus were considered, including a MIRV ban. Most offensive force options included a limit on missile numbers at the level the United States had at the time, 1,710, although one included a proposal for reductions. All offensive force options included sublimits on heavy ICBMs aimed at restricting Soviet SS-9 deployments, and a "one-way freedom to mix"—to move the missile force to sea by replacing ICBMs with SLBMs on a one-for-one basis.

Moscow was no less busy, though probably burdened less with studies of details of various alternatives than Washington. From the mass of studies and options, however, choices had to be made on which proposals to present to each other initially. Both sides chose opening positions that had no chance of acceptance by the other without significant modification. The choices of opening positions were important in outlining future negotiating directions, but were less important than the decisions made after the opening positions were rejected.

The United States presented two alternative opening proposals for limiting offensive systems. One was a comprehensive arrangement, which would have placed a ceiling of 1,710 on ICBM and SLBM launchers[1] with a sublimit on large ICBM launchers. It would also have limited heavy bombers, cruise missiles, and Soviet MRBMs and IRBMs. The sublimit on large ICBMs would be supported by limitations on silo modifications. (The MLBM and IRBM provisions were submitted as an opening gambit in deference to the desires of U.S. NATO allies.) The comprehensive option would ban MIRV testing and deployment—but with a requirement for on-site inspection—and would not restrict MIRV production or stockpiling. The second U.S. option for offensive limitations was less comprehensive in scope but did call for a reduction over a number of years from an initial ceiling of 1,710 strategic missiles to a lower level of 1,000. This option did not limit MIRVs. As with all U.S. proposals during SALT I that envisaged equal total aggregates of strategic delivery vehicles, one-way freedom to mix from land to sea launchers was permitted by both proposals.

The Soviets rejected both U.S. proposals. The second U.S. proposal,

[1] As was the case with all proposals for numerical limitations, missiles would be controlled not by a limitation on the missiles themselves but by a limitation on missile launchers or silos, which could be verified by each side's national technical means of verification. Throughout this chapter, references to ICBM and SLBM numbers refer in fact to numbers of ICBM or SLBM launchers.

the reduction option, was considered by the Soviets as hardly worth comment. Whereas the United States was primarily interested in slowing the increasing deployment of Soviet land-based ICBMs, and particularly of the large SS-9s, which were, together with SLBMs, the major ongoing Soviet strategic offensive programs, the Soviets were primarily interested in preventing the installation of MIRVs on U.S. missiles, the only ongoing U.S. strategic offensive program. The Soviets had little interest in an American proposal that would limit Soviet strategic programs but place no limits on the American MIRV program. Not only would the reduction proposed preserve a MIRV advantage to the United States; it would also force the Soviet Union to move the bulk of its strategic force to sea, where the United States was seen to have an advantage because of greater experience, more favorable geography, and foreign submarine bases. (The United States had two such bases, Rota in Spain and Holy Loch in Scotland.) Moreover, reductions in central strategic systems would increase the strategic importance of U.S. FBS deployments.

The Soviets also rejected the comprehensive U.S. option, but gave more attention to it than to the reduction proposal. The Soviets objected to the comprehensive proposal's limitation on IRBMs and MRBMs as outside the scope of the negotiations. They also objected to the proposed sublimits on missiles and to the collateral restrictions on silo modifications. They further objected to the U.S. requirement for on-site inspection against MIRVs as unnecessary and contrary to the ground rules of the negotiations and argued that the U.S. MIRV proposal was one-sided. By prohibiting testing, the U.S. proposal would prevent the Soviet Union from developing MIRV technology. The United States, however, having tested MIRVs, would be permitted to continue to manufacture and stockpile MIRVs and be prohibited only from deploying them on its missiles. The Soviets therefore viewed the proposal as one that would enable the United States to rapidly deploy MIRVs at some future date.

The Soviets' opening proposal for offensive limitations reflected general views they had expressed earlier in Helsinki. They wanted FBS counted as part of the strategic balance and proposed a radical solution of the FBS problem through the withdrawal of forward-based nuclear-armed aircraft and associated facilities. Later, they suggested an alternative approach of some reduction and of "compensation" for the FBS in determining permitted Soviet force levels. They also proposed elimination of foreign bases for nuclear submarines, such bases giving an advantage to the United States by increasing the portion of the submarine force that can be on station at any one time. The Americans repeatedly asked the Soviets to suggest an aggregate total number of delivery vehicles to be permitted; the Soviets refused, arguing that numbers could not be discussed until the question of FBS was settled. The Soviets also broke the silence of Helsinki on MIRVs. The Soviets proposed the dismantling of existing MIRVs and a ban on their production and deployment. This Soviet proposal did not include either on-site inspection or a ban on MIRV testing; thus the Americans could not be sure the Soviets would not deploy MIRVs. When the Americans argued that a MIRV test ban was necessary, the Soviet delegation avoided responding on the issue.

If the initial positions on offensive limitations showed great differences, those on ABMs offered promise. The United States took the lead by presenting two alternative ABM proposals. The first would limit ABM deployments to one site around each nation's "National Command Authority" (Washington and Moscow). The proposal, which became known as the NCA option, would have restricted radars and limited the number of interceptor missiles at the one site. The reason advanced for this proposal was that ABMs, as limited, would be unable to threaten the deterrent capability of the other side's forces, and would not even protect the capitals from attack by a large number of missiles, but could still afford some protection against an accidental or unauthorized launch of a few missiles and therefore reduce the risk that such a launch would trigger a large-scale nuclear exchange. In shaping the proposal, the United States also judged that the Soviet Union would probably be unwilling to dismantle its Moscow ABM site, which was already partly constructed. Shortly after presenting the NCA option, the United States advanced a ban on all ABMs as an alternative proposal with equal standing. This proposal became known as the Zero-ABM option.

The Soviets surprised the Americans by agreeing to the general idea of an NCA limitation even before the Zero option was presented. But the Americans presented the Zero option anyway. This sequence of two ABM proposals in rapid succession created some Soviet uncertainty about U.S. ABM preferences. Uncertainty was compounded by the fact that the U.S. government, while proposing NCA and Zero ABM, was building two ABM sites far from Washington and asking Congressional authorization for two more sites.

The session was broken by a short recess in June 1970 to allow each side to review its position after hearing the other's initial proposals. During the recess, the Nixon Administration began to doubt the desirability of its NCA proposal, in part because it feared that Congress would not approve plans for an ABM site around Washington. Senate opposition to area defense had been growing. In July 1970 the Senate Armed Services Committee would reject the Administration's request for four new Safeguard sites for area defense, sites that would have supplemented the two previously approved sites. Some in the Administration also feared that Congress would be concerned about adverse voter reactions to an ABM system that covered only Washington. A plan to cover only Washington might give the impression that the government was concerned only with protecting itself, while allowing the rest of the country to remain unprotected. In some Administration quarters there was also opposition to abandoning the political and monetary capital that had been invested in the Safeguard sites already under development. In addition, some military circles strongly opposed abandonment of the Safeguard program. These concerns increased pressures within the United States to revise the ABM proposal. However, those who sought to achieve an ABM ban, or at least to restrict ABMs to the NCA deployment, prevailed at the time, and the U.S. position was not changed.

Some of the U.S.-Soviet differences on offensive limitations reflected efforts to shape the agenda in ways favorable to each side, and could be expected to disappear in the natural course of further negotiations. Thus, the United States shortly gave up its proposed limitation on IRBMs and MRBMs and the Soviets ultimately withdrew their opposition to sublimits on large ICBMs. The FBS problem, however, was one on which the United States was unprepared to make any compromise move, both for reasons of substance and because of concerns of U.S. NATO allies. No clear solution of the issue was apparent. Some of the more optimistic in Washington estimated that the Soviets would ultimately ignore the issue if the total offensive limitation package were attractive enough and if there were assurances that FBS would not be used to circumvent SALT limitations.

The key element in the offensive arms equation was MIRV. The United States had never expected its MIRV proposal to be acceptable to the Soviets, and there was great opposition to submitting one that would be acceptable. President Nixon himself had decided to require on-site inspection as part of the U.S. MIRV proposal; those who wished to stop MIRVs had argued that the way for the United States to verify a MIRV ban was through a MIRV test ban rather than through on-site inspection. A real effort to stop MIRVs would probably have required a new proposal dropping the on-site inspection requirement, including a production and stockpiling ban (a ban that would affect only the United

States as the only side in a position to produce and stockpile), and pressing the Soviets to agree to a MIRV test ban, as the most practical verification procedure. Despite arguments that the Soviets might well accept a MIRV test ban, the United States decided to abandon the effort for a MIRV ban and to put aside such qualitative limitations on offensive arms for a later SALT negotiation. This decision was taken after only two months of actual negotiation and only a month after the Senate, concerned about the potentially destabilizing effects of MIRVs, had passed a resolution urging a prompt U.S.-Soviet freeze on further deployments of offensive and defensive strategic weapons. Yet the decision was to have a significant effect on Soviet willingness to limit offensive arms. The U.S. five-year program for offensive strategic arms was exclusively devoted to increasing the number of reentry vehicles by MIRVing, a fact that was public knowledge and was known to the Soviets. The United States began to deploy MIRVed Minuteman III ICBMs in June 1970 and later deployed MIRVed Poseidon SLBMs. From this time on, therefore, the U.S. proposals on offensive limitations ignored the most important on-going U.S. strategic missile programs. They did not stimulate the Soviet Union's interest in restricting its offensive forces.

After the two delegations returned to Vienna, the Americans presented a new package for numerical limitations on offensive forces. The new plan would set equal totals for strategic missiles and bombers, but would place no limits on MIRVs. On ABMs, the Americans again proposed NCA or Zero ABM as equally acceptable alternatives. Considerable time was spent in technical explanations of the provisions of the package. Although they did not respond formally before the end of the session, the Soviets showed little interest in the proposal. They again raised the FBS issue and argued that U.S. forward-based aircraft and carrier-based aircraft would have to be considered part of the American aggregate of strategic forces. Even before the end of this session, the Soviets began to indicate their view that the positions of the two sides on offensive limitations were so far apart that the negotiators should first seek a separate agreement on ABMs.

During this session, the Soviets also emphasized a concern about "provocative attacks" by third powers, aimed at causing a U.S.-Soviet nuclear exchange, suggesting that the two nations agree to joint arrangements to prevent or to retaliate against such attacks. The proposal was clearly aimed against China; there had been conflict along the Sino-Soviet border the previous year. The United States managed to prevent the proposal from becoming an explicit part of the SALT negotiations, although certain of the provisions of the 1971 agreement on measures to reduce the risks of nuclear war could be said to deal with the issue. The session ended on August 14, 1970, with an announcement that the talks would resume on November 2, 1970, in Helsinki.

Session 3

The third and shortest session of SALT in Helsinki was to last only 46 days. There were no real negotiations; the session was rather a debate. The United States continued to argue for its previous proposal on offensive limitations. The Soviets debated offensive limitations but made it clear that the U.S. August proposal was unacceptable. They wanted FBS to be taken into account and MIRVs to be banned, but were unresponsive to U.S. efforts to discuss details of offensive limitations provisions. This has been a traditional Soviet negotiation approach: discussion of details and of specific elements of an agreement must await agreement on general provisions and on what systems are to be covered.

The Soviets were also interested in obtaining U.S. agreement that ABMs be limited to Washington and Moscow. Toward the end of the session, they proposed that the two nations first negotiate an NCA-type ABM agreement and then proceed to negotiate an agreement on offensive weapons. The United States, however, was becoming increasingly concerned about the build-up of Soviet offensive missiles and particularly about the possible counterforce capabilities of the growing Soviet SS-9 force in case it should be MIRVed. The United States therefore resisted: it linked its ABM proposals to its proposals on offensive limitations.

Session 4

During the three-month recess preceding the fourth session, which would start in March 1971, Washington debate turned away from the details of limitation proposals and focused instead on broader questions concerning the "ABM-first" proposal, the type of ABM limitations, and the desirability of new approaches to offensive forces limitations. The recurring effort to develop a serious MIRV proposal once again failed.

Early in the recess, the fact that the Soviets had made an ABM-first proposal was leaked to the press, and was widely welcomed by anti-ABM forces in the United States. The White House was concerned, however, about the growing Soviet ICBM deployment. The Administration feared that unless offensive forces were limited at the same time that an ABM agreement was reached, it would have little leverage to apply to the Soviets to obtain offensive limits in subsequent negotiations.

At the same time, even though there was increasing recognition that Safeguard could not defend ICBMs effectively, there was pressure to maintain an ICBM-oriented ABM system in any SALT agreement. A decision was therefore made early in the recess to continue to reject the ABM-first approach, and the Soviets were so informed. The United States also decided to change its ABM proposal to one that would allow the Soviets one NCA ABM site and allow the Americans four ABM sites to cover ICBM fields. This proposal reflected a real U.S. interest toward use of ABMs to defend ICBM fields; the four-to-one balance caused the proposal to be generally regarded in Washington as a holding operation.

When the fourth session began in Vienna, the Soviets had tabled a draft ABM treaty embodying the NCA option. This draft treaty clarified the Soviet position: it accepted the concept of limiting each site to 100 interceptor launchers but did not include specifics on radar limitations. The United States then presented its four-to-one ABM proposal, defending it as restricting each side to the ABM program it already had under way. To no one's surprise, the Soviet reaction was strongly negative. The Soviets argued that they had accepted the U.S. proposal for an NCA option but that now the United States was backing off from its own proposal. The Soviets also maintained that the U.S. proposal, which would allow the Americans 400 interceptor missile launchers and the Soviets only 100, was unequal and would permit the United States to lay the base for a nation-wide ABM system. The Soviet position, maintained throughout Salt I, was that any ABM limitations must be the same for each side.

The main activity of this session took place in "back channel" exchanges between Presidential adviser Henry Kissinger and Anatoly Dobrynin, the Soviet ambassador to the United States. These exchanges, kept closely secret, aimed at reconciling the differing priorities of the two sides toward offensive and defensive limitations. Reflecting these exchanges, the Soviet delegation in Vienna hinted in early May that an ABM treaty could be accompanied by a freeze on ICBMs, pending a permanent agreement on offensive limitations. Complications were feared, since the U.S. delegation was not aware of the back-channel exchanges, and the fourth session was recessed in mid-May for a short period. On May 20, 1971, the back-channel results were made known through a joint public U.S.-U.S.S.R. statement. The statement said the two governments had agreed to concentrate that year on working out an ABM agreement and that, "together with concluding an agreement to limit ABMs, they will agree on certain measures with respect to the

limitation of offensive strategic weapons." How Dr. Kissinger was able
to obtain this agreement was not made public. It is worth noting, however, that a Congress of the Communist Party of the Soviet Union was
held during March and April 1971. The Soviet leaders announced a new
policy at this congress: that the U.S.S.R. economic base required an infusion of foreign science and technology and that the way to obtain
this infusion was through an era of détente. Since SALT would be a
significant component of détente, the interests of the Soviet leadership
may have coincided with Kissinger's aims.

Probably the most important aspect of the May 20 joint statement was
that it demonstrated the political commitment of both governments to
achieve a SALT agreement. The public statement and the secret, high-
level communications that lay behind it also moved the negotiations
forward, but left major issues to be resolved in future negotiations. What
had been agreed in effect was that ABM limitations would be definitively
settled first, leaving an overall settlement on strategic offensive arms
for a subsequent negotiation. The ABM agreement would be accompanied by some limitation of offensive arms, but the meaning of the "certain
measures" to be taken on offensive arms was far from resolved. The
Soviets were prepared to deal in some fashion with American concerns
about ICBMs, including the Soviet SS-9. But even here there was no
agreement on the point at which Soviet deployments would be restricted.
Even more important, there was no agreement on what other offensive
systems would be covered, although it was clear that the FBS issue
would be temporarily put aside. After a brief second phase, the fourth
session ended on May 28. Agreement was reached to resume negotiations
in Helsinki on July 8.

Session 5

Intense activity in both capitals, particularly in Washington, marked
the recess before the fifth session. In the U.S. government, one major
issue was whether the "certain measures" on offensive weapons should
include restrictions on SLBMs. The United States had not pressed for
limitation of SLBMs in the back-channel negotiations, for fear of creating another stalemate and perhaps provoking the Soviets to raise again
the FBS issue. Consequently, the agreement in principle achieved in
those back-channel negotiations was for a freeze on only ICBMs.

Nevertheless, military officials and the Defense Department were
pressing for an offensive freeze on SLBMs as well. In mid-1971, the
Soviet Union had 22 operational nuclear missile submarines and was
building another 15, while the United States had 41 such submarines

operational. At its construction rate of about eight new nuclear submarines per year, the Soviets could have obtained in five years a submarine fleet about twice as large as that of the United States. This Soviet advantage would have been in number of submarines, not in number of submarine-launched warheads. Although the United States was building no new boats, it was extensively modifying its submarines to replace Polaris missiles with MIRVed Poseidon missiles that carried 10 warheads each.

Proponents of an SLBM limitation argued that an SLBM freeze was necessary to prevent Soviet superiority in both ICBMs and SLBMs. They suggested that Congress might balk at an offensive agreement that gave the Soviets superiority in ICBMs and allowed them to greatly increase their submarine force as well. Others argued that Soviet ICBMs, not SLBMs, had been the threat that prompted U.S. ABMs. Moreover, the Soviets would not accept an arrangement precluding them from coninuing their SLBM program while the United States was free to continue its MIRV program. These officials also maintained that expanding the scope of the temporary offensive limitations would tend to formalize the temporary limitations and make them appear more permanent. The final U.S. decision was that the United States should seek Soviet agreement to freeze SLBMs at the levels existing at the time. Submarines under construction could be completed but no new SLBM construction could be initiated.

At the SALT negotiations themselves, the Soviets reacted negatively to the U.S. insistence that SLBMs be limited by the "certain measures" on offensive limitations. They also objected to U.S. efforts to base a freeze on current-force levels, insisting that freezes be based on the deployment levels existing at the time an agreement would actually be signed. As time passed, the United States was gradually to modify its proposals in this regard, and the Soviet view ultimately prevailed.

There were also differences over the character of the undertaking on offensive limitations. The Soviets wanted the undertaking to be a simple informal understanding, of short duration, arguing that it was intended to be only a temporary arrangement to be followed in the near future by a formal, comprehensive, permanent agreement. The United States insisted that the interim undertaking be formal and treaty-like in language, detailed, and of five years' duration. In taking this position, the U.S. government was perhaps driven by its publicly stated opposition to the ABM-first approach. The United States may also have judged that it would not be able to deploy new or additional missiles for at least five years in any event.

Tactical differences also slowed down progress during the fifth session. The Soviets wanted to focus on the ABM agreement; the Americans were reluctant to modify their ABM position very rapidly before the parties reached a greater area of agreement on offensive limitations. In fact, however, most of the fifth session focused on discussion of ABM limitations. During the initial part of the session the Americans set forth a modified position on ABM limitation. They proposed that each side be allowed a choice of either one NCA site or three sites at ICBM fields. Since it was highly unlikely that the Soviets would dismantle their Galosh system around Moscow, this proposal was a less than subtle way to give the United States 300 interceptors for its three Safeguard sites while the Soviet Union would have only 100 interceptors around Moscow. Subsequently, the United States proposed an arrangement by which each side could choose between one NCA site or two ABM sites covering ICBM fields.

The Soviets rejected both U.S. ABM proposals in turn. It argued that any ABM agreement had to permit equality in numbers and in kinds of ABM, and pressed for a straight NCA agreement as the way to solve the ABM issue. Later in the session, however, the Soviets proposed a one-plus-one arrangement. Under this plan, the Soviets would retain Galosh and have the right to build one other site, probably at an ICBM field. The United States would retain its Safeguard site at Grand Forks, North Dakota, and have the right to build an NCA site around Washington. The United States rejected this proposal at the time, partially because of the proposal's ambiguities, but also because of strong bureaucratic pressures to retain two Safeguard sites. Moreover, the United States chose not to accept parity in ABM sites until an agreement on offensive weapons had been reached. (Later, the United States did accept a similar two-to-two arrangement under which each side could build or retain one NCA site and one site for an ICBM field.)

Within the U.S. government, the arguments for and against the various ABM options were being made on strategic grounds, but the negotiations became dominated by politics rather than by strategy. Congressional support for the Safeguard program had become very shaky, and there was increasing realization within the Executive branch that even a three-site ABM deployment using the Safeguard system would contribute little to the protection of the Minuteman ICBM force. The real issues, therefore, were becoming those of appearance of equality in an ABM agreement and of assuring that the systems permitted to the Soviet Union could not provide the radar base for subsequent rapid expansion. In this political context, reinforced by the lack of significant progress in reaching an ABM agreement, two opposite ABM limitation approaches arose at the fifth session. Either could have changed the course of the negotiations, but both were stopped before they had progressed very far.

One approach arose from an effort made by those in the United States who favored a hard-site ABM defense of ICBMs. Such a system would differ in design from the Safeguard system, which, despite its public rationale, was oriented more toward limited area defense. The group favoring a hard-site system wanted an ABM agreement that distinguished between the systems. In contrast to an ABM site located at Moscow or Washington, an ABM site at an ICBM field could have a large number of small radars and many more than 100 interceptor missiles. During the fifth session in Helsinki, U.S. defense officials discussed this concept with Soviet military officials, and the latter began to show increasing interest in the idea. The concern then developed that stimulating Soviet military interest in the hard-site defense concept in this way would eventually either preclude an ABM agreement or produce one that would only divert ABM development toward ICBM defense systems. This development did not take place, however; the United States decided to stand by its position that an ABM site in an ICBM field should be permitted to have only the types and numbers of radars and interceptors then being deployed in Grand Forks.

The opposite development was a near resurrection of the Zero-ABM option. The Zero-ABM option had swirled around just below the surface of the negotiations ever since the Soviets had accepted the NCA option in the second session. The Soviets had said their acceptance of the NCA option indicated it was their preference, but Zero-ABM advocates in the United States argued that the Soviets had not ruled out Zero and that a return to the Zero option would offer a way out of the ABM impasse and help obtain a better arms control agreement. Ambassador Gerard Smith was authorized to raise the possibility of the Zero option with the Soviets. The response was that the Soviet Union was interested and would like to hear specific U.S. views on the option. The military on each side, however, was opposed to a complete ABM ban, and some in the United States doubted that the Soviets would ever agree to dismantle the Moscow system. Although the Soviets repeated their interest in hearing U.S. views on Zero ABM, the United States decided to cut off further exploration of this option and to seek a mutually acceptable arrangement that would allow both sides to retain some ABM deployment. The Americans did indicate to the Soviets, however, that Zero ABM remained an ultimate U.S. objective to be pursued in negotiations following SALT I.

Although the two sides remained divided on the ABM deployments to be allowed, some progress was made during the session in developing the detailed provisions that would be necessary for any ABM agreement. In particular, the Soviets indicated more willingness to accept some of the technical approaches to radar restriction for which the Americans had been pressing. The United States also made a long delayed decision to press for a ban on deployment of future "exotic" ABM systems as part of the agreement. Unless, for example, ABM systems using laser beams rather than interceptor missiles were prohibited, any ABM agreement might rapidly become obsolete. Agreement on this point came in the subsequent session.

The fifth session in Helsinki also brought to fruition a side negotiation that had been in process throughout most of SALT. Two executive agreements were concluded and subsequently signed: the Accident Measures Agreement and the Revised Hot Line Agreement. These arrangements, discussed in more detail in Chapter 6, reflected a mutual awareness of the risks inherent in the nuclear-missile age and a common interest in joint efforts to reduce those risks.

The fifth session ended on September 24, 1971, with the Soviets awaiting U.S. moves on ABMs and the United States awaiting Soviet moves on interim limitation of SLBMs.

Session 6

During the fifth session, there had been dramatic improvements in U.S.-Chinese relations, reflected in such steps as eased U.S. trade and travel restrictions, Peking's invitation to the U.S. table tennis team, and Kissinger's visit to Peking in July 1971. President Nixon pointed out that only the United States and not the Soviet Union could take the initiative to end China's "isolation." Nevertheless, the U.S. moves also suggested a triangular politics, under which the United States would seek friendly relations with both China and the Soviet Union, in a sense playing the two nations off against each other. The policy was reflected again in Kissinger's second visit to China in October 1971 and in Nixon's visit in February 1972.

This U.S. policy aroused Soviet fear of a possible U.S.-China alliance and created pressures on the Soviets to improve relations with the United States to counter the U.S.-Chinese thaw. This, on top of the Soviet concern about provocative attacks by third powers, increased the Soviets' desire for a bilateral strategic arms agreement with the United States. An arms agreement would further U.S.-U.S.S.R. détente and would demonstrate that the world was still bipolar with respect to major strategic issues. Nixon also strongly desired an arms agreement to demonstrate the success of his efforts for an "era of negotiation" and to improve his standing at the polls in the November 1972 elections. These motivations provided much of the political will needed to overcome the major remaining obstacles to agreement on offensive and defensive weapons. A summit meeting was planned for May 1972 in Moscow at which both Premier Brezhnev and President Nixon hoped to sign a SALT agreement. This served to provide a deadline and increased the pressures on both sides to settle outstanding issues.

At the sixth session, which began November 15, 1971, the delegations drafted language for both the offensive and defensive agreements, using brackets to provide alternative language for the unresolved questions like ABM levels, ABM radar controls, SLBMs, and the dates for beginning the offensive freeze. Midway in the session, the Soviets formally accepted the concept of a sublimit on heavy ICBMs, the SS-9s. Agreement was also reached on banning the deployment of "exotic" ABM systems.

Perhaps because of the Administration's preoccupation with Nixon's trip to China, little progress was made on the content of ABM limitations. ABM discussions became somewhat ridiculous. New positions were offered by each side, and the United States proposed that the Soviets keep Galosh and it keep the two Safeguard sites under construction. The Soviets proposed that the United States retain its Grand Forks Safeguard site, while the Soviets keep Galosh and build an additional site for the defense of ICBMs.

Nor was there much progress on the SLBM issue. The United States argued that SLBMs must be included in the offensive arrangement and that there should be approximate parity in both the number of submarines and the number of launchers, or "tubes." The Soviets did not admit that SLBMs should be limited, but did make clear that any such limitation should give them an advantage in numbers to make up for the longer times their submarines must take to transit from port to deployment stations. The SLBM issue remained unresolved in this session, and was worked out only in later back-channel negotiations.

During this session, the Soviets showed no willingness to ban mobile ICBMs either, a position that contributed to unhappiness in Washington. The sixth session ended on February 4, 1972, with some in the United States doubting whether agreement could be achieved or should even be sought before the summit meeting.

Session 7

The seventh and final session of SALT I began in Helsinki on March 28, 1972. It was an exceedingly hectic session, during which both sides attempted to work out an agreement in time for the Moscow summit scheduled to begin May 22.

In this session, the United States presented a new ABM proposal that was linked to the SLBM issue. The United States proposed that the two sides have equality in ABMs—two sites for the Americans, at Grand Forks, North Dakota, and Malmstrom Air Force Base, Montana, and two sites for the Soviets, at Moscow and an ICBM site—but only if the Soviets agreed to limit SLBMs. The Soviets were unwilling to allow the Americans to defend twice as many ICBMs as they could, and again proposed a one-plus-one arrangement. Under this proposal, the Americans would keep their Grand Forks site and be allowed to build an NCA site, while the Soviets would keep their Galosh site and be allowed to build one ICBM defense site. Thus there was still disagreement over the ABM and SLBM issues; disagreement also remained over the duration of the interim offensive agreement.

In late April 1972, after returning from China, Kissinger made a secret visit to Moscow to negotiate with the Soviet leaders on some of the unresolved issues. This visit led to agreement that the Soviets would accept inclusion of a freeze on SLBMs but only at the then current levels of deployment or construction and with the right to exchange older ICBM launchers for additional SLBM launchers. The Soviet Union would be permitted to convert to up to 62 SLBM submarines with 950 launchers or tubes, and the United States up to 44 SLBM submarines and 710 SLBM launchers or tubes. With respect to ABM, agreement in principle was reached to limit each side to one NCA site and one ICBM site.

Senior members of the Soviet delegation had returned to Moscow at the time of Kissinger's visit. Shortly after his return to Washington, senior members of the U.S. delegation also returned to their capital for discussions. There they were given instructions to present a proposal that in effect incorporated the results of the Kissinger visit, though at the time they were unaware that this was the case.

Discussions resumed in Helsinki only three weeks before the summit meetings, with most of the outlines of the agreement nearly complete but many specific issues still unresolved. On SLBMs, the Americans claimed that the Soviets had about 640 tubes operational or under construction in May 1972, and maintained that the Soviets could increase their number of tubes past this level only by retiring one pre-1964 ICBM or older SLBM for each new tube added in excess of the number of tubes operational or under construction in May 1972. This replacement condition was designed to ensure that the combined number of Soviet ICBMs and SLBMs would not increase once the freeze took effect, even if the Soviets built up to their SLBM ceiling of 950 tubes. The Soviets accepted this replacement condition, but disagreed with the U.S. estimate of the size of the Soviet submarine fleet. The United States claimed that the Soviets had from 41 to 43 submarines, but the Soviets sought credit for 48 submarines operational or under construction as of May 1972. Since older missiles would have to be retired for only those SLBMs on submarines begun after May 1972, the larger Soviet number implied that the Soviets would have had to forfeit fewer older weapons to reach their maximum SLBM-launcher total of 950 tubes. Disagreement continued over this point, which was not settled until the day the SALT I agreements were signed.

With respect to ABM, the Soviet Union had agreed, in principle, to locate its second ABM site east of the Urals and away from major population centers. The United States had insisted that this second ABM site be around an ICBM field and away from any major cities so that it would have no overlapping city-defense capabilities. The Soviets refused to accept treaty language specifically stating that the ICBM site would have to be east of the Urals, but did accept a requirement that each side's ICBM defense site be at least 1,300 kilometers from its NCA site. Since it is 1,300 kilometers from Moscow to the back of the Ural Mountains, this was a de facto acceptance of the U.S. "east of the Urals" requirement for the second ABM site. The Soviets also agreed to a ban on all large ABM-type radars, subject to certain exceptions such as those at the sites permitted under the treaty. The United States had argued that such a ban was important to assure each side that the other was not laying a radar base for a future expanded ABM system.

When the summit meeting began in Moscow, negotiations continued in Helsinki as well. The result, in spite of communications between the delegations and their heads of government, was some overlapping and confusion, intensified by time pressure. As the frantic pace of negotiations continued in both cities, most of the remaining issues were resolved.

The Soviets agreed that silo dimensions could not be "significantly increased." This ban on significant silo modifications was intended to prevent replacement of light ICBMs, like SS-11s, by much heavier missiles. It was later clarified by an understanding that "significantly increased" meant an increase in excess of 10 to 15 percent of present dimensions, but there has been some argument whether the 10 to 15 percent can be applied to several linear dimensions at the same time.

The United States had pressed in earlier SALT sessions for a ban on the deployment of mobile ICBMs, i.e. ICBMs that would be placed on trucks or railway cars and moved about. Mobile ICBMs would be less vulnerable than fixed ICBMs, whose location can be readily detected via satellite, but the United States strongly opposed the deployment of mobile ICBMs because they could not be counted as well through national technical means and their use would preclude adequate verification of an offensive limitation. The Soviets, however, were unwilling to give up the right to mobile ICBMs because the vast geographical size of the Soviet Union would be so well suited to their deployment.

As noted above, there had been disagreement in Helsinki over the number of Soviet submarines and tubes operational or under construction in May 1972. During the summit, the Soviets claimed that they had 768 tubes operational or under construction, while the United States claimed that the Soviets had only 640. On May 26, the day the agreements were signed, the two nations compromised the difference between their estimates and accepted 740 as the number of Soviet tubes operational or under construction in May 1972. To build past this baseline number of 740 tubes toward their permitted ceiling of 950 tubes, the Soviets would have to retire one old missile for each new SLBM tube added. The two sides drafted a Protocol to the Interim Offensive Agreement, specifying the numbers of SLBM launchers and submarines to be permitted and the terms for replacing older ICBM and SLBM launchers with new SLBM launchers.

A crash effort was required to complete the final texts of the agreements. The signing ceremony was originally scheduled for 5 P.M. on May 26, but had to be postponed until 11 P.M. that evening to give the two delegations additional time to draft and type the protocol and to fly from Helsinki to Moscow on an American military plane. The rush produced several minor grammatical and typographical errors that could not be corrected in time for the signing ceremony. At 11 P.M. Nixon and Brezhnev signed the ABM Treaty and the Interim Agreement on offensive arms. The next morning certain of the documents were retyped to correct the errors; Nixon and Brezhnev signed the new copies in private that day.

The SALT I Agreements

Four agreements were reached in the SALT I negotiations: the Agreement on Measures to Reduce the Risk of Outbreak of Nuclear War Between the United States of America and the Union of Soviet Socialist Republics (the Accident Measures Agreement), the Agreement Between the United States of America and the Union of Soviet Socialist Repub-

198   *The Negotiation of SALT I*

lics on Measures to Improve the U.S.-U.S.S.R. Direct Communication Link (the Revised Hot Line Agreement), the Treaty Between the United States of America and the Union of Soviet Socialist Republics on the Limitation of Anti-Ballistic Missile Systems (the ABM Treaty), and the Interim Agreement Between the United States of America and the Union of Soviet Socialist Republics on Certain Measures with Respect to the Limitation of Strategic Offense Arms (the Interim Offensive Arms Agreement).[2] The Accident Measures Agreement and the Revised Hot Line Agreement were executive agreements signed at Washington September 30, 1971, and entered into force the same day. The ABM Treaty and the Interim Offensive Arms Agreement were signed at Moscow on May 26, 1972, and entered into force on October 3, 1972, the date of exchange of instruments of ratification for the Treaty and notices of acceptance for the Interim Agreement.

As a treaty, the ABM agreement required approval by two-thirds of the Senate; the Interim Agreement was submitted to both Houses of Congress to obtain an expression of support in accordance with the ACDA Act provision mentioned in the previous chapter. Congressional approval occurred only after considerable controversy; this controversy will be discussed in the next chapter. Supplementing the texts of the ABM Treaty and the Interim Offensive Arms Agreement and its Protocol, there was a series of "agreed interpretations," "common understandings," and "unilateral statements." The "agreed interpretations" and "common understandings" are additional statements, accepted by both parties, which clarify or elaborate on certain points of each agreement. They are as binding on the Soviet Union and the United States as the texts of the agreements themselves. The "unilateral statements," on the other hand, are not binding and do not necessarily reflect mutual agreement, but were intended to clarify one side's interpretation of or reservation about some aspect of the agreement.

ABM Treaty

The ABM Treaty, by far the most significant achievement of SALT I, is a carefully drafted agreement in which each nation agrees not to build an ABM system for the "defense of the territory of its country," and not to build a defense for an individual region except for systems at two allowed sites. In effect, each nation agrees to build neither a nationwide ABM defense nor the radar base for such a defense. An ABM system is defined as "a system to counter strategic ballistic missiles or their

---

[2] The texts of all these agreements, agreed interpretations, common understandings, and unilateral statements are given in Appendix C.

elements in flight trajectory." This general language is backed up by specific and verifiable limitations on system components.

The ABM Treaty limits each side to two ABM sites, one around the national capital and one around an ICBM site. Thus the United States could retain its Grand Forks ABM site and build one around Washington. Construction was stopped on the Malmstrom ABM site and its dismantling ordered. The Soviet Union could retain its Moscow ABM site and build one at an ICBM site. The treaty further provides that there be no more than 100 ABM launchers and interceptor missiles at each site. Each site is to be deployed within an area with a radius of not more than 150 kilometers, and the ICBM-ABM site is to be at least 1,300 kilometers away from the national capital site. The number and capabilities of permissible radars for each ABM site are limited. In addition, each side is limited to a total of no more than 15 ABM launchers at current or additionally agreed test ranges.

The development, testing, or deployment of sea-based, air-based, space-based, or mobile land-based ABM systems is prohibited, as is the development, testing, or deployment of ABM launchers capable of launching more than one ABM interceptor missile at a time and ABM launchers capable of carrying MIRVed missiles. The development, testing, or deployment of automatic or semiautomatic systems for rapid reloading of ABM launchers is also prohibited.

The location and orientation of large early-warning radars is limited to preclude the development of a radar base that could support a rapid-ABM-missile-launcher deployment. Conversion of other systems, such as antiaircraft surface-to-air missiles, to ABM use is also prohibited, as is the testing of such systems in an ABM mode. This limitation was designed to assuage U.S. fears that the Soviets could upgrade their extensive antiaircraft system for use as an ABM system. Modernization and replacement of fixed land-based ABM systems are permitted, but the deployment of so-called exotic ABM systems, i.e. ABM systems "based on other physical principles," is prohibited.

The transfer to other countries of ABM systems or their components is prohibited, as is the deployment of any ABM system outside of each party's national territory. According to an agreed statement, this provision also restricts the transfer of technical descriptions and blueprints to other nations.

The ABM Treaty is to be verified by national technical means of verification; the treaty specifically prohibits each nation from interfering with or using deliberate concealment measures against the other's national technical means of verification. Thus, each side has agreed not to interfere, for example, with the other's satellites used for verification of the treaty.

The treaty provides for the establishment of a U.S.-U.S.S.R. Standing Consultative Commission (SCC). This commission, mentioned in the previous chapter, was actually set up through a later agreement reached in December 1972, and is a forum to work out procedures for implementing the treaty, to consider problems arising under the treaty, and, if appropriate, to consider further measures for limiting strategic arms. The SCC is to meet at least twice a year and also on call of either party.

The treaty is of unlimited duration and is to be reviewed every five years. Each party has the right to withdraw from the treaty if it decides that "extraordinary events related to the subject matter of this Treaty have jeopardized its supreme interests." Before withdrawing, a party must give six months' notice and indicate what extraordinary events have occurred to endanger its supreme national interests. The United States made a unilateral statement indicating that U.S. supreme interests could be jeopardized unless a more complete offensive strategic arms agreement were reached within five years, i.e. by 1977. Thus, the United States suggested that failure to control offensive forces in SALT II would be grounds for withdrawing from the ABM Treaty.

Interim Offensive Agreement and Protocol

In contrast to the ABM Treaty, the Interim Offensive Arms Agreement and its Protocol are less polished. The Interim Agreement is also to be verified by national technical means of verification. Although these means, such as reconnaissance satellites, are sufficient to count missile launchers, they are unable to count the missiles themselves. The agreement therefore limits the launchers rather than the missiles. Since a missile cannot be fired without a launcher, the limitation on launchers is a de facto limitation on operational missiles.

The Interim Agreement prohibits both parties from starting construction of additional fixed, land-based ICBM launchers after July 1, 1972. Thus the United States can have no more than 1,054 ICBMs operational or under construction, and the Soviet Union can have no more than 1,618. The parties are also prohibited from converting light ICBM launchers or launchers for ICBMs deployed prior to 1964 into land-based launchers for heavy ICBMs of types deployed after 1964. This provision prohibits the Soviets from replacing their light SS-11s with heavy missiles such as SS-9s. As a result, the Soviets are limited to 313 large missiles, the number they had operational or under construction on May 26, 1972.

The SLBM tube and modern ballistic submarine limitations are spelled out primarily in the Protocol. The United States is limited to a total of 710 SLBM launchers and 44 modern ballistic missile submarines, and the Soviet Union to 950 launchers and 62 submarines. However, to build past the number of tubes agreed to be operational or under construction in May 1972 up to these limits, each side must dismantle or destroy an equivalent number of ballistic missile launchers of older types deployed prior to 1964 or of SLBM launchers on older SLBM submarines. Thus, the United States had 656 tubes operational or under construction on May 26, 1972. To build up to its allowed total of 710 tubes, the United States would have to dismantle or destroy 54 older ICBM launchers (or older SLBM tubes) in exchange for the 54 new SLBM tubes it would be adding. The Soviet Union was deemed to have 740 tubes operational or under construction on May 26, 1972. To build up to their allowed total of 950 tubes, the Soviets would have to dismantle or destroy 210 older ICBM launchers (or SLBM tubes) in exchange for the new SLBM tubes they would be adding.

In a unilateral statement about SLBM launchers, the Soviets said they agreed that the United States and its NATO allies could together have up to 50 modern ballistic submarines, with a total of 800 SLBM launchers. They also stated that if the U.S. allies in NATO should increase their number of SLBM submarines or SLBMs beyond the level operational or under construction on May 26, 1972, the Soviets would have the right to a corresponding increase in the number of submarines. The Soviet statement went on to say that the question of liquidating U.S. submarine forward bases would have to be resolved in subsequent negotiations, since the Interim Agreement's solution of the SLBM submarine question only partially compensated for the strategic imbalance in submarine deployment patterns. The United States replied that it did not accept the validity of this Soviet claim to compensation for SLBM submarines belonging to third countries and for U.S. submarine forward bases.

Modernization and replacement of strategic offensive ballistic missiles and launchers are permitted, but the dimensions of land-based ICBM silo launchers cannot be significantly increased, i.e. they cannot be increased by more than 10 to 15 percent. The agreement places no limitations on qualitative improvement of missiles such as MIRVing or improving accuracy, unless the improvements significantly enlarge silo size or conflict with the sublimit placed on modern heavy ICBMs. The Americans had pushed for a ban on land-mobile ICBM launchers, but agreed to defer the issue to subsequent negotiations for more complex limitations on strategic offensive arms. They made a unilateral statement, however, that they would consider the deployment of such land-mobile ICBM launchers during the period of the Interim Agreement as being inconsistent with the objectives of that agreement.

The agreement commits the parties to continue active negotiations for limitations on strategic offensive arms, and provides that its terms are not to prejudice the scope or terms of any future offensive agreement. The agreement is to remain in force for five years unless replaced earlier by an agreement on more complete measures limiting strategic arms. As with the ABM Treaty, each party has the right to withdraw from the agreement upon six months' notice if it decides that extraordinary events related to the subject matter of the agreement have jeopardized its supreme interests. Verification provisions are the same as those of the ABM Treaty, and the SCC is to be used in support of the Interim Agreement as well as of the ABM Treaty.

Significance of the SALT I Agreements

The ABM Treaty is clearly the most important of the agreements reached in SALT I. In this treaty, each country renounced the right to build certain defenses. Such a renunciation is unprecedented.

Thus, the United States and the Soviet Union have effectively accepted the mutual-hostage relationship that is generally considered essential for a stable deterrent relationship. A stable balance of deterrence requires that each side be confident that its retaliatory second strike can inflict unacceptable damage on an opponent who has struck first. By reducing each side's vulnerability to the other's retaliatory forces, ABM systems threaten to weaken the latter's confidence in its deterrent forces. As a result, ABM deployments can create crisis instability and strengthen incentives to build compensatory offensive weapons. The restrictions in the ABM Treaty preclude nationwide ABM systems. Moreover, the ABM systems permitted under the treaty are so limited that they can easily be penetrated (if only by exhaustion through targeting more than 100 warheads against each site). Thus even the allowed ABM systems cannot effectively protect population or industry. The ABM Treaty has, then, enhanced the deterrent value of each power's retaliatory forces by ensuring that these forces will be able to penetrate any missile defenses and reach their targets. Many thought that it would therefore reduce pressure to build new offensive forces.

Though its effects were in many respects limited, the Interim Agreement also contributed somewhat to the stability of deterrence. The sublimit on Soviet heavy ICBMs limited concerns relating to the dangers that might arise if these high-yield weapons were made more accurate and MIRVed so as to be effective against Minutemen. The provisions for permitting conversion of pre-1964 ICBM launchers into new SLBM launchers may also tend to contribute to deterrence. Fear that many of the pre-1964 ICBM launchers might not survive a first strike increases pressures to make a preemptive first strike or to launch on warning, and thus decreases crisis stability. The Interim Agreement permits both sides to replace these vulnerable older missiles with new SLBMs, the most survivable missile forces.

SALT I not only recognized and supported deterrence; it also recognized a parity or rough balance between the two superpowers. This recognition was especially important to the Soviet Union, which had for a long time held a second-best position in strategic nuclear weapons. For the Soviets, SALT I symbolized achievement of a long-sought goal of equality. This interest in equality was reflected in SALT's almost slavish acceptance of symmetry, especially in ABMs.

For many in the United States, acceptance of parity was bitter medicine. Recognizing the end of U.S. superiority seemed dangerous and likely to weaken U.S. policy in subtle ways. Many criticized SALT I, and especially the Interim Agreement, for allowing the Soviets superiority in both SLBMs and ICBMs. Many argued that superiority might, after all, be important when strategic weapons are bargained during crisis. Supporters of SALT I emphasized traditional deterrence theory and responded by noting that the Interim Agreement was to be in effect for at most five years. There was no chance that the Soviets could achieve a first-strike capability during that period and little chance that the U.S. superiority in number of reentry vehicles could be overcome. Moreover, the United States is allowed to develop new systems such as the B-1 bomber and the Trident submarine. Supporters also emphasized those balances that favor the United States. The SALT I agreements did not restrict the U.S. strategic bomber force, for example, and the United States had about three times as many strategic bombers as the Soviet Union. Although the Soviets had an advantage of about two and a half to one in deliverable megatonnage, counting only missiles, the two sides were approximately equal in megatonnage if strategic bomber forces are included in the comparison. Moreover, with its MIRVed forces, the United States had an advantage in number of reentry vehicles.

SALT I did play a role in restricting the arms competition, but this effect was limited. Thus, the freeze on ICBMs and SLBMs perhaps prevented further buildups of strategic forces, but also allowed each side to continue major ongoing programs. The Soviet Union could continue its SLBM building program for some time and could test and deploy MIRVs. The United States could continue to deploy MIRVs and to develop new bomber and submarine systems. The failure to restrict accuracy improvements or qualitative improvements in offensive weapons, such as MIRVs, was a particularly serious drawback of the Interim Agreement. As noted in Chapter 7, highly accurate MIRVs might threaten the survivability of land-based ICBM forces. Although this threat could not be realized within the five-year period of SALT I, it could speed further arms construction.

On the ABM side, those concerned about arms competition could criticize SALT I as "arms control upward," because it permitted each side to build a new site. Moreover, some suggest that Congress might not have approved the U.S. ABM had not SALT I been in progress. Nevertheless, the ABM Treaty did effectively diminish strategic concerns about building or penetrating missile defenses. This was a result of the agreement itself and of the bureaucratic consensus on ABM capabilities reached during the agreement process. Both powers could therefore save the considerable resources that might otherwise have been used for additional ABM deployments or additional offensive deployments aimed at countering an opponent's ABM deployment.

Moreover, both nations agreed to ban certain qualitative ABM improvements such as ABM missiles carrying multiple warheads. They thereby demonstrated the possibility of achieving qualitative as well as quantitative restrictions on strategic weapons. Similarly, by agreeing to ban the deployment of "exotic" ABM systems, the two nations agreed to forgo yet undeveloped weapons technologies. The significance of these decisions should not be underestimated. They mount a significant challenge to the frequent policy of developing every weapon system or technique that appears technically feasible. The idea of control at the development phase rather than the deployment phase may weaken a crucial driving force in an arms competition that has become increasingly qualitative rather than quantitative.

The ABM Treaty also established important precedents for future arms control negotiations. By specifying that the agreement was to be verified by national technical means and promising not to interfere with each other's national technical means, both nations acknowledged and sanctioned the use of such systems as reconnaissance satellites. They thereby indicated their confidence in these systems and recognized that the sytems are mutually beneficial. They also demonstrated that on-site inspections are not necessary for some types of arms control agreements. Some critics of SALT I have argued, however, that certain of the restrictions on systems development might be essentially unverifiable by national technical means, and they feared that SALT I sets a precedent for unverified agreements.

The Standing Consultative Commission (SCC) is also an important precedent for the future. Except for the International Atomic Energy Agency (IAEA), it is the only functional equivalent of an international disarmament organization. It should provide valuable experience in the processes of assurance, dispute settlement, and problem resolution under a complicated and technical arms control agreement.

SALT I also showed that serious U.S.-U.S.S.R. negotiations were possible in an area as sensitive and complex as strategic weaponry. Negotiations dealt with central issues of national power that were often still being debated in the national capitals. Information and strategic concepts were successfully exchanged in a process of mutual education. This exchange should help in further negotiations; it may also help each nation understand the other's motivations and thus reduce the chances for mistakes in crisis decisions and arms construction decisions.

At the same time, third nations and many of the U.S. and U.S.S.R. public may become somewhat suspicious of the two superpowers working together so closely. Some critics feared that the negotiations were the beginning of an alliance by the executives of the two nations against their publics and the U.S. Congress. Stories have emerged from SALT of the U.S. negotiators presenting U.S. intelligence estimates of Soviet force strength to the U.S.S.R. negotiators; the U.S.S.R. negotiators had not known their own nation's military strength. What is more significant in suggesting the changing political pattern is that the Soviet military representatives are then said to have remonstrated with the U.S. representatives for revealing military information to the *Soviet civilian* representatives.

SALT I also had a political effect, which was outside the strategic arms area but was perhaps the most important effect. In a hard-to-define way, suggested by the alliance aspect of the negotiators, the agreement changed the manner in which the two superpowers and the rest of the world viewed each other. Although the Soviets probably looked to SALT as a step toward world condominium with the United States, SALT I did not produce such condominium, for the United States retained its ties with China and many new power centers were emerging. The United States was probably less enthusiastic about world condominium. Nevertheless, SALT I was a step in this direction, as suggested by the agreement on the Basic Principles of Relations Between the United States of America and the Union of Soviet Socialist Republics. For the Soviets and for many observers outside the superpowers, this agreement, signed three days after the SALT I accords, was politically coupled with those accords.

Although the Basic Principles explicitly recognized the sovereign equality of all states and denied any special right for the United States and the Soviet Union, they did suggest that the two nations would co-ordinate their policies for mutual benefit:

> The USA and the USSR attach major importance to preventing the development of situations capable of causing a dangerous exacerbation of their relations. . . .
> Both sides recognize that efforts to obtain unilateral advantage at the expense of the other, directly or indirectly, are inconsistent with these objectives. The prerequisites for maintaining and strengthening peaceful relations between the USA and the USSR are the recognition of the security interests of the Parties based on the principle of equality and the renunciation of the use or threat of force.
> The USA and the USSR have a special responsibility, as do other countries which are permanent members of the United Nations Security Council, to do everything in their power so that conflicts or situations will not arise which would serve to increase international tensions. . . .

Soviet diplomats find much more satisfaction in such broad language than do U.S. scholars. To the Soviets, the language probably symbolized U.S. recognition of both U.S.-U.S.S.R. parity and of a form of special cooperation, or at least restraints on competition, between the two nations. The agreement did not separate the United States from its European allies or from China; it was, however, at least a symbol of détente and an indication of a new form of U.S.-U.S.S.R. cooperation.

World reactions to SALT I were generally apathetic, even in Europe. Strategically, the restriction on U.S.S.R. ABMs assured the European nuclear nations and China that their small nuclear forces could penetrate Soviet defenses. SALT I's resolution of the issue of the Forward-Based Systems (FBS) also favored the defense of Europe. It may therefore have helped satisfy Chinese and European strategic concerns that were among the barriers to expanding SALT to include all nuclear nations. But the strategic calculations were generally subordinate to political judgments. Some were concerned at the U.S. acceptance of missile numbers below those of the Soviet Union. It was, after all, those in Europe and Japan who placed reliance on a U.S. nuclear umbrella to protect them from conventional attack. Others were disappointed at the relative weakness of the agreements in restricting arms construction, although public opinion was generally pleased at the indications of détente.

In most of the third world, SALT was not even a major news item. Many of those who had opinions had looked to SALT as the place where the superpowers could fulfill their Non-Proliferation Treaty commitment to reduce vertical proliferation, and were disappointed by the agreement. China, in particular, strongly criticized SALT I, calling it a sham and a manifestation of the efforts of the superpowers to dominate the world. Chou En-lai said that "the agreements marked the beginning of a new stage in the arms race." The sharpness of his reaction perhaps emphasizes that SALT I was extremely significant for U.S.-U.S.S.R. relations.

Although the SALT I negotiations were the most significant and dramatic arms control negotiations to date, they left a substantial agenda for further efforts at arms control. The Interim Agreement was, by its character, temporary and would have to be reshaped in response to new weapons. The United States already viewed its new weapons programs as bargaining chips for the SALT II round, which would begin in November 1972, and the offensive missile problem was one that the parties were unable to solve in their first period of strategic arms negotiations. SALT I left a difficult agenda for SALT II.

CHAPTER TEN

SALT, 1972-1975

SALT I was a secret negotiation, dominated by bureaucratic pressures and high-level executive decision-making. Once the SALT I agreements were brought back to the United States, however, Congressional and public politics began to play a greater role in setting the stage for SALT II. These political pressures continued through SALT II and substantially affected the U.S. bargaining.

Ratification of SALT I—The Jackson Amendment

President Nixon's transmission of the SALT agreements to Congress emphasized the role that SALT would play in furthering détente between the United States and the Soviet Union. At the same time that the President sought approval of the SALT agreements as being in the national interest, he also sought approval of the B-1 bomber and the Trident missile submarine.[1] Secretary of State Kissinger defended the agreements on their own merits; Secretary of Defense Melvin Laird directly linked the desirability of the agreements to Congressional approval of the new weapons programs.

The Senate readily approved the ABM Treaty (88–2) on August 3, 1972. The President had decided to submit the Interim Offensive Arms Agreement to both houses; not being a formal treaty, it did not require a two-thirds vote in either house. Hints of dissent were contained in news reports that Senator Henry Jackson, a Democrat from Washington, would work with several powerful Republicans to attach reservations to the Interim Agreement.

---

[1] The B-1 was a supersonic bomber designed to replace the B-52. It would have a low altitude penetration capability and a larger payload than the B-52. The Trident was a large nuclear submarine, designed to carry 24 missiles rather than the 16 carried by Polaris and Poseidon. It would carry a new longer-range missile; some of the new missiles would also be retrofitted on several of the Poseidon ships.

The day the ABM Treaty was passed, Senator Jackson did in fact send the Senate Committee on Foreign Relations a copy of his proposal—an amendment to the declaration authorizing the President to approve the Interim Agreement. The amendment had three important features: (1) that Congress would consider Soviet actions endangering the survivability of the U.S. deterrent to be contrary to the supreme national interest of the United States—and therefore grounds for abrogation—whether or not the Soviet actions were consistent with the Interim Agreement, (2) that Congress would urge the President to seek a future treaty that "would not limit the U.S. to levels of intercontinental strategic forces inferior to the limits" for the Soviet Union, and (3) that a vigorous research and development and modernization program should be pursued.

What was interesting was that earlier the same day the White House had also sent a copy of the proposal to the Foreign Relations Committee. Over the weekend of August 5–6, Senator Jackson worked together with White House representatives and produced a revised version in which the first point was drastically weakened. The revised version picked up one of the U.S. unilateral statements made during negotiation and said that failure to achieve a follow-up agreement during the Interim Agreement's five-year term could jeopardize the U.S. supreme national interest if U.S. missile survivability were threatened as a result. In this revised form the amendment received White House support on August 7, in a statement calling it consistent with the undertakings in Moscow.

Confusion increased the following day. Several of the amendment's Congressional supporters interpreted it in public statements, saying, for example, that the amendment's definition of equality required equality of throw-weight in future strategic agreements and prohibited the inclusion of European-based systems in counting what was to be equal. The White House responded by reaffirming its endorsement of the Jackson amendment but denying any endorsement of "separate elaborations" of the amendment.

This was the position when the amendment was finally debated on the floor of the Senate. The Jackson amendment debate was surrealistic, reflecting the Administration's support for the resolution conditioning its own treaty. For example, the Democratic opposition accused the amendment's Republican supporters of lack of confidence in the arrangements made by the Republican President in Moscow. And the debate often spilled over into criticism of the haste that marked the final SALT I negotiations and into discussions of the credibility of the Soviets' past statements. The actual vote was delayed until September 14, because of Senator Fulbright's opposition and the impossibility of obtaining a procedural compromise between the two senators. The Senate accepted the amendment 56–35 and then approved the agreement 88–2. The House fell in line about two weeks later.

The Senate's desire for equality in future agreements was expressed quite strongly, even in the face of criticism that such an expression would tie the hands of future U.S. negotiators. Many of the discussions rejected pure deterrence theory in favor of counterforce capabilities and the need for equality to maintain the confidence of allies. Most strongly, the Senate seemed determined to give the President a warning that could be passed on to the Soviets—that equality was essential in any long-term strategic agreements. The meaning of "equality" was only slightly clarified. From a vote rejecting an amendment to strike the word "intercontinental" one can say fairly confidently that the Senate "intended" that European systems not be included in the balance. There were no grounds for persuasive argument, however, that the Senate chose any specific parameter for equality—warhead numbers, missile numbers, or throw-weight. Moreover, there was some legal question whether the Congressional action was binding on future negotiations; the agreements produced in such negotiations would, after all, be submitted to Congress.

The Jackson amendment's effect on U.S. negotiators—whether read as strengthening or tying their hands—was probably its most important long-term effect. But the amendment may have been politically coupled with another extremely important short-term action—a purge of most of those (except Nixon and Kissinger) who had had anything major to do with SALT I. During the year following SALT I, all the senior Arms Control and Disarmament Agency officials resigned or were replaced. Gerard Smith resigned as Director of ACDA and U.S. SALT negotiator. Fred Ikle was appointed the new ACDA director, but he would not be the chief SALT negotiator. A career diplomat, U. Alexis Johnson, was assigned this latter task. And many of the State and Defense Department officials who had participated in negotiations were also replaced.

The Issues for SALT II

The key task for SALT II was to convert the interim SALT I offensive force agreements into a more permanent restriction on offensive forces. To do so, the negotiations would eventually have to come to grips with three problems: (1) extension of quantitative restrictions in a form acceptable to both Congress and the Soviet Union, (2) application of qualitative restrictions to missile technology and particularly to MIRVs, and (3) recognition of the effects of bombers and anti-submarine warfare (ASW) on the strategic balance.

Quantitative Restrictions

The Jackson amendment called for equality between the United States and the Soviet Union in "levels of intercontinental strategic forces," but left unanswered or gave only partial answers to the definitions of "forces" and "equality."

Design of an agreement to achieve parity or equality was clearly difficult in the face of the asymmetries following SALT I. The Americans had many more deliverable warheads. The Soviets had about 50 percent more ICBMs, but the Americans had about four times as many strategic bombers as the Soviets. Whereas the Soviets had about a 4-to-1 superiority over the Americans in deliverable payload if only ICBMs and SLBMs were counted, the two nations had roughly equivalent deliverable payloads if bombers were also included in the balance. And, although Congress had spoken on the FBS (forward-based systems) issue, the Soviets still held to their position as well.

The inclusion of bombers could be a step toward equal starting points. Even if bombers were included, however, it would still be difficult to design an agreement that gave both nations the same number of each kind of weapon: ICBMs, SLBMs, and strategic bombers. For example, if the negotiators were to decide to limit ICBMs, they would have to decide whether to have the Soviet Union reduce its ICBMs to the U.S. level or to have the United States increase its ICBMs to Soviet levels. If the Soviets had to reduce their ICBM force to match the U.S. level, it is likely they would demand a comparable reduction in other U.S. strategic forces. But what reduction would be comparable? This type of exchange is difficult to negotiate, since there is no obvious way to compare different types of weapons systems.

Strictly symmetrical limitations would also tend to ignore asymmetries that exist in the weapons themselves and in the basing facilities for the weapons. Thus, the U.S. forward bases for submarines make it easier for the United States to deploy its submarines within range of the Soviet Union than for the Soviets to deploy their submarines on station off U.S. shores. U.S.S.R. development of longer-range SLBMs would reduce this advantage of U.S. submarine bases abroad, but the status of U.S. forward bases for aircraft was an issue that would be likely to come up in reply. Similarly, the Soviets could be expected to argue that they should be compensated for the U.S. advantages in MIRV technology and superiority in numbers of warheads. It would be difficult to compensate for these asymmetries if each side were limited to equal numbers of each type of strategic system.

Some of the problems caused by the asymmetries could be met by limiting each side to an aggregate level of forces and thus allowing it to deploy whatever combination of forces it preferred within this aggregate. Thus, one might count each ICBM, SLBM, and strategic bomber as one unit in the aggregate, and then allow each side to use its own judgment to determine how many of each type of weapon to maintain or perhaps to shift from one force type to another within defined limits.

Even if the two nations were to agree to negotiate such aggregate limits rather than separate limits on separate weapon types, it might still be necessary, when setting each side's aggregate, to take into account such factors as the differences in basing facilities and weapons technology. As a result, the aggregate levels agreed upon might not necessarily be equal for each side, although they would be equivalent in a broad strategic sense. Alternatively, the negotiators might conclude that these asymmetries balanced out, at least at a particular stage of technology.

The achievement of parity would not necessarily imply the achievement of reductions; the process of reducing force levels could intensify the effects of the asymmetries that have just been reviewed. The fixing of parity might no longer be politically costly to either side; both were committed to détente, which may require parity, and recognized that strategically significant inequality is probably technologically impossible. But any process of reduction would face bureaucratic hurdles in both nations, the use of bargaining chip strategies by one or both sides, and eventually the desire to maintain a strong position against third nations such as China. Hence, parity would as likely be achieved by equalizing up as equalizing down.

Qualitative Restraints

In order to control the strategic arms competition, it would also be necessary to restrict qualitative improvements in strategic weapons, and particularly MIRVs. The United States and the Soviet Union were both actively involved in MIRV programs, and each viewed the other's program as a threat to its land-based ICBMs. Thus limiting, if not banning, the deployment of MIRVs would be a continuing topic in SALT II.

Verification of MIRV limitations would be a problem, but not necessarily an insurmountable one. Before deploying a MIRVed missile, a nation must test it, and these tests can be monitored. The Soviet Union tested its MIRVs on new large missiles for which silo modifications would have to be made. These silo modifications would be detectable. Therefore, partly by happenstance, it would remain possible to verify a MIRV limitation by national technical means alone.

There were also balance problems. The United States was substantially ahead of the Soviet Union in MIRV technology, and it was unlikely that the Soviets would agree to a ban on MIRVs until they had mastered MIRV technology as an "insurance" measure. Moreover, the new ICBMs that the Soviets were testing with MIRVs were extremely large. The much greater Soviet throw-weight caused many in the United States to argue that in time the Soviets would be able to have either more or larger MIRVs than the United States. Whether this "throw-weight problem" could be balanced by the U.S. advantages in technology and accuracy would depend upon the strategic judgments of each side. And, once again, there was the issue of what to equalize: number of MIRVed missiles, number of MIRV warheads, or throw-weight.

Another important qualitative improvement was increased accuracy; if techniques of inertial guidance improve sufficiently, a single warhead will be able to eliminate any fixed target with high probability. This is partly a result of improved inertial guidance technology. Maneuverable reentry vehicles (MARVs) may also become available to provide even greater accuracy through sensing the target location and maneuvering to home on it. Since both the Americans and the Soviets appeared committed to large MIRV programs, the number of available, accurately deliverable warheads on each side could eventually greatly exceed the number of fixed land-based missiles, and these missiles themselves become vulnerable.

At first approximation, this development would not affect the current state of symmetrical deterrence, because both sides retain missile-carrying nuclear submarine fleets, whose positions remain unknown and which carry a sufficient number of missiles to ensure massive retaliation against aggression. Nevertheless, such missile advance might create strategic instabilities of the type noted by Secretary of Defense Schlesinger. He argued that the Soviets might launch an attack on the Minuteman force and then deter a U.S. response against Soviet cities by threatening to strike U.S. cities in return. To prevent this type of action, Schlesinger argued that the United States needs an accurate counterforce capability to respond in kind to a Soviet attack on U.S. missiles.

As noted in Chapter 7, many have criticized this concept and Schlesinger's conclusions from it. Many doubt that the Soviets could carry out a first strike capable of destroying all U.S. Minuteman forces. For example, there are serious problems of fratricide—damage to one incoming reentry vehicle through the explosion of another. Moreover, such an attack would kill a substantial number of people, and therefore the Soviets could never be certain that the United States would not react by retaliating with an all-out strike on Soviet cities. The United States would certainly be capable of such a strike, since it would retain SLBMs and bombers even if all ICBMs were destroyed. In light of this risk, what strategic or political requirements would motivate the original attack? Others criticize a solution based on increasing U.S. missile accuracy. The accuracy required to hit soft military targets—which might be the targets in some forms of strategic war—is less than the accuracy necessary to destroy a missile in a hardened silo. If the United States improves accuracy to the point that it can destroy hardened silos, then it may give the Soviets the impression that it is preparing for a first strike. Soviet confidence in its deterrent might then be weakened, leading to further weapons construction.

Thus, many hoped that accuracy improvement would be restricted at SALT II. Nevertheless, the verification problems were quite difficult. The observer of a missile test can tell where the missile went but is unlikely to know where it was aimed.

One way to restrict both accuracy and MIRV development has often been suggested: to limit the number of missile test firings each year. If both countries were limited to about ten firings a year, for example, new weapons development might be slowed, since no country would want to stockpile an inadequately tested weapon. Such a restraint could also reduce fears of a first strike, since any first-strike force would have to be tested extensively to ensure the necessary levels of accuracy and reliability. Such proposals have faced considerable military opposition, however. Frequent tests are argued to be necessary to ensure the reliability of existing systems as well as to develop new systems. Moreover, the Soviet testing philosophy may be different from that of the United States, leading to another asymmetry problem.

It appeared most likely, then, that MIRV restrictions would take the form of numerical limits on deployed systems. It was unlikely that either the Americans or the Soviets would accept a total MIRV ban. It might, however, be possible to negotiate a restriction allowing each side to MIRV a given number or proportion of its missiles, but the level of these restrictions would be important, as would their verification features.

Bomber and Submarine Systems

The combination of MIRVs and increased missile accuracy suggested to many that fixed land-based ICBMs were becoming obsolete. Therefore, alternative systems would be likely to attract greater attention from both force designers and arms control negotiators.

For bomber systems, the biggest arms control issues were those of definition. How does one draw a dividing line between a long-range strategic bomber and a short-range tactical aircraft also capable of carrying nuclear weapons? Can an arms control agreement create a balance that is effectively dependent on where forces are based without intolerable inspection and instability problems, let alone political conflicts with the nations where the forces are based? And how does one count missile-carrying aircraft, especially if the aircraft carry several missiles of a range adequate to penetrate air defense systems?

On the submarine side, the problem was a different one—the possible vulnerability of nuclear submarines to anti-submarine warfare (ASW). Both nations had already developed techniques for the tracking and destruction of ASW submarines in order to protect merchant shipping and surface warships from attack by conventional submarines. There is considerable overlap in the technology of ASW against conventional and nuclear submarines. Moreover, the missions of protecting merchant shipping and surface warships remain extremely important to navies. It is very difficult to design restrictions that effectively permit the one form of ASW and prohibit the other.

What makes ASW itself difficult is that the seas, unlike the atmosphere, are relatively opaque. Most electromagnetic radiations are very strongly absorbed. Sound is less strongly absorbed and is the basis of sonar detection technology. Nevertheless, sound-generating and receiving systems are often large and cumbersome, difficult to deploy and maintain, and impossible to disguise or hide. The oceans are far from homogeneous, and contain a great variety of noise sources. Because of the many sources of noise and confusion, there are many ways for a submarine to create plausible decoys or to deceive or jam detection devices. Since the problem of ASW, like that of the ABM, is one of devising a means of detection and destruction that stays ahead of the counter-measures, the effectiveness of submarine decoys and of similar technologies is a crucial issue for the feasibility of ASW defense systems.

To be effective as a "first-strike" system against a submarine deterrent, the ASW system must be able to find and track not simply a given nuclear submarine but a large number of submarines. Only then can a large fraction of the opponent's nuclear submarine force be suddenly and simultaneously eliminated. Most experts consider the ASW problem to be so difficult that submarine-based missile systems will continue to be fully reliable deterrents at least well into the 1980's.

Nevertheless, the search for more effective ASW devices continues, and it is possible that, sooner or later, one side or the other will deploy more advanced systems—whether intended against missile submarines or against tactical submarines—that are viewed by the opponent as threatening underseas missile forces. Once this happens, uncertainty concerning the invulnerability of SLBM systems will be introduced into the worst-case analyses; countermeasures will be taken, and a new arms competition will possibly develop. It is unlikely that any installation or system large enough to have any real effectiveness can be deployed in secret; its detection would probably be accomplished by readily available national means. Hence, the opponent would have warning early enough to take effective countermeasures to protect its SLBM deterrent. But even if preemption is unlikely, expanded arms competition would be relatively likely.

To avoid such underseas arms competition, many suggest agreements between the nuclear superpowers to limit deployments of systems that could have an ASW capability against missile submarines. One element of such an agreement might restrict the installation of systems of sonar arrays in the oceans. Another element might designate areas of the ocean in which each superpower would be free to place its SLBMs; the opponent would be prohibited from any ASW activity in the area. Another element might place limits on so-called hunter-killer submarines, i.e. submarines designed to track and destroy other submarines. An effective attack on either side's nuclear submarine force would require the use of a large number of hunter-killer submarines, so it might be possible to restrict them to a number large enough to satisfy the tactical requirements of protecting merchant shipping and surface ships, but small enough to prevent an effective coordinated attack on the entire nuclear fleet.

Arrangements to control bombers or to increase the survivability of SLBM systems are relatively likely responses to the increasing vulnerability of fixed land-based ICBMs. Whether the United States and the Soviet Union would explicitly agree to reduce the level of ICBMs is another question; such an explicit agreement would raise serious bureaucratic problems of interservice rivalries. Negotiations probably are more likely to lead to overall limits that permit interservice adjustments to be made as part of the domestic budget process in each nation.

SALT II—The Nixon Phase

SALT II began on November 21, 1972, in Geneva, which would be its long-term seat. The first session is said to have been unproductive. The United States fielded its new negotiating team early in 1973; there must have been time lags as the U.S.S.R. delegates and the new U.S. delegates assessed one another. The new appointees in Washington must also have needed time to develop negotiating positions. Major changes were occurring in the Soviet Union as well. For example, in a shift from the recent pattern, the Soviet Defense Minister was admitted in 1973 to full membership in the Politburo, the key decision-making group.

Although data on the negotiations are not as easy to obtain as is information on SALT I, it appears likely that the Soviets made an early proposal to freeze new strategic programs; the Americans did not pursue this proposal, presumably because it would halt the new B-1 and Trident efforts. In rejecting the proposal, the Americans probably lost an opportunity to halt the Soviets' new programs to develop large MIRVed missiles. These new U.S.S.R. programs created concern in Washington and led to a U.S. proposal to freeze MIRV testing and deployment. Naturally, such a proposal was unacceptable to the Soviets.

At some point, the negotiators moved past this phase of proposing freezes that might have differential effects and began to examine various forms of aggregate equality. There was probably a U.S. proposal to extend the Interim Agreement, adding a limitation to equal throw-weight for MIRVed ICBMs. The Soviets, however, must have rejected the proposal because their larger missile size would imply fewer missiles, and probably no SLBMs, could be MIRVed under such a limitation. They apparently replied with a proposal to retain the unequal missile totals of the Interim Agreement but to place equal limits on the total number of MIRVed missiles. This balance would not be acceptable to the United States. Unsuccessful efforts seem to have been made to adjust the concept by permitting the United States more MIRVed missiles than the Soviets and restricting the Soviets' SS-18 (one of the new large MIRVed missiles) while still permitting them to retain their overall missile number superiority. It was apparently impossible, however, to define a compromise of this type that might not provide the basis for unbalanced construction when the agreement lapsed. There was apparently no effort to limit MIRV launchers to levels low enough to require large reductions in the U.S. force.

At the June 1973 summit, the leaders promised agreement in 1974 and issued a statement of principles, couched in terms of an eventual permanent agreement and separate measures in the meantime. President Nixon's position at home then became increasingly weaker as the Watergate issue came to dominate domestic politics. The President went to Moscow in June 1974, hoping to honor the pledge that he and Brezhnev had made a year earlier to reach a SALT II agreement during 1974.

Kissinger said that the discussion was conducted with a frankness that would have been considered inconceivable two years earlier (i.e. at the time of SALT I) and at a level of detail that would have been considered as violating intelligence codes in previous periods. The best the parties were able to do, however, was to issue a communiqué that an agreement to cover the period until 1985 and dealing with both qualitative and quantitative limitations should be completed before the 1977 expiration of the Interim Agreement.

Kissinger presented this 1985 date as a major advance, pointing out that, until late in the summit talks, consideration had been given only to short-term or permanent agreements. Short-term (two or three years) agreements would be too sensitive to current programs, and permanent agreements would be too sensitive to the unpredictability of technology. Hence, he argued, the new idea of agreeing for about a 10-year term would open up new options for agreement design.

Essentially, however, there was only failure in the midst of leaks of discord between Kissinger and Secretary of Defense Schlesinger. Critics suggested that President Nixon's political position was so weak that he was unable to resolve the dispute between the two men. Kissinger rather bitterly stated that agreement was essential within 18 months or there would be "an explosion of numbers and of technology," that both the United States and the Soviet Union would have to "convince their military establishments of the need for restraint," and that one of the questions we would then have to ask ourselves was "'What in the name of God is strategic superiority?'"

The leaders did find it possible to reach several subsidiary arms control agreements, agreements that critics called cosmetic or worse than nothing. One of these was a treaty to restrict each side to its existing ABM systems. The asymmetry between the U.S. missile-defense ABM system and the U.S.S.R. city-defense system—an asymmetry that had been such a barrier in SALT I—was then accepted as it became clear that neither side had any intention of building its additional permitted ABM systems. This agreement alleviated any concerns based on an expanded radar base had either party exercised its second-site option. To permit flexibility, each side was permitted to shift its ABM system once between national capital defense and missile defense. A second agreement was the threshold test ban treaty, discussed in Chapter 6, which was heavily criticized because the threshold was so high and because the treaty was not to become effective until 1976. It was said that the delay was to permit necessary additional arrangements to be worked out on the testing of peaceful nuclear explosions. The Senate approved the ABM agreement in November 1975, but at that time, the other treaty had not yet been submitted to the Senate for its advice and consent.

Two other subsidiary arms control arrangements were more technical. These new arrangements were secret technical protocols involving the dismantling and replacing of missiles and had been worked out by the Standing Consultative Commission. Kissinger said they were made secret at the request of the Soviet Union but that they would be submitted to the appropriate Congressional committees. Finally, discussions were to begin toward control of environmental modification as a tool of warfare, and the two nations indicated their support for an agreement on the most dangerous lethal means of chemical warfare.

SALT II—The Ford Phase and Vladivostok

Under deepening pressure from Watergate, President Nixon announced his resignation on August 8, 1974, and Gerald Ford assumed the office the following day. Preparatory work for negotiations had been essentially impossible during the last months of Nixon's Presidency, so preparations had to begin anew under the new President.

The new negotiations were oriented toward a 10-year agreement. Evidently, several combinations of quantitative and qualitative limitations were considered, proposals were exchanged in October and discussed during Kissinger's visit to Moscow that month, and one combination was finally accepted in outline form by Ford and Brezhnev at their November Vladivostok summit meeting. Under the agreement, in principle, each side would be limited to 2,400 strategic delivery vehicles, including long-range bombers as well as ICBMs and SLBMs. Each side would be allowed to MIRV no more than 1,320 of its ICBMs and SLBMs. These new arrangements would cover the period from October 1977, when the Interim Agreement would expire, to December 31, 1985. The Interim Agreement would remain in force in the meantime.

The contents of this package were released in several steps. A joint statement, issued in Vladivostok, gave the framework but did not give the numbers. The numbers were released several days later; this gave the leaders time to brief their governments before the numbers were publicly released. Secretary Kissinger's press conference in Vladivostok added several other points that might not be clear from the bare text of the joint statement. The Soviets had—for this agreement—deferred their demand to be compensated for forward-based systems (FBS). Kissinger suggested the Soviets conceded on the FBS issue in part because those systems were not suitable for a significant attack. Moreover, the force levels were set so high that the FBS could have only marginal effect. The Soviets subsequently indicated, however, that the FBS issue was left open in the event of future agreements at lower force levels. Subject to SALT I constraints, the two sides could mix their forces among ICBMs or SLBMs and heavy bombers. The understanding did not prohibit mobile land-based missiles. The SALT I constraints on the number of heavy missile launchers were to be carried over until 1985, presumably along with the SALT I restrictions on increase in silo dimensions. And the Soviet Union accepted a balance with the United States in missile numbers. This concession may have reflected a U.S.S.R. judgment that it would retain an advantage in missile throw-weight through 1985. The key U.S. concession was probably in precisely this area—accepting a limit on MIRV launcher numbers rather than MIRV launcher throw-weight.

The Vladivostok agreement in principle was criticized by both arms controllers and military theorists. For the arms controllers, the agreement was objectionable because it neither increased stability nor reduced force levels to any appreciable extent, if at all. Although there was some doubt about the exact force levels, the total number of U.S. delivery systems in January 1975 was about 2,130, counting ICBMs, SLBMs, and long-range bombers. Of the missiles, about 822 were MIRVed. The corresponding total for the Soviets was about 2,393 or perhaps about 100 higher, depending on whether obsolescent bombers were counted; U.S.S.R. MIRVed systems were just beginning to be deployed. Thus, substantial new MIRVing was permitted and the new ceilings would not significantly reduce force levels. They might even have had little effect on future deployment plans; if the United States went ahead with its 10 Trident boats, its total of MIRVed launchers would be 1,286 short of the agreement's 1,320. Secretary Kissinger responded that it was valuable to place a ceiling on strategic offensive systems and that the limitations would be beneficial by permitting each nation to plan with the knowledge that its opponent's forces would not exceed the agreed ceiling during the term of the agreement.

A generally different group of critics argued that the agreement was dangerous to the United States. In spite of continuation of the Interim Agreement's limitation on heavy missiles, the Soviet Union could have a potential three-to-one advantage in throw-weight, and could conceivably convert this throw-weight advantage into one of MIRV numbers during the agreement's lifetime. The sublimit on MIRVed missiles was so large that it would not forestall development of an arguable threat to Minuteman. Senator Jackson combined both criticisms: because the agreement did not resolve the Minuteman vulnerability issue, it should be renegotiated with lower force levels. He suggested that the parties should avoid modernizing 700 of their vehicles, presumably looking toward a future reduction from 2,400 to 1,700. Secretary Kissinger's off-the-record response was to downgrade the importance of throw-weight. On the record, both he and Schlesinger emphasized the agreement's importance to détente and the possibility that the dangers and costs would be much greater without the agreement—positions disputed by many.

At Vladivostok, Kissinger had judged there was a strong possibility that the agreement in principle could be converted into a treaty during 1975. Some of the remaining issues would probably be noncontroversial —e.g. rules for mothballing old forces. Several important issues, however, were left to the detailed negotiations, which were to be conducted in the regular SALT framework.

One such issue was verification, particularly verification of the number of MIRVed missiles. The Soviets had made this problem easy by testing their MIRVed systems only on new missiles the deployment of which required silo changes. The U.S. expectation was that the Soviets would then agree that any missile successfully tested in a MIRV mode could be counted as being MIRVed—the number of MIRVed missiles would then be counted as the number of modified silos. If this principle were applied neutrally, however, the entire U.S. Minuteman force would have to be counted as MIRVed. The Soviets resisted strict application of this principle, because they had tested one of their new large missiles, the SS-18, in both MIRVed and single warhead modes and wished to deploy some of each mode.

The definition of long-range bomber became another important issue. This issue centered around a U.S.S.R. bomber with the range to fly over the United States and then land in Cuba, but without the range to make a round-trip between the Soviet Union and the United States. The United States wanted the aircraft counted against the Soviet Union's 2,400 vehicle ceiling, whereas the Soviet Union did not.

Finally, cruise missiles became a subject of controversy. These missiles use conventional air-breathing engines and can be designed to fly long ranges. They are essentially pilotless aircraft and can use new guidance systems to achieve very high accuracy. The Vladivostok understanding was apparently to count air-launched missiles with a range of over 600 miles as strategic delivery vehicles subject to the 2,400 ceiling. The Soviets interpreted "air-launched missiles" as including cruise missiles, whereas the Americans argued that only ballistic missiles were affected. Both sides have developed such systems; the United States is well ahead in the technology and its planned versions would be long-range systems that can be placed on aircraft or submarines and can fly at low altitudes to avoid radar detection.

The detail negotiations did not go well during 1975, so the planned deadline was not met. There may have been political problems in the Soviet Union. In December 1973, that nation had angrily withdrawn a trade agreement after Congress amended trade legislation to require the Soviet Union to permit more free emigration of Jewish residents. This Soviet action, coupled with an illness of Secretary Brezhnev at about the same time, might have suggested a breakup of the Soviet coalition that favored arms control as a *quid pro quo* for increased technology from the West. Such a breakup probably did not occur, but the Communist victory in Southeast Asia and the subsequent international debate over U.S. commitment gave additional grounds for doubt about Soviet interest in an agreement. A "hawk" in the Soviet leadership might argue against an agreement that codified parity when superiority seemed to be within reach; many in the West felt that such motivations were important to the Soviets and that the Soviet Union was seeking superiority through SALT. This sinister interpretation is unlikely to be correct. Most specialists agree that the Soviet leaders view parity as reducing risks of confrontation and are willing to support further agreements—such as SALT—which help maintain that parity. Continued agreements with the United States could help discourage the United States from seeking the buildup of a third power such as China, Western Europe, or Japan. The Soviet leaders have tended to prefer low-risk over high-risk situations. Moreover, the problem of scarce resources continues to argue in favor of arms control and détente.

The domestic U.S. political situation was also hardening. Defense Secretary Schlesinger left the government late in 1975; his departure triggered criticism that the nation's strategic weapons plans were inadequate, criticisms likely to be repeated during the coming election year. A general disillusion with détente was also developing, and there had been charges that the Soviet Union was not complying with the side understandings (unilateral statements) of SALT I, for example, by deploying larger missiles. There was also discussion of earlier Soviet use of a radar in violation of the ABM Treaty, and Soviet preparation of new sites that looked like ICBM sites, but the radar use was stopped after SCC discussion and the sites were said to be designed for command and control installations. And the cruise missile program gained political support in the United States and made agreement design more difficult.

The MIRV verification issue had evidently been resolved during 1975, and some progress was announced at a January 1976 meeting, reported to be based on a U.S.S.R. proposal that would set a minimum range at which cruise missiles would have to be counted against force ceilings, and would modify the U.S. and U.S.S.R. ceilings to allow for U.S. aircraft carrying cruise missiles and for the Soviet bombers that were in dispute. Nevertheless, it was not clear whether the differences between the requirements of the Soviet Union and those of the U.S. Congress and the election campaign would leave Kissinger adequate room to negotiate an agreement.

The Future of SALT

Assuming that a Vladivostok-style agreement were successfully achieved, what would be the possible future of SALT? Clearly, there were several technical issues unlikely to be resolved in the Vladivostok detail agreement—the anti-submarine warfare (ASW) question and probably the cruise missile question. The crucial issue of missile accuracy was left open, perhaps even intensified by the Vladivostok numbers. All that a Vladivostok agreement would achieve would be to limit strategic delivery vehicle launchers quantitatively. The agreement would in no way restrict qualitative improvements; it might even increase the incentive toward such improvements. MIRVs would be more "permitted" than "limited." Thus, concern about vulnerability of fixed land-based forces would continue. The SALT III agenda would be substantial, even before consideration of serious reductions.

But the longer-term picture was much less clear: would the negotiations retain central attention and proceed toward actual force reductions or drop to a secondary role as issues like nuclear proliferation gained greater attention? Would the negotiations expand to include other nuclear powers?

SALT will retain central attention only if actual force reductions and the slowing of technological innovation are considered. The U.S. Congress might press the President toward such reductions; whether the President or the Soviet Union will be interested is much less clear, although regular meetings of U.S. and U.S.S.R. leaders have become an institution, and arms control is a likely subject of discussion and public movement. If SALT does deal with reductions, Vladivostok will probably be seen as a necessary phase in which formal parity is regained and a high but symmetrical restriction is imposed. The restriction could then be gradually lowered, probably cutting most heavily against ICBMs. A parallel slowing of technology would require either restriction on testing or quite complex and detailed negotiations.

The alternative is for Vladivostok's 1985 deadline to appear so distant and force reduction so unlikely that there is little political pressure to continue significant negotiations. Although Secretary Kissinger has suggested that the effort may begin earlier, there is so far no formal obligation to begin negotiating a follow-up until 1980–81. Political pressures to deal with nuclear proliferation are likely to be stronger than those to deal with strategic arms reductions. Many of those enthusiastic about arms control fear that SALT negotiations speed the arms race through encouraging procurement of weapons as bargaining points. Thus it is possible that SALT may drop to a secondary role until sometime in the early 1980's, perhaps meeting, but dealing with only relatively minor issues.

Any estimate of the future of SALT also requires consideration of its possible expansion to include other nuclear powers, particularly France and China, whose recent participation in arms control has been minimal. Although the strategic doctrine of neither nation is parallel to that of the United States or the Soviet Union, they probably seek a minimum strategic capability in order to deter both a nuclear first strike and a massive conventional invasion. As a result, they can both be expected to refuse to limit their strategic testing and deployment programs until they feel they have achieved this minimum capability.

The attainment of minimum capability was facilitated by the ABM limitations required under the 1972 ABM Treaty, which increases the probability that a Chinese or French missile will penetrate defenses and land on target. The French and, to a lesser extent, the Chinese, however, consider their nuclear forces as deterrents against both nuclear and conventional attack; hence their willingness to limit their nuclear forces will also be affected by the conventional threats they face. As will be discussed in Chapter 12, De Gaulle's decision to build a *force de frappe* was prompted, at least in part, by his fears that the United States would fail to respond with nuclear weapons to a massive Soviet conventional attack on Europe for fear this would cause a retaliatory Soviet nuclear strike on the United States. In a similar way, Chinese fears of a possible Soviet conventional attack can affect China's willingness to limit its strategic forces. Although the Chinese nuclear force may not be sufficient to prevent a large-scale Soviet conventional attack, this condition does make such an attack much more risky. Despite Chinese pledges not to be the first to use nuclear weapons, the Soviets could never be sure that the Chinese might not react to a massive Soviet conventional attack by firing nuclear missiles against Soviet cities. As a result, even the remote possibility of Chinese nuclear retaliation makes a Soviet conventional invasion potentially very costly, and thus presumably less likely.

Thus, although the attainment of a minimum strategic force appears to be a precondition for French and Chinese willingness to negotiate limits on strategic weapons, it is by no means a guarantee of that willingness. In both cases, the resolution of political tensions and the success of arms control negotiations aimed at reducing conventional force levels could have an important impact on decisions to limit or increase nuclear force levels. Moreover, strategic arms have political import; these nations might refuse to accept any permanent arrangement that would freeze them at inferior levels. A commitment on the part of the superpowers to move toward staged general disarmament might or might not help; it will take major U.S.-U.S.S.R. changes to persuade France and China that SALT is not essentially a way to maintain superpower hegemony. Thus the future of SALT, if not SALT III, might lead back to the comprehensive issues discussed in the multilateral forums of the 1950's.

An expansion of SALT to include new nations would also require changes in the negotiation forum to avoid the appearance that the new nations were joining SALT as lesser partners. The U.S.-U.S.S.R. negotiation style of broad exchange of technical information would have to be modified. Not only might there be security difficulties in the new data exchanges; there would even be problems deriving from the likelihood that China and France would lag in intelligence technology. In the mid-1970's, however, the problem was that of persuading these nuclear powers even to enter into any talks with the others. Several efforts within the U.N. context had produced little more than acrimony between China and the Soviet Union.

Conclusion—The SALT Process

By the time of SALT II, the U.S.-U.S.S.R. strategic arms negotiations had become an institutionalized part of détente and had clearly helped support a special relationship between the two nations. Any dispute in either the field of diplomacy or the field of strategic arms negotiations was immediately examined for its effect on the other field. The negotiations had become procedurally independent of other nations; Europe and China were not yet playing a direct role and were not particularly interested either.

But, at least in the United States, interest in SALT had broadened. Congress was playing a more active role through the Jackson amendment and threats of similar future actions. Political support for détente led Presidents to seek a continuing stream of successes, although this attitude was in question again by mid-decade.

Two important features of the bargaining process deserve special comment. One was the bargaining chip concept—the idea that weapons programs should be started in order to stimulate the other side's interest in negotiations. This may explain the Soviet Union's missile buildup during the late 1960's; it certainly helps explain the U.S. ABM program during SALT I and the U.S. B-1 and Trident programs. Many argue that the concept was important in helping obtain the SALT I agreements if not the Vladivostok accord.

Nevertheless, the concept is substantially responsible for the SALT pattern of agreements without force reductions or (except for ABM) stringent limitations. The bargaining chip cannot always be cashed in. The other side may not be willing to halt programs in exchange for a halt in the bargaining chip program. And as development and deployment of the bargaining chip program continue, bureaucratic pressures for and vested interests in the system grow. As a result, it may be impossible to negotiate away the system. The building of the bargaining chip program may also cause the opponent to doubt the builder's sincerity and even lead the opponent to initiate new programs in response. After the program is built, the opponent may even refuse to stop while in an inferior position. The approach can then stimulate not strategic arms limitations but strategic arms competition.

A second feature is the heavy use of bargaining deadlines. Regular meetings between U.S. and Soviet leaders have become an established ritual, and probably serve many useful purposes. Within the arms control field, for example, they create deadlines for internal and international negotiation. However, the number of summit meetings has exceeded the number of important agreements, so that there is political pressure to announce agreements in principle or plans to complete an agreement by a publicly announced time. Many feel that the United States is at a disadvantage in negotiating under such a public deadline; the political costs of failure to agree are viewed as greater for the United States, so that it is more likely to make concessions. In response, one might point to the advantage of preliminary announcements such as that of Vladivostok; the announcement permits public criticism and evaluation before the agreement is reduced to final form.

These features are a reflection of the internal political processes that affect strategic arms negotiations: bureaucratic pressures in both nations supporting continued arms procurement, Congressional desires for greater participation, a poorly understood Soviet coalition for arms control. These processes changed greatly between SALT I and SALT II; they will have to change still more if SALT is to become a forum for substantial force reductions. And expansion of SALT to include the other nuclear nations will require substantial changes in those nations themselves as well as in the motivations that move the United States and the Soviet Union and in the way the negotiations are conducted.

CHAPTER ELEVEN

The Economics of Arms and Arms Control

Economics influences arms and arms control in many ways. Economic interests may fuel arms races or operate against arms control through beliefs that military expenditures give jobs, promote industrial development and technology, and stimulate growth.

Economic interests can also promote arms control. Reducing the burdens and the dangers of arms is a classic objective of arms control. Economic measurements can reveal what these burdens are, and what benefits, in the sense of better living standards for society at large, might be available through arms control. Economic alternatives help to extend the horizons of "national security," through belief that economic strength is important to national security, along with military strength.

Economic actions by governments can smooth the transition from military to civilian production, and economic techniques of measurement and analysis might help to verify compliance with agreements. Trade arrangements have been politically coupled with arms control negotiations, while economic sanctions could be a means of discouraging violations. Budgetary limitations might offer an arms control approach that actually reduces military expenditures.

This chapter focuses on the links between arms control and the economy. It first examines the economic magnitude of arms procurement: what resources do arms command, how big a burden are they to society, how important are they in the national and world economy? It then reviews the domestic and international economic processes at work in arms procurement. These discussions provide the background for evaluating the adjustments that substantial arms control would entail and for considering concepts of arms control through budgetary limitations. A caution must be inserted: accurate data are difficult to obtain, eco-

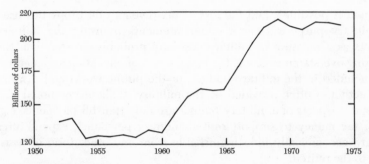

Fig. 6. Total world annual military expenditures, in constant 1970 dollars (*SIPRI Yearbook, 1974*, pp. 206–7, and *1975*, pp. 120–21).

nomic sources often disagree with one another, and there have been few careful estimates of post-1972 world arms expenditures.

Dimensions of Arms Procurement

The World Economy

The most commonly used single measure of the size of the military economy is the national government's total annual military expenditures. Governments are not wholly agreed on the activities and programs that come under this budgetary rubric, but a total of national budgets can give an *approximate* measure of world economic costs. By the beginning of the 1970's, this total was more than $225 billion (in 1972 dollars) a year on military programs.[1] This number had been growing very rapidly through the 1960's (even after correction for inflation). Its growth in real terms tapered off to zero in the early 1970's (see Figure 6), but may have resumed in the 1975–76 era. The total is about the same as the total income of the poorest half of the world's population.

Although the sum is awesome, it does not adequately reflect full military costs, in either budgetary or economic terms. Defense budgets frequently do not include such costs as veterans' benefits, which can be quite substantial, nor do they cover interest charges on national debts resulting from past years. Other military-related costs do not appear in budgetary outlays, e.g. the loss of income by draftees who are serving in the armed forces at less than market wages (assuming that other em-

[1] Except as noted, the sources of the numbers in this chapter are *SIPRI Yearbook, 1975* (Stockholm International Peace Research Institute, 1975), and R. Sivard, *World Military and Social Expenditures* (New York: Institute for World Order, 1974). As explained in the text, there is dispute over both the magnitude and the meaning of the various numbers.

ployment is possible), and the loss of tax revenues on properties used for military purposes. These understatements in using the military budgets as a measure of military costs are probably greater than the offsetting overstatements, e.g. the many forms of education and medical care included in the military budget, or the public works and disaster relief activities often provided by the military. It should be noted also that many aspects of a military budget are only transfer payments, e.g. use of tax money to support retired military personnel, expenditures that are economically indistinguishable from any other form of assistance to the retired.

Military expenditures are frequently compared with gross national product (GNP), a measure that sums up the value of an economy's total output of goods and services. In the mid-1960's, world military expenditures represented about 7 to 8 percent of world GNP, but fell to about 5½ percent by 1972. In a historical sense, these numbers are relatively high; the corresponding percentages in 1913 and the early 1930's, before World Wars I and II respectively, were around 3 to 3½ percent.[2]

Because the ratio of military expenditures to GNP is an often cited measure, it is well to note its limitations. First, as world product expands, there is no logical reason to assume that threats to the security of nations, and therefore military expenditures, should grow in proportion. During the decade of the 1960's, as world product doubled, world military outlays took a share of that product that was declining only very slowly. Looking at the ratio alone, one could miss the fact that a relatively steady growth of GNP also implied a substantial increase in arms expenditures.

As a measure of *burden* on the economy, the ratio to GNP must also be used with care. An economy with a high per capita income (e.g. the United States—about $5,500) should be able more easily to bear a particular defense burden than an economy with a low per capita income (e.g. Indonesia—about $86). In the poorer country, even a small drain of resources away from the civilian economy bites more heavily into the necessities of life.

In addition to military expenditures and their ratio to GNP, other measures may contribute to an understanding of the scope of the military economy. One such measure is the manpower employed in defense and defense-related activities. The regular armed forces of the world number over 20 million. One can add the armed border guards, gendarmerie, and other paramilitary forces that are significant in some

[2] *SIPRI Yearbook*, 1968/69, p. 27.

countries. The result would still not include reservists, who serve for a short period in the year, nor would it include the many civilians employed in defense ministries. These civilian staffs are probably growing more rapidly than are uniformed forces, and in some countries they represent a large component of the personnel in military departments. The U.S. Department of Defense, for example, employs about 1.1 million civilians, compared to about 2.1 million military. Supplementing the manpower directly employed by the defense ministries are the many workers who directly or indirectly provide the products and services that the military needs. There is no precise count of their numbers even in the United States. It is very roughly estimated, however, that they may be equal to those directly employed in the armed forces—suggesting that the total manpower involved in the world's military economy is at least 50 million.

A fourth measure of the dimensions of the military economy is the amount of research and development (R&D) resources devoted to it. One U.N. estimate was that world annual R&D expenditures were about $60 billion, of which about $25 billion was for military R&D.[3] Defense, then, represents about 5½ percent of world GNP, but it absorbs a much larger proportion—25 to 40 percent—of all expenditures, both government and private, for research and development. Although some of this defense research has side benefits for the nonmilitary portions of the economy, much does not.

Arms expenditures have been highly concentrated in a relatively few countries, largely the more economically advanced. The United States and the Soviet Union alone account for over 60 percent of the world total. Their allies in the NATO and Warsaw military pacts, plus China, bring the proportion to a little below 90 percent. It is these countries that largely determine the dimensions of overall world military spending.

But the most important *trends* are in the developing world. In contrast to the expenditures of the major powers, the military outlays of the developing world are still small in aggregate. For the countries generally classified as developing, total military expenditures in the early 1970's were approximately $30 billion annually, about half the

[3] *Disarmament and Development, Report of the Group of Experts on the Economic and Social Consequences of Disarmament,* ST/ECA/174 (1972), p. 16. Because of the difficulty of defining "R&D" and because of special difficulties in estimating U.S.S.R. military R&D expenditures, R&D numbers are particularly unreliable. SIPRI estimates of world military R&D are substantially lower: $15–16.5 billion annually during the 1960's. SIPRI, *Resources Devoted to Military Research and Development* (1972).

military budget of the United States alone. (The number would be about $20 billion if China were excluded.) The level in developing nations was about 4½ percent of GNP, lower than that in developed nations. But what is significant is that, albeit from a low base, these numbers are the most rapidly increasing ones. During the 1963–72 era, the growth rate of military expenditures in the developed world was 2 percent per year, corrected for inflation. The corresponding number for the developing world (including China) was 7.2 percent.[4] In 1955, the developing world was spending about 5.2 percent of the world's military budget; in 1973 it was spending about 14.4 percent. This rapid growth is not shared by all nations; it is often the result of large increases in particular nations. For example, a world arms expenditure upturn in the 1974–75 era would likely be in part a result of the rapidly increasing expenditures of nations such as Iran and Saudi Arabia, which are buying arms with oil profits.

The United States

With an annual GNP of about $1,300 billion—some 35 percent of the world's total—the United States probably ranks number one in the world in the budget it devotes to military programs, and certainly ranks number one in the size and sophistication of its arms industry and in the technology that goes with it.

The official U.S. budget for national defense covers the budgets of the Department of Defense, foreign military assistance, atomic energy, and a relatively minor group of defense-related activities. As corrected for inflation, it is shown in Figure 7. It totaled about $87 billion in current dollars in 1975. It was generally declining, in real terms, from the Vietnam war peak of the late 1960's, but appeared likely to begin to rise again about 1976.

The official defense budget does not include all the military costs, and the Joint Economic Committee of the Congress has suggested a more comprehensive definition. Some of the elements that are now omitted from the official budget but could reasonably be included are veterans' benefits and services, interests on debts for past wars (perhaps $20 billion, assuming that two-thirds of annual interest payments on the public debt are war-related), and space research and technology ($3 billion). Broadening the definition of defense along these lines could add over 40 percent to the budget as presently announced.

A comparison with GNP in 1973 showed U.S. defense spending ac-

[4] U.S. Arms Control and Disarmament Agency (ACDA), World Military Expenditures and Arms Trade, 1963–1973, p. 14.

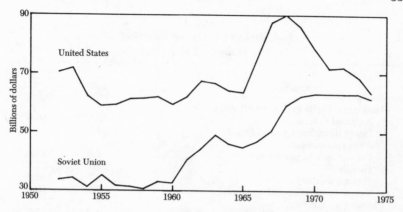

Fig. 7. U.S. and U.S.S.R. annual military expenditures, in constant 1970 dollars (*SIPRI Yearbook, 1974*, pp. 206–7, and *1975*, pp. 120–21). Earlier SIPRI yearbooks give substantially lower estimates for the Soviet Union. Secretary Schlesinger's Report to Congress on the Fiscal Year 1976 Budget (Feb. 5, 1975) shows substantially higher estimates for the Soviet Union, crossing the U.S. level in about 1970. ACDA's Soviet estimate (*World Military Expenditures and Arms Trade, 1965–74*) is higher than SIPRI's but lower than Secretary Schlesinger's, crossing the U.S. level between 1970 and 1971.

counting for about 6 percent of the gross national product under the traditional budget definition and closer to 10 percent under broader budgetary concepts. The defense share of GNP, based on the official budget, was the lowest in two decades, but double the ratio that was common in peacetime before World War II.

The ratio of defense spending to all federal government spending is another indicator frequently used in the United States. The most common approach compares the defense budget with the federal budget as a whole (Table 3). In the mid-1970's this ratio was about 24 percent, down from a Vietnam war peak of about 43 percent. This is sometimes cited as evidence of a "reordering of national priorities" in favor of "human resources."

The conclusion is accurate, but the change is not as dramatic as suggested. One reason is that Vietnam itself produced a hump. Constant-price expenditures have not fallen back to quite the pre-Vietnam level, although the proportion of the budget or of GNP has fallen back to well below the pre-Vietnam levels. Another reason is the definition problem already discussed, particularly the exclusion of veterans' benefits and interest on debts. Expenditures for veterans have been rising rapidly and are included in the "human resources" category of the budget.

Finally, there is the expansion of the budget base. The federal budget

TABLE 3

U.S. *Budget Outlays by Function*

(Billions of dollars)

Category	Fiscal years	
	1965	1975
National security and international affairs:		
National defense	49.6	86.6
International affairs and finance	4.3	4.4
Human resources:		
Education and manpower	2.3	15.2
Health	1.7	27.6
Income security	25.7	108.6
Veterans' benefits and services	5.7	16.6
Physical resources:		
Agriculture and rural development	4.8	1.7
Natural resources and environment	2.1	9.5
Commerce and transportation	7.4	16.0
Community development and housing	.3	4.4
Space research and technology	5.1	3.1
Interest	10.4	30.9
Other (net)	−1.0	0.2
Total expenditure	118.4	324.6

SOURCE: *The Budget of the U.S. Government, Fiscal Year 1965 and 1975.*

includes more than the administrative budget; it also includes large trust funds for which the government acts as caretaker or banker. Social security is the largest of these funds and is also the largest element in the human resources part of the budget. It has been growing rapidly since the 1950's, giving a major push to the overall federal budget, and to the human resources category. It is not, however, subject to annual administration reviews. The result of its increase is to make the defense budget look smaller and smaller in comparison with an enlarged budget base. Even if social security and the national debt are excluded, however, the ratio of the defense budget (as narrowly defined) to the total budget has fallen since Vietnam.

Other measures, however, show a continued preponderant role of defense in U.S. government functions, and an important role in the U.S. economy as a whole. Of the 5.1 million employees of the federal government (1974), active-duty military numbered 2.1 million and Department of Defense civilians 1.1 million. Thus, defense-related employees in the federal government were about 65 percent of all federal employment.

For a comparison with all people employed in the United States (about 88 million in 1974), defense-related jobs in private industry as well as in government must be considered. It has been roughly estimated that about another 3.5 million jobs in U.S. private industry are defense-related.[5] Adding that total to the 3.2 million in government defense jobs means that almost one person in 12 in the United States is working in the military part of the economy.

In the government sector, military R&D still takes by far the largest portion of research expenditures, even though civilian-category research has been growing. In the mid-1970's federal outlays were about $10 billion for defense R&D and under $3 billion for space, as against almost $7 billion for civilian research. In short, about 50 percent of the government's research funds still went to defense, more if space research is considered defense-related. In the economy as a whole, military R&D accounted for over a quarter of all expenditures on R&D, more if space research is added.[6]

The Soviet Union

Although U.S. military expenditures have been relatively constant (in real terms) in recent years, those of the Soviet Union probably increased rapidly over the same era, perhaps reaching a plateau in the early 1970's. This development is shown in Figure 7.

The figure should, however, be read only with great caution. It reflects attempts to correct for two major problems in interpreting the Soviet defense budget, but no one can be confident of the proper magnitude of corrections to be used.

The first problem is that the published U.S.S.R. numbers are themselves clearly incomplete. For example, military research and development are not included in the published defense budget. Moreover, the bulk of the defense industry is not subject to the Ministry of Defense. Its costs can therefore be reflected in the budgets for other ministries. Western analysts usually resolve this problem by examining the budgets of all areas to look for "residuals"—elements in overall budgets that are not explained by detailed budgets. The total of these "residuals" ranges up to over 40 percent of the stated defense budget. The analyst then estimates what portion of the residuals can be attributed to defense and adds that amount to the stated defense budget to obtain a measure comparable to the Western understanding of defense budget.

The second problem is converting the number just developed—a number stated in rubles—into dollars. There is an official dollar-ruble

---

[5] Data derived from *Statistical Abstract of the United States, 1975*, pp. 243, 321–23. The estimate of private industry defense jobs is for 1972.

[6] *Statistical Abstract of the United States, 1975*, pp. 546–48.

exchange rate. Prices in the Soviet Union are not, however, set by economic principles analogous to those of the West. Instead they are set by central planners and are designed to affect and shape the economy. Thus the relationships among wages and industrial prices can be completely different from those in the West. Trade between the East and the West does not bring the price relationships into line because trade occurs only as decided by the central planners and at prices that can be set administratively. Hence, the Western analyst has to estimate "real" exchange rates in place of the official rates. These "real" exchange rates may be different for military salaries, for military hardware, and for consumer goods. These calculations can be supplemented by efforts to inventory the Soviet military manpower and force components and to evaluate the cost of supporting an analogous establishment in the West.

It is clear, then, that the numbers of Figure 7 (and to a lesser extent their trend) are subject to considerable uncertainty. Assuming, however, that the early 1970's plateau of $63 billion is approximately correct, one can attempt to calculate ratios analogous to those of the United States.[7]

The U.S.S.R. GNP was approximately $600 billion in 1972. (The GNP estimate is subject to some of the same problems as the defense budget estimate.) Thus, the Soviet Union may be devoting over 10 percent of its GNP to defense, a ratio considerably higher than the world average.

Total military manpower was 3.37 million, about 1.3 percent of the population. This compares with about 1.1 percent in the United States and 0.6 percent in the world as a whole. Extension of the U.S.S.R. figure to allow for civilian defense officials or employment analogous to defense-industry employment is so uncertain as not to be worthwhile.

Finally, Soviet R&D levels are among the most doubtful of the numbers, because estimates rest almost entirely on the "residuals" discussed above. The 1973 total Soviet R&D expenditures were about 15.5 billion rubles—between $18 billion and $31 billion, depending on the exchange rate chosen. Estimates of military expenditures run on the order of 35–37 percent of this amount, a proportion lower than the U.S. federal government's proportion and higher than the U.S. overall proportions.

---

[7] The ratio of defense expenditures to national budget will not be estimated. Any comparison between it and Western numbers, particularly the U.S. number, would be meaningless. The Soviet government budgets include a much greater part of the society's overall economic activities than do Western government budgets. Moreover, the U.S. federal budget calculation overstates the role of defense in the overall government budget because it ignores the role of state and local governments.

Domestic Economic Processes

The aggregate data that have just been discussed show the importance of military expenditures to most societies. This importance is reflected in electoral and bureaucratic constituencies; a significant number of employment possibilities do depend on military expenditures. From the opposite viewpoint, the amount of resources that substantial arms control could free is most impressive. Nevertheless, the aggregates conceal several important phenomena that are crucial for anyone examining arms control and economics.

The Uses of Military Expenditures

The first significant phenomenon is suggested by Figure 8. Expenditures for strategic weapons form a relatively small portion of the military

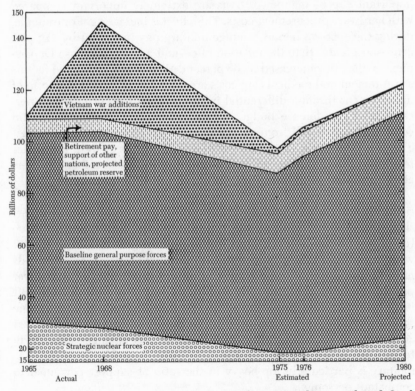

Fig. 8. Distribution of U.S. Department of Defense expenditures, selected fiscal years, in constant 1974 dollars. (Data from B. Blechman et al., *Setting National Priorities, the 1976 Budget*, Washington, D.C.: Brookings, 1975, p. 91.)

budget. What dominates the military budget are the costs of general purpose forces—the traditional Army, Navy, and Air Force functions. The figure in part simply reflects the fact that the United States has recently been modifying strategic systems rather than deploying basically new systems. Strategic expenditures, in real terms, are therefore substantially lower than those of the late 1950's and early 1960's. An upturn in the strategic area would be likely if the United States chooses to modify its strategic position heavily in the post-SALT II era. The fundamental implication of the figure is, however, correct: for arms control to affect military costs substantially, it must find ways to reduce tactical forces. (It does not necessarily follow that arms control should concentrate on tactical forces; one may reasonably argue that the cumulative efforts of sustained strategic expenditures are more dangerous.)

A different breakdown of the defense budget would show another important effect—manpower costs are extremely important compared with hardware procurement costs. This effect is increasing. For example, during the 1968–74 period, average military pay increased by 113 percent—far greater than the inflation rate—and average Defense Department civilian pay increased by 66 percent. When such additional factors as retirement and medical care costs are added, it is clear that a form of disarmament through differential inflation rates is occurring. The percentage of the defense budget available for procurement, R&D, and construction thus fell from 42 percent in 1968 to 30 percent in 1974.[8] The phenomenon is likely to occur in other societies as well. Pay scales tend to be raised to keep up with inflation and to make military careers attractive, particularly in nations in which the draft is abolished.

As noted in Chapter 4, costs of individual weapons have also been rising. These increase rates are enormous—factors of over 20 in aircraft since World War II and around 10 in destroyers, increases well above the general inflation level. Thus, with a relatively fixed budget, fewer weapons systems can be procured. In the United States, these two trends have balanced out in the direction of an increased level of manpower per combat unit. Thus, the total number of people—in the combat unit itself and in tracing, procurement and the like—needed to support one ship or one aircraft has increased by proportions often on the order of 40 percent in the 1964–74 decade.[9] Whether this balance is shared in foreign forces is not clear; there is some reason to believe that the U.S. military is particularly top-heavy in the ratio of support personnel to combatant personnel.

[8] *The Budget of the U.S. Government Fiscal Year 1975*, p. 62.

[9] E. Fried et al., *Setting National Priorities, The 1974 Budget* (Washington, D.C.: Brookings, 1973), p. 299.

Defense Procurement

Having seen that defense procurement is a part—but only a part (on the order of $30 billion in the United States in the mid-1970's)—of the defense budget, one is ready to examine the defense industry component of the military economy.

Defense spending is widely dispersed throughout the United States, but is most heavily concentrated on the West Coast and in the South. These two areas probably account for half the contract awards. The defense money flows into every industry including the service trades, but represents a significant share of total employment in relatively few—primarily ordnance, communications equipment, electronics, aircraft, and other transportation equipment.

Over two-thirds of defense prime contract awards go to 100 large contractors, some of them the giants of American business. Defense orders for most (but not all) of the top 100 represent a relatively small share of their sales volume. Much of the work is passed on to subcontractors for actual performance. Thus there is an extremely broad network of firms involved in defense business.

In many cases, the government provides plant, equipment, and working capital for the prime contractor. Manufacturers usually enjoy the added benefit of regular progress payment from the government. Moreover, in the United States, the bulk of defense contracts are awarded on a negotiated basis rather than through competitive bid. A profit, usually based on a percentage of the original bid price, is included. This profit appears relatively low as a return on sales. Nevertheless, because the manufacturer often supplies proportionately little capital, profits as a return on private investment capital tend to be higher than the average in manufacturing industry. It is this last measure that is more significant economically.

R&D plays a larger role in defense contracts than it does in most civilian industries. Compared with civilian employment in general, defense-associated employment includes relatively more professionals and skilled and semiskilled workers, fewer managers and proprietors, and appreciably fewer sales and service personnel.

This importance of research and of particularly skilled employees is a worldwide characteristic of defense industry and helps to explain the worldwide pressures to export weapons. A large research investment is needed to produce a new weapon at all. If this research investment can be spread over many sales of the new weapon, the unit price can be lowered. Even the manufacturer's government itself can purchase the weapons more cheaply if some of the production run is exported. Moreover, since each R&D and production facility requires skilled employees, governments fear that such facilities could not be established quickly in national emergencies. They therefore believe it necessary to continue giving contracts to each facility in order to have the facility ready for an emergency. Once again, if the facility can be kept operating through export sales rather than through national expenditures, so much the better. These pressures, well known in the United States, operate especially strongly on the smaller national defense industries, such as those of Western Europe.

Economic Consequences of Military Spending

How does the defense sector affect the pace of overall development? The direction in which a society grows? Innovation and new technology? In attempting to make such assessments, one is on soft ground. Military spending has often been said to be beneficial to the U.S. economy; in contrast, the relative absence of defense spending has often been said to be beneficial to the Japanese economy. Research on such critical questions as the relationship between military spending and economic growth, or the effects of military R&D on civilian technology, is limited and inconclusive. Conclusive factual evidence in support of specific conclusions is seldom available.

Clearly, the intended effect of military expenditures is an important one. These expenditures are intended to provide the protection and political stability that an economy needs to stay healthy and grow. One may question whether military expenditures are an effective way of maintaining peace. Nevertheless, in the absence of an international system of security, national forces are generally believed to have an essential role in preserving order and protecting the society and the economy.

Military expenditures also have major macro-economic effects, i.e. effects on the level of production and employment and on the growth rate of the economy. As an obvious point, they create jobs; societies ranging from that of the United States to those of developing nations often have severe underemployment problems. Nevertheless, defense expenditures may create fewer jobs than many alternative forms of public spending. For example, equivalent expenditures for health care and education provide more jobs than do military contracts. Moreover, the economic effects of public expenditure for job creation are sometimes dubious, depending, for example, on the status of the economy and on whether the public expenditures are supported through taxation or through borrowing. In particular, military expenditures may sometimes be inflationary through creating buying power without creating consumer goods and services on which the income can be spent.

There are also what economists call allocative effects. Military spending often provides roads, bridges, and dams. It puts to use plant capacity that might otherwise be idle. Nevertheless, what is built may not accord with either rational development plans or the desires of consumers. In this sense, military spending draws resources and skills away from the civilian economy. Such resources and skills are important to both developing and developed countries. Similarly, military demand takes from consumption by diminishing the quantity and quality of resources available to meet basic human needs for food, housing, and health care.

Military research has direct benefits for the civilian economy through spin-offs, new scientific or technical information that helps society in many ways. Major technological breakthroughs, such as atomic power, radar, and computers, are the result of military R&D. In these cases, military programs also often bear initial development costs, making commercial application more feasible. This technological spin-off argument, however, has been greatly overemphasized. Firms specialized for operating in a military environment often find it extremely difficult to apply their technology to the civilian market. Productive results could have been achieved more efficiently and economically if commensurate R&D outlays had been applied directly to civilian needs.

There are also many special effects depending heavily on the particular military programs and the particular sociological characteristics of the society. For example, military programs may use immense amounts of nonrenewable resources. They may encourage new approaches to production which are then transferred to the civilian society, e.g. the concept of a production line developed for Civil War military production or the concept of large-scale team research which was a by-product of World War II. On a different scale, the military often provides contact among persons from all parts of a society. Such contact was an important effect of World War II in the United States. It is an explicit goal of the military in the form of "nation building" in some of the developing nations.

Many claim that military needs are unique in their power to mobilize resources and provide an impetus to the economy. The assumption is that society is more prepared to bear a tax burden and legislators are more ready to allocate funds for military defense than for other social-economic programs. The historical record appears to give some support to this argument, at least in the United States. It is especially in the defense area that political authorities can, for example, channel contracts to depressed areas or fields of endeavor. By the same token, however, public authorities are tempted to use defense budgets unwisely as economic props or to confer economic favors. Traditionally less subject to citizen review than are social programs, defense budgets are especially susceptible to sectional and industry lobbying and to corruption, resulting in programs that are essential for neither military nor economic purposes. It is here that one can reasonably speak of a Military-Industrial (or perhaps a Military-Industrial-Congressional) Complex. Public concern about governmental honesty (which may be felt most heavily in the United States) and increased legislative willingness to support social expenditures (which is probably a worldwide phenomenon) may deprive defense spending of this privileged role as an economic tool.

The upshot of all these factors clearly leads to no general answer on the economic effect of defense spending. Any answer depends on estimates of the alternative ways the resources might be used—a political judgment fraught with difficulty—and on estimates of the employment, growth, and inflation consequences of the various alternatives— an economic judgment also fraught with difficulty. The military budget is generally viewed as buying an extremely important form of security, and it often provides valuable by-products. Nevertheless, what it buys are goods and services which often have no value to society for direct consumption purposes or for production of consumption goods in the future. In developed nations, the balance of these factors is almost certainly such that military spending decreases real economic growth. In developing nations, the balance may possibly be in the opposite direction.[10]

The International Arms Economy

The arms economies of different nations are linked. Of the various couplings, the most important one is probably the comparisons that each nation makes between its own arms level and those of other nations. The character of this arms competition phenomenon—and the arguments that the phenomenon may not be as important as is often suggested—are explored elsewhere in this book. But this coupling is not the only one.

Another substantial linkage lies in the international production of weapons. In general, the United States and the Soviet Union produce

[10] For a careful and surprising analysis including nontechnical case studies, see E. Benoit, *Defense and Economic Growth in Developing Countries* (Lexington, Mass., 1973).

their own weapons. Many smaller nations, however, are constrained to buy at least some of their weapons from abroad because their requirements are too small to support a full-scale defense industry. Nevertheless, they wish to have some defense industry, and they seek the employment benefits that come from domestic production. The result is to buy weapons from abroad with some of the manufacturing done locally, typically through an agreement in which a local industry is licensed by the original manufacturer to do part of the work. This is the pattern of the more elaborate international arms sales. Competition for the contracts is severe and often deviates from normal ethical business practices as governments seek to assist their national industry by diplomatic pressure, by providing credit, and by side deals to help the manufacturers lower prices. Moreover, military advisers will sometimes attempt to sell their own nation's equipment.

International economic factors provide other motivations for arms exports. Many nations find that selling arms is a relatively easy way to increase exports and improve their balance of payments. The most spectacular examples derive from the oil crisis, which began in 1973. During the following year, sellers of arms such as France and the United States and buyers such as Iran and Saudi Arabia entered large military sales contracts, some on the order of $10 billion over five years. In effect, the arms sellers were paying for oil with weapons.

Finally, nations often seek self-sufficiency in some aspects of military supplies, for fear that supplies might be cut off in time of crisis. This desire for self-sufficiency sometimes leads to uneconomically small national industries. It can lead to development of substitutes, such as the artificial rubber developed during World War II. It can also lead to a politics of stockpiling or protecting access to scarce resources such as oil and chromium. In many of these cases, national insecurity over the possibility of war deprives the world economy of the benefits of specialization.

Economic Consequences of Arms Control

An arms control measure may release resources for peaceful uses. These released resources, or "savings," represent the positive, or beneficial, consequences of arms control in an economic sense. There are also shorter-term economic consequences that have a more negative connotation in that they represent the readjustment of the economy to the changes that arms control requires. The term "impact of arms control" usually refers to these problems of economic adjustment.

An important requirement in estimating arms control savings is to define the two states of the world that are to be compared. One might, for example, consider post-agreement reductions in resource use for military purposes as compared with pre-agreement levels of such use. But, with some imprecision, one can compare the levels of resource use after the agreement with those that might have occurred had technology and production continued to develop as appeared likely with-⁂ out the agreement. These savings are hard to measure because future trends in prices, in weaponry, and in national procurements are quite uncertain. One can conjecture, for example, what a 4-site or 12-site ABM system might have cost the United States if there had been no SALT I agreement. In this sense, SALT I clearly saved money—a major portion of $40 billion for the 12-site system—but usually any estimate of such savings through forestalled expenditures is highly tentative. A third savings estimate could allow also for side effects. Arms control might damp down some aspects of military expenditures while leaving others uncontrolled. "Bargaining chips" might be procured during the negotiations. Each such side effect, however, will be controversial in that only some will judge it to be a cost of the arms control agreement. Others will judge that the procurement was properly justified on its own merits. When these possible side effects (ABM continuation during SALT, the B-1, the Trident) are considered, some doubt that SALT I produced any economic savings.

These savings are only potential savings; whether or not a reduction in defense spending would really result in a corresponding increase in the supply of other goods and services is itself a complex economic problem that depends on the wider economic status of the society and on the actions of governments, business, and consumers. As a small but important example, military research and development expenditures declined substantially in real terms during the 1968–72 period. Civilian R&D rose somewhat during the period but not enough to fill the gap.[11] Similarly, in the period of defense cutbacks after the Korean war, civilian public expenditures were cut as well but taxes were held high. There followed some years of slow economic growth.

The impact of an adjustment problem posed by arms control represents the effect on particular industries and communities as procurement is curtailed. It is economically indistinguishable from shifts in demand that accompany the rapid changeovers in weapons technology. In other words, adjustment to arms control is not a unique phenomenon as far as the overall economy is concerned. The economy is constantly

[11] Data derived from National Science Foundation, *National Patterns of R&D Resources, 1953–1972*, NSF 72–300, Dec. 1971.

undergoing evolutionary changes in demand which pose similar problems.

The nature of those international arms control agreements under active consideration implies a disarmament process that is more gradual than abrupt, and selective rather than broad-based. Even a gradual reduction process, however, is not without problems. In the United States and other major military powers, the relatively high concentration of arms orders in particular regions and industries suggests that the effects of defense cutbacks could be especially severe in some localities and among some types of skilled workers.

An example is provided by a detailed study of the economic effects of the SALT I treaty that was undertaken in 1972 and updated in 1974 under the auspices of the U.S. Arms Control and Disarmament Agency.[12] The study considered localized impact, effects on regions and communities in which production and deployment had been concentrated, and overall consequences for the U.S. defense budget.

Except for three areas—Huntsville, Alabama; Taunton, Massachusetts; and Conrad, Montana—the regional economic hardship caused by the treaty was found to be negligible or nonexistent. The principal reason for the limited impact on jobs in other areas was that most of the major companies involved in Safeguard were large and well diversified, and Safeguard represented a relatively small share of total business. Follow-up studies showed that two years after the treaty there had been successful readjustment for the most part in the three impacted areas. The adjustment process had been helped by federal government assistance and energetic local action. Locally run industrial development programs were under way, including an effort to convert one Safeguard site to an industrial park to provide a more stable economic base than the military installation would have. Although the study showed a generally satisfactory outcome for the communities, it also recommended more effective government planning and action to assist the transition in similar cases. In particular, it pointed to the need to identify impacts beforehand and to develop plans for alleviating them.

Various measures, described as offset programs, can be taken to ease the transition process. Offset programs could be designed more effectively for arms control agreements than for meeting structural shifts resulting from technological and civilian market changes. This is because defense orders come from one customer, government. Therefore government can develop precise information on the location and nature

[12] *The Economic Consequences of SALT I* (3 vols.), ACDA/E-224, General Research Corporation, Aug. 1973 and April 1974.

of defense impact: where the business goes and what resources it uses. Government also has advance knowledge of the nature and timing of arms control agreements that would affect the military economy. For effective policy actions, this information base is critical, although it is not yet as adequate as it could be.

Government policies in the transition period following arms control measures have two basic tasks: to maintain aggregate demand and to avert hardship to regions, industries, and individuals most affected by the disarmament agreements. To maintain aggregate demand, governments have available a variety of options, including tax reductions, expansionary monetary policy, and increases in spending on civilian programs. The choice of options and the emphasis on each will depend on the general state of the economy, as well as on public priorities and practical politics. Governments are, however, finding it more difficult to manage aggregate demand in this way without creating inflation.

To avert hardship to particular regions and industries, policy-makers could have in reserve a selection of compensatory programs. These could be designed to match, at least roughly, the resource requirements and regional patterns of the defense programs being phased out. Precise matching of that sort would not be feasible in the United States at present, since detailed information on the characteristics of offset programs compared with defense demand is not yet at hand. Approximations are, however, possible to some extent. Many economists will argue that explicit subsidy aid is a better approach. The critical barriers to any approach are those of political feasibility and doubt about the economic desirability of the offset programs in an era of combined inflation and unemployment. The political issues are suggested by the post–Korean war experience; the economic issues by the concerns of all economic decision-makers in the mid-1970's.

Substantial arms control would also produce international economic impacts as trade patterns in military goods and supplies change. The developed world would decrease its imports of some raw materials; the developing world would decrease imports of some weapons systems. The growth rate of the developed countries would be likely to increase more rapidly than that of the poorer countries under such arms control. This is because the percentage of GNP spent on arms is lower (although growing more rapidly) in the developing nations than in the developed. Moreover, the effect of arms spending may be more likely to slow economic growth in the developed than the developing world. Thus, unless there were a substantial increase in economic aid, the income gap between developed and developing nations would be likely to widen under substantial arms control. For this reason and because enormous developed-world resources could be freed through arms control, many have argued that the money not spent on arms should be spent instead on economic aid. So far, however, no such coupling has proved politically feasible.

The conclusion seems clear for both the domestic and the international aspects of arms control. In both areas, there is some doubt in the mid-1970's whether any economic problems are tractable at all. If they are tractable, the problems of adjusting to arms control are at worst complicating factors rather than decisive factors and the key limitations are those of politics rather than economics.

Budget Limitations as Arms Control Measures

The Russians, who are credited with one of the first proposals for the limitation of military expenditures—a proposal at the Hague Peace Conference in 1899 for a short-term budgetary freeze—have often suggested the concept as a relatively simple and effective way to curb the arms race. Between 1948 and 1964, the Soviet Union alone made 20 such proposals, usually to accompany provisions for the reduction of forces and armaments. The Soviet draft treaty for general and complete disarmament (GCD) provided that military expenditures would be reduced proportionately to the physical reduction in arms under the treaty, and that inspectors would be given unimpeded access to legislative and financial records. Other proposals would establish an independent agreement on budgets generally calling for a 10 to 25 percent reduction from existing levels and not spelling out verification procedures. A variant, however, was proposed by French Premier Faure in 1955, a requirement that the parties to the treaty contribute an agreed portion of the savings to foreign aid.

Despite the variety of proposals for formal multilateral agreement on budget limitation, it was an informal arrangement rather than a treaty agreement that represented the only achievement in this field during the post–World War II period. In 1963–65, the Soviet Union and the United States made a limited and tentative series of parallel moves, involving statements on each side, of their intent to limit military budgets. (The U.S. statements were made only privately.) The spirit of mutual example was reflected in the relative constancy of military expenditures in this period. Further progress was abruptly halted by developments in Vietnam; after 1965, the U.S. budget rose rapidly and the Soviet budget followed it. Secretary Brezhnev urged negotiations of reduction of military expenses in his address to the 24th Party Congress of the Soviet

Union in March 1971. Then, in 1973 the U.N. Assembly overwhelmingly approved a U.S.S.R. resolution, calling for a 10 percent reduction of the military budgets of all five permanent members of the Security Council and the allocation of a portion of the savings to development assistance. China labeled the resolution an exercise in Soviet propaganda and made clear that it would have no part of it. The United States abstained, stating that there was no common standard for measuring states' military budgets, that there was no system for verifying budget cuts, and that it was opposed to a direct linkage between budget reductions and increased aid.

The same year Mexico sponsored a resolution, also overwhelmingly approved, calling for a study by experts, and a report to the next General Assembly, on the reduction of military budgets and the allocation of part of the savings to development assistance. Despite a history of opposition to Western suggestions for experts' discussions of military budget limitations, the Soviets voted in favor of the resolution. The U.S. statement on the Mexican resolution suggested essential questions for the experts to study. The study was completed in 1974, the first international study of the concept since the World Disarmament Conference of 1932.

A key benefit of such agreements is that the central trade-offs would be relatively simple to negotiate. The interminable hassles about quality and quantity factors that arise in balance of forces agreements could be left to domestic budgetary processes. Moreover, the agreement could be comprehensive. Limiting of spending puts a restriction on research and development and on qualitative upgrading in a way that may not otherwise be practical. Finally, such limitations could actually affect the financial burdens of arms and reinforce popular support for disarmament by providing tangible benefits the public can share.

Against these advantages are very difficult verification problems and equally difficult definition problems. Nations would have to negotiate to find a common concept of what a defense budget should include. Problems of price changes, differing rates of inflation, and the relative valuation of differing national currencies would all have to be resolved.

The advantages appear likely to arise from either a formal treaty or an informal understanding; the disadvantages would be more pressing under a formal treaty than under an informal approach. Some analysts therefore favor the informal arrangements and the U.N. experts suggested a step-by-step approach. Whether the technical problems of more formal agreements are surmountable is not yet known; budget limitations have been a relatively neglected area of study.

CHAPTER TWELVE

Regional Arms Control: The European Example

REGIONAL ARMS control arrangements are often suggested as a step toward global arrangements and as a way to defuse specific areas of conflict. Among those seriously proposed have been a number of European arrangements, nuclear free zones in Latin America, the Mediterranean, the Mideast, Africa, and the Indian Ocean Zone of Peace. The only one of these proposals to eventuate in full agreement is the Latin American Nuclear Free Zone, which will be discussed in Chapter 14 on nuclear proliferation. The European area, however, has been the subject of a long series of negotiations and will be discussed here as a case study in regional arms control.

Other regions would reveal different phenomena because political motivations toward arms control differ drastically among different regions. The European case shows an interplay of traditional U.S.-U.S.S.R. arms control motivations—reducing costs, defusing potential conflicts, confirming détente—with a more complex pattern of motivations on the part of the regional nations—protecting borders, supporting traditional strategic interests, shaping détente for national benefit. Traditional alliances and their possible evolution dominate the politics of this example. In some of the other cases, however, the role of alliances and of the superpowers is much weaker. For example, the concept of the Indian Ocean Zone of Peace is essentially an effort to keep the influence of the United States and the Soviet Union out of the area. The relative roles of détente, great power diplomacy, regional power diplomacy, and U.N. diplomacy will clearly differ radically in such a case.

Regional arms control is also at the frontier of what is commonly called arms control. It shades into arms-control-like arrangements that evolve from traditional diplomacy. The Cuban missile crisis, for example, produced an "agreement" that the United States would not attack Cuba and the Soviet Union would not introduce missiles into Cuba. The latter commitment was even verified unilaterally. Similarly, several of the Arab-Israeli interim resolutions included provisions that forces would be thinned or withdrawn from defined cease-fire lines and provided for U.N. observers to verify these commitments. These arrangements are logically indistinguishable from arms control.

The European Background

At the conclusion of World War II, the peoples of Western Europe deeply desired to avoid another holocaust. Unfortunately, they could not simply sit back and hope that war weariness would be enough to maintain peace. The rapid transformation of the states of Eastern Europe into Soviet satellites in the first three years after the war, particularly the Communist takeover in Czechoslovakia in 1948, made it appear likely that Soviet power would be projected into Western Europe as well. If it were, there would presumably be resistance and war, but war in the worst possible circumstances. British and American troops had been largely withdrawn from Western Europe, and the existing armies of the other Western European countries would be powerless to stop a major Soviet attack. Europeans talked bleakly in 1948 of the possibility of a swift Russian conquest of the entire continent, a belated response by the United States and Great Britain, and then a bloody liberation of Western Europe by the Western allies—a process that would again devastate all Europe.

To prevent such a development, the Western European governments (Great Britain, Belgium, the Netherlands, Luxembourg, and France) committed themselves to mutual defense by signing the Brussels Treaty in March 1948. Later that year President Truman endorsed the purpose of the Brussels Treaty, and negotiations were started that ultimately led to the North Atlantic Treaty Organization (NATO). The NATO Treaty was signed in April 1949 by the five powers at Brussels plus Denmark, Norway, Italy, Portugal, Iceland, Canada, and the United States. Greece and Turkey acceded in 1952. West Germany acceded in 1954, as described below. Created as a defensive body, NATO was designed to preserve peace not by reducing arms but by building them up and by threatening a U.S. nuclear response to any U.S.S.R. attack on Western Europe.

Rearmament of Germany and the Failure of the Initial Arms Control Response

From the beginning, NATO was plagued with problems. The West Europeans were hesitant to expand their conventional forces, and it did not prove easy to reach the combined military strength that strategists thought necessary to deter the Russians. These problems prompted decisions to deploy American troops in the NATO line of battle and to impose an American-controlled command structure; to rearm Germany, a decision hedged by the integration of German forces into NATO and by a German commitment not to build nuclear weapons; and to deploy tactical nuclear weapons as part of NATO's weaponry.

Politically, the most significant of these steps was the rearmament of Germany. It followed an effort, at a time when dreams of Western European political unification were strong, to create a unified Western European army, the European Defense Community. By subordinating its arms to such unified structure, West Germany could rearm against the Soviet Union without creating Western fear of its power. Nevertheless, in 1954 the French Assembly defeated these plans for the European Defense Community. The French action promised to cause complete disarray in NATO's plans for European defense, but this threat was removed by skillful diplomatic maneuvers by Sir Anthony Eden and the British Foreign Office, assisted behind the scenes by Secretary of State John Foster Dulles. The result was the rearmament of Germany through the London and Paris Treaties of 1954, which admitted West Germany to NATO through amendment of the Brussels Treaty and authorized Bonn to raise an army of 500,000 men.

From the Eastern viewpoint, the resulting situation was quite dangerous. The Soviet Union had not lost its fear of German militarism and was probably pleased that World War II had left Germany divided. It not only feared German rearmament; it also feared German reunification, an often-stated political goal of Konrad Adenauer, the Chancellor of West Germany from 1949 to 1963. And Poland had special additional reasons to fear Germany: in the territorial settlement imposed on Eastern Europe after World War II, the Soviet Union had taken some of Poland's prewar eastern territory and compensated Poland by giving it the part of prewar Germany east of the Oder-Neisse line. Thus, Germany had territorial claims against Poland—claims that Adenauer still formally asserted on behalf of the future unified Germany, whose division he did not accept.

The Eastern response was two-pronged: to form a military alliance, the Warsaw Pact, analogous to NATO but more centralized, and to propose a series of disarmament arrangements and European settlements. As already discussed in Chapter 5, these proposals, initiating in the mid-1950's, may have indicated a fundamental shift in Soviet attitudes toward disarmament. Nevertheless, they were also designed to benefit the Eastern position in Europe. Thus, the typical pattern would include the elimination of foreign bases, the withdrawal of occupying forces from Germany, a nonaggression pact between NATO and Warsaw Pact countries, a "significant reduction" of great-power forces in NATO and Warsaw Pact countries, and the permanent denuclearization of Germany. The military components of such proposals were oriented substantially toward reduction of Western power in Germany. The nonaggression pact was viewed as a way to obtain Western acquiescence in the division of Germany and in the new Polish boundary on the Oder-Neisse line. These issues were central to all the general debates on arms control of the mid-1950's.

In response, British Prime Minister Eden in 1955 proposed the establishment of a system for controlling armaments in Germany and neighboring countries and the creation of a demilitarized zone between the East and West, but only as part of a general plan for German reunification. For the West, the questions of European security and German reunification were "two sides of a single coin."

Polish Foreign Minister Rapacki then in 1957 presented the first of a series of proposals for regional arms control measures for Europe. He suggested the denuclearization of East and West Germany, Poland, and Czechoslovakia, and again suggested a nonaggression pact between NATO and Warsaw Pact countries. Although there was considerable British interest, the United States, France, and West Germany rejected the Rapacki Plan as tending to perpetuate the division of Germany, and as too limited in scope to provide a dependable basis for the security of Europe or for reducing the danger of nuclear war. The United States also argued that the Rapacki Plan would create a serious military imbalance by eliminating Western nuclear weapons in Germany without restricting the widely deployed conventional and nuclear forces of the Soviets.

Variants were suggested in the early 1960's. In 1963 Polish Communist leader Gomulka proposed a freeze on nuclear armaments in Central Europe, but this was opposed by West Germany, which stated in 1965 that it would consent to such an agreement only if the agreement provided for effective control, preserved the overall balance of power, and was linked with substantial progress in the solution of political problems in Central Europe. In 1964 the Soviets emphasized the reduction and eventual withdrawal of all foreign troops stationed in Europe. The West refused to accept the concept except as part of a larger package. In part the West feared that the Soviet Union, geographically closer to Europe, would be in a better strategic position to move back into Central Europe on short notice than the United States. Western opposition also reflected the fears of some European leaders that special areas of limitation in Europe could lead to discrimination among different European nations and to the demilitarization and neutralization of Europe.

The decline of these negotiations was probably a result of the general strategic climate and of their inherent difficulty: the problems of tactical force balance and of satisfying many nations made agreement design much more complex than in the strategic area. The Americans and the Soviets soon found it both easier and more rewarding to negotiate bilaterally about more technical issues as they shifted their attention to the agreements of the 1960's. But the key barriers in the late 1950's were clearly the Western preferences for security through alliance over security through agreement and for linking the reunification of Germany with arms control, preferences in which the West followed Adenauer's lead.

Germany may have been a serious concern to the East. But recurrent crises provoked by the East over Berlin—a Western island in the middle of East Germany—continually reminded West Germany also of the danger of its position. In the face of this danger, Adenauer was convinced that the only way to maintain peace and eventually usher in a general détente was by following a policy of strength and Western European unity. He worked hard to win Western permission to rearm his country within the framework of a Western defense system, and it was a proud day for him when the Federal Republic was brought into NATO in 1955.

This policy was *not* unanimously supported by the German people. In the eyes of many Germans, particularly of the younger citizens, any form of German rearmament—within an international body or not— was anathema. In 1954, as the issue of rearmament reached a head, indignation meetings sprouted throughout Germany. The Defense Minister tried to argue in favor of rearmament in a public meeting in Munich and beer steins were hurled at him. Thoughtful people argued that if Germany really did become a member of NATO the result would be to invite a Soviet attack. NATO would be unable to resist, and Germany would either be devastated or, at least, be divided indefinitely, leaving Berlin permanently exposed.

German public concern over Adenauer's policy increased after NATO's decision to deploy tactical nuclear weapons. The United States introduced these weapons in 1953, followed by Soviet ground force adoption in 1957. The NATO maneuvers of 1955 tested the capabilities of tactical nuclear weapons against enemy bases and lines of communication: some 3,000 planes flew simulated sorties and dropped 335 simulated bombs. Observers calculated that if the raids had really taken place, 1,700,000 Germans would have been killed, 3,500,000 wounded, and an unknown number affected by radiation. Played up in the press, these figures horrified the German public and seemed to prove the utter pointlessness of rearming Germany and the senselessness of NATO's strategy, which was, according to Field Marshal Montgomery, to resort to atomic weapons immediately in any attack. Why then raise 500,000 troops? The government did not persuade its critics by arguing that having troops available would make immediate resort to nuclear weapons unnecessary.

It was in the midst of this debate that the East was making its proposals for disengagement and arms control. Chancellor Adenauer rejected them almost immediately as Soviet maneuvers to destroy NATO and to prepare the way for Soviet domination of Europe. The Socialists were more receptive. The right way to reduce the possibility of interstate friction was political, the Socialists argued, and they continued to discuss disengagement until late 1958, when Khrushchev's note on Berlin and a subsequent crisis undercut their beliefs that the Soviets were ready to make political concessions on Germany.

Moreover, in July 1958 the Chancellor's party had received a majority in a vote in North Rhine–Westphalia, a region that includes one-third of all the voters in the Federal Republic. One observer said, "The majority of the voters of North Rhine–Westphalia have announced that their confidence in Adenauer is greater than their fear of misuse of atomic weapons." German rearmament went forward.

The champions of Adenauer's policy argued that his efforts and his stubbornness sensibly strengthened NATO and to this extent prevented the outbreak of war; that his pro-French tendency, which culminated in the French-German Alliance of January 1963, laid the ghost of an old enmity that had caused repeated wars in the past; and that his efforts in building up the West European community promised, if carried further, to supplement NATO's essentially military functions with useful new instruments of collaboration. The critics of his policy pointed out that his policy could not and did not intimidate the Russians or persuade them to change their position in any way on vital German issues. Nevertheless, his position was accepted, the possibility of reunification was stalemated, Berlin was still a center of recurrent crisis, and the East's arms control proposals failed.

The Era of Alliance Weakening and Non-Proliferation Negotiations

Despite the National Assembly's defeat of the treaty creating the European Defense Community in 1954 and France's inability to keep its NATO contingent at agreed strength, there was no question of France's loyalty to the alliance during the early 1950's. Nevertheless, the forces leading to an independent policy were developing and would lead first France and later much of Europe to a more flexible policy than that of Dulles and Adenauer.

The critical event was probably the Suez crisis of 1956, in which France and England, together with Israel, invaded the Suez Canal area of Egypt. The action had not been cleared with the United States, and both the United States and the Soviet Union reacted sharply and forced France and England to withdraw their troops. The crisis occurred at almost exactly the same time as the Soviet invasion of Hungary, whose liberalization went too far for the Soviet leadership; perhaps for this reason no U.S.-U.S.S.R. rapprochement resulted from their joint Suez position. But the United States and its European allies found that their interests were no longer strictly parallel.

France was finding additional reasons to diverge from U.S. policy. England had worked with the United States in the World War II program to build nuclear weapons, and had gone on to test its own weapons. France, however, was not the beneficiary of close cooperation with the United States in the development of nuclear weapons. In France during the 1950's, the lower-level officials in charge of the nuclear power program kept open an option to develop nuclear weapons. Successive governments accepted this lower-level activity, and France conducted its first nuclear test in 1960 after General de Gaulle came to power. This interest in nuclear weapons colored its arms control positions, even though it participated fully in negotiations of the early and mid-1950's. One of France's consistent positions during this period was that a nuclear test ban would be unacceptable unless coupled with a halt of the existing nuclear powers' production of fissionable materials for weapons purposes. Otherwise, it argued, nuclear arms control would be simply a way for the current nuclear nations to protect their monopoly rather than a step toward world disarmament. As it became clear that the United States and the Soviet Union were seriously considering a separable nuclear test ban, France lost interest in arms control negotiations. By 1962, General de Gaulle decided not to participate in the Geneva Conference.

De Gaulle, however, went further. From the time of his assumption of power in 1958, the General had made clear his dissatisfaction with the predominant role of the United States in NATO. Within a few months, he told U.S. Secretary of State Dulles that France would shortly become a nuclear power and urged on the United States a proposal for cooperative strategic planning on a worldwide scale by the United States, Great Britain, and France. President Eisenhower rejected the proposal, concerned about the reaction of other allies to such an arrangement.

With the failure of this effort, De Gaulle proceeded to develop a French deterrent force. He may have persuaded himself that the Western allies were unreliable. Certainly he believed that an American force, or even a NATO force under American control, was not the best way of deterring a Soviet attack on France or even on Europe as a whole. The use of American nuclear weapons to defend Europe was unlikely, he argued, because it would invite Soviet retaliation and devastation of the United States. Thus, in a press conference in 1963, he said:

In these conditions, no one in the world—particularly no one in America—can say if, where, when, how, and to what extent the American nuclear weapons would be employed to defend Europe. Moreover, this does not in the least prevent the American nuclear weapons from remaining the essential guarantee of world peace. . . . But it remains that the American nuclear power does not necessarily and immediately meet all the eventualities concerning Europe and France.

De Gaulle's emphasis on an independent nuclear deterrent for France was attributed by many to vanity. That the General possessed his share of this quality is doubtless correct. It is also likely that his rather old-fashioned nationalism—his belief in France's natural superiority and its right, in consequence, to complete equality of status with the super-powers—influenced him in following the nuclear course. But his thinking was probably more complicated than that. A man who is considered to have been one of De Gaulle's chief military strategists, General André Beaufre, later articulated what may have been at the bottom of De Gaulle's decision. Even if one could count upon American support in the event of a Soviet attack, Beaufre argued, it might come belatedly. American strategy at that time, with its emphasis on second-strike capacity and on centralized command and control arrangements, tended to downgrade the use of deterrence to defend Europe. To the extent that the United States was giving the impression that it would not strike first in response to a conventional Soviet attack in Europe and was reinforcing this impression by adopting a graduated response strategy, it had, according to Beaufre, created a dangerous instability at the non-nuclear level. This instability could invite a conventional Soviet attack. This is probably what De Gaulle was talking about when he said that "the American nuclear power does not necessarily and immediately meet all the eventualities concerning Europe and France." If the nuclear response was to be forthcoming, it would have to come from Europe. Only Europe's nuclear capacity could restabilize the balance in areas vital to Europe. France would provide this by creating an independent *force de frappe*. Nor would this be a negligible weapon. "The French force," De Gaulle said, "from the very beginning of its establishment, will have the sombre and terrible capability of destroying in a few seconds millions and millions of men. This fact cannot fail to have at least some bearing on the intents of any possible aggressor."

At the same time, De Gaulle argued, so long as the Western stand was firm and unequivocal in the face of Soviet threats, there would be no real danger of war in Europe. Once firmness were demonstrated, it would be possible to work toward a real détente that would solve other problems and in the end transform Europe into a continent of free nations. This was to be accomplished, De Gaulle believed, by Europeans, not by Americans. If Western Europe were to become a truly independent power and not a mere adjunct of the United States, the basis for a properly European cooperation would have to be laid. This would not necessarily mean the end of Atlantic cooperation, but it would certainly imply that Western Europe was independent of American strategic power and American leadership, and was capable of dealing as an equal with the Soviet Union. This would facilitate an approach to the Soviet Union, which, caught between the United States and China, would eventually have to admit that it too was European.

In 1966 De Gaulle went still further and announced France's military withdrawal from NATO. He did not, however, withdraw from the political alliance, which he continued to believe was valid and would assist France in case of attack. He did take French army and navy units out of NATO and force it to move its headquarters from Paris to Brussels, with a consequent loss in NATO's manpower, logistical support, and strategic depth.

De Gaulle and his successors carried out his military plans. By the 1970's, the French nuclear force consisted of nine squadrons of Mirage-IV, as well as 18 land-based medium-range missiles and two nuclear submarines, each carrying 16 missiles. France was also examining MIRV technology and in 1974 was equipping some of its land forces with tactical nuclear missiles. One may argue about the strategic importance of small nuclear forces. The total *force de frappe* comprised 86 carriers containing a total of about 21 megatons—inferior in number of warheads to one advanced U.S. submarine and in explosive power to the four

10-megaton bombs carried by one B-52. Nevertheless, particularly after the ABM Treaty, the force may well be enough to deter attack upon France.

And De Gaulle rounded out his strategic concept by diplomatic openings to the East, to both Moscow and Peking, seeking trade relationships and frequent meetings. The Soviet Union, driven perhaps by the hope of dividing NATO or perhaps by the need to come to terms with an increasingly powerful Western Europe, proved willing to participate.

For the United States, France's new diplomacy posed the problem of nuclear proliferation. The United States wanted to ensure that NATO would have access to nuclear weapons under United States control, but wanted also to keep other nations and particularly Germany from following France's lead. It improved NATO consultation arrangements on nuclear targeting, thus giving the European nations less reason to build their own nuclear weapons. Another approach, which the United States sought to protect in its non-proliferation negotiations with the Soviet Union, was to create a multilateral nuclear force with its European allies. Such a force would control European nuclearization, just as the European Defense Community, a decade earlier, might have controlled German rearmament. Although it was later abandoned, the new concept heavily colored U.S.-European relationships, particularly during the Kennedy years.

Great Britain's policies were essentially unchanged. It had always accepted American membership in and leadership of NATO as absolutely necessary. This acceptance dated back to 1946–47, when Great Britain had to appeal to Washington to take over the burden of maintaining the security of Greece and Turkey against Soviet pressure. After the 1956 debacle in the Suez, Britain's strategy became largely subordinated to America's, a fact illustrated all too plainly during the Bermuda Conference in December 1962, when Prime Minister Harold Macmillan agreed to a U.S. technical decision to abandon the Skybolt program, which would have supplied England with missiles. Instead England would receive Polaris submarine missiles. The British submarines armed with these missiles were to be assigned, along with British bombers, to the joint NATO multilateral force that never came to fruition. Macmillan's critics at home accused him of surrendering Britain's independence in military affairs. But, given Britain's economic difficulties and its still far-flung responsibilities in the world, there was no acceptable alternative. If peace was to be preserved in Europe, it had to be accomplished by NATO under American leadership and backed by American nuclear power. This was the view of the Conservative government of Macmillan, and was not substantially changed when the Labour government of Harold Wilson assumed power in 1964. In spite of some doubts about the British nuclear program that it had expressed during the election campaign, Labour continued the nuclear program, as have all successor governments, despite a continuing reduction in Britain's conventional forces and commitments. England built four nuclear submarines, buying the missiles and some of the electronics from the United States but building the submarines and the nuclear warheads itself. This force is subordinate to NATO command, but England has the right to withdraw it when "supreme national interests" are at stake. In addition, England has a number of aircraft with nuclear capability.

In Germany, in contrast, the traditional policies began to change. Even Adenauer's last Foreign Minister, Gerhard Schröder, began to feel that Adenauer's strategy had outworn its usefulness and that something new must be tried. The long-term aftermath of the building of the Berlin Wall in August 1961 and of the Cuban missile crisis was a lowering of tension in Europe and a widespread belief that the Cold War might be ending. Schröder's views were felt even more strongly by Willy Brandt, leader of the Socialist Party, and they were put into effect when Brandt became Foreign Minister in the Grand Coalition government that came to power in 1966. Brandt did not immediately reverse Adenauer's policies and he firmly subscribed to the belief that German security depended upon NATO. Nevertheless, his policy, both during the Brandt-Kiesinger coalition government and later in the Socialist–Free Democratic Party government that came to power in October 1969, showed new movement and independence from the United States.

The policy changed only slowly on nuclear weapons. Germany showed some interest in the multilateral force; some U.S. critics have argued that the concept actually increased Germany's interest in nuclear weapons. Nevertheless, Germany went along with the abandonment of the force. The non-proliferation treaty itself first came up for discussion during this period of transition. The German government regarded the draft treaty as an instance of the superpowers negotiating over the heads of Europeans. It also argued publicly against the technological handicaps that a non-proliferation treaty might impose upon West Germany's atomic energy program. But, by 1967, Germany generally, if reluctantly, accepted the idea of the Non-Proliferation Treaty. When Brandt became Foreign Minister, he pushed the treaty, almost as a first step of *Ostpolitik*, a program of diplomatic moves toward the East designed to test all of the opportunities available for broadening the prevailing détente and for advancing toward German unification and a Berlin settlement. Germany signed the treaty in November 1969, and ratified it in 1975 after the completion of negotiations on International Atomic Energy Agency inspection.

Toward Negotiations: West European Unification, Détente, and Ostpolitik

Ostpolitik was perhaps the most important of the changes that made renewed regional arms control discussions possible in the early 1970's, but it was not the only one. In France, General de Gaulle neared the end of his rule as he faced workers' strikes and student riots in May 1968. Despite artful political maneuvers, he held on only until April of the following year. De Gaulle's successor as President, Georges Pompidou, immediately announced that he intended to follow De Gaulle's policies, but it did not take long for Pompidou, supported by Brandt, to approve Great Britain's entry into the European Common Market on January 1, 1973. Less than a decade earlier, De Gaulle, pointing to the Skybolt cancellation, had argued that Great Britain could never be independent of the United States and would always be a barrier to the political unity envisaged as eventually growing from the Common Market. But now England entered the market; its commitment would be successfully tested in the June 1975 referendum, and the concept of a European community was firmly in place.

A pattern of growing Western European independence was expressed in a series of disagreements with the United States, primarily over economic policy, but by 1973 over issues as crucial to security as the approach to take to the Mideast conflict. Europe feared antagonizing its Arab oil suppliers and refused to permit the United States to use European bases to supply Israel. These tensions were reinforced by the U.S.-U.S.S.R. bilateral SALT and détente diplomacy, which Europe feared would ignore its interests. France took the lead in European criticism of U.S.-U.S.S.R. bilateral arrangements, most heavily criticizing the San Clemente declaration of June 1973, which, it feared, amounted to a no-first-use agreement that would destroy the credibility of the U.S. nuclear guarantee to Western Europe. Europeans began to argue that they would have to enter into the arms control negotiations to ensure that their interests were protected.

Ostpolitik, however, was the critical new step. Brandt had evidently decided to abandon past claims to the territory east of the Oder-Neisse line and to the continued formal unity of the two Germanys. Instead he would seek to negotiate toward the ultimate goal of German unification, starting from the situation of the world as it was. His position reflected a new realism and an increased doubt about the effectiveness of the Adenauer policies on the credibility of the U.S. commitment. The opening salvo in his new campaign was to visit Erfurt in East Germany in March 1970 to begin talks with Willi Stoph, the chairman of East Germany's Council of Ministers. As Brandt stated on May 21, 1970, these talks were designed to lead to a "treaty regulating relations between the two States in Germany, improving contacts between the populations of the two States, and helping to eliminate existing disadvantages." The atmosphere of enthusiasm and hope that surrounded the Brandt-Stoph talks was somewhat dampened as they resumed in Kassel, West Germany, two months later, but there was nevertheless a widespread belief in Germany that something important was happening. As the Hamburg *Die Zeit* said in a headline, "After Erfurt everything is different."

Over the next several years the initiative bore fruit. German Foreign Minister Walter Scheel and Soviet Foreign Minister Gromyko signed a treaty renouncing the use of force in the two nations' mutual relations. The momentum achieved through the "blitz" diplomacy was continued through a West German treaty with Poland, designed to normalize relations between the two nations on the basis of German renunciation of its claims to the former German territory east of the Oder-Neisse line. The new agreements were ratified in May 1972. (Talks had proceeded toward an analogous treaty with Czechoslovakia, but were stalled until 1973.) The climax came in 1972—in a treaty initialed in November with East Germany. This treaty was preceded by an important accord among the four World War II occupying powers (France, Great Britain, the United States, and the Soviet Union) still formally supervising Berlin. The East German treaty gave rise to a brutal political battle in Bonn, but was finally ratified. It opened the way to normalization of relations between the two Germanys and their participation in the United Nations, beginning in the 1973 session.

Brandt's Ostpolitik thus enjoyed much more success than had De Gaulle's "Free Europe to the Urals" policy or Adenauer's more military policy. It brought a flexibility of maneuver into European diplomacy that had been lacking in the 20 years of Cold War and alliance-building. Nowhere was this more true than in Eastern Europe. East Germany had been, in effect, recognized. Poland's territorial anxieties were alleviated. The Eastern European nations felt freed to begin to formulate constructive policies. They had been reminded of their lack of freedom by the 1968 Soviet invasion of Czechoslovakia and the Brezhnev doctrine under which the Soviet Union asserted the right to intervene in any Socialist nation to protect socialism. But they felt that Ostpolitik had opened up new maneuvering room for their policies, and they sensed the economic competition of the enlarging Common Market.

This is the background against which the East and West practically stumbled into two parallel negotiations, the Conference on Security and Cooperation in Europe (CSCE) and the Mutual Force Reduction (MFR) talks. Responding to its traditional interests of a pre-Ostpolitik era, the East had proposed a security conference as early as 1967. Presumably such a conference would deal with the legitimization of the European order and the status of Germany. The West, acting through NATO, opposed the concept for the traditional reasons that had motivated Adenauer and Dulles and suggested force reduction talks instead. By 1970, it had become clear that the West would participate in a security conference only if there were parallel force reduction talks. The West was also becoming interested in force reduction talks because of fear that the U.S. Congress would make unilateral reductions in the U.S. forces in Europe. Many Americans believed that the current levels of U.S. forces in Europe were no longer needed in an era of détente, that balance-of-payment problems and domestic needs required a substantial reduction in U.S. overseas forces, and that the European allies should make a more substantial contribution to their own defense. There was corresponding pressure in Congress for unilateral reductions, resulting in the Mansfield amendment, which would have required a cut in U.S. overseas forces.

If the Western leadership was willing to negotiate out of fear of the U.S. Congress, the Eastern leadership must also have sensed the same fear. The East had looked upon Western interest in force reduction talks as an attempt to stall the security conference, but Brezhnev announced a more positive position in the spring of 1971—just in time for the Mansfield amendment's U.S. opponents to make the argument that bilateral reductions were possible and would be better than unilateral reductions. The amendment was defeated. Brezhnev may have reasoned that passage of the Mansfield amendment would so frighten an increasingly independent and economically powerful Europe that Europe itself might become a formidable military opponent.

As the success of the Ostpolitik became clear, the obvious trade-off was arranged during Kissinger's visit to Moscow in September 1972. Preparatory talks for a security conference were to begin in November 1972 and preliminary discussion on force reductions in January 1973.

Conference on Security and Cooperation in Europe

The East's desired agenda for the security conference had been formulated at a conference of foreign ministers of the Warsaw Pact in

January 1972, and included three subjects. The first was a set of principles such as nonintervention and respect for sovereignty. These principles, which would have effectively confirmed East Germany's status and the post–World War II German borders, had been the original thrust of Eastern interest in a security conference. Because of Ostpolitik, they were now much less controversial, at least vis-à-vis Germany. They did, however, contain the potentially sensitive issue of the Brezhnev doctrine and intervention in Eastern Europe. Probably, however, only Rumania had any serious hopes that the principles could help protect Eastern Europe against the Soviet Union. The second subject area was less controversial: economic, technological, scientific, and cultural exchange. The third subject area was establishment of a permanent organization to further European security. This would presumably be a way to begin to transcend the existing bloc organization; it might also help weaken NATO. The Soviet hopes of weakening NATO were not absurd: the United States did not fully support Ostpolitik; France sought a more independent Europe; all tended to weaken alliance commitments during times of détente.

The West's proposed agenda included areas similar to the first two of the Eastern proposal but had a different third point: the freer movement of people, ideas, and information. This was an attack on the Iron Curtain; it was also an approach to creating the underlying contacts that could ultimately transcend the bloc patterns of Europe.

Preliminary discussions were held in Helsinki from November 1972 until June 1973 and were ratified at the foreign minister level in July. Participation included nearly the whole of Europe plus the United States and Canada. The West held firm and was successful in maintaining the free movement topic on the agenda. The result was a plan for a second stage to begin at Geneva at the specialist level in three commissions. The results would then be approved in a third stage at the foreign minister level at least—planned at the time for 1974.

The three commissions would roughly follow the Western agenda. The first commission had the task or "basket" of developing a statement of principles on international conduct. Gromyko made it quite clear, however, that these principles would not give the West any right to interfere in future Eastern European disputes. The first commission was also to deal with "confidence-building measures"—arms-control-like measures such as prior notification procedures for large military maneuvers and the exchange of foreign observers for such maneuvers. The limits of CSCE responsibility were carefully defined in this area out of sensitivity to the French, who participated in the CSCE as a natural extension of their traditional diplomacy but still refused to participate in the MFR talks as too close to arms control. The second commission would deal with economic and technological cooperation. The third commission had responsibility for cultural cooperation and the very sensitive issues of free movement and communication. The institutional follow-on issue was left to a coordinating committee.

The CSCE meeting had great symbolic importance for the Soviet Union as a kind of peace treaty to settle World War II and legitimize the Soviet position in Eastern Europe. Nevertheless, after accepting the free movement issue as an agenda item, the East hardened its substantive position on the issue itself. The issue was a crucial one for those Eastern governments that felt their stability depended on public conformity; the Soviet Union itself was hardening its position against internal dissenters.

Brezhnev, however, strongly sought a heads-of-state ceremony to sign such an agreement, perhaps for internal political reasons almost like those in U.S. politics. Nearly every communiqué issued on the occasion of a major East-West visit or summit called for such a meeting. After several postponements and much last-minute negotiation, the West agreed to hold such a ceremony in Helsinki. The East made some concession on free movement, but the force of these concessions was weakened by agreement that the document would not be legally binding. Thirty-five nations signed the 30,000 word document on August 1, 1975. Most of the Conference on Security and Cooperation in Europe, Final Act, was platitudinous; provisions were, however, included for notification of military maneuvers exceeding a total of 25,000 troops.

Mutual Force Reduction

Although the preparatory talks for MFR began in November 1972, they were soon adjourned until the end of January, and then lasted until June 1973. The delay reflected what are perhaps best described as several important tests of will.

One such test of will was over the title of the conference. Prior to this session, the West had been using the title Mutual and Balanced Force Reduction talks. The Soviets objected to the term "balanced," as suggesting that the East might have to cut its forces more than the West. The United States first refused to drop the term but finally conceded and then had difficulty persuading its allies. The new term, Mutual Reduction of Forces and Armaments and Associated Measures in Central Europe (MURFAAMCE), or Mutual Force Reductions (MFR) for short, was not fully accepted until Brezhnev's summit trips in the late spring. Apparently, however, the terminology discussion was the occasion for

Western agreement upon the objectives to be pursued during the talks. The second test of will was over the membership of the planned conference. The West had sought to include seven Western nations—the United States, Great Britain, Canada, West Germany, Holland, Belgium, and Luxembourg—and five Eastern nations—the Soviet Union, Poland, East Germany, Czechoslovakia, and Hungary. The Soviet Union objected to the inclusion of Hungary, because this would include Soviet troops in Hungary—and therefore all its troops deployed abroad—among those theoretically subject to negotiation. In contrast, it argued, only some of the U.S. troops deployed abroad were included in the negotiation. Therefore, if Hungary was included, Italy should also be included. The compromise was to create two classes of members. A first class consisted of the West's original list less Hungary and would participate fully in the meeting. The second class included Denmark, Greece, Italy, Norway, Turkey, Belgium, Bulgaria, and Rumania, with Hungary as a special-status nation whose status would be questioned by the West at a later date. This class would have the right to address subjects under discussion but not to raise new subjects. The compromise thus protected the Soviet Union from embarrassing proposals that might be raised by Rumania. It also essentially recognized the Soviet position on Hungary. The United States' NATO allies strenuously objected to the compromise, pointing to the strategic importance of the Soviet forces in Hungary, but conceded under U.S. and U.S.S.R. pressure.

The military picture in central Europe was generally assumed to favor the Warsaw Pact. Although other figures are often cited, the estimate used in Western presentations was that, in the central region, NATO had 777,000 ground forces (including 193,000 U.S. troops) and the Warsaw Pact had 925,000 ground forces (including 496,000 U.S.S.R. troops). Again on the central front, NATO had 6,000 tanks and the Warsaw Pact had 15,500 tanks. The actual numbers, however, are uncertain. They are also dependent on how each side's support troops and the troops of the East European nations are counted. Moreover, the numbers would change rapidly during mobilization. There are many other asymmetries. The characteristics of corresponding Eastern and Western aircraft, tanks, and even military division structures are radically different. Resupply and redeployment capabilities are different—across the Atlantic in one case and across Eastern Europe in the other. Tactics are different —the East was deployed for rapid offensive war; the West for a longer defensive war and in a geographical pattern that dated back to the occupation of Germany after World War II. Moreover, in some areas—for example, anti-tank capabilities—military technology was changing so rapidly that force balances accurate for one year could become imbalanced a few years later. Finally, the level of agreement among experts on the likely outcome of a tactical engagement was much less than for strategic engagements. The task of formulating rational balances or making trade-offs among different kinds of forces was therefore much more difficult than with SALT.

Not surprisingly, it proved difficult for either side to define intelligible negotiating objectives. In the West, some did believe that the MFR talks could lead to measures that would improve Western security or make escalation of accidental conflict less likely. Most European leaders, however, had the same reservations voiced in the past about the small prospects for improvement in the Western security position in Europe as a result of arrangements limited to Europe. Many leaders seriously feared a "Finlandization," a need to adjust their policies to U.S.S.R. desires, particularly in the wake of SALT's recognition of strategic parity. Britain under Labour and Germany under Brandt were the only substantial supporters of MFR. Otherwise, it was political concern about possible Congressionally imposed U.S. withdrawals, rather than a great anticipation of improved Western security arrangements, that motivated the West to begin MFR negotiations. To a lesser extent, parallel European concerns about public support for the rising cost of maintaining forces in Europe may have contributed to European interest in MFR. Although their doubts had not yet been expressed in major Parliamentary debate, West European publics tended to regard the Communist threat much less seriously than their leaders.

The NATO countries therefore professed a goal of achieving a more stable military balance in Europe at lower levels of force while maintaining undiminished security for all parties. In some respects, forces were still deployed in Europe in ways that encouraged preemption. Specifically, the West hoped to equalize ground forces on the central front so that neither the Warsaw Pact nor NATO could launch a successful surprise ground attack. The discussions of ways to achieve these goals did encourage NATO and European force designers to consider cheaper and more effective defenses. Not all the ideas were implemented, but a new flexibility emerged within the military planning itself.

One important example was the U.S. nuclear weapons in Europe, numbering about 7,000 by the late 1960's. These weapons had first been deployed in the 1950's, when it appeared likely that any European war could escalate to the strategic nuclear level. They were justified at first as helping in the postulated ground engagement. Later, as European allies began to doubt the United States' willingness to escalate to strategic nuclear war in defense of Europe, the weapons were justified as making that escalation more likely, thereby deterring Soviet conventional attack. In the meantime, the Soviet Union had also deployed tactical nuclear weapons, and Soviet doctrine suggested that these would be used in great number and possibly even preemptively. The tactical advantage of the U.S. weapons was therefore illusory and the weapons might invite escalation too quickly. Congress and many others questioned the deployment on military grounds and out of fear that terrorists might seize the weapons; European leaders, however, tended to view the weapons as a symbol of U.S. commitment. NATO did not initially propose their reduction at MFR talks, but Western politicians began to consider changes in the nuclear deployments.

The Soviet motivations for MFR were largely political. MFR would contribute to Brezhnev's policy of détente, and would, the Soviets hoped, give the Soviet Union increased influence in Western security matters. It would also complement Soviet efforts in the CSCE, which was still a high-priority objective for the Soviets. On the more strictly military side, MFR might allow the Soviets to transfer more troops to the Sino-Soviet border, and might result in a reduction in U.S. tactical nuclear weapons, a long-sought Soviet goal. It is probable, however, that the Soviet Union was much more interested in the CSCE than in the MFR.

Eastern European attitudes toward MFR were mixed. Nations such as East Germany (whose military budget was one of the most rapidly growing in the world) and Poland probably viewed the Soviet presence as a form of commitment to their defense and as a form of defense cheaper than maintaining their own forces. Hence they would prefer cutting their own forces to cutting U.S.S.R. forces. The Hungarian and Czech leaderships—owing their power to the Soviet invasions of 1956 and 1968, respectively—probably felt dependent on the Soviet military presence but might welcome partial U.S.S.R. withdrawals. And Rumania sought comprehensive disarmament goals such as nuclear-free zones, withdrawal of troops from foreign soil, and the eventual phasing out of military blocs.

The Warsaw Pact countries sought to leave the relationship of forces unchanged. Initially, they argued for equal reductions on each side, which would enhance the force level asymmetry. Then, at the working session that began in Vienna in October 1973, they proposed that NATO and the Warsaw Pact make equal percentage reductions in all types of forces, except naval, in three stages, after an initial, small, equal reduction. In the first stage, each side, including allied forces, would reduce its forces by 20,000 men. In stage two, to be carried out in 1976, each side would reduce its forces by 5 percent, and in stage three, in 1977, each side would reduce by 10 percent. Thus, by the end of 1977, NATO ground and air manpower would be reduced from 1,000,000 to 820,000 (in the whole of Europe) and Warsaw Pact manpower from 1,300,000 to 1,150,000. Air forces and tactical nuclear weapons would also be reduced under this proposal. It was apparently Eastern European nations that sought to minimize the size of the reductions proposed. Although the Warsaw Pact accepted controls on reinforcements and maneuvers in principle, the Soviet Union tended to consider such restrictions an infringement on the Soviets' ability to control their allies in Eastern Europe.

NATO responded with a two-stage mutual reduction plan. In stage one, the United States would withdraw 29,000 men and the Soviet Union would withdraw 69,000 men. The Soviet Union would also withdraw one of its tank armies from East Germany. No allied troops would be reduced by either side in stage one. In stage two, both NATO and the Warsaw Pact countries would reduce to a common ceiling of 700,000 ground troops on the central front, applicable to the allied forces on both sides as well as to the Americans and the Soviets. The Western proposal called for reductions only in ground forces, on the theory that ground forces were the most important because they were the only ones that could be used to seize and hold territory. There would also be restrictions on maneuvers and reinforcements in stage two, but there would be no limits on tactical nuclear weapons or on air forces.

Perhaps the most important disagreement between the NATO and Warsaw Pact proposals was whether to make equal percentage reductions and thereby preserve existing disparities (as proposed by the Warsaw Pact), or whether to make unequal reductions toward a common ceiling (as proposed by NATO). The NATO position presupposed Warsaw Pact conventional superiority. This assumption has been challenged by a number of arms control experts who maintain that NATO has overall conventional equality with the Warsaw Pact. The Warsaw Pact superiority in tanks, which has caused considerable NATO concern, could, for example, become less important as a result of recent advances in anti-tank weapons. These tactical arguments are, however, quite controversial.

There was also disagreement on the type of reductions. NATO proposed that only ground forces should be reduced, whereas the Warsaw Pact proposed that ground and air forces should also be reduced, as should specific armaments, and particularly some of the 7,000 NATO tactical nuclear weapons deployed in Europe. Before agreement could be reached to limit specific armaments, it would be necessary to resolve the complexities of comparing and weighing differing systems.

The United States stated that reductions should be accompanied by adequate verification procedures, with safeguards against violations of the agreement, and by measures to reduce the risk of miscalculation and the fear of surprise attack, measures closely related to those then under discussion at the CSCE. It is not clear what types of observation posts or inspection would be required. Although the Soviets normally oppose on-site inspection and any verification scheme that does not rely solely on national technical means of verification, they have in the past proposed the idea of observation posts in Eastern Europe and the western borders of the Soviet Union.

According to press reports in late 1975, the United States was seeking NATO approval for a proposal to withdraw 1,000 of the U.S. tactical nuclear warheads in return for Soviet withdrawal of 1,700 tanks and associated troops. Whether this proposal would succeed was unclear— the issues were so complex as to make negotiations difficult. But the critical questions were those of political motivations, and these motivations were evolving. NATO had to decide how large a reduction in U.S. forces would be necessary to stave off pressures in Congress for unilateral U.S. reductions, and Congress was torn between the desire to reduce defense spending and the desire to show U.S. credibility. It was not clear whether analogous domestic pressures would lead European NATO countries, which were disagreeing with the United States over Mideast policy, to reduce military expenditures also. France, under new leadership, was retaining its nuclear forces and continuing to avoid arms control negotiations, but it seemed less intransigent than in the past. And the Soviet Union had to decide what concessions it was willing to make to the West to further détente, an evaluation dependent on both the course of Ostpolitik after Brandt's 1974 resignation and the course of U.S.-U.S.S.R. relations after Nixon's resignation and the 1975 Southeast Asia dénouement. And the 1975 conclusion of a purely symbolic CSCE agreement might remove one of the more important U.S.S.R. reasons for negotiating in MRF. The Soviet Union had in many respects hardened its position between the early days of Ostpolitik and the negotiations of 1973–75; its concessions at the preparatory conference for both MRF and CSCE proved illusory in the actual negotiations. Some Western observers even argued that U.S.S.R. policy had entered a new phase of concentrating on the developed world, particularly Europe, rather than on the developing world.

Conclusion

The European example shows the enormous political complexity of regional arms control negotiations. Strategic arms negotiations were relatively separable from politics, since these arms relate primarily to other strategic arms in a technical dialectic that becomes detached from actual conflict. The regional arms are, however, often viewed as protecting broad security and political interests. Thus, serious arms control negotiations could come in Europe only in conjunction with serious negotiations and a new flexibility in the political and security areas.

Although the U.S. Congress played a crucial role, Ostpolitik was clearly a major factor in making negotiation possible. The Ostpolitik example is perhaps the best counterargument to "bargaining chip" arguments; by giving up several traditional diplomatic bargaining points, Chancellor Brandt initiated a new era in Europe. Nevertheless, agreements stabilizing the new era had not been reached by mid-1975, and some argued that the difficulty of MFR and CSCE lay precisely in the fact that the West had given away its bargaining position.

Just as SALT led to bureaucratic rethinking of the ABM, the European negotiations led to some rethinking of the role and deployment of military forces in Europe, at least within NATO. Military doctrines were reexamined more deeply than they had been since the early 1950's. Preparation for negotiations may then have forced more rational planning.

Finally, it is hard to exaggerate the ambiguity of the role of the United States and the Soviet Union in regional arms control negotiations. SALT led both nations' allies to desire renewed participation in arms control and to fear that their interests were being forgotten. When regional negotiations were finally achieved, the United States and the Soviet Union found themselves aligned against the allies of both on a number of important issues. On several issues, the small nations felt that the larger nations were ignoring their interests. Regional arms control may imply overall limitations for the regional nations; if it is to imply more than redeployments for the United States and the Soviet Union, these latter nations must also negotiate their global force balances. This pattern of diverging interests, like the other patterns suggested in this conclusion, is likely to characterize any future regional negotiations, such as those suggested for the Mideast or the Indian Ocean.

CHAPTER THIRTEEN

Control of Conventional Arms

Except as part of Mutual Force Reduction (MFR), no major state has developed a serious arms control policy for conventional forces since the early 1960's. This is a serious deficiency in arms control efforts. Conventional forces continue to be used in warfare. Many conventional wars have taken place during the era, and the numbers and capabilities of conventional weapons are expanding enormously. Conventional forces constitute the major portion of military budgets; relief from the economic burdens of military establishments will require renewed attention to conventional limitations. Finally, there are direct relationships between strategic nuclear arms control and conventional forces; if a nuclear war were to take place, it would probably be through escalation of a conventional war.

Lack of governmental attention is one reason, but not the only reason, why this text can do no more than outline some of the issues of conventional arms control. Evaluations of conventional force engagements and outcomes are extremely difficult to make; little civilian expertise is available to balance military expertise, and the military experts often disagree among themselves. Facts are often unavailable or unreliable —many armament levels and arms transfers are kept secret. The possibilities of agreement, like those for regional arms control, are dependent on subtle political forces. Verification is likely to be difficult. Hence, this chapter will be less a discussion of what is known than of what is not known.

Conventional Arms in the 1970's

Even cursory information, however, shows that the world's conventional arms situation is evolving at a rate that is dizzying compared with that in the nuclear area. The technologies are changing extremely

rapidly—so rapidly as often to be undigested by military establishments
—and the relative capabilities of different nations are changing just
as rapidly.

The Conventional Arms Technologies

Many conventional weapons—tanks, aircraft, naval vessels—are
showing continued improvement in traditional directions: greater speed,
greater payload, more effective weaponry, better armor protection,
and the like. These changes are undoubtedly significant in themselves,
but the changes that have attracted the greatest attention outside the
military community go even further. Two can be singled out as examples: the precision-guided munition (PGM) and the electronic battlefield.

PGM weaponry, sometimes also called "smart" weaponry, resulted
from a series of small technological developments that combined to produce a major tactical development: relatively small weapons, sometimes
able to be fired by one or two infantrymen and able to reach a target at
substantial distances with great precision. Some of the weapons use
infrared or electronic homing technology. Others use a TV camera,
laser beam, or a link, by wire or radio, to a controller who guides the
weapon onto target. Some of the weapons are essentially rockets; others
are bombs guided from aircraft. Some of the weapons are cheap and
the technology is becoming readily accessible to developing nations—
nearly as accessible as, say, the technology of the hand-held calculators
spreading through the world. The tactical potential is that an infantry-
man can, with high probability, destroy a tank or an aircraft. There
could then be a major equalizing effect among different forces and different nations. It might also become possible to attack military targets
with less collateral damage to nearby civilian targets and to use conventional warheads in situations where nuclear warheads had previously
seemed essential.

Another development that might be important is the electronic battlefield, most typically proposed as a defensive barrier. What is involved
physically is a variety of prelocated sensor devices that detect people
or equipment and transmit the information by radio. These data on
movements in the area would go to a computer, which would then direct
air action or possibly detonate prelocated munitions. The concept can be
combined with traditional barriers such as barbed wire and minefields.
The concept was tried, without notorious success, in Vietnam; its deployment has also been discussed in southern Oman as a barrier against
the Dhofar rebels.

The growth of the U.S.S.R. navy is a different kind of important conventional force development. The strategic nuclear role of naval forces has already been discussed. Navies have more conventional missions as well: to protect their own merchant shipping and overseas military operations, to deny the same capabilities to an opponent, and to "show the flag"—a traditional naval function to support a diplomatic initiative through signaling that a military operation *could* be undertaken. The Soviet Union has developed a worldwide fleet to fulfill at least the ocean denial and the flag-showing roles. Its fleet was expanded during the 1960's to become numerically larger than the U.S. fleet in submarines, cruisers, and frigates. The Soviet fleet was, however, weaker in destroyers and had virtually no aircraft carriers. Moreover, the Soviet ships were generally smaller than their U.S. counterparts. The Soviet emphasis was on ships that carry missiles, often anti-ship missiles, as contrasted with the U.S. emphasis on aircraft carriers. The strategic design of the fleet was therefore quite different from that of the U.S. fleet.

These are not the only new tactical developments, or necessarily the most important ones. They do, however, show the possibility of tactical changes comparable with those following upon the introduction of the tank and of aircraft. The effects on warfare may differ from region to region and from war type to war type. For example, the PGM technology was enormously effective in the 1973 Mideast war, but it is dependent on weather and might do less well in Central Europe. Nevertheless, there is at least a chance that the new technology implies that on land the defense will become dominant over the offense because the tank and the aircraft might become vulnerable. Thus future land conflict might resemble the static warfare of World War I rather than the dynamic warfare of World War II. This could imply an era of greater stability; conceivably, however, there could be greater temptation to use nuclear weapons to avoid a stalemate analogous to World War I. The likely effect on naval warfare is opposite: ship-to-ship missiles might become effective enough to encourage a nuclear or conventional first strike between naval forces in time of tension. A further possible effect is to weaken the relative power of the United States and the Soviet Union. The threat of great-power intervention has often affected local conflicts such as those in the Mideast. But this threat would normally be implemented with aircraft or naval forces—and those forces may become vulnerable to PGMs.

The availability of new technology does not guarantee its acceptance; military institutions are relatively resistant to technological change, as shown by the slow adoption of air power between the two world wars and the slow phasing out of horse cavalry. This institutional resistance may affect the spread of the new technologies; it will certainly affect the development of the tactics to which the new weapons are most suited. The institutional barriers occasionally cut the other way: many have argued that the supersonic aircraft being widely purchased by developing nations are not at all suited to the conflicts likely to be faced by these nations, and thus represent a waste of military resources. These institutional barriers imply that some nations will adopt new tactics more quickly than others and—of critical importance for the likelihood of war—that different nations will make different evaluations of the outcomes of possible wars. Moreover, since the detailed tactics may affect war outcomes and since some of the electronic weapons

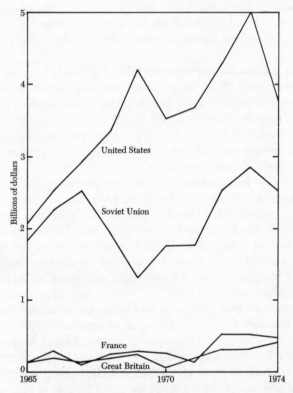

Fig. 9. Total arms exports of major exporters, in constant 1972 dollars. (Data from U.S. ACDA, *World Military Expenditures and Arms Transfers, 1965–1974.*)

are vulnerable to countermeasures if their characteristics are known, a premium may be placed on military intelligence about tactics and weapons characteristics.

The Arms Trade

In the midst of these tactical changes, an unprecedentedly large quantity of tactical weapons has been flowing across international boundaries. This flow of arms is not quite the same as that carried on by the "merchants of death" in the early twentieth century; in the post–World War II era, governments have become deeply involved. Nearly all the transfers have been transacted on a government-to-government basis or otherwise controlled by both recipient and supplier governments. The major exception, the magnitude of which is unknown, is supply of small arms to insurgent groups, a trade that is usually, however, regulated by the supplier's government.

The exports of the major suppliers are estimated in Figure 9, which is based on estimates of all arms transfers except those to insurgent groups. The four nations shown supplied about 86 percent of all arms exported in 1974. The other nations that exported more than $100 million worth of arms in 1973 or 1974 were Canada, China, Czechoslovakia, the Federal Republic of Germany, and Italy. This group was likely to expand; nations such as Brazil were seeking to enter the international arms market. The trend of the chart—a substantial increase occurring primarily in U.S. exports—would be reinforced if accurate data were available showing the effect of sales made in the 1974–75 period for later delivery. During that time, both the United States and France contracted for sharply increased sales—of $8–12 billion in the U.S. case and of $2–3 billion in the French case.

The destination of the arms was primarily the developing world by the early 1970's. In 1963, exports had been split about half and half to the developed and the developing world, reflecting U.S. and U.S.S.R. supplies to their European allies. By 1974, around 72 percent of the greatly expanded exports went to the developing world. The imports of the developed world had remained roughly constant in real terms; those of the developing world had risen from $3.0 billion to $6.0 billion between 1965 and 1974. Moreover, as Table 4 shows, these imports were concentrated among relatively few nations. On the left can be seen all those nations importing more than $100 million worth of arms during 1974; arms imports of these nations represent about 78 percent of all arms imports. On the right are all those nations whose military

TABLE 4
Comparison of Major Arms Importers with Nations Rapidly Expanding Their Military Establishments

Nations with substantial imports[a]	Imports, 1974 (millions of 1973 dollars)	Military budget, 1974 (millions of 1973 dollars)	Constant-dollar growth rate of military budget, 1965–74 (percent per annum)	Nations with substantial and rapidly expanding military budget[b]
	$ 64	$1,720	9.4%	Brazil
Bulgaria	104	1,410	4.3	
Cambodia	274	85	9.0	
Canada	103	2,530	0.7	
	32	15,400	6.1	China (Mainland)
China (Taiwan)	114	738	4.4	
Czechoslovakia	249	2,780	2.0	
Egypt	107	1,910	12.4	Egypt
Germany (East)	372	3,150	6.3	
Germany (West)	426	12,500	1.7	
Greece	153	621	8.3	Greece
Hungary	118	1,230	2.7	
India	117	2,180	0.7	
	32	545	11.2	Indonesia
Iran	789	4,780	29.0	Iran
Iraq	323	945[c]	9.4	Iraq
Israel	577	3,480	28.1	Israel
Italy	165	4,190	3.5	
	83	3,320	7.4	Japan
Korea (South)	103	582	12.5	Korea (South)
Libya	143	373	27.8	
	8	771	23.0	Nigeria
Poland	263	3,900	3.9	
	17	820	8.0	Portugal
Saudi Arabia	356	1,320	28.1	Saudi Arabia
	42	918	9.3	South Africa
	75	2,060	8.7	Spain
Syria	422	443	6.2	
Turkey	186	871	3.7	
United States	105	77,900	0.8	
Vietnam (North)	363	263	−5.7	
Vietnam (South)	603	347	−4.6	

SOURCE: U.S. ACDA, *World Military Expenditures and Arms Transfers, 1965–1974.*
   [a] Greater than $100 million in 1974 (1973 dollars).
   [b] Greater than $500 million in 1974 and expanding more rapidly than 7 percent per annum in constant dollar terms over the 1965–74 period.
   [c] Less reliable data.

budget is already greater than $500 million and rapidly expanding. There is clearly a substantial correlation between the two groups. Most of the expansion and most of the arms supply are in areas where war has occurred or is especially feared: Central Europe, Southeast Asia, and, above all, the Mideast.

The numbers given above and in Figure 9 and Table 4 are attempts to measure total arms trade. Of that total trade, in the 1967–71 period, jet aircraft and tactical missiles comprised more than 40 percent by value; naval craft and land equipment such as tanks made up about another 20 percent. This proportion of major weapons systems probably increased during the mid-1970's with large sales to Mideast nations. The remainder of the trade represents items such as ammunition and small arms; however, little is known about this aspect of the arms trade.

The arms trade numbers do not reflect a wide variety of other ways in which military capability is transferred from one nation to another. In 1973, for example, U.S. sales of military equipment totaled between $4 and $5 billion. Those sales, however, were only part of a much more elaborate program of military assistance totaling somewhere in the $10 to $12 billion range during fiscal year 1974. The largest portion of the difference was direct subsidy aid, money supplied to another nation to help it support its military establishment. Some of these funds were intended to help support arms purchases, but this form of arms transfer by gift was probably not nearly as important in the 1970's as in the 1960's. Other important components ranged from training of foreign officers in U.S. military schools to supply of U.S. advisers to work with foreign military units. Little is known about these categories of transfer of military capability. Even the U.S. programs are difficult to analyze accurately because of extremely confusing budgetary presentation. Other nations have similar programs: the Soviet Union assists many nations; European nations often support their families of former colonies. Even less is known about these programs. By the mid-1970's, private U.S. firms had entered this area and were selling packages of training services in the military and internal security areas. It is probable that an analysis of these "intangible" military transfers would show them to be strategically more important than the arms trade in major weapons.

Chapter 11 discussed some of the economic motivations of arms suppliers. For the businesses involved, profit is at stake. For their governments, employment, a favorable balance of payments, and econo-

mies of scale in the industry are all perceived as benefits. These economic factors were probably dominant in Europe in the 1960's and
became dominant in the United States by the mid-1970's. The balance-
of-payments pressures resulting from the oil crisis were so strong that
each government wanted to export all it could, including arms. Under
the forces of competition—the argument that another nation would
make the sale anyway—the arms industries were able to remove nearly
all restraints that their governments had imposed. There followed a
quantum jump of widespread sales of the most sophisticated weapons.
The extremely high level at which any restraint was being applied is
suggested by a French decision of 1974 not to sell nuclear-powered
submarines.

But in the sales of the Soviet Union, in those of the United States
before the mid-1970's, and in nearly all of the military assistance, strategic and political factors were probably more important than economic
factors. Both powers often saw strategic reasons why a particular nation
should be helped to become more powerful. Thus, the United States
and the Soviet Union each supported their respective friends in the Mideast, Vietnam, Korea, and Europe. Each side saw itself forced to provide
weapons to its friends to rebalance the two sides after the opponent
had provided weapons. The effect was usually a balance of military
power at an ever-increasing level. Similarly, but more covertly, opposing outside suppliers would sometimes support an insurgent movement
or the counterinsurgency program designed to contain it. This kind of
military assistance and arms sale sometimes supplemented direct involvement; by 1969 under the Nixon Doctrine, it was offered as a replacement for involvement. Thus, President Nixon hoped, the United
States would be able to help contain a Communist thrust without having
to commit U.S. troops.

It is not always reasons based on economics or on a military balance
of power that lead a supplier to give military support or to encourage
arms sales. Nearly all suppliers have broader political reasons, typically
a hope that the military assistance will encourage the recipient government to follow the supplier's policies. Soviet military advisers are often
viewed as agents of influence. U.S. advisers have sought to support
U.S. policies in Latin America, and U.S. sales of new arms have been
seriously supported as ways to distract the Latin American military
from intervention in government. In a slightly different way, suppliers
and advisers can utilize their control over deployments and over the
flow of spare parts to affect a military action. The location and range

of the Soviet-supplied surface-to-air missiles were an important factor in permitting Egypt to have some—but not unlimited—success in the 1973 Mideast war. The Indo-Pakistan war of 1965 probably ended as quickly as it did because of embargoes on spare parts. In a still different way, the Soviet Union traditionally gave arms as a form of reward to those who were already friendly. The Castro regime in Cuba and the Sukarno regime in Indonesia received Soviet arms after their shifts toward a Soviet orientation.

The buyers and recipients of military support have their own reasons to acquire arms. Sometimes their motivations are essentially a fascination with the mystique of advanced weapons. Sometimes bureaucratic pressures dominate. For example, during the 1950–70 period in Argentina, one could track whether a military or civilian government was in power by whether arms were being bought for the Navy (the more conservative service) or for the Air Force. Ambitions toward great-power status probably dominate arms procurements in nations like Iran and Brazil, and in nearly all arms-importing nations the weapons are more sophisticated than can be justified by likely military conflicts. Nevertheless, perceptions of a real military threat nearly always play an important role in military purchases. Sometimes, this is a domestic threat of rebellion. But very often it is a major international threat, as evidenced by the fact that the major arms-importing nations are nearly all located in areas of great conflict potential. Even Iran's naval procurements, for example, could be explained as a response to possible instability in the Persian Gulf and to U.S.S.R. intrusion into the Indian Ocean.

The Effects of the Growth and Spread of Conventional Arms

Lack of information about the arms themselves makes it difficult to estimate the effects of their growth and spread. The processes that support arms transfer are generally likely to keep different nations in tactical balance in areas of possible conflict, so that aggressive war is by no means a necessary result of the diffusion of advanced military technology. Hence, the effects of the arms on war are likely to be somewhat subtle. And any generalization that is made is likely to fail in special cases, because of wide variations in both tactical and political conditions.

One generalization that requires great caution is that arms purchases or large military budgets encourage military government in developing nations. A long series of statistical studies on Latin America gives mild support to this hypothesis.[1] There are some effects; for example, a large increase or decrease in military spending is likely to be followed by a military coup. Moreover, flow of internal security technology—advanced systems for identifying and keeping track of dissidents—has expanded only recently and might be more closely coupled with authoritarian government. Careful analysis of the political patterns of the nation and of the political role of the military in individual cases is, however, necessary before one can estimate the domestic political effects of a transaction.

Neither is it possible to argue persuasively that the arms trade has a major negative effect on developing-nation economic growth. The overall size of the arms trade is itself small compared with overall military budgets, as can be seen from Table 4. On a worldwide basis, the developing nations had total military budgets of $42.3 billion in 1973, but spent $7.7 billion on imported arms the same year. Thus, less than 20 percent of their total budget was spent on imported arms. These imports may, however, increase maintenance and training costs; moreover, they may affect neighbors' arms budgets. The negative effects of the arms trade are likely to be less significant than the indeterminate effects of domestic military budgets. Many of the purchases are made by oil-rich nations or through military assistance provided by the supplier nation, and hence are likely to have little economic effect in the developing nation.

However, one can confidently say that the spread of conventional weapons will change the character of war in the developing world. For a time, it looked as if the spread of supersonic aircraft might encourage relatively short preemptive war, such as the various Mideast wars. That conclusion may have to be reversed with the possible defense dominance suggested by the PGM. The character of guerilla warfare might also change. Advanced technology has often not been very useful in conflicts with guerilla forces. Acquisition of PGMs by guerillas might help them substantially, however, and lead to the breakdown of central governments—unless the new internal security technologies cut the other way. The direction of change is not at all clear, but the likelihood of change and the likelihood of greatly increased casualties both seem high.

Finally, the spread of conventional arms probably does increase the

[1] L. Einaudi et al., *Arms Transfers to Latin America: Toward a Policy of Mutual Respect* (RAND R-1173-DOS, June 1973), pp. 30–32; E. Hyman, "Soldiers in Politics: New Insights on Latin American Armed Forces," *Political Science Quarterly*, 87 (1972): 401.

probabilities of war. Most actors will seek to keep conflict areas in balance, which would, with traditional diplomacy, ensure peace. But the technologies are so novel and the force levels are changing so rapidly that different nations are bound to evaluate particular balances differently. The chances for miscalculation of possible war outcomes are likely to grow and the chances for diplomatic misunderstanding are also likely to grow as more nations begin to interact strategically with one another.

Limitations on Conventional Forces

Arms control proposals based on distinctions like that between offensive and defensive weapons were considered during the 1920's. After World War II, limitations on conventional forces were discussed briefly in the 1940–48 period, in the 1950's in the London Subcommittee discussions, and again in the early 1960's in connection with discussions on the U.S. and Soviet General and Complete Disarmament proposals. Among these post–World War II discussions, the only serious negotiations were those in the London Subcommittee. The Mutual Force Reduction talks have examined proposals for limiting particular kinds of weapons in particular regions. The Geneva law-of-war discussions have considered barring certain weapons such as napalm and antipersonnel fléchettes as inhumane. And there have been a few special arrangements such as the 1972 U.S.-U.S.S.R. Agreement on the Prevention of Incidents on and over the High Seas. But fundamentally, nations have not yet carefully analyzed the technical characteristics of conventional weapons from an arms control viewpoint in the way that they have analyzed strategic weapons. And, except for a few unofficial proposals for naval arms control, arms control analysts have also tended to ignore the problems of conventional arms balances.

National Restrictions on Arms Transfers

Most nations, however, have developed their own national restrictions on arms exports and international military assistance, generally designed to ensure that the actions accord with national goals. In the United States, these restrictions are predominantly legislative, deriving from Congress's effort to control the Executive. They include, for example, ceilings on the total amount of certain categories of military sales to Latin America, ceilings on the number of foreign military personnel that can be trained in the United States, limitations on the grant of credit for foreign military purchases, and prohibitions on the transfer of sophisticated weapons to developing nations. Most of these restrictions can be waived by the President upon findings such as that the action would benefit national security. Relatively recently, Congress has acted to restrict arms flows to particular nations when it is dissatisfied with U.S. policy toward those nations, e.g. in Southeast Asia and Turkey. The legal patterns of authority to transfer arms and of restrictions on arms transfers are both complex; the Executive has been quite ingenious in finding alternative statutory authority for arms transfers.

The rules, when effective, are enforced by standard procedures such as mandatory export licenses designed both to control the ultimate disposition of the arms traded and to protect the sellers' patents and licenses. End-use certificates are often used to guarantee that the weapons arrive and remain within the country named on the export license. Some suppliers, including the United States, require that clauses restricting the resale of equipment be written into arms sales agreements. Such clauses are, however, extremely difficult to enforce.

Supplier governments sometimes adopt ad hoc restrictions on arms sales in response to specific security or political considerations. During the 1965 war over Kashmir, for example, the United States placed a total embargo on all arms shipments to both India and Pakistan. Similarly, France imposed an embargo on arms sales to the Mideast in 1967, when its policy was shifting to favor the Arab side and the embargo would benefit that side. In 1974, the embargo—now preventing sales to the Arab side—was lifted in favor of case-by-case review of each sale. The United States also long sought informally to keep supersonic aircraft out of Latin America.

Arrangements to Register Transfers and to Reduce Incentives for Arms Transfers

Proposals for the international control of arms transfers have tended to take three forms: efforts such as registration of arms transfers to encourage public opinion pressures against arms sales, arrangements among supplier countries to restrict shipments of arms to certain areas, and arrangements among recipient countries to limit imports of armaments.

Since World War II, several nations have proposed registration of and publicity about international arms transactions. In 1965 Malta introduced a draft resolution in the U.N. General Assembly requesting the Eighteen-Nation Disarmament Committee (ENDC) to consider the question of arms transfers and to submit to the next General Assembly proposals for the establishment through the United Nations of a system of publicity on sales and transfers of arms. This proposal was rejected, with the United States and 38 other countries abstaining. In 1967, as one of President Johnson's five principles for peace in the Middle East, the United States proposed the reporting to the United Nations of all arms shipments to the Middle East. This proposal encountered strong opposition from the Soviet Union, the Arab states, and some Western nations. It was not put to a vote. In 1968, Denmark, Iceland, Malta, and Norway submitted a joint resolution to the General Assembly to request the Secretary-General to investigate the views of U.N. members on the registration of all exports and imports of conventional arms and on publishing information on arms transfers. A number of developing countries strongly opposed this proposal, and the sponsors decided not to bring it to a vote.

Proponents of arms registration argued that the secrecy surrounding the acquisition of armaments increased the insecurity of neighboring states and could cause these states to overreact by acquiring an excessive number of additional weapons. Registration and publicity, they argued, would reduce this uncertainty, assuage the suspicions of neighboring countries, and thereby prevent excessive responses to arms acquisitions in neighboring countries. Supporters of arms registration and publicity also suggested that publicity about arms transfers would help public opinion in the supplier states to discourage transfers.

Opponents of arms registration argued that the proposals to register arms transfers were discriminatory in that they would reveal the arms acquisition activities of nonproducing states but allow arms-producing states to continue producing and deploying their own weapons secretly. They also questioned the proponents' proposition that secrecy encouraged arms acquisition, suggesting that public disclosure would be just as likely to stimulate competitive acquisitions as to restrain them. This would be particularly true in regions where the military inventories were so low that small acquisitions might appear threatening to rival states and create pressures for new acquisitions to redress the perceived imbalances.

Some analysts have made the closely related suggestion that arms suppliers agree to a standardized form of end-use certificate to prevent retransfers without the approval of the original supplier government. Not all suppliers require such agreements against retransfers of their exported arms. End-use agreements, under which the original supplier would buy back exported weapons or provide the recipient with an economic incentive to scrap weapons rather than reexport them, have also been proposed to reduce trade in "secondhand" weapons. Finally, a few experts have proposed restructuring the U.S. and European arms industries to reduce the economic incentives to export arms.

Arrangements Among Supplier States

Proposals for arrangements among supplier states to control arms transfers have been directed primarily to controlling the export of arms to specific areas. Some of these were U.N.-sanctioned embargoes of arms shipments to certain countries, such as Rhodesia and South Africa, designed not so much to control arms transfers per se as to punish and modify undesired state behavior. In general, these embargoes were only moderately successful in restricting the flow of arms and were unsuccessful in persuading the target nations to change their behavior. Most of the embargo proposals, however, were oriented toward conflict areas.

During the Palestine conflict in 1948, for example, the U.N. Security Council adopted a British draft resolution that called for a Palestine cease-fire and urged all countries to refrain from importing or exporting war matériel into or from the Middle East. The three principal suppliers of arms to the Middle East—Great Britain, France, and the United States—modified the arrangement in 1950 with a joint declaration that all Arab and Israeli applications for arms would be considered "in the light of defense needs of the area as a whole." This suppliers' arrangement successfully restricted the flow of arms to the Middle East for several years. It broke down in 1955, when Egypt concluded an agreement to barter Egyptian cotton for Czech arms after learning it could not receive U.S. military aid "unconditionally." The Soviet Union sought to revive the Middle East arms embargo in 1956 and 1957, as did the United States in the 1967–72 period, but both efforts failed.

The United States unilaterally embargoed arms shipments to India and Pakistan during the 1965 war over Kashmir. After lifting this embargo in 1967, the United States still limited deliveries to nonlethal equipment and to spare parts for the lethal equipment it had previously provided. This policy remained in effect until 1971, when the United States responded to the Bangladesh war with another total embargo on military shipments to both India and Pakistan. In 1973, the United States reverted to its earlier policy of delivering only nonlethal equipment and spare parts for previously supplied lethal equipment. China and the Soviet Union, however, placed no restrictions on their arms shipments to the subcontinent during this period and continued to provide substantial military aid in the form of combat aircraft, tanks, and other equipment.

The United States and its principal allies have also restricted trade in arms and other strategic materials with Communist countries. Seven NATO members, including the United States and Great Britain, established a Consultative Group on East-West trade policy in November 1949. This group was later expanded to include Japan and all NATO countries except Iceland. A Coordinating Committee (COCOM) began functioning in 1950 as a forum for the exploration of control questions, to consider and recommend specific control measures, and to maintain lists of arms and other strategic materials to be embargoed to all Communist countries except Yugoslavia. Although all COCOM countries accepted these lists as their minimum standards for control, each country maintained its own list of restricted exports and its own system for administering the strategic trade controls. The COCOM control system maintained fairly strong controls on strictly military items, but in the moves toward greater East-West trade in the late 1960's and early 1970's, it substantially weakened its restrictions on goods such as computers and civilian aircraft.

Arrangements Among Recipient States

At the Conference of the Committee on Disarmament (CCD) a number of Western and nonaligned countries, as well as Rumania, have expressed their willingness to cooperate in controlling international arms traffic, but their proposals for arrangements among recipient states have elicited little response. In 1966 and 1968, President Johnson proposed the exploration of regional arrangements to limit arms transfers in messages to the ENDC, and in 1971 President Nixon urged the CCD to give increasing attention to conventional arms measures. Mexico, Sweden, and Yugoslavia also submitted a draft comprehensive disarmament program which stressed the need for regional conferences to consider conventional arms limitation. Opponents, however, argued that supplier countries were the ones responsible for conventional arms races and that the problem of arms transfers could be solved only in the context of worldwide disarmament. None of the efforts were successful.

Both the Paris Agreement on Ending the War and Restoring Peace in Vietnam, signed in January 1973, and the Laotian cease-fire agreement, signed in February the same year, included specific restrictions on arms transfers. Under the Paris Agreement, the two South Vietnamese parties agreed not to accept the introduction of armaments, munitions, and war matériel into South Vietnam, except as required for periodic replacement on a piece-for-piece basis of items that were destroyed, damaged, worn out, or used up after the cease-fire. The Laotian cease-fire agreement included a prohibition against bringing any foreign-made weapons or war matériel into Laos, except for those armaments specified as necessary for the defense of Laos in the Geneva agreements of 1954 and 1962. These agreements were probably violated extensively on both sides. They were rapidly overtaken by the Communist successes in Southeast Asia.

The most serious negotiations of the mid-1970's were those in Latin America, a region almost completely dependent on imported arms. In the 1958–60 period, Costa Rica and Chile had proposed discussions on the limitation of arms in Latin America. These proposals were considered by the Organization of American States (OAS), but no significant action was ever taken. The issue was raised in general terms in the Punta del Este Summit Declaration of 1967. The nations expressed "their intention to limit military expenditure," just as the U.S. policy of keeping supersonic aircraft out of Latin America was breaking down with a French sale to Peru. Over the next several years, Argentina, Brazil, Colombia, and Venezuela soon also bought the French Mirage.

In this context, Colombia took the initiative at the OAS in 1971 to implement the Punta del Este declaration. Venezuela and Argentina argued that the United Nations, not the OAS, was the right forum. Brazil also argued that Latin American arms expenditures were minimal and Peru doubted that Latin American armaments hurt economic development. Application of the Punta del Este declaration was eventually held to be "the exclusive responsibility of each government in its own territory"—a way of saying that there would be no international agreement.

The philosophy of Peru's government changed, however, and it took up the concept again in early 1974. By December, eight Andean nations issued the Declaration of Ayacucho, which called for the creation of conditions for an effective limitation of arms. A mixed diplomatic and military working group held its first meeting in February 1975 to work toward arms limitations.

Conclusion

There has been little real progress in controlling conventional arms or the trade in such arms. This lack of progress can be explained in large part by the lack of consensus on the desirability of arms control in particular regions and the nearly prohibitive difficulties of worldwide conventional force limitations. Conventional weapons are already present in almost every nation, and are used to promote a wide variety of national objectives; agreements are therefore difficult to achieve. The arms trade is particularly difficult to control because countries that cannot produce their own arms tend to consider restrictions on arms transfers an infringement on their right and duty to provide for their external defense and internal security.

Perhaps the prime reasons, however, derive from the fact that the control of conventional weapons seriously tests the philosophical premises underlying arms control. Few conventional weapons create the automatic horror that nuclear weapons do. Most arms controllers can think of areas of conflict (e.g. southern Africa) in which they might wish to favor one side through supplying conventional weapons. Control of conventional weapons could affect a government's ability to control its own population—raising another controversial dimension not raised by strategic arms control discussions. And there is no doctrine analogous to deterrence theory that suggests when *both* sides have enough.

Interests within nearly every nation are, however, divided. Thus, the militaries are often divided on which of the new arms are desirable and even on whether the sophisticated tanks and aircraft—which have made up a large portion of the weapons growth—are militarily useful in many contexts. Many developing nations, including some of those under military rule, sense an acute conflict between military demands and economic demands. Some military leaders, for example, believe that economic development is a crucial form of military defense. Conventional arms can be very expensive. The supplier nations are also torn. Economic and foreign policy officials tend to support arms sales for their economic benefits and their use for diplomatic bargaining. But strands of questioning are developing within the military over the possibility that the buying nations might sometime use the weapons against the supplying nations' interests. These divisions suggest the possibility of new political alignments supporting conventional arms control and encouraging the careful tactical analysis needed for both regional and worldwide conventional force limitations. This possibility is reinforced by the likelihood that continuation and expansion of strategic arms negotiation will require renewed attention to the interactions between strategic and conventional forces.

CHAPTER FOURTEEN

Control of Nuclear Proliferation

Efforts to control nuclear proliferation began with the first case of proliferation—the U.S. development of the fission bomb during World War II. That development was conducted in the framework of the Manhattan Project, a secret program costing approximately $2 billion and lasting approximately six years. The program was enormous for the time and was one of the first historical examples of large-scale, defense-oriented research-and-development activity. The program's magnitude and secrecy have shaped attitudes toward proliferation, even in the 1970's. Yet, after allowing for inflation, the program does not seem so large when compared with typical 1970's development costs of $10 billion for a major new airplane. Since the Manhattan Project, development of a nuclear weapon has also become much easier. Much better data have become publicly available on the fundamental physical constants, data that had to be developed and measured as part of the Manhattan Project. Some of the calculations for the first atom bomb were made by banks of clerks sitting at desk calculators programmed to work together in much the way a regular computer is programmed. Computers with thousands of times the capability have become widely available. The nuclear materials themselves have been spread around the world through peaceful nuclear programs. Thus, the economic cost of a nuclear weapons program has substantially fallen.

To ask, as many did in 1945, who has the atomic secret was and is particularly misleading. The question should be how long would it take a particular society with a particular level of resources to build and test an atomic bomb. This question was infrequently posed in 1945. Instead, public controversy then and ever since has been cast to a great extent in terms of who has the nuclear secret. The illusion was widely maintained that if the secret could be hidden, the weapon would be controlled.

Secrecy made up only part of the initial efforts to control atomic weapons. The first arrangements were those within the United States to establish a domestic atomic control system. Secretary of War Henry Stimson had appointed a panel to deal with this problem before the first nuclear explosion. The panel's report drew Congressional controversy and scientific criticism but ultimately led to the statute creating the Atomic Energy Commission (AEC). This agency was governed by a commission of five civilians appointed by the President but not removable by him. Under the initial proposal, the Commission would have had several military representatives, but Congress balked. Instead, the military received what was eventually called a Division of Military Application within the AEC, and a special committee appointed by the Secretaries of War and Navy called the Military Liaison Committee. Also, the General Manager, who was subordinate to the commission itself, was traditionally a military officer. The second major decision was to combine military and peaceful uses of atomic energy under a government monopoly, with security arrangements to prevent release of nuclear information. The government monopoly concept was nearly unique in American history. Finally, the bill created the Joint Atomic Energy Committee, a committee of both Houses, with carefully defined and rather substantial powers over the AEC. The long-term tendency was that the AEC and the Joint Committee would work together to become the common developers and proponents of atomic energy. Atomic energy was thus given a Congressional watchdog, which sometimes became a Congressional advocate.

The early approach on the international side also sought an international monopoly as a way to supplement secrecy. Such a monopoly was proposed in the Baruch plan, but, as described in Chapter 5, this plan failed. Control thus depended on the U.S. nuclear monopoly alone, but the monopoly was short-lived. In September 1949 the Soviet Union tested its first nuclear weapon and the monopoly was broken. Great Britain, which had cooperated with the United States during World War II, followed in 1952. The advantage of secrecy was becoming less attractive. The U.S. domestic politics of nuclear energy also changed: the potential of peaceful uses of atomic energy was becoming clear, particularly for electrical power production and for medicine. Beneath the surface was the old political controversy between private and public ownership of electrical utilities. If the AEC continued to develop nuclear power under its monopoly, it would become the great public power agency in the United States. The international secrecy concept and the economic monopoly role of the AEC were thus both under question.

One result of these developments was the 1954 amendments to the Atomic Energy Act, amendments that substantially modified the effective character of the AEC. They allowed the AEC to release data more easily to allies and to industry. They also allowed private nuclear power development, although the AEC would have regulatory authority in such areas as materials, protection of classified data, and safety hazards. The AEC, originated as an agency to control and prevent the spread of nuclear understanding and technology, became instead an agency to spread nuclear materials and technology, although with legal safeguards. It retained this character until 1974, when it was divided into two agencies, one to regulate and one to conduct research, development, and promotion.

The corresponding international development was announced in December 1953, when President Eisenhower delivered his Atoms for Peace speech in the United Nations. Eisenhower said that it was necessary to end the nuclear arms race, and that it would be useful toward this goal if peaceful development of nuclear energy by all the countries of the world were encouraged and if the nuclear powers contributed some of their fissionable materials for such development. This would reduce the nuclear stockpiles, still somewhat limited, that the United States and Russia were then building up. To the extent that these materials would be diverted to peaceful uses, they would be unavailable for missiles and bombs. The nuclear powers could also demonstrate their interest in using nuclear energy for peace. A new international agency would be created as a channel for spreading the peaceful uses of nuclear energy.

Secretary of State John Foster Dulles played a leading role in negotiating the creation of the new agency, eventually named the International Atomic Energy Agency (IAEA). In January 1954 he began bilateral negotiations with the Soviet Union, the nation with whom agreement was most critical. These negotiations were conducted through an exchange of memoranda, kept confidential until late that year. At first the Soviet Union wanted to tie the agency to a general disarmament scheme; at the time it was behind in nuclear materials. This seemed much like the Soviet response that Baruch had received a decade earlier. The Soviets accepted the U.S. position in September, however, for several reasons. First, during the summer of that year the AEC Act revisions were passed. These revisions made clear that the United States would have its own peaceful international nuclear programs and that any outside influence over these would have to be through the international agency. Second, the fall meetings of the U.N. Assembly were to discuss the issue, so the Soviet Union did not want to be in too awkward a position before other nations. Third, and perhaps most important, the United States had organized a group of "principally involved" powers: Great Britain, Canada, France, South Africa, Belgium, Australia, and Portugal—major world suppliers of uranium. The United States had a good bargaining position with these nations, because of its own bilateral program, under which it could supply processed nuclear material for peaceful purposes under AEC-imposed controls. Dulles was thus able to obtain a draft agreement from these supplying nations and submit it confidentially to the Soviet Union. Not surprisingly, he obtained Soviet agreement, and then worked the draft through broader and broader U.N. groups. The treaty was finally completed in November 1956 at a formal negotiating session of 81 nations; at this point, they could make only minor changes.

The International Atomic Energy Agency was set up with some nuclear materials of its own, an elaborate control scheme and decision-making system, and a bureaucracy of its own. The major way the IAEA concept differed from the Acheson-Lilienthal plan was that it did not give the international body a monopoly. Nuclear materials were given to the IAEA as voluntary donations from countries—the United States immediately agreed to contribute approximately 5,000 kilograms of nuclear material—but there was no requirement that all nuclear materials be transferred to the IAEA. The IAEA set up a "safeguards" system, with inspectors to detect the diversion of nuclear materials to military purposes. Although the United States at first used bilateral safeguards rather than IAEA safeguards, IAEA inspection has since been applied to a large proportion of the materials and facilities transferred to non-nuclear nations. The IAEA safeguards, however, cover only a portion of the nuclear materials in recipient nations, and in no way cover the materials that the Americans and the Soviets reserve for their own military purposes. Thus the IAEA became one of several parallel ways to transmit nuclear materials from countries that have them to the countries that do not. In retrospect, the Atoms for Peace effort may have stimulated interest in peaceful nuclear technology before a full control system was available.

The inspection and organization structure of the IAEA was, nevertheless, to become an important element of the Non-Proliferation Treaty of 1968. The technology spread by the IAEA and bilateral agreements in the 1950's would define the framework for the proliferation issues of the 1970's. The proliferation of the early 1960's, however, resulted from independent and Soviet-assisted technological advances.

France exploded its first nuclear device in 1960, for reasons discussed more fully in Chapter 12. France felt left out by U.S.-British nuclear cooperation. It felt that an independent deterrent was necessary for the defense of Western Europe. And it perhaps felt that French grandeur required a nuclear capability—a capability easily acquired because the officials guiding France's peaceful nuclear power program had designed this program to make military applications easily realizable.

The next nuclear nation was China, which exploded its first device in 1964. Since Western nations were entering their own nuclear assistance arrangements in the mid-1950's, the Soviet Union also gave nuclear assistance to China. An October 1957 agreement appeared to include weapons development assistance as part of this program; but by 1959 the Sino-Soviet split became sharp and the Soviet physicists were called home. China continued its nuclear program on its own—possibly orienting it at first toward protection against the United States but soon orienting it clearly toward protection against the Soviet Union.

The Agreements of the 1960's

In the early part of the 1960's, there was widespread world sentiment against proliferation, sentiment reinforced by the nuclear explosions of France and China. Negotiations to restrict nuclear weapons went forward in three major forums, but in only one of these did the United States and the Soviet Union play a major role.

One effort was in Africa, where there was worry over the fallout dangers posed by French nuclear testing. France conducted four atmospheric tests in the Sahara in 1960 and 1961, and then carried out underground tests in the same area until 1965, when it moved its test range to the Pacific. The African nations responded with a series of resolutions in the United Nations and in the Organization of African Unity, calling on all nations to abstain from testing, building, using, or installing nuclear weapons on the African continent. Follow-up negotiations to convert these resolutions into formal agreements never occurred, presumably because the Non-Proliferation Treaty negotiations intervened.

The Latin American Nuclear Free Zone Treaty

This concept of designating an area as off limits for nuclear weapons was often suggested in other proposals for nuclear free zones. These proposals constitute an attempt to separate a particular part of the world from the nuclear arms race by prohibiting the introduction of nuclear weapons into the area and by prohibiting the use of nuclear weapons against nations in the area. The only proposal to be embodied in a treaty, however, was that for a Latin American nuclear free zone.

The Cuban missile crisis was the immediate origin for the interest of a number of Latin American countries in the creation of a Latin American nuclear free zone. In November 1962, Bolivia, Brazil, Chile, and Ecuador submitted a Draft Resolution on a Latin American Denuclearized Zone to the First Committee of the General Assembly. This draft resolution, which was not put to a vote during that session, would have led to an international framework in which the countries of Latin America would agree not to manufacture, receive, store, or test nuclear weapons. The sponsors hoped that Cuba could thus more easily commit itself not to permit Soviet missiles on its territory.

In April 1963 the presidents of Bolivia, Brazil, Chile, Ecuador, and Mexico declared their readiness to sign a multilateral agreement undertaking not to manufacture, receive, store, or test nuclear weapons or nuclear launching devices. That fall, by a vote of 91–0, with 15 abstentions (including Cuba and the Soviet Union), the General Assembly adopted a resolution urging all Latin American states to initiate studies of measures to achieve the denuclearization of Latin America called for in the April 1963 Declaration. A Preparatory Commission for the Denuclearization of Latin America was established; it held a series of working meetings in 1965 and 1966 and submitted a draft treaty on the denuclearization of Latin America in May 1966.

Since the first discussions, however, a military government had taken power in Brazil, and that nation expressed several reservations about the treaty concept. Its key reservations were that the right to use peaceful nuclear explosions (PNEs) would have to be preserved, and that the treaty could not enter into force unless all Latin American nations were bound and all nuclear nations had committed themselves not to introduce or use nuclear weapons in Latin America. The negotiation of the treaty was in large part the work of the Mexican diplomat García Robles, who sought to define a compromise that would be both effective and acceptable to Brazil. The final Treaty for the Prohibition of Nuclear Weapons in Latin America (the Latin American Nuclear Free Zone Treaty [LANFZ] or Treaty of Tlatelolco)[1] was signed at Mexico City in February 1967. It entered into force for all signatories except Brazil, Chile, and Trinidad and Tobago in April 1968. Argentina did not ratify the treaty, and because of the treaty's implications for a territorial dispute, Guyana did not sign. Nor has Cuba signed.

The LANFZ Treaty provides, *inter alia*, that the signatory nations

[1] See Appendix C for the text of the treaty.

are to use the nuclear material and facilities under their jurisdiction for exclusively peaceful purposes; that the signatory nations are to prohibit and prevent in their respective territories the testing, use, manufacture, production, or acquisition of nuclear weapons, and the receipt, storage, installation, deployment, or possession of nuclear weapons. The treaty established a control agency and placed all peaceful nuclear activities in the zone under the safeguard system of the International Atomic Energy Agency.

The treatment of PNEs was left ambiguous. Mexico and most other signatories hold that the treaty prohibits peaceful nuclear explosions, except by states already possessing nuclear weapons, which are asked to undertake peaceful projects requiring the use of nuclear explosions. This is also the U.S. interpretation. Brazil, Argentina, and Nicaragua do not agree with this view, and they maintain that the treaty permits production of a PNE if in the future it becomes technologically possible to create such a nuclear explosive device that cannot be used as a weapon.

Relations with nations outside Latin America are governed by two protocols to the treaty. (The United States is outside Latin America for the purposes of the treaty.) Protocol I, designed for the nations still having colonial possessions in Latin America, calls on nations outside the area having *de jure* or *de facto* territories in the Latin American area to place these territories under the restrictions of the treaty. The Netherlands and Great Britain have ratified Protocol I, but the United States has refused to accept denuclearized status for its possessions in the area, which include Puerto Rico, the Virgin Islands, and the Guantánamo base in Cuba.

Protocol II is for the signature of the nuclear powers and commits them to respect the denuclearization of Latin America and not to use or threaten to use nuclear weapons against any of the contracting parties to the treaty. This protocol has been ratified by the United States and Great Britain and signed by France and China. This is the only arms control agreement that either France or China has been willing to sign; their actions are a reflection both of their political interests in the area and of Mexican President Echeverría's diplomacy. This protocol is also the only formal limitation on the use of nuclear weapons that the United States has become party to, though the U.S. signature was accompanied by a formal statement that the United States would consider that an armed attack by a party assisted by a nuclear weapon state would be incompatible with the parties' obligations under the treaty.

The treaty was written to enter into force only after four conditions had been fulfilled: ratification of the treaty by all members of the geographic area covered by the treaty; ratification of Protocol I by all parties outside the region with territories in the region; ratification of Protocol II by all powers possessing nuclear weapons; and conclusion of bilateral or multilateral safeguard arrangements with IAEA. Signatories, however, have the right to waive any of these requirements. Of the 19 states that have ratified the treaty, only Brazil, Chile, and Trinidad and Tobago have not waived the requirements. The treaty is therefore not in force in these three states.

It is unlikely that all the missing ratifications will be completed during the 1970's. The Soviet Union has persistently refused to sign Protocol II. Cuba has also refused to participate, although it might change its position as part of its general rapprochement with Latin America. But Argentina has not ratified and Brazil will not be bound until all these actions are completed. The treaty is therefore unlikely to forestall the serious potential of Argentinian and Brazilian nuclear programs, a potential heightened by Brazil's decision in mid-1975 to acquire uranium enrichment facilities from Germany.

The Non-Proliferation Treaty

Although non-proliferation provisions were included in U.S. and Soviet comprehensive proposals of the late 1950's, early proposals for a separate Non-Proliferation Treaty (NPT) came from small nations, particularly Ireland, during the 1958–61 era. The proposals took the form of U.N. resolutions, and were made against the backdrop of discussions about U.S. nuclear weapons in Europe and the form of control that NATO should have over those weapons. For the United States, such weapons were an important part of the defense of Europe; for the Soviet Union, they were threats that verged on a nuclear West Germany.

This split was shown on the U.N. resolutions. A major Irish resolution was overwhelmingly approved in November 1959, with the Soviet Union abstaining. This resolution urged negotiations to prevent the wider spread of nuclear weapons, but the Soviets objected that the resolution did not "even mention prohibiting States from having nuclear weapons outside their own territory." The next year, a modified Irish resolution asked states *inter alia* "to refrain from relinquishing control of [nuclear] weapons to any nation not possessing them." Again the resolution was approved, but this time the United States abstained, pointing out that the resolution would call for an unverified halt to such transfers during the period of negotiation. Finally, in 1961, a compromise formula was found, and the General Assembly unanimously approved an Irish resolution calling for an agreement under which the nuclear powers would not transfer nuclear weapons or their control to non-nuclear-weapon states, and the non-nuclear-weapon states would not manufacture or otherwise acquire nuclear weapons.

By 1962 the United States and the Soviet Union had begun private discussions on a non-proliferation agreement as a possible separable measure. The NATO issues, however, were not fully resolved by the 1961 U.N. resolution, and they blocked progress between the two nations until 1965. The Soviets opposed any non-proliferation agreement that would permit the establishment of a multilateral nuclear force (MLF) in Europe. The MLF would consist of ships or submarines manned by crews drawn from all NATO nations and would carry nuclear weapons under some form of NATO control. To its Western proponents, the MLF was a way to advance European unity and to avoid proliferation of nuclear weapons among the Atlantic nations. To its opponents in the West, the MLF was only a way to finesse the real issues of responsibility in the Atlantic alliance on nuclear matters, or, alternatively, a scheme to avoid serious arms control. And to the Soviet Union the MLF was an attempt to give the Federal Republic of Germany some form of control over nuclear weapons, a development to which Moscow was violently opposed.

The drafts of the era reflected this U.S.-U.S.S.R. division. The U.S. draft, tabled in the ENDC in August 1965, would have prohibited the dissemination of nuclear weapons by the nuclear states into the "national control" of non-nuclear-weapon states, as well as prohibiting the development or acquisition of nuclear weapons by the non-nuclear-weapon states. The words "national control" would have permitted an MLF, and were opposed by the Soviets for that reason. The Soviets' draft NPT, submitted to the General Assembly in September, had more comprehensive nontransfer and nonacquisition clauses that would have prohibited the creation of an MLF.

The U.S. position changed at the end of 1965. The U.S. government was itself divided on the choice between an NPT and the MLF. The State Department, presumably responding to concerns over NATO, supported the MLF. ACDA favored a formula that would achieve an NPT agreement. The Defense Department generally supported ACDA, in part because the NPT was looked upon as preferable to a comprehensive test ban as a way to discourage proliferation, and in part because it was skeptical of the MLF concept. Difficulties in the effort to move forward on the MLF increased, many of the NATO countries had lost their enthusiasm for the project, and President Johnson concluded, after discussions with Congressional leaders, that Congress would not support the scheme. Anxious to make progress in controlling proliferation, Johnson and Secretary of State Rusk decided in effect to abandon the MLF. The United States was now prepared to agree that nuclear weapons should not be transferred to non-nuclear states, whether directly or indirectly, through third countries or groups of countries, or through units of the armed forces under any military alliance.

Johnson's decision was reinforced early in 1966 with the introduction and passage of the Pastore Senate Resolution. This resolution cited the dangers involved in the spread of nuclear weapons, commended urgent efforts to negotiate an agreement, and supported the principle of "additional efforts by the President which are appropriate and necessary in the interest of peace for the solution of nuclear proliferation problems."

A break in the U.S.-U.S.S.R. impasse was thus in sight, but problems were arising on other fronts. Most countries had over the years voiced strong support for a non-proliferation agreement as an important step in limiting the dangers of a nuclear world. Thus the United States, and probably the Soviet Union as well, assumed that if the two countries could agree on the terms of an arrangement, the rest of the world would sigh with relief and be eager to associate itself. At meetings of the ENDC in Geneva in 1966, however, it became evident that many other states did not view the proliferation problem in quite the same way as the United States or the Soviet Union did. Representatives of many non-nuclear nations demanded that a non-proliferation agreement do more than commit the non-nuclear states not to obtain nuclear weapons and commit the nuclear states not to provide these weapons to the non-nuclear nations. These representatives called for a package arrangement that would place more substantial responsibilities and obligations on the nuclear states. Further, they doubted the simple division of countries into nuclear and non-nuclear. Instead, as Alva Myrdal, the Swedish delegate, suggested, there was a "spectrum of positions," including those of the nuclear superpowers, of other powers currently possessing nuclear weapon capabilities, of states with potential weapon capabilities, and of definitely non-nuclear-weapon countries. "Can we really hope," she asked, "to encompass these highly different situations in one and the same treaty?" In response, Adrian Fisher of the United States, Deputy Director of ACDA, suggested that the negotiations should not "link the entry into force of one measure with that of another for fear that we might not get either" and said that it was a mistake to assume that a "non-proliferation treaty is advantageous to nuclear weapons States." The Soviet delegate similarly argued that "it would hardly be conducive to our purpose to tie up a series of measures in a single package. . . . In our opinion this would complicate negotiations which are difficult enough already."

The demands of the non-nuclear powers increased in intensity during the following year. The non-nuclear states insisted that the two superpowers accept obligations to take steps to reduce the "vertical proliferation" of their nuclear arsenals. Some non-nuclear states asked how their own security would be protected if they renounced nuclear weapons. They also demanded assistance from the nuclear powers in the peaceful uses of nuclear energy such as nuclear power and PNEs. Some of these objections resulted from genuine concerns on the part of the non-nuclear states; some came from reservations about or concealed opposition to the NPT itself.

The implication of these objections and of the link—albeit attenuated after 1965—between the NPT and NATO nuclear issues was that three overlapping negotiations were required before the NPT could be signed: that between the United States and the Soviet Union, that between the United States and its NATO allies, and that between the two superpowers on the one hand and the nonaligned non-nuclear states on the other hand. Negotiations centered on the ENDC and private meetings in Geneva, but they extended far beyond that forum. Many meetings of NATO's North Atlantic Council in Brussels were devoted to the negotiations; special U.S. missions were dispatched to Japan, West Germany, Italy, South Africa, and Australia. The Japanese and Indian governments sent special envoys to Washington for consultations; lengthy bilateral consultations with special teams from various NATO countries took place in Washington. The Soviet Union sent missions to certain capitals and also met with its allies, one of whom, Rumania, had raised numerous objections in ENDC sessions. The nonaligned nations in the ENDC met frequently to formulate their views and present them to the co-chairman. And a World Conference of Non-Nuclear Nations was held in 1968, after the treaty was negotiated but before many had ratified it.

The United States and the Soviet Union resolved the basic Article I and II issues—the scope of the treaty—during 1966 and 1967, negotiating at the ENDC, in private sessions of the two co-chairmen, and through meetings between Secretary Rusk and Foreign Minister Gromyko in New York in 1967. Several differences had remained after the United States gave up the MLF in late 1965. The Soviets were still worried that U.S. proposals would permit West Germany access to or control over U.S. nuclear weapons through participation in NATO defense arrangements. The Soviets wanted a prohibition barring co-ownership or co-possession. The United States assured the ENDC that under existing NATO defense arrangements the United States retained control over the right and the ability to fire its nuclear weapons, and had no intention of changing this policy, which indeed was required by U.S. domestic law. The United States was prepared to reflect this position by letting Article I prohibit transfer of nuclear weapons not only to the national control of non-nuclear states but also to the control of an association of such states.

A further issue was raised by the "European option," the possibility that the nuclear nations of Western Europe might create a future European federation of states and turn their nuclear arsenals over to that federation. This issue was resolved in favor of the United States, and the two nations presented identical drafts with a blank safeguards article on August 24, 1967. Article I, together with its mirror image Article II concerning obligations of non-nuclear states, is for the United States and the Soviet Union the heart of the treaty. Article I states:

Each nuclear-weapon State Party to the Treaty undertakes not to transfer to any recipient whatsoever nuclear weapons or other nuclear explosive devices or control over such weapons or explosive devices directly, or indirectly; and not in any way to assist, encourage, or induce any non-nuclear-weapon State to manufacture or otherwise acquire nuclear weapons or other nuclear explosive devices, or control over such weapons or explosive devices.

The language of both Articles I and II was incorporated in the final treaty without change. The United States has publicly interpreted the language as permitting European nations to create a European nuclear force if sovereignty is transferred to the European federation. The Soviet Union has not publicly objected. The two nations agree that the language prohibits the MLF.

The problem of Article III was not anticipated by either nation at the beginning of the negotiations, but it was to cause more difficulty than any other issue except Article I. The United States and the Soviet Union both favored the use of the IAEA safeguards system. However, the countries of the European Atomic Energy Community (EURATOM) wished to use the EURATOM safeguard system for NPT inspection arrangements for EURATOM countries. EURATOM had been created as part of the initial drive toward European integration, and it safeguarded the nuclear materials that the United States had transmitted to Western Europe for peaceful purposes. Many feared that if the EURATOM safeguard system were relinquished to the IAEA, EURATOM might collapse, with adverse consequences for European integration. In deference to its allies, the United States supported their views. The Soviets refused to accept EURATOM safeguards for the NPT, calling EURATOM a form of self-inspection. In addition, non-EURATOM countries objected to preferential treatment for the EURATOM states. After a lengthy and complex negotiation, this issue was finally resolved by an arrangement that would allow utilization of the EURATOM system but would bring its activities under the wing of the IAEA through an agreement between EURATOM and the IAEA. Even this arrangement offered some legal difficulties because France was a member of EURATOM but would not sign the NPT and objected to discrimination by European Economic Community (EEC) institutions between different EEC members. The legal problem became still more tangled later when Great Britain entered the EEC and became part of EURATOM as an NPT nuclear weapons party.

To help assure non-nuclear countries that NPT safeguards would not cause them any commercial disadvantages in their peaceful nuclear programs, the United States also announced in December 1967 that it would permit IAEA safeguards to be applied to all nuclear activities in the United States except those with direct national-security significance. Great Britain made a similar offer. The Soviet Union, arguing that such inspections would serve no purpose, refused to make such an offer.

But the non-nuclear-weapon nations had other difficulties with the August 1967 drafts. At their insistence, the United States and the Soviet Union revised their positions and presented a joint draft to the ENDC on January 18, 1968. Under the new draft, the superpowers would promise to negotiate in good faith toward ending the arms race and toward a treaty on general and complete disarmament. They would promise to make arrangements to provide PNEs and to facilitate the transfer of peaceful nuclear technology. These provisions were the heart of the treaty for the non-nuclear nations. The right to create nuclear free zones would be expressly reserved. Finally, a review process and a twenty-five-year limitation on the treaty (unless readopted by majority vote) would be designed to give the non-nuclear nations greater control over the future of the treaty.

Even these changes were not enough, and Sweden particularly criticized the draft, acting as the spokesman for the nonaligned nations. New amendments were made: support in the preamble for a comprehensive test ban and for a halt to the arms race, and inclusion in the text of a plan for a regular review conference to be held every five years. The ENDC transmitted the amended draft to the General Assembly in March. New changes were made to strengthen the assurances to non-nuclear states that they would benefit from the development of peaceful uses of nuclear energy. Finally, on June 12 the General Assembly overwhelmingly passed a resolution commending the treaty and asking that it be opened for signature.

There was still a further problem, long since raised by the non-nuclear nations, the problem of security assurances to protect those nations that were being asked to give up the right to possess nuclear weapons. They initially sought negative assurances parallel to those of Protocol II to the LANFZ. Switzerland and Rumania, for example, proposed that the NPT include a clause forbidding nuclear-weapon states from using or threatening to use nuclear weapons against the signatories to the treaty. Since the treaty would permit the United States to deploy nuclear weapons in Germany, the Soviet Union found the clause unacceptable, arguing that it could not then retaliate against Germany following a U.S. attack with nuclear weapons from West Germany. The Soviets proposed a clause designed to meet this problem by exempting states that had nuclear weapons on their territory from the benefit of the negative assurance. The clause was understandably unacceptable to Germany, and negotiations toward negative assurances failed.

The United States, Great Britain, and the Soviet Union therefore chose a different tack: to make parallel declarations, recognizing that the threat or use of nuclear weapons would put the peace and security of all states in doubt and create a qualitatively new situation. As members of the Security Council, they pledged that they would take action in accordance with the U.N. Charter to assist the threatened states and to counter the threat on use of nuclear weapons. These general declarations were submitted to the Security Council with an equally general resolution of approval. Although regarded as too weak by some non-nuclear nations, the resolution was approved on June 19, 1968, by a vote of 10 to 0 with 5 abstentions.

On July 1, 1968, the Treaty on the Non-Proliferation of Nuclear Weapons[2] was signed in Washington, Moscow, and London, and the United States announced that agreement had been reached with the Soviet Union to enter discussions on strategic arms limitations.

Nuclear Proliferation and Its Control After the Non-Proliferation Treaty

The NPT went into effect on March 5, 1970. On that date, 97 nations had signed it and 47 had ratified it. By the time of the first Review Conference in 1975, there were 111 signatories, including 96 full parties.

[2] For the text of the treaty, see Appendix C.

Of the six nuclear powers, three, the United States, the Soviet Union, and the United Kingdom, had ratified the treaty. France has declared that it will abide by its terms. The People's Republic of China has also refused to join, but it has given no indication that it will encourage nuclear proliferation. Although the United States and the Soviet Union were the principal negotiators and sponsors of the treaty, they delayed ratification until December 1969. This delay was probably due to a Soviet decision not to ratify until after the West German government had signed; the desire to prevent West German acquisition of nuclear weapons was a principal motivation for Soviet support of the treaty. The United States, in turn, withheld ratification until Soviet approval was assured.

Among the non-nuclear powers that have or are planning significant nuclear industries, only Australia, Canada, Iran, Mexico, Sweden, and most of the nations of Europe, including the Federal Republic of Germany, ratified the treaty by the time of the Review Conference. Japan's Diet voted to ratify the treaty in 1976. Most of the other nations with comparable programs had not signed: Argentina, Brazil, India (if it is not counted as a nuclear nation), Israel, Pakistan, Saudi Arabia, and South Africa. Egypt had signed but not ratified, and it appeared unlikely that it would ratify. Thus the treaty failed to obtain the support of many of the nations whose support was the most important.

The negotiation of the IAEA safeguards required by the treaty proved less difficult than anticipated. Concern had been expressed that these safeguards would prove both costly and intrusive, but scientists in Germany and the United States helped develop simplified and automated inspection devices for nuclear reactors. The agreement between the IAEA and EURATOM was successfully negotiated. This agreement made ratification by Germany and other EURATOM states possible and also removed one of the barriers to Japan's ratification.

The abstention of so many important nations therefore rested on grounds deeper than the cost and intrusiveness of safeguards. Probably the key difficulty was the inherent asymmetry of the treaty. The treaty divided the world into two groups of nations and placed much heavier burdens on one group than on the other. Naturally, the non-nuclear nations, which were being asked to bear heavier burdens, objected, particularly since the political division of the world was tending to shift from an East-West pattern to a North-South pattern that paralleled the nuclear versus non-nuclear division. The United States and the Soviet Union did not enhance the treaty's attractiveness with their SALT agreements, which did not seem that substantial to many non-nuclear nations. The U.S.-U.S.S.R. failure to reach a comprehensive test ban antagonized some nations, and the U.S.S.R. interest in PNEs contributed to non-nuclear-nation interest in PNEs. The U.S.-U.S.S.R. assurance structure seemed weak. And the NPT's safeguard system had an understandable but unfortunate disincentive built into it. If a non-nuclear nation joined the NPT, it had to submit *all* its peaceful nuclear facilities to IAEA safeguards. But if the nation stayed out of the NPT, only those facilities supplied internationally would generally be subject to IAEA safeguards.

Specific strategic and political issues were, however, more important than these general factors for almost every major nation. Attitudes toward the NPT varied from country to country as a function of such factors as economic and technical development, geostrategic position, and political ambitions. The attitudes ranged from outright indifference to intense support or opposition. Consequently, when proliferation is discussed, it is more useful to examine the specific considerations affecting the decisions of particular non-nuclear powers than to attempt to outline a largely nonexistent "non-nuclear-nation position" on proliferation. Three examples—India, Israel, and Japan—will be discussed to illustrate the reasons why nations have chosen to reject the NPT or found it difficult to accept. All three have advanced nuclear industries. Both India and Israel have uneasy borders. India has a "peaceful nuclear device," Israel is generally assumed to be able to conduct a nuclear explosion anytime it chooses, and Japan is very unlikely to develop nuclear weapons but also found it very difficult to ratify the NPT.

In May 1974 India conducted an underground test of a "peaceful nuclear device" and became the first nation to cross the nuclear threshold after negotiation of the NPT. India's device used plutonium derived from India's own uranium in a natural uranium reactor supplied by Canada. Indian officials said they tested a "nuclear device," not a nuclear weapon, and they claim they will not develop nuclear weapons but rather will use the "devices" for peaceful purposes such as mining. Through this distinction between military and peaceful devices, and through use of its own uranium, India argued that it did not violate the safeguard agreements covering the Canadian-supplied reactor. There is, however, little if any scientific or technical difference between a "device" and a weapon, and India's neighbors have viewed the device as giving India a weapons capability. The degree to which the Indian action has weakened the NPT, however, is difficult to judge: Pakistan is the nation most directly affected, and it has been negotiating the purchase of reprocessing facilities but is still far from a nuclear capability. Other nations are influenced only indirectly by the effect of India's action on the climate for proliferation, an effect that is quite difficult to evaluate.

India's motives in acquiring the device are probably quite complex. India has had uneasy relations with its neighbors, particularly Pakistan and China. The military threats to India from Pakistan, however, decreased after India's victory in the 1971 war. India nevertheless continues to fear the possibility of a Chinese conventional or nuclear attack, a fear deriving from the Chinese victory in its 1962 war with India in the Himalayas. The nuclear powers' assurances at the time of NPT negotiations gave India little confidence of outside support against China, and any confidence India might have had of U.N. enforcement action was taken away when China entered the Security Council as a permanent member able to veto such action. The actual role of nuclear weapons in protecting India against China is unclear. Tactical nuclear weapons or nuclear land mines might help repulse a possible invasion across the Himalayas. It has also been suggested that Indian nuclear weapons might be used to counter a possible Chinese threat of nuclear war by ensuring that India could retaliate. The ability of India to deter a possible Chinese nuclear attack would, however, depend upon the nature of the Indian nuclear arsenal: it is unlikely that India could develop an invulnerable second-strike capability without an intolerable strain on scarce resources. A less advanced force might still have deterrent value; it might also be destabilizing. Moreover, there exists some opposition to large nuclear programs among Indian military officials, who fear that the costs of such programs would necessitate drastic cuts in conventional forces, as they did in France.

The Indian nuclear test was also seen as having significant prestige value. The first Chinese atomic explosion resulted in a great increase in developing-world respect for China, and India may hope to secure a similar increase in prestige. In addition, Indian nuclear weapons could be seen as helping to give India the psychological equality it desires for future détente with China. The Indian test also brought the government substantial domestic political advantages.

Some within the Indian government have also directly supported the economic role of peaceful nuclear explosions for purposes such as excavation and oil retrieval, but many experts doubt that such explosions would be economically useful for India (or any other nation). The "peaceful uses" identification of the explosion may well have been designed to gain some of the benefits of nuclear status without imposing the cost of an ambitious nuclear weapon and delivery system program. Whether India will continue in this halfway position or be tempted into a substantial nuclear weapons program cannot be foreseen.

Security concerns are paramount to Israel, a state of about three and one-half million people in running conflict with states with a total population of about 40 million. With the military capability of the Arabs' side growing, some in Israel fear that Israel might be destroyed in a future war. A small Israeli nuclear arsenal, capable of hitting several Arab cities and the Aswan High Dam, could be argued to deter such Arab action. Even rumors of a possible Israeli ability to use nuclear weapons as a last resort are seen as important ways to deter the Arabs from exploiting any battlefield victory too far.

Although the possession of nuclear weapons might have military advantages to Israel, it would also have high military and political costs. An Israeli atomic bomb test would almost certainly decrease chances for a long-term peaceful settlement in the Middle East. The Soviets might respond by increasing their conventional aid to Egypt, by strengthening the Soviet nuclear fleet in the Mediterranean, and even possibly by deploying Soviet armed forces in Egypt or Syria. An Israeli decision to go nuclear would also alienate the United States and might well result in a U.S. disengagement from its previous commitments to Israel; Israel would thus be faced with the choice of trading its main source of strength, the tie with the United States, for an overt nuclear capability that would increase tensions and would not be usable except in a last-resort situation.

Israel probably has a plutonium-reprocessing plant in Beersheba and at least the capability to build a nuclear weapon in a matter of months or even weeks. The political costs of going nuclear are unlikely to be incurred unless Israel actually detonates an atomic weapon, and Israeli scientists can probably be confident of needed weapons designs without conducting such a test. It is likely that the most advantageous position for Israel is therefore to develop a standby capability and to leave this capability ambiguous, relying on Arab suspicions and fears of possible Israeli nuclear weapons as deterrents against any massive Arab incursions into Israeli territory. This strategy of nuclear ambiguity is inconsistent with signature of the NPT. The ambiguity may also be viewed as an implied threat to go nuclear unless the United States provides adequate conventional military aid. Although there may be other ways to analyze Israel's strategy, its NPT position is clearly intertwined with its relations with the United States and with the entire Mideast conflict.

Analysis of Japan's position must begin with Article 9 of its constitution, imposed by the U.S. occupation forces after Japan's defeat in 1945:

Aspiring sincerely to an international peace based on justice and order, the Japanese people forever renounce war as a sovereign right of the nation and the threat or use of force as means of settling international disputes.

In order to accomplish the aim of the preceding paragraph, land, sea and air forces, as well as other war potential, will never be maintained. The right of belligerency of the state will not be recognized.

By the time the occupation ended in 1952, the United States was fighting a war in Korea and was more concerned about U.S.S.R. and Chinese militarism than about Japanese militarism. It urged rearmament upon Japan and a construction of Article 9 that would permit such rearmament. Japan now has a defense force, although this force is much smaller than one would expect for the world's third largest economic power. In 1953, the United States also entered into a Mutual Security Agreement with Japan, effectively placing the latter within the U.S. nuclear umbrella. This agreement helped permit Japan to emphasize economic growth, but was also the occasion for a series of disputes over issues such as U.S. bases in Japan and U.S. rights on Okinawa.

Nevertheless, the framework provided by the Mutual Security Agreement persisted and the parallel special relationship remained, even though disturbed by the "Nixon shocks" of the early 1970's. These were the U.S. devaluation of the dollar in 1971, which seriously affected the Japanese economy; President Nixon's opening to China, a nation that the United States had encouraged Japan to fear; and the San Clemente communiqué of 1973, which led some Japanese to doubt the credibility of the U.S. nuclear defense guarantee. These actions were apparently taken without prior consultation with Japan, and they had a serious effect on Japanese public opinion.

Japan's diplomatic response was to continue its effort to maintain the special relationship with Washington, while striving to walk a tightrope between the Soviet Union and China. Premier Tanaka visited China and opened expanding relationships with Peking. Corresponding efforts were made to set up relationships with the Soviet Union. In both cases, economic relationships were emphasized, and the rapprochement with China progressed more easily than with the Soviet Union.

Japan signed the NPT in early 1970 but delayed ratification, both because of fears that the safeguard requirements might hurt the economic competitiveness of its nuclear industry, and because of some public opinion opposition to the treaty. The safeguard concerns were alleviated after the pattern of the IAEA-EURATOM safeguard agreement became clear, but the Nixon shocks and the U.S. withdrawal from Southeast Asia intervened. In this new strategic environment, it was easy to make Gaullist-type arguments that the U.S. guarantee lacked credibility. The government faced opposition to the NPT within parts of the bureaucracy, within factions of the ruling Liberal Democratic Party, and from some of the opposition parties. Submission of the NPT to the Diet was considered but rejected several times in 1974 and early 1975, but both houses finally approved the treaty in 1976.

In the examples just reviewed, the decision whether or not to build nuclear weapons was taken primarily on political and strategic grounds. In this sense, technical and economic issues are of lesser importance. The technical and economic factors are, however, leading to a greater and greater diffusion of the ability to develop nuclear weapons.

These technical and economic factors derive from the spread of nuclear power through the world, a spread that accelerated with the oil crisis following the 1973 Mideast war. As the price of oil rose, nuclear reactors became more attractive economically as alternative electricity sources. International sales of nuclear reactors increased drastically, as did competition among the different suppliers. Most of the reactors sold were of types that could be useful in weapons programs only if spent fuel were retained by the recipient nation and the plutonium were extracted from that fuel in a reprocessing plant. The nuclear-technology-exporting parties to the NPT agreed in 1974 to require safeguards on all fuel processed through reactors they supplied. France, however, not a party to the NPT, did not participate in this understanding, and the agreement came too late to prevent the Indian explosion.

What was probably more important than the sales of reactors was a series of 1975 arrangements to sell enrichment and reprocessing facilities and to build enrichment plants in new nations. Thus, Brazil and South Africa were planning enrichment facilities, and Pakistan, South Korea, and Taiwan were planning reprocessing facilities. Some of the new facilities were under safeguards, but the technology was clearly becoming widely available, and the technology involved was adequate for weapons. An enrichment plant can produce weapons-grade uranium from natural uranium, although it would normally be operated to produce low-enriched uranium that is suitable for most reactors but not for weapons. And a reprocessing plant, combined with a reactor in which the nation has control over the disposition of the used fuel, can produce plutonium for weapons. Thus, the spread of this second wave of nuclear technology was crucial from the proliferation viewpoint, albeit the acquisition of enrichment capabilities was understandable from the energy security viewpoint. Nations feared that their nuclear fuel supplies would be cut off the same way their oil supplies had been cut off; they therefore sought to ensure that the critical facilities would be under their control.

During 1975, some efforts were made to negotiate a halt to the transfer of these facilities and to bring France, as an important supplier, into the control network, but the efforts were not totally successful. Some doubted whether such transfer restrictions were negotiable or would be effective if negotiated, and suggested economic or political ways to discourage the sales. Others pointed to the growing public concern over the safety and environmental dangers of nuclear power and the possibility of terrorist seizure of nuclear power, and suggested that this public concern could in some way be harnessed to strengthen international control over nuclear power.

It was clear, however, that the primary way to prevent nuclear proliferation was to create a world political and strategic order in which nations would not want to build nuclear weapons. After all, political and strategic factors were crucial in nations' actual weapons development decisions. But there were at least two drastically different schools of thought on the way to create such a world order.

One school emphasized the arguments used in the French decision to build nuclear weapons. It suggested that firm U.S. nuclear and military commitments would give nations such as Japan and Israel the confidence not to build nuclear weapons. Similarly, in a world in which the strategic predominance of the superpowers was assured, nations such as Brazil and Iran would recognize that they could not increase their political prestige through acquiring nuclear weapons. Members of this school suggested that SALT itself might have encouraged nuclear proliferation, and they tended to oppose any U.S. force reductions.

The other school pointed to the arguments that had frequently been made in arms control negotiations—that success in superpower arms control would strengthen the climate of nuclear restraint and would therefore make a decision to proliferate politically more difficult. A failure of the superpowers to fulfill their obligations under Article VI of the NPT to control their own arms race could be exploited by nonnuclear states to justify not signing the treaty. Negotiating a comprehensive test ban could help remedy the rather hypocritical position of the United States and the Soviet Union, that of urging non-nuclear powers to refrain from developing and testing nuclear weapons while continuing to conduct active test programs themselves. The nuclear nations could also enter no first-use agreements regarding nuclear weapons as a way to show that they did not believe such weapons to be viable and useful. Similarly, by refusing to grant special favors or recognition to nations, like India, that do build nuclear devices, they could show that acquisition of nuclear weapons does not bring prestige.

Nearly all from both schools agreed on one point—that the current U.S. and U.S.S.R. position on PNEs encourages proliferation. The Americans and, more especially, the Soviets have carefully protected their own opportunity to test PNEs, but have not given any other nations assistance in using PNEs. The superpowers should either admit—as many argue—that PNEs are uneconomical and completely discontinue their own programs, or alternatively conduct research on the economical applications and assist developing nations by making PNEs available under proper safeguards. By doing neither, they leave non-nuclear nations able to argue that PNEs must bring important benefits and that these benefits can be made available only through national nuclear development programs.

The Indian nuclear explosion, followed by debates about the spread of peaceful nuclear facilities and the sales of these facilities after the 1973 oil crisis placed non-proliferation near or at the top of the arms control agenda. For many, it became more important than U.S.-Soviet bilateral negotiations, for the spread of nuclear weapons appeared likely to be dangerous and likely to make negotiation of any substantial arms control more difficult.

CHAPTER FIFTEEN

Toward an Evaluation of Arms Control: Unanswered Questions

THE PRECEDING chapters have described the course of arms control through several decades, from the scattered efforts made before World War II to the central role it has taken in the diplomacy of the 1970's. We have tried also to present a balanced discussion of both the motivations for arms control and the factors affecting the success or failure of the various negotiations. In reflecting on this history we can suggest many high-priority issues for future arms control planners—nuclear proliferation, perhaps, or bringing China into the negotiations, or revising the way in which bureaucratic structures help shape arms control agreements. We might also question arms control on its own terms: Can effective agreements be negotiated swiftly enough to keep pace with the changing weapons technology?

Underlying these important issues, there are deeper questions centering around the possible benefits of arms control: Can arms limitations help save money? Can they help prevent war? Can they help improve relations between nations such as the United States and the Soviet Union? Are they steps toward a unified disarmed world? Each of these questions suggests an intuitively plausible benefit of arms control; none of the questions, however, can yet be answered very confidently.

This concluding chapter reviews several of these areas of uncertainty. (The question of the economic benefits of arms control was discussed in Chapter 11 and is not therefore considered here.) This chapter first considers the possible war-prevention benefits of arms control. It then reviews the role of arms control in détente and U.S.-U.S.S.R. understanding. Finally, it examines the long-term goals of an arms control policy, asking whether some new international order—perhaps disarmament or more powerful international organization—is necessarily associated with substantial arms control. The issues raised in this chapter are controversial; they deserve scholarly analysis and political debate.

Can Negotiable Arms Control Help Prevent War?

Even though few of the arms control agreements reached so far place very substantial limitations on nations' force levels, the agreements are generally designed around an underlying assumption that they will help prevent war through modifying international diplomatic and strategic relationships. As noted in the first chapter, there is a tendency to begin by asking whether arms are the cause of war or are merely symptoms of the underlying conflicts that cause war. To pose the question this way is, however, to create a false dilemma and to ignore the complex interactions that exist between the levels and types of armaments and the political decision to go to war. Arms can sometimes cause war and sometimes reflect the causes of war. The naval arms race between Britain and Germany and the ready availability of arms for the Balkan Wars in 1912 and 1913 were probably contributing factors to World War I. On the other hand, greater U.S., British, and French weapons procurements in the 1930's might have prevented World War II, suggesting that arms are sometimes obtained to prepare for or even to try to prevent an impending war. The result of these two inverse effects is that there is a high correlation between arms levels and the likelihood of some kinds of war, but that that correlation does not imply that arms necessarily cause war.

Arms control can *directly* affect only a nation's military capability. A decision-maker, however, does not decide to go to war just because he has the capability to do so, but instead because he has the intention to do so. Indirectly, perhaps, a decision-maker's capabilities may affect his own intentions; he may decide to go to war, in part because he believes that his nation has the capability to win a war that he had previously been considering. Thus, one argument against nuclear proliferation is the chance that some nation might decide that possession of nuclear weapons gives it the decisive power to settle an old dispute.

The effect of capabilities on a possible opponent's intentions is probably stronger. Unless a nation has clear and reliable information about its opponent's intentions, the nation will tend to use worst-case analysis and to assume that its opponent intends to do all the harm that it is capable of doing. The nation may respond with actions that suggest to its opponent that its intentions cannot be trusted either. In this sense, an arms competition can develop a momentum of its own so that it not only reflects existing political conflict but also creates new conflict. Even though weapons procurement may be intended defensively, it may give the opponent additional reason to believe that one is aggressive. In the Middle East, for example, basic conflicts of interest caused the Arabs and Israelis to build up their armed forces, but the forces and deployments themselves created added suspicions, since each side viewed increments in the opponent's forces as suggestive of aggressive intent. Similarly, in the era before World War I, arms buildups, new alliances, and even the construction of strategic railroads became sources of new suspicion. These tensions created by arms might be reduced by arms control efforts. A reduction or control of arms would not remove the basic conflicts in the Middle East; it might remove some of the tensions and uncertainties caused by the weapons themselves and might decrease the risks and consequences of diplomatic miscalculation.

Arms control might also be beneficial through providing greater certainty about different nations' force levels. A balance of power, such as that in the Mideast or before World War I, is stable so long as each nation expects that victory in war would be doubtful or extremely costly and also knows what actions are or are not likely to provoke a war. Weapons can sometimes help stabilize such situations through maintaining a balance of powers or adding credibility to commitments. When force levels are rapidly increasing, however, it becomes easier to misjudge whether they are balanced. Arms control can provide knowledge and planning information to help stabilize these balances.

Arms control arrangements can also reduce the probability that incidents will occur. With military activity banned in the Antarctic, war in the area becomes less likely. The rules for prevention of incidents at sea decrease the chances of a naval incident that might escalate into war. Non-proliferation arrangements might help prevent terrorist groups from obtaining nuclear materials and creating international incidents. Unilateral or internationally agreed improvements in command and control of nuclear weapons can reduce the risk of unauthorized or accidental use of such weapons. Analogous concepts were long applied by diplomats in serious conflict areas by setting up weak or neutralized nations as buffer zones between contending powers. A nation protected by such a zone need not be quite so suspicious of another nation's actions.

Finally, arms control can improve the stability of military deployments and reduce incentives to attack first or to escalate quickly. The SALT I agreements were designed in part to meet this goal, in keeping with the rules of deterrence theory, and stability between nuclear powers is clearly a crucial achievement. Conventional arms limitations could be similarly dealt with, both to reduce incentives to preempt and to afford political decision-makers better control of their military forces.

Nevertheless, there remain some types of conflict that by their very nature cannot be affected, let alone prevented, by arms control agreements. One example is revolutionary struggle, which will not be directly affected by state-to-state agreements designed to stabilize the international system and prevent war. In many parts of the world there are revolutionary groups whose desire to remedy basic inequities outweighs their concern for the stability of the international system. Some of these groups, demanding self-determination, seek to fulfill their aims by revolutionary wars of national liberation, viewing order as the goal of the more advanced and more satisfied. The coincidence of post-colonial nationalism with the emergence of modern economic systems and the rise of Communist movements has produced a powerful combination for continued struggle. Such struggles are likely to be little affected by agreements to limit or prohibit the use of sophisticated weapons systems, although they might be affected by the spread of or limitations on the new conventional technologies and materials suitable for terrorism.

Deeply felt conflict can also arise internationally or become international. The case of the Arabs and the Israelis or that of Greece and Turkey over Cyprus or that of Black and White in southern Africa shows the potential. Conflicts of this type are sometimes all but forced on political leaders by the attitudes of their supporters, and low initial military-force levels are unlikely to limit the struggle.

The probability that some wars cannot be stopped by arms limitations raises a further question: can arms control keep the unavoidable wars from becoming nuclear wars? The limited wars of the recent past did not escalate into nuclear wars, but the danger of escalation into a full nuclear exchange was always present, and persists today. So far, this danger has probably been relatively slight, and arms control can help keep it slight. The possession of highly sophisticated weapons systems by the major powers may even have inhibited their freedom of action and willingness to intervene in conflict, and thereby indirectly made certain types of conflicts "safer" to wage. With the spread of nuclear weapons and the growth of more flexible nuclear-targeting doctrines, however, one may perhaps be more pessimistic and fear that escalation will become more likely. If, again, the threat of escalation is a barrier to conventional war, it might follow that success in inhibiting the deployment and use of nuclear weapons could make non-nuclear war more likely—"safer" as a means of policy and therefore more feasible. One might also argue that conventional war provides a less dangerous alternative to nuclear war, and therefore conventional disarmament should not be allowed to lead to elimination of this alternative. It is this sort of argument that can be used to favor strong conventional forces in Europe.

This review leads one toward the conclusion that arms control agreements can help prevent some wars, although only some. Whether enough arms control agreements are actually negotiable to play a major role in war prevention is another question. As the text has shown, the barriers to both unilateral arms reduction and negotiation of arms control agreements are quite substantial. Those favoring the maintenance of military forces are often placed in strong bureaucratic and political positions. Reductions of important arms are much harder to negotiate than are agreements not to build up unimportant arms. Asymmetries and imbalances among different nations limit arms control possibilities. Some critics—often ardent arms controllers—have gone further to conclude that the bureaucratic and political pressures surrounding arms control negotiations are so strong that the negotiations are likely to lead to increased force levels.

At most, an arms control agreement, like any peacetime treaty, can generally only strengthen and confirm preexisting intentions of governments. No treaty will be accepted unless it is in the interests of all parties. Arms control has thus tended to become a tool of stabilizing very specific military balances and of coordinating national military intentions. It is likely to be very difficult to decrease force levels drastically.

Greater effort and increased political support *might* help arms control to go further to obtain broader agreements that appear strategically desirable but are stalled by current limits on negotiability. If such far-reaching agreements are to be obtained, they will probably be negotiated in a single package. One of the lessons of history is that incrementalism—the use of a series of small steps—is a questionable strategy (although negotiations between radically different political systems might be an important exception to this judgment). The general tendency, as with the 1922 Naval Accord, the Limited Test Ban, and SALT I, is to agree first on what is easy. The second step is usually disappointing. And, although they have not yet had this effect, the easy withdrawal clauses that are essential to contemporary agreements might make first agreements weak bases on which to build further agreements. One is strongly tempted, therefore, in order to gain the benefits of arms control, to pursue extensive agreements like those sought in the negotiations of the 1950's. Conceivably, such agreements might be possible during times of particularly favorable political balances in the various nations.

Arms Control in Its Political Context: The U.S.-U.S.S.R. Case

The arguments just presented assume that arms control does not remove the basic conflicts that initially cause nations to build weapons; it reduces only those conflicts arising from the existence of the weapons themselves. But much broader agreements have also been made; the process of reaching agreements can itself develop a friendship that indirectly helps prevent war. In other words, arms control would in some way change the goals that nations pursue—goals that are assumed fixed in most diplomatic and strategic arguments. Moreover, limited arms control might change the political framework to make more substantial agreements politically feasible. When President Nixon brought the SALT package home from Moscow in 1972, he did not emphasize the details of strategic theory in presenting it to the public; instead, he presented the agreement as a symbol of détente.

It does seem the case, more often than not, that negotiations with another nation, on almost any important issue, will decrease the likelihood of war. The mechanism is much less clear. Perhaps it is simply that the two sides come to understand one another's motivations and actions more clearly. Perhaps the process of negotiation sometimes creates a sense of cooperation in working out shared problems. Perhaps political constituencies develop in each nation in favor of accommodation with the other.

The process does not always work so beneficially. A nation may react antagonistically if it believes that the other nation's diplomats are not negotiating seriously. A one-sided agreement can also hurt the cause of peace. In the Washington Naval Conference, heavy diplomatic leverage was applied against Japan to force it to accept a lower battleship limitation than that imposed on the United States and Great Britain. Over the next decade, Japan's view of this treaty as a humiliating containment of its power contributed to the development of its militarism before World War II. Senator Jackson reacted to SALT I in a comparable but less violent way. He viewed the agreement as imbalanced against the United States and judged that the Soviet Union was attempting to take advantage of the United States. To the extent that an arms control agreement is likely to create such a reaction, it may intensify suspicion between the parties and increase the ultimate likelihood of war.

One can hope, however, that balanced and seriously negotiated agreements will usually be beneficial. The test in the U.S.-U.S.S.R. case rests on the changes that have occurred in the two societies during their negotiations. The idea of changes was raised during the era of the containment doctrine, long before any arms control agreements. The hope was to maintain peace between the two powers through a military balance for long enough that the political structure of the two sides would change and allow peace to be maintained politically, as it is, for example, between the United States and Great Britain.

The underpinnings of this theory were suggested very early after World War II, with an argument that the United States and the Soviet Union might develop to resemble one another—that they might converge. Harold Lasswell wrote in 1946: "As modern science and technology move toward universality, certain uniformities are imposed upon world attention, and attitudes are molded in similar ways." This convergence might eventually make peace possible. Lasswell again wrote that if there were no war, the societies, in spite of their intense militarism, might eventually "feel secure enough to expand the thin trickle of contact between the 'two worlds.' As the area of contact and confidence gradually extends, a movement toward 'one world' would gradually get under way."[1] Andrei Sakharov in the Soviet Union wrote much more recently that convergence was the only alternative to annihilation.[2] Lasswell also noted, however, that "homogeneity of social structure does not necessarily carry with it either uniformity of doctrine or a single state."

The two societies have converged rather substantially. This convergence is much more than the commonly noted phenomena of an increased economic role for the U.S. government and an increased role of profit-like motivations in the U.S.S.R. economy. The convergence also reaches arms control and military policies. The SALT accords showed some developing similarity in the way the two nations understand strategic theory and the roles of different weapons systems. The two nations found their interests closely aligned in NPT negotiations.

The same convergence appeared in the way military policy is made. Both nations face substantial internal pressures toward arms expenditures. Khrushchev wrote:[3]

I know from experience that the leaders of the armed forces can be very persistent in claiming their share when it comes time to allocate funds. Every commander has all sorts of very convincing arguments why he should get more than anyone else. Unfortunately there's a tendency for people who run the armed forces to be greedy and self-seeking. They're always ready to throw in your face the slogan "If you try to economize on the country's defenses today, you'll pay in blood when war breaks out tomorrow." . . .

Apparently the control of military spending is a universal problem. I remem-

---

[1] Harold D. Lasswell, "The Interrelations of World Organization and Society," *Yale Law Journal*, 55 (1946), 903, 898.

[2] *Thoughts on Progress, Coexistence and Intellectual Freedom* (New York, 1968).

[3] *Khrushchev Remembers* (Boston, 1970), p. 519.

ber a conversation I once had with President Eisenhower when I was a guest at his dacha at Camp David. We went for walks together and had some useful informal talks. During one of these talks, he asked, "Tell me, Mr. Khrushchev, how do you decide the question of funds for military expenses?" Then, before I had a chance to say anything, he said, "Perhaps first I should tell you how it is with us."

Against the demands for military expenditures, there are competing demands for other expenditures, and both nations have developed elites of scientists and intellectuals criticizing the military expenditures. There are many differences between and within the U.S. and U.S.S.R. opposition elites, but the two groups are in contact with each other in places like the Pugwash meetings and international scientific meetings, and often make essentially similar arguments to their governments. Arms control negotiations undoubtedly speeded the convergence process through the sharing of strategic ideas and the encouragement of the recognition of common political and strategic interests.

But at least two points should restrict one's optimism about this convergence. The first is that many on both sides, including most of their opposition elites, are strongly committed to the view that arms limitation is more a part of military security than a restriction on it. In other words, arms control, for many, is a way to stabilize and to lower the cost of a military balance of power, not the beginning of a way to replace that balance of power by some different political structure or a friendship in which the power became unnecessary. This narrow view of arms control, which is shared by the corresponding elites in some of the developing nations, can be contrasted with, for example, that of Western European leaders after World War II. These leaders sought to revise the military and political structure of Western Europe so that war between France and Germany would become unthinkable—and succeeded to the extent that plans for a Franco-German war are probably not even written, let alone taken seriously. Relations between the United States and the Soviet Union are far from that point.

The more telling point about convergence is the character of the society it may have encouraged in the Soviet Union. Many have argued that détente, which seems necessarily associated with U.S.-Soviet arms control, leads through the internal dynamics of the Soviet system to increased repression. It has certainly shown few signs of leading to democracy. Thus, at a 1973 news conference, Andrei Sakharov, the developer of the Soviet H-bomb, referred to the dangers of "détente without democratization."[4] And as détente proceeded, both he and his fellow dissenter, Aleksandr Solzhenitsyn, were increasingly harassed by

[4] "Sakharov: Teetering at the Brink," *Science*, 181 (Sept. 28, 1973), 1228.

the U.S.S.R. government, the latter to the extent of being forced into exile. The two were divided, however, on the policy to be taken toward arms control. For Solzhenitsyn, any form of U.S.-U.S.S.R. détente, including arms control, should be rejected. The right policy for the West would be to avoid all actions that might through trade or through arms control alleviate the burdens on the Soviet economy. The Soviet system would then eventually change under the weight of its internal inefficiencies. Sakharov accepted the same general argument, but would make an exception for arms control, arguing that the possibility that arms control could help prevent nuclear war overrides all the other considerations. And Roy Medvedev, yet another Soviet intellectual, evaluated the effect of détente differently, suggesting that it would be more helpful than harmful to freedom in the Soviet society.

One is left with a sense that arms control negotiations have importantly affected Soviet society—far more than they have affected U.S. society. It is an effect that could favor incrementalism via the hope that a series of small agreements with the Soviet Union could eventually help change that society, which has been a major barrier to substantial arms control. But one can equally argue that incrementalism in its current détente framework is delaying change in the Soviet Union. The interplay of economic and ideological and strategic factors is too complex to evaluate these effects without far more knowledge of the internal workings and motivations of the Soviet leadership than anyone in the West possesses.

Arms Control and Change in the International Order

Although large percentages of nuclear arms and lesser percentages of conventional arms could conceivably be eliminated on the strength of agreements of the current form, the situation eventually encounters limitations deriving from national perceptions of minimum essential force levels and from asymmetries among the forces of different nations and groups of nations. One answer to this problem is international organization. The military forces of a central body might provide the security that national forces currently provide; deeper cuts in national forces would then be possible. Most of the proposals for general and complete disarmament (although probably not offered seriously) suggested such an international group. In the preliminary discussions within the United States government during the early part of World War II, a disarmament system was to be set up along with the United Nations to make sure no small nation could effectively oppose the United Nations. But the disarmament concept was lost before the beginning of serious negotiations toward the United Nations. More recent proposals would restrict the forces each nation could have, and would set up a decision-making body to interpret the limitations and revise them as technology changes. There would also be an enforcement arrangement such as an international police force.

As discussed in Chapter 2, the United Nations was itself established with a procedure for enforcing its decisions against the less powerful nations, but shifted to a peacekeeping mode of operation in which it avoided direct enforcement and sought instead to help defuse particular controversies. Building on the experience of either the enforcement or the peacekeeping model of international organization, one could outline international structures to complement arms control agreements for non-nuclear weapons and eventually for nuclear weapons. Under the enforcement model, one would try to ensure the supremacy of the international force. Under the peacekeeping model, one would try to limit weapons that lead to quick or rapidly decisive wars. And there are also possible regional patterns. Under any model, however, there is complex politics. No pattern has to date been worked out in any detailed way that is responsive to today's force or political patterns, or even to the presence of nuclear weapons. Yet, it should be clear that substantial arms control progress will eventually require great attention to this interplay between arms control and international organization.

It is very difficult to design and organize a credible and far-reaching enforcement system. No one knows how to guarantee that the enforcement power is used properly. No nation will want to risk having its government tried by a court that is set up by another country. There would even be political and constitutional difficulties if U.S. citizens became subject for certain arms control purposes to an international criminal tribunal. Even the right to withdraw raises questions; it is significant that the U.S. Constitution does not say what to do if a state repudiates it. Politically, those opposed to arms races are not necessarily the same as those who want to transfer substantial authority to an international body. The international community does not yet arouse loyalty or patriotism. One is back to the problem that people often see military force as a way to defend their liberty.

Agreements working toward international organization or disarmament are therefore not being seriously considered. Nor does it yet seem likely that the political coalitions supporting arms control will readily evolve into political coalitions supporting such agreements. The U.S.-Soviet negotiations may even have increased the relative power of the two nations' governments at the expense of international organization and of the citizens of both nations.

Yet serious consideration of far-reaching international organization is probably essential to the control of war. If so, the economic, sociological, and technological character of the nation-state system will have to change more deeply. This system may in many ways currently encourage war. The nation-state system helps to maintain inequalities, such as those between developed and developing nations. These inequalities can perhaps lead to war. The unification and internal success of a nation, such as that of Germany in the late nineteenth century, can sometimes lead the nation to an expansionist course. National governments, like that of the Soviet Union or those of the Reformation, can come to symbolize particular ideologies or religions, and war can be seen as a way to spread a certain ideology or religion. Each of these features of the nation-state system that can lead to international conflict is also viewed as beneficial by some of each nation's citizens, who therefore have reason to resist international organization.

The character of this nation-state system is in fact changing. Citizens have come to demand that their governments satisfy economic needs in ways that would not have been considered appropriate in the late nineteenth century. New forms of international organization have evolved to meet specific technical problems. Ideologies have become internationalized through movements such as international communism and Christian democratic political parties in Europe. The elites of many of the developing nations identify more with elites in the developed world than with the people of their own nations.

There is no guarantee, however, that the current changes will lead in a compatible direction. The arms control designer must therefore hope for a combination of changes in arms, in international organization, and in the way citizens think of the nation. All would have to change together, just as they did in the past when nations became unified. In the United States, for example, the Civil War marked a major transition from a relatively loose federation in which the states played a strong role to a much closer federation in which the federal government played the stronger role. In the process, the central government assumed a substantial monopoly over the armed forces, the Constitution was amended to give citizens (as distinct from state governments) an important stake in the central government, and the national political party system became much more firmly established. One cannot imagine any of these developments occurring without the others taking place also.

The outlining of an analogous process for today's world—necessarily without world civil war—is an urgent task, essential if arms control is to proceed very far and probably essential if nuclear war is to be averted.

The design of the process will have to reflect insights traditionally considered as belonging to economics, to constitutional theory, to sociology, and even to philosophical theory, as well as insights deriving more obviously from international relations. Arms control might be an important part of the process. So also might national political restrictions on the military, the development of parallel political interests among the military or arms controllers or economic groups in different nations, or the emergence of international interests in solving technological or social problems that cross national boundaries.

The implication for the citizen is that the maintenance of peace rests on more than formal arms control negotiations and defense budget decisions. It perhaps rests also on the reorganization of the United Nations, on the encouragement of international political parties, on a judgment of the levels and areas of competence that can safely be ascribed to the professional diplomat—issues and questions that are often beyond the control of governments. The citizen must evaluate arms control in this broader context of changing institutions and changing political beliefs. And the citizen can play an important role in many other areas of the broader context as well as in arms control itself.

Glossary of Abbreviations

ABM	Anti-Ballistic Missile
ACDA	Arms Control and Disarmament Agency
AEC	Atomic Energy Commission
ASW	Anti-Submarine Warfare
BMD	Ballistic Missile Defense
BW	Biological Weapons (or Biological Warfare)
CCD	Conference of the Committee on Disarmament
CEP	Circular Error Probable
COCOM	Coordinating Committee
CSCE	Conference on Security and Cooperation in Europe
CTB	Comprehensive Test Ban
CW	Chemical Weapons (or Chemical Warfare)
DOD	Department of Defense
EEC	European Economic Community
ENDC	Eighteen-Nation Disarmament Committee
EURATOM	European Atomic Energy Community
FBS	Forward-Based System
FOBS	Fractional Orbital Bombardment System
GCD	General and Complete Disarmament
GNP	Gross National Product
IAEA	International Atomic Energy Agency
ICBM	Intercontinental Ballistic Missile
IGY	International Geophysical Year
IRBM	Intermediate-Range Ballistic Missile
JCS	Joint Chiefs of Staff
KT	Kiloton (1,000 tons)
LANFZ	Latin American Nuclear Free Zone Treaty
LTB	Limited Test Ban
MARV	Maneuverable Reentry Vehicle
MFR	Mutual Force Reduction

MIRV	Multiple Independently Targetable Reentry Vehicle
MRBM	Medium-Range Ballistic Missile
MLF	Multilateral Force
MRV	Multiple Reentry Vehicle
MSR	Missile Site Radar
MT	Megaton (1,000,000 tons)
NATO	North Atlantic Treaty Organization
NCA	National Command Authority
NPT	Non-Proliferation Treaty
OAS	Organization of American States
OPANAL	Agency for the Prohibition of Nuclear Weapons in Latin America (Spanish acronym)
PAR	Perimeter Acquisition Radar
PGM	Precision-Guided Munition
PNE	Peaceful Nuclear Explosive
SAC	Strategic Air Command
SALT	Strategic Arms Limitation Talks
SCC	Standing Consultative Commission
SLBM	Submarine-Launched Ballistic Missile
U.K.	United Kingdom
ULMS	Underwater Long-Range Missile System
U.N.	United Nations
UNAEC	United Nations Atomic Energy Commission
U.S.	United States
U.S.S.R.	Union of Soviet Socialist Republics
WDC	World Disarmament Conference

The Disarmament Forums, 1945–1975

Past Forums No Longer Functioning

1946–52 *U.N. Atomic Energy Commission* (New York). The U.N. General Assembly established this forum, composed of the members of the U.N. Security Council plus Canada. Early efforts to achieve international control over nuclear weapons took place in this commission. In 1952, its functions were taken over by the U.N. Disarmament Commission.

1947–52 *Commission for Conventional Armaments* (New York). Established by the U.N. Security Council, this body was composed of the members of the Security Council. In 1952, its functions were taken over by the U.N. Disarmament Commission.

1954–57 *Subcommittee on Disarmament* (London). This body was established by the U.N. Disarmament Commission and was the principal negotiating forum for three years. Its members were Canada, France, Great Britain, the Soviet Union, and the United States.

1958 *Conference of Experts to Study the Possibility of Detecting Violations of a Possible Agreement on the Suspension of Nuclear Weapons Tests* (Geneva). This group was composed of experts from Canada, Czechoslovakia, France, Poland, Rumania, Great Britain, the Soviet Union, and the United States. It was established as a result of a U.S.-U.S.S.R. agreement that scientific experts be appointed to study the verification of a possible comprehensive test ban agreement. It met for two months and produced an agreed report which led to the three-power political Conference on the Discontinuation of Nuclear Weapons Tests.

NOTE: This list includes only the negotiating forums. It therefore excludes such organizations as the International Atomic Energy Agency (IAEA) and the Agency for the Prohibition of Nuclear Weapons in Latin America (OPANAL), established to administer the Latin American Nuclear Free Zone Treaty.

1958 *Conference of Experts for the Study of Possible Measures Which Might Be Helpful in Preventing Surprise Attack and for the Preparation of a Report Thereon to Governments* (Geneva). This group, which recessed after only six weeks, comprised experts from Canada, France, Great Britain, and the United States, and representatives from Albania, Czechoslovakia, Poland, Rumania, and the Soviet Union.

1958–62 *Conference on the Discontinuation of Nuclear Weapons Tests* (Geneva). The members of this conference, which was a central negotiating group for the partial test ban, were Great Britain, the United States, and the Soviet Union. In 1962 its functions were taken over by the ENDC's "Subcommittee on a Treaty for the Discontinuation of Nuclear Weapons Tests."

1960 *Ten-Nation Committee on Disarmament* (Geneva). This group was established as a result of U.S.-U.S.S.R. agreement and was composed of an equal number of states on each side from NATO and the Warsaw Pact. It ceased to function when the Warsaw Pact members walked out.

1963 *Tripartite Moscow Test Ban Negotiations.* This was the group, including Great Britain, the United States, and the Soviet Union, that negotiated final aspects of the Limited Test Ban Treaty in Moscow. It resulted from a heads-of-government agreement of the three nuclear powers that had been negotiating on a test ban in the ENDC.

1963–67 *Preparatory Commission for the Denuclearization of Latin America.* This group was established by the Latin American countries. Its work resulted in the 1967 Treaty of Tlatelolco, which established a nuclear free zone.

1973–75 *Conference on Security and Cooperation in Europe* (Geneva and Helsinki). The focus of this conference was on security issues, machinery for peaceful settlement of disputes, increased exchange of information, industrial and scientific cooperation, environmental cooperation, freer movement and contact among individuals and organizations, and future European institutional arrangements. It was composed of 33 states of Europe plus the United States and Canada. Some arms control questions, such as prior notification of military maneuvers and exchange of observers at military exercises, were considered.

Current Forums

1945– *U.N. General Assembly* (New York). The General Assembly is the U.N. organ in which all members participate. It serves as a forum for general policy debate during its annual session. On occasion, private discussions held in conjunction with the formal General

Assembly sessions have been significant for arms negotiations. The General Assembly also receives reports from the Conference of the Committee on Disarmament (CCD) and through its resolutions attempts, with varying degrees of success, to influence negotiations. In this way, it affords an important way for states who are not members of the CCD to express their views.

1945– *U.N. Security Council* (New York). On occasion, the Security Council, the U.N. organ that represents the great powers, has engaged in discussion of arms control matters. Its meetings have also sometimes afforded opportunity for private discussions which have contributed to negotiations. Under the U.N. Charter, the Security Council was to have responsibility for formulating plans for the regulation of armaments, but its role in this regard since the early 1950's has been less than that of the General Assembly.

1952– *U.N. Disarmament Commission* (New York). This body was established by the General Assembly. From 1952 to 1954, its membership consisted of Security Council members plus Canada, and it was the principal negotiation forum. In 1954, significant negotiations shifted to its Subcommittee on Disarmament. In 1959, the commission was expanded to include all U.N. members. It met irregularly during the 1960's, usually prior to consideration of disarmament matters by the General Assembly, and has been primarily a forum for general discussion rather than for negotiation. It has not met in recent years.

1962– *Eighteen-Nation Committee on Disarmament (ENDC) and Conference of the Committee on Disarmament* (CCD) (Geneva). This has been one continuing forum, with a name change in 1969, when the group was enlarged beyond the original 18 members. It was established as a result of a U.S.-U.S.S.R. agreement in which the two countries, in effect, invited the others to participate. The United States and the Soviet Union serve as permanent co-chairmen. The body is not technically a U.N. body, although the General Assembly endorsed its creation. The U.N. Secretariat services the conference, and the conference submits annual reports to the General Assembly. For 14 years this body has been the central forum for multilateral arms control negotiations. A large portion of the arms control agreements of the post–World War II period have been negotiated in this conference or, if concluded elsewhere, have been the product of its efforts. In 1975, it was composed of the following 26 members: the United States and six states allied with it (Canada, France [which has never occupied its seat], Great Britain, Italy, Japan, the Netherlands), and the Soviet Union and six allied states (Bulgaria, Czechoslovakia, Hungary, Mongolia, Poland, Rumania), plus

12 nonaligned countries from the various geographical areas of the world (Argentina, Brazil, Burma, Egypt, Ethiopia, India, Mexico, Morocco, Nigeria, Pakistan, Sweden, Yugoslavia).

1969– *Strategic Arms Limitation Talks* (SALT) (Helsinki and Vienna during the first phase [SALT I], 1969–72; Geneva for the second phase [SALT II]). This bilateral forum, established by the United States and the Soviet Union, produced the SALT I agreements. Meetings are secret; each side keeps its own records, and no reports are submitted to the United Nations.

1972– *Standing Consultative Commission* (Geneva). This group, composed of U.S. and U.S.S.R. representatives, was established pursuant to the Anti-Ballistic Missile (ABM) Treaty. Its primary function is to help implement the SALT I agreements. It is envisaged as a permanent body that will in the future be responsible for consideration of amendments to the ABM Treaty and for "proposals for further measures aimed at limiting strategic arms." While SALT II continues, however, it will not have a negotiating function for new agreements. Meetings are held at least twice a year and also on call of either party.

1973– *Negotiations on the Mutual Reduction of Forces and Armaments and Associated Measures in Central Europe* (Vienna). This is a conference concerned with arms and related security arrangements in Central Europe. The participants with full decision-making status are Belgium, Canada, the Federal Republic of Germany, Great Britain, Luxembourg, the Netherlands, and the United States from the North Atlantic Treaty Organization (NATO); and Czechoslovakia, the German Democratic Republic, Poland, and the Soviet Union from the Warsaw Pact. Special-status participants without decision-making rights are Denmark, Greece, Italy, Norway, and Turkey from NATO; and Bulgaria, Hungary (subject to review of its status), and Rumania from the Warsaw Pact.

Texts of Major Arms Control Agreements

"Hot Line" Agreement (1963)   330

"Hot Line" Modernization Agreement (1971)   333

"Accidents Measures" Agreement (1971)   338

Antarctic Treaty (1959)   340

Outer Space Treaty (1967)   346

Seabed Arms Control Treaty (1971)   351

Limited Test Ban Treaty (1963)   355

Threshold Test Ban (1974)   358

Geneva Protocol (1925)   362

Biological Weapons Convention (1972)   363

SALT I Accords (1972)   368

Basic Principles of Relations (1972)   383

Standing Consultative Commission (1972)   385

ABM Protocol (1974)   388

Vladivostok Accord (1974)   390

Conference on Security and Cooperation in Europe,
    Final Act (1975) (excerpts)   391

Treaty for the Prohibition of Nuclear Weapons in
    Latin America (1967)   396

Non-Proliferation Treaty (1968)   414

Memorandum of Understanding Between the United States of America and the Union of Soviet Socialist Republics Regarding the Establishment of a Direct Communications Link

Signed at Geneva June 20, 1963
Entered into force June 20, 1963

For use in time of emergency the Government of the United States of America and the Government of the Union of Soviet Socialist Republics have agreed to establish as soon as technically feasible a direct communications link between the two Governments.

Each Government shall be responsible for the arrangements for the link on its own territory. Each Government shall take the necessary steps to ensure continuous functioning of the link and prompt delivery to its head of government of any communications received by means of the link from the head of government of the other party.

Arrangements for establishing and operating the link are set forth in the Annex which is attached hereto and forms an integral part hereof.

Done in duplicate in the English and Russian languages at Geneva, Switzerland, this 20th day of June, 1963.

FOR THE GOVERMENT OF THE
UNITED STATES OF AMERICA:

Charles C Stelle

Acting Representative of the United
States of America to the Eighteen-
Nation Committee on Disarmament

FOR THE GOVERNMENT OF THE
UNION OF SOVIET SOCIALIST
REPUBLICS:

Acting Representative of the Union of
Soviet Socialist Republics to the
Eighteen-Nation Committee on
Disarmament

(SEAL)

Annex

To the Memorandum of Understanding Between the United States of America and the Union of Soviet Socialist Republics Regarding the Establishment of a Direct Communications Link

The direct communications link between Washington and Moscow established in accordance with the Memorandum, and the operation of such link, shall be governed by the following provisions :

1. The direct communications link shall consist of:

   a. Two terminal points with telegraph-teleprinter equipment between which communications shall be directly exchanged ;

   b. One full-time duplex wire telegraph circuit, routed Washington-London-Copenhagen-Stockholm-Helsinki-Moscow, which shall be used for the transmission of messages ;

   c. One full-time duplex radiotelegraph circuit, routed Washington-Tangier-Moscow, which shall be used for service communications and for coordination of operations between the two terminal points.

If experience in operating the direct communications link should demonstrate that the establishment of an additional wire telegraph circuit is advisable, such circuit may be established by mutual agreement between authorized representatives of both Governments.

2. In case of interruption of the wire circuit, transmission of messages shall be effected via the radio circuit, and for this purpose provision shall be made at the terminal points for the capability of prompt switching of all necessary equipment from one circuit to another.

3. The terminal points of the link shall be so equipped as to provide for the transmission and reception of messages from Moscow to Washington in the Russian language and from Washington to Moscow in the English language. In this connection, the USSR shall furnish the United States four sets of telegraph terminal equipment, including page printers, transmitters, and reperforators, with one year's supply of spare parts and all necessary special tools, test equipment, operating instructions, and other technical literature, to provide for transmission and reception of messages in the Russian language.

The United States shall furnish the Soviet Union four sets of telegraph terminal equipment, including page printers, transmitters, and reperforators, with one year's supply of spare parts and all necessary special tools, test equipment, operating instructions and other technical literature, to provide for transmission and reception of messages in the English language.

The equipment described in this paragraph shall be exchanged directly between the parties without any payment being required therefor.

4. The terminal points of the direct communications link shall be provided with encoding equipment. For the terminal point in the USSR, four sets of such equipment (each capable of simplex operation), with one year's supply of spare parts, with all necessary special tools, test equipment, operating instructions and other technical literature, and with all necessary blank tape, shall be furnished by the United States to the USSR against payment of the cost thereof by the USSR.

The USSR shall provide for preparation and delivery of keying tapes to the terminal point of the link in the United States for reception of messages from the USSR. The United States shall provide for the preparation and delivery of keying tapes to the terminal point of the link in the USSR for reception of messages from the United States. Delivery of prepared keying tapes to the terminal points of the link shall be effected through the Embassy of the USSR in Washington (for the terminal of the link in the USSR) and through the Embassy of the United States in Moscow (for the terminal of the link in the United States).

5. The United States and the USSR shall designate the agencies responsible for the arrangements regarding the direct communications link, for its technical maintenance, continuity and reliability, and for the timely transmission of messages.

Such agencies may, by mutual agreement, decide matters and develop instructions relating to the technical maintenance and operation of the direct communications link and effect arrangements to improve the operation of the link.

6. The technical parameters of the telegraph circuits of the link and of the terminal equipment, as well as the maintenance of such circuits and equipment, shall be in accordance with CCITT and CCIR recommendations.

Transmission and reception of messages over the direct communications link shall be effected in accordance with applicable recommendations of international telegraph and radio communications regulations, as well as with mutually agreed instructions.

7. The costs of the direct communications link shall be borne as follows :

a. The USSR shall pay the full cost of leasing the portion of the telegraph circuit from Moscow to Helsinki and 50% of the cost of leasing the portion of the telegraph circuit from Helsinki to London. The United States shall pay the full cost of leasing the portion of the telegraph circuit from Washington to London and 50% of the cost of leasing the portion of the telegraph circuit from London to Helsinki.

b. Payment of the cost of leasing the radio telegraph circuit between Washington and Moscow shall be effected without any transfer of payments between the parties. The USSR shall bear the expenses relating to the transmission of messages from Moscow to Washington. The United States shall bear the expenses relating to the transmission of messages from Washington to Moscow.

Agreement Between the United States of America and the Union of Soviet Socialist Republics on Measures To Improve the U.S.A.–U.S.S.R. Direct Communications Link With Annex, Supplementing and Modifying the Memorandum of Understanding With Annex, of June 20, 1963

Signed at Washington September 30, 1971
Entered into force September 30, 1971

The United States of America and the Union of Soviet Socialist Republics, hereinafter referred to as the Parties,

Noting the positive experience gained in the process of operating the existing Direct Communications Link between the United States of America and the Union of Soviet Socialist Republics, which was established for use in time of emergency pursuant to the Memorandum of Understanding Regarding the Establishment of a Direct Communications Link, signed on June 20, 1963,

Having examined, in a spirit of mutual understanding, matters relating to the improvement and modernization of the Direct Communications Link,

Have agreed as follows :

Article 1

1. For the purpose of increasing the reliability of the Direct Communications Link, there shall be established and put into operation the following:

(a) two additional circuits between the United States of America and the Union of Soviet Socialist Republics each using a satellite communications system, with each Party selecting a satellite communications system of its own choice,

(b) a system of terminals (more than one) in the territory of each Party for the Direct Communications Link, with the locations and number of terminals in the United States of America to be determined by the United States side, and the locations and number of terminals in the Union of Soviet Socialist Republics to be determined by the Soviet side.

2. Matters relating to the implementation of the aforementioned improvements of the Direct Communications Link are set forth in the Annex which is attached hereto and forms an integral part hereof.

Article 2

Each Party confirms its intention to take all possible measures to assure the continuous and reliable operation of the communications circuits and the system of terminals of the Direct Communications Link for which it is responsible in accordance with this Agreement and the Annex hereto, as well as to communicate to the head of its Government any messages received via the Direct Communications Link from the head of Government of the other Party.

Article 3

The Memorandum of Understanding Between the United States of America and the Union of Soviet Socialist Republics Regarding the Establishment of a Direct Communications Link, signed on June 20, 1963, with the Annex thereto, shall remain in force, except to the extent that its provisions are modified by this Agreement and Annex hereto.

Article 4

The undertakings of the Parties hereunder shall be carried out in accordance with their respective Constitutional processes.

Article 5

This Agreement, including the Annex hereto, shall enter into force upon signature.

Done at Washington on September 30, 1971, in two copies, each in the English and Russian languages, both texts being equally authentic.

FOR THE UNITED STATES   FOR THE UNION OF SOVIET
OF AMERICA: SOCIALIST REPUBLICS:

Annex to the Agreement Between the United States of America and the Union of Soviet Socialist Republics on Measures To Improve the U.S.A.–U.S.S.R. Direct Communications Link

Improvements to the USA–USSR Direct Communications Link shall be implemented in accordance with the provisions set forth in this Annex.

I. CIRCUITS

(a) Each of the original circuits established pursuant to paragraph 1 of the Annex to the Memorandum of Understanding, dated June 20, 1963, shall continue to be maintained and operated as part of the Direct Communications Link until such time, after the satellite communications circuits provided for herein become operational, as the agencies designated pursuant to paragraph III (hereinafter referred to as the "designated agencies") mutually agree that such original circuit is no longer necessary. The provisions of paragraph 7 of the Annex to the Memorandum of Understanding, dated June 20, 1963, shall continue to govern the allocation of the costs of maintaining and operating such original circuits.

(b) Two additional circuits shall be established using two satellite communications systems. Taking into account paragraph I(e) below, the United States side shall provide one circuit via the Intelsat system and the Soviet side shall provide one circuit via the Molniya II system. The two circuits shall be duplex telephone band-width circuits conforming to CCITT standards, equipped for secondary telegraphic multiplexing. Transmission and reception of messages over the Direct Communications Link shall be effected in accordance with applicable recommendations of international communications regulations, as well as with mutually agreed instructions.

(c) When the reliability of both additional circuits has been estabilshed to the mutual satisfaction of the designated agencies, they shall be used as the primary circuits of the Direct Communications Link for transmission and reception of teleprinter messages between the United States and the Soviet Union.

(d) Each satellite communications circuit shall utilize an earth station in the territory of the United States, a communications satellite transponder, and an earth station in the territory of the Soviet Union. Each Party shall be responsible for linking the earth stations in its territory to its own terminals of the Direct Communications Link.

(e) For the circuits specified in paragraph I(b):

—The Soviet side will provide and operate at least one earth station in its territory for the satellite communications circuit in the Intelsat system, and will also arrange for the use of suitable earth station facilities in its territory for the satellite communications circuit in the Molniya II system. The United States side, through a governmental agency or other United States legal entity, will make appropriate arrangements with Intelsat with regard to access for the Soviet Intelsat earth station to the Intelsat space segment, as well as for the use of the applicable portion of the Intelsat space segment.

—The United States side will provide and operate at least one earth station in its territory for the satellite communications circuit in the Molniya II system, and will also arrange for the use of suitable earth station facilities in its territory for the satellite communications circuit in the Intelsat system.

(f) Each earth station shall conform to the performance specifications and operating procedures of the corresponding satellite communications system and the ratio of antenna gain to the equivalent noise temperature should be no less than 31 decibels. Any deviation from these specifications and procedures which may be required in any unusual situation shall be worked out and mutually agreed upon by the designated agencies of both Parties after consultation.

(g) The operational commissioning dates for the satellite communications circuits based on the Intelsat and Molniya II systems shall be as agreed upon by the designated agencies of the Parties through consultations.

(h) The United States side shall bear the costs of: (1) providing and operating the Molniya II earth station in its territory; (2) the use of the Intelsat earth station in its territory; and (3) the transmission of messages via the Intelsat system. The Soviet side shall bear the costs of: (1) providing and operating the Intelsat earth station in its territory; (2) the use of the Molniya II earth station in its territory; and (3) the transmission of messages via the Molniya II system. Payment of the costs of the satellite communications circuits shall be effected without any transfer of payments between the Parties.

(i) Each Party shall be responsible for providing to the other Party notification of any proposed modification or replacement of the communications satellite system containing the circuit provided by it that might require accommodation by earth stations using that system or otherwise affect the maintenance or operation of the Direct Communications Link. Such notification should be given sufficiently in advance to enable the designated agencies to consult and to make, before the modification or replacement is effected, such preparation as may be agreed upon for accommodation by the affected earth stations.

II. TERMINALS

(a) Each Party shall establish a system of terminals in its territory for the exchange of messages with the other Party, and shall determine the locations and number of terminals in such a system. Terminals of the Direct Communications Link shall be designated "USA" and "USSR".

(b) Each Party shall take necessary measures to provide for rapidly switching circuits among terminal points in such a manner that only one terminal location is connected to the circuits at any one time.

(c) Each Party shall use teleprinter equipment from its own sources to equip the additional terminals for the transmission and reception of messages from the United States to the Soviet Union in the English language and from the Soviet Union to the United States in the Russian language.

(d) The terminals of the Direct Communications Link shall be provided with encoding equipment. One-time tape encoding equipment shall be used for transmissions via the Direct Communications Link. A mutually agreed quantity of encoding equipment of a modern and reliable type selected by the United States side, with spares, test equipment, technical literature and operating supplies, shall be furnished by the United States side to the Soviet side against payment of the cost thereof by the Soviet side; additional spares for the encoding equipment supplied will be furnished as necessary.

(e) Keying tapes shall be supplied in accordance with the provisions set forth in paragraph 4 of the Annex to the Memorandum of Understanding, dated June 20, 1963. Each Party shall be responsible for reproducing and distributing additional keying tapes for its system of terminals and for implementing procedures which ensure that the required synchronization of encoding equipment can be effected from any one terminal at any time.

III. OTHER MATTERS

Each Party shall designate the agencies responsible for arrangements regarding the establishment of the additional circuits and the systems of terminals provided for in this Agreement and Annex, for their operation and for their continuity and reliability. These agencies shall, on the basis of direct contacts:

(a) arrange for the exchange of required performance specifications and operating procedures for the earth stations of the communications systems using Intelsat and Molniya II satellites;

(b) arrange for testing, acceptance and commissioning of the satellite circuits and for operation of these circuits after commissioning; and,

(c) decide matters and develop instructions relating to the operation of the secondary teleprinter multiplex system used on the satellite circuits.

Agreement on Measures To Reduce the Risk of Outbreak of Nuclear War Between the United States of America and the Union of Soviet Socialist Republics

Signed at Washington September 30, 1971
Entered into force September 30, 1971

The United States of America and the Union of Soviet Socialist Republics, hereinafter referred to as the Parties:

Taking into account the devastating consequences that nuclear war would have for all mankind and recognizing the need to exert every effort to avert the risk of outbreak of such a war, including measures to guard against accidental or unauthorized use of nuclear weapons,

Believing that agreement on measures for reducing the risk of outbreak of nuclear war serves the interests of strengthening international peace and security, and is in no way contrary to the interests of any other country,

Bearing in mind that continued efforts are also needed in the future to seek ways of reducing the risk of outbreak of nuclear war,

Have agreed as follows:

Article 1

Each Party undertakes to maintain and to improve, as it deems necessary, its existing organizational and technical arrangements to guard against the accidental or unauthorized use of nuclear weapons under its control.

Article 2

The Parties undertake to notify each other immediately in the event of an accidental, unauthorized or any other unexplained incident involving a possible detonation of a nuclear weapon which could create a risk of outbreak of nuclear war. In the event of such an incident, the Party whose nuclear weapon is involved will immediately make every effort to take necessary measures to render harmless or destroy such weapon without its causing damage.

Article 3

The Parties undertake to notify each other immediately in the event of detection by missile warning systems of unidentified objects, or in the event of signs of interference with these systems or with related communications facilities, if such occurrences could create a risk of outbreak of nuclear war between the two countries.

Article 4

Each Party undertakes to notify the other Party in advance of any planned missile launches if such launches will extend beyond its national territory in the direction of the other Party.

Article 5

Each Party, in other situations involving unexplained nuclear incidents, undertakes to act in such a manner as to reduce the possibility of its actions being misinterpreted by the other Party. In any such situation, each Party may inform the other Party or request information when, in its view, this is warranted by the interests of averting the risk of outbreak of nuclear war.

Article 6

For transmission of urgent information, notifications and requests for information in situations requiring prompt clarification, the Parties shall make primary use of the Direct Communications Link between the Governments of the United States of America and the Union of Soviet Socialist Republics.

For transmission of other information, notifications and requests for information, the Parties, at their own discretion, may use any communications facilities, including diplomatic channels, depending on the degree of urgency.

Article 7

The Parties undertake to hold consultations, as mutually agreed, to consider questions relating to implementation of the provisions of this Agreement, as well as to discuss possible amendments thereto aimed at further implementation of the purposes of this Agreement.

Article 8

This Agreement shall be of unlimited duration.

Article 9

This Agreement shall enter into force upon signature.

Done at Washington on September 30, 1971, in two copies, each in the English and Russian languages, both texts being equally authentic.

FOR THE UNITED STATES
OF AMERICA:

FOR THE UNION OF SOVIET
SOCIALIST REPUBLICS:

The Antarctic Treaty

Signed at Washington December 1, 1959
U.S. ratification deposited August 18, 1960
Entered into force June 23, 1961

The Governments of Argentina, Australia, Belgium, Chile, the French Republic, Japan, New Zealand, Norway, the Union of South Africa, the Union of Soviet Socialist Republics, the United Kingdom of Great Britain and Northern Ireland, and the United States of America,

Recognizing that it is in the interest of all mankind that Antarctica shall continue forever to be used exclusively for peaceful purposes and shall not become the scene or object of international discord ;

Acknowledging the substantial contributions to scientific knowledge resulting from international cooperation in scientific investigation in Antarctica ;

Convinced that the establishment of a firm foundation for the continuation and development of such cooperation on the basis of freedom of scientific investigation in Antarctica as applied during the International Geophysical Year accords with the interests of science and the progress of all mankind ;

Convinced also that a treaty ensuring the use of Antarctica for peaceful purposes only and the continuance of international harmony in Antarctica will further the purposes and principles embodied in the Charter of the United Nations ;

Have agreed as follows :

Article I

1. Antarctica shall be used for peaceful purposes only. There shall be prohibited, *inter alia*, any measures of a military nature, such as the establishment of military bases and fortifications, the carrying out of military maneuvers, as well as the testing of any type of weapons.

2. The present Treaty shall not prevent the use of military personnel or equipment for scientific research or for any other peaceful purpose.

Article II

Freedom of scientific investigation in Antarctica and cooperation toward that end, as applied during the International Geophysical Year, shall continue, subject to the provisions of the present Treaty.

Article III

1. In order to promote international cooperation in scientific investigation in Antarctica, as provided for in Article II of the present Treaty, the Contracting Parties agree that, to the greatest extent feasible and practicable :

(a) information regarding plans for scientific programs in Antarctica shall be exchanged to permit maximum economy and efficiency of operations;

(b) scientific personnel shall be exchanged in Antarctica between expeditions and stations;

(c) scientific observations and results from Antarctica shall be exchanged and made freely available.

2. In implementing this Article, every encouragement shall be given to the establishment of cooperative working relations with those Specialized Agencies of the United Nations and other international organizations having a scientific or technical interest in Antarctica.

Article IV

1. Nothing contained in the present Treaty shall be interpreted as:

(a) a renunciation by any Contracting Party of previously asserted rights of or claims to territorial sovereignty in Antarctica;

(b) a renunciation or diminution by any Contracting Party of any basis of claim to territorial sovereignty in Antarctica which it may have whether as a result of its activities or those of its nationals in Antarctica, or otherwise;

(c) prejudicing the position of any Contracting Party as regards its recognition or non-recognition of any other State's right of or claim or basis of claim to territorial sovereignty in Antarctica.

2. No acts or activities taking place while the present Treaty is in force shall constitute a basis for asserting, supporting or denying a claim to territorial sovereignty in Antarctica or create any rights of sovereignty in Antarctica. No new claim, or enlargement of an existing claim, to territorial sovereignty in Antarctica shall be asserted while the present Treaty is in force.

Article V

1. Any nuclear explosions in Antarctica and the disposal there of radioactive waste material shall be prohibited.

2. In the event of the conclusion of international agreements concerning the use of nuclear energy, including nuclear explosions and the disposal of radioactive waste material, to which all of the Contracting Parties whose representatives are entitled to participate in the meetings provided for under Article IX are parties, the rules established under such agreements shall apply in Antarctica.

Article VI

The provisions of the present Treaty shall apply to the area south of 60° South Latitude, including all ice shelves, but nothing in the present Treaty shall prejudice or in any way affect the rights, or the exercise of the rights, of any State under international law with regard to the high seas within that area.

Article VII

1. In order to promote the objectives and ensure the observance of the provisions of the present Treaty, each Contracting Party whose representatives are entitled to participate in the meetings referred to in Article IX of the Treaty shall have the right to designate observers to carry out any inspection provided

for by the present Article. Observers shall be nationals of the Contracting Parties which designate them. The names of observers shall be communicated to every other Contracting Party having the right to designate observers, and like notice shall be given of the termination of their appointment.

2. Each observer designated in accordance with the provisions of paragraph 1 of this Article shall have complete freedom of access at any time to any or all areas of Antarctica.

3. All areas of Antarctica, including all stations, installations and equipment within those areas, and all ships and aircraft at points of discharging or embarking cargoes of personnel in Antarctica, shall be open at all times to inspection by any observers designated in accordance with paragraph 1 of this Article.

4. Aerial observation may be carried out at any time over any or all areas of Antarctica by any of the Contracting Parties having the right to designate observers.

5. Each Contracting Party shall, at the time when the present Treaty enters into force for it, inform the other Contracting Parties, and thereafter shall give them notice in advance, of

(a) all expeditions to and within Antarctica, on the part of its ships or nationals, and all expeditions to Antarctica organized in or proceeding from its territory ;

(b) all stations in Antarctica occupied by its nationals ; and

(c) any military personnel or equipment intended to be introduced by it into Antarctica subject to the conditions prescribed in paragraph 2 of Article I of the present Treaty.

Article VIII

1. In order to facilitate the exercise of their functions under the present Treaty, and without prejudice to the respective positions of the Contracting Parties relating to jurisdiction over all other persons in Antarctica, observers designated under paragraph 1 of Article VII and scientific personnel exchanged under subparagraph 1(b) of Article III of the Treaty, and members of the staffs accompanying any such persons, shall be subject only to the jurisdiction of the Contracting Party of which they are nationals in respect of all acts or omissions occurring while they are in Antarctica for the purpose of exercising their functions.

2. Without prejudice to the provisions of paragraph 1 of this Article, and pending the adoption of measures in pursuance of subparagraph 1(e) of Article IX, the Contracting Parties concerned in any case of dispute with regard to the exercise of jurisdiction in Antarctica shall immediately consult together with a view to reaching a mutually acceptable solution.

Article IX

1. Representatives of the Contracting Parties named in the preamble to the present Treaty shall meet at the City of Canberra within two months after the date of entry into force of the Treaty, and thereafter at suitable intervals and places, for the purpose of exchanging information, consulting together on matters of common interest pertaining to Antarctica, and formulating and considering and recommending to their Governments, measures in furtherance of the principles and objectives of the Treaty, including measures regarding :

(a) use of Antarctica for peaceful purposes only ;

(b) facilitation of scientific research in Antarctica ;

(c) facilitation of international scientific cooperation in Antarctica ;

(d) facilitation of the exercise of the rights of inspection provided for in Article VII of the Treaty ;

(e) questions relating to the exercise of jurisdiction in Antarctica ;

(f) preservation and conservation of living resources in Antarctica.

2. Each Contracting Party which has become a party to the present Treaty by accession under Article XIII shall be entitled to appoint representatives to participate in the meetings referred to in paragraph 1 of the present Article, during such time as that Contracting Party demonstrates its interest in Antarctica by conducting substantial scientific research activity there, such as the establishment of a scientific station or the despatch of a scientific expedition.

3. Reports from the observers referred to in Article VII of the present Treaty shall be transmitted to the representatives of the Contracting Parties participating in the meetings referred to in paragraph 1 of the present Article.

4. The measures referred to in paragraph 1 of this Article shall become effective when approved by all the Contracting Parties whose representatives were entitled to participate in the meetings held to consider those measures.

5. Any or all of the rights established in the present Treaty may be exercised as from the date of entry into force of the Treaty whether or not any measures facilitating the exercise of such rights have been proposed, considered or approved as provided in this Article.

Article X

Each of the Contracting Parties undertakes to exert appropriate efforts, consistent with the Charter of the United Nations, to the end that no one engages in any activity in Antarctica contrary to the principles or purposes of the present Treaty.

Article XI

1. If any dispute arises between two or more of the Contracting Parties concerning the interpretation or application of the present Treaty, those Contracting Parties shall consult among themselves with a view to having the dispute resolved by negotiation, inquiry, mediation, conciliation, arbitration, judicial settlement or other peaceful means of their own choice.

2. Any dispute of this character not so resolved shall, with the consent, in each case, of all parties to the dispute, be referred to the International Court of Justice for settlement; but failure to reach agreement on reference to the International Court shall not absolve parties to the dispute from the responsibility of continuing to seek to resolve it by any of the various peaceful means referred to in paragraph 1 of this Article.

Article XII

1. (a) The present Treaty may be modified or amended at any time by unanimous agreement of the Contracting Parties whose representatives are entitled to participate in the meetings provided for under Article IX. Any such modification or amendment shall enter into force when the depositary Government has received notice from all such Contracting Parties that they have ratified it.

(b) Such modification or amendment shall thereafter enter into force as to any other Contracting Party when notice of ratification by it has been received by the depositary Government. Any such Contracting Party from which no notice of ratification is received within a period of two years from the date of entry into force of the modification or amendment in accordance with the provisions of subparagraph 1(a) of this Article shall be deemed to have withdrawn from the present Treaty on the date of the expiration of such period.

2. (a) If after the expiration of thirty years from the date of entry into force of the present Treaty, any of the Contracting Parties whose representatives are entitled to participate in the meetings provided for under Article IX so requests by a communication addressed to the depositary Government, a Conference of all the Contracting Parties shall be held as soon as practicable to review the operation of the Treaty.

(b) Any modification or amendment to the present Treaty which is approved at such a Conference by a majority of the Contracting Parties there represented, including a majority of those whose representatives are entitled to participate in the meetings provided for under Article IX, shall be communicated by the depositary Government to all the Contracting Parties immediately after the termination of the Conference and shall enter into force in accordance with the provisions of paragraph 1 of the present Article.

(c) If any such modification or amendment has not entered into force in accordance with the provisions of subparagraph 1(a) of this Article within a period of two years after the date of its communication to all the Contracting Parties, any Contracting Party may at any time after the expiration of that period give notice to the depositary Government of its withdrawal from the present Treaty ; and such withdrawal shall take effect two years after the receipt of the notice by the depositary Government.

Article XIII

1. The present Treaty shall be subject to ratification by the signatory States. It shall be open for accession by any State which is a Member of the United Nations, or by any other State which may be invited to accede to the Treaty with the consent of all the Contracting Parties whose representatives are entitled to participate in the meetings provided for under Article IX of the Treaty.

2. Ratification of or accession to the present Treaty shall be effected by each State in accordance with its constitutional processes.

3. Instruments of ratification and instruments of accesssion shall be deposited with the Government of the United States of America, hereby designated as the depositary Government.

4. The depositary Government shall inform all signatory and acceding States of the date of each deposit of an instrument of ratification or accession, and the date of entry into force of the Treaty and of any modification or amendment thereto.

5. Upon the deposit of instruments of ratification by all the signatory States, the present Treaty shall enter into force for those States and for States which

have deposited instruments of accession. Thereafter the Treaty shall enter into force for any acceding State upon the deposit of its instrument of accession.

6. The present Treaty shall be registered by the depositary Government pursuant to Article 102 of the Charter of the United Nations.

Article XIV

The present Treaty, done in the English, French, Russian and Spanish languages, each version being equally authentic, shall be deposited in the archives of the Government of the United States of America, which shall transmit duly certified copies thereof to the Governments of the signatory and acceding States.

IN WITNESS WHEREOF, the undersigned Plenipotentiaries, duly authorized, have signed the present Treaty.

DONE at Washington this first day of December, one thousand nine hundred and fifty-nine.

Treaty on Principles Governing the Activities of States in the Exploration and Use of Outer Space, Including the Moon and Other Celestial Bodies

Signed at Washington, London, Moscow, January 27, 1967
U.S. ratification deposited October 10, 1967
Entered into force October 10, 1967

The States Parties to this Treaty,

Inspired by the great prospects opening up before mankind as a result of man's entry into outer space,

Recognizing the common interest of all mankind in the progress of the exploration and use of outer space for peaceful purposes,

Believing that the exploration and use of outer space should be carried on for the benefit of all peoples irrespective of the degree of their economic or scientific development,

Desiring to contribute to broad international co-operation in the scientific as well as the legal aspects of the exploration and use of outer space for peaceful purposes,

Believing that such co-operation will contribute to the development of mutual understanding and to the strengthening of friendly relations between States and peoples,

Recalling resolution 1962 (XVIII), entitled "Declaration of Legal Principles Governing the Activities of States in the Exploration and Use of Outer Space", which was adopted unanimously by the United Nations General Assembly on 13 December 1963,

Recalling resolution 1884 (XVIII), calling upon States to refrain from placing in orbit around the Earth any objects carrying nuclear weapons or any other kinds of weapons of mass destruction or from installing such weapons on celestial bodies, which was adopted unanimously by the United Nations General Assembly on 17 October 1963,

Taking account of United Nations General Assembly resolution 110 (II) of 3 November 1947, which condemned propaganda designed or likely to provoke or encourage any threat to the peace, breach of the peace or act of aggression, and considering that the aforementioned resolution is applicable to outer space,

Convinced that a Treaty on Principles Governing the Activities of States in the Exploration and Use of Outer Space, including the Moon and Other Celestial Bodies, will further the Purposes and Principles of the Charter of the United Nations,

Have agreed on the following:

Article I

The exploration and use of outer space, including the moon and other celestial bodies, shall be carried out for the benefit and in the interests of all countries, irrespective of their degree of economic or scientific development, and shall be the province of all mankind.

Outer space, including the moon and other celestial bodies, shall be free for exploration and use by all States without discrimination of any kind, on a basis of equality and in accordance with international law, and there shall be free access to all areas of celestial bodies.

There shall be freedom of scientific investigation in outer space, including the moon and other celestial bodies, and States shall facilitate and encourage international co-operation in such investigation.

Article II

Outer space, including the moon and other celestial bodies, is not subject to national appropriation by claim of sovereignty, by means or use of occupation, or by any other means.

Article III

States Parties to the Treaty shall carry on activities in the exploration and use of outer space, including the moon and other celestial bodies, in accordance with international law, including the Charter of the United Nations, in the interest of maintaining international peace and security and promoting international co-operation and understanding.

Article IV

States Parties to the Treaty undertake not to place in orbit around the Earth any objects carrying nuclear weapons or any other kinds of weapons of mass destruction, install such weapons on celestial bodies, or station such weapons in outer space in any other manner.

The moon and other celestial bodies shall be used by all States Parties to the Treaty exclusively for peaceful purposes. The establishment of military bases, installations and fortifications, the testing of any type of weapons and the conduct of military maneuvers on celestial bodies shall be forbidden. The use of military personnel for scientific research or for any other peaceful purposes shall not be prohibited. The use of any equipment or facility necessary for peaceful exploration of the moon and other celestial bodies shall also not be prohibited.

Article V

States Parties to the Treaty shall regard astronauts as envoys of mankind in outer space and shall render to them all possible assistance in the event of accident, distress, or emergency landing on the territory of another State Party or on the high seas. When astronauts make such a landing, they shall be safely and promptly returned to the State of registry of their space vehicle.

In carrying on activities in outer space and on celestial bodies, the astronauts of one State Party shall render all possible assistance to the astronauts of other States Parties.

States Parties to the Treaty shall immediately inform the other States

Parties to the Treaty or the Secretary-General of the United Nations of any phenomena they discover in outer space, including the moon and other celestial bodies, which could constitute a danger to the life or health of astronauts.

Article VI

States Parties to the Treaty shall bear international responsibility for national activities in outer space, including the moon and other celestial bodies, whether such activities are carried on by governmental agencies or by non-governmental entities, and for assuring that national activities are carried out in conformity with the provisions set forth in the present Treaty. The activities of non-governmental entities in outer space, including the moon and other celestial bodies, shall require authorization and continuing supervision by the appropriate State Party to the Treaty. When activities are carried on in outer space, including the moon and other celestial bodies, by an international organization, responsibility for compliance with this Treaty shall be borne both by the international organization and by the States Parties to the Treaty participating in such organization.

Article VII

Each State Party to the Treaty that launches or procures the launching of an object into outer space, including the moon and other celestial bodies, and each State Party from whose territory or facility an object is launched, is internationally liable for damage to another State Party to the Treaty or to its natural or juridical persons by such object or its component parts on the Earth, in air space or in outer space, including the moon and other celestial bodies.

Article VIII

A State Party to the Treaty on whose registry an object launched into outer space is carried shall retain jurisdiction and control over such object, and over any personnel thereof, while in outer space or on a celestial body. Ownership of objects launched into outer space, including objects landed or constructed on a celestial body, and of their component parts, is not affected by their presence in outer space or on a celestial body or by their return to the Earth. Such objects or component parts found beyond the limits of the State Party to the Treaty on whose registry they are carried shall be returned to that State Party, which shall, upon request, furnish identifying data prior to their return.

Article IX

In the exploration and use of outer space, including the moon and other celestial bodies, States Parties to the Treaty shall be guided by the principle of co-operation and mutual assistance and shall conduct all their activities in outer space, including the moon and other celestial bodies, with due regard to the corresponding interests of all other States Parties to the Treaty. States Parties to the Treaty shall pursue studies of outer space, including the moon and other celestial bodies, and conduct exploration of them so as to avoid their harmful contamination and also adverse changes in the environment of the Earth resulting from the introduction of extraterrestrial matter and, where necessary, shall adopt appropriate measures for this purpose. If a State Party to the Treaty has reason to believe that an activity or experiment planned by it or its nationals in outer space, including the moon and other celestial bodies, would cause potentially harmful interference with activities of other States Parties in the peaceful exploration and use of outer space, including the moon and other celestial bodies, it shall undertake appropriate international consultations before proceeding with any such activity or experiment. A State Party to the Treaty which has reason to believe that an activity or experiment planned by another State Party in outer space, including the moon and other celestial bodies, would cause potentially harmful interference with activities in the peaceful exploration and use of outer space, including the moon and other celestial bodies, may request consultation concerning the activity or experiment.

Article X

In order to promote international co-operation in the exploration and use of outer space, including the moon and other celestial bodies, in conformity with the purposes of this Treaty, the States Parties to the Treaty shall consider on a basis of equality any requests by other States Parties to the Treaty to be afforded an opportunity to observe the flight of space objects launched by those States.

The nature of such an opportunity for observation and the conditions under which it could be afforded shall be determined by agreement between the States concerned.

Article XI

In order to promote international co-operation in the peaceful exploration and use of outer space, States Parties to the Treaty conducting activities in outer space, including the moon and other celestial bodies, agree to inform the Secretary-General of the United Nations as well as the public and the international scientific community, to the greatest extent feasible and practicable, of the nature, conduct, locations and results of such activities. On receiving the said information, the Secretary-General of the United Nations should be prepared to disseminate it immediately and effectively.

Article XII

All stations, installations, equipment and space vehicles on the moon and other celestial bodies shall be open to representatives of other States Parties to the Treaty on a basis of reciprocity. Such representatives shall give reasonable advance notice of a projected visit, in order that appropriate consultations may be held and that maximum precautions may be taken to assure safety and to avoid interference with normal operations in the facility to be visited.

Article XIII

The provisions of this Treaty shall apply to the activities of States Parties to the Treaty in the exploration and use of outer space, including the moon and other celestial bodies, whether such activities are carried on by a single State Party to the Treaty or jointly with other States, including cases where they are carried on within the framework of international inter-governmental organizations.

Any practical questions arising in connection with activities carried on by international inter-governmental organizations in the exploration and use of outer space, including the moon and other celestial bodies, shall be resolved by the States Parties to the Treaty either with the appropriate international organization or with one or more States members of that international organization, which are Parties to this Treaty.

Article XIV

1. This Treaty shall be open to all States for signature. Any State which does not sign this Treaty before its entry into force in accordance with paragraph 3 of this article may accede to it at any time.

2. This Treaty shall be subject to ratification by signatory States. Instruments of ratification and instruments of accession shall be deposited with the Governments of the United States of America, the United Kingdom of Great Britain and Northern Ireland and the Union of Soviet Socialist Republics, which are hereby designated the Depositary Governments.

3. This Treaty shall enter into force upon the deposit of instruments of ratification by five Governments including the Governments designated as Depositary Governments under this Treaty.

4. For States whose instruments of ratification or accession are deposited subsequent to the entry into force of this Treaty, it shall enter into force on the date of the deposit of their instruments of ratification or accession.

5. The Depositary Governments shall promptly inform all signatory and acceding States of the date of each signature, the date of deposit of each instrument of ratification of and accession to this Treaty, the date of its entry into force and other notices.

6. This Treaty shall be registered by the Depositary Governments pursuant to Article 102 of the Charter of the United Nations.

Article XV

Any State Party to the Treaty may propose amendments to this Treaty. Amendments shall enter into force for each State Party to the Treaty accepting the amendments upon their acceptance by a majority of the States Parties to the Treaty and thereafter for each remaining State Party to the Treaty on the date of acceptance by it.

Article XVI

Any State Party to the Treaty may give notice of its withdrawal from the Treaty one year after its entry into force by written notification to the Depositary Governments. Such withdrawal shall take effect one year from the date of receipt of this notification.

Article XVII

This Treaty, of which the Englisn, Russian, French, Spanish and Chinese texts are equally authentic, shall be deposited in the archives of the Depositary Governments. Duly certified copies of this Treaty shall be transmitted by the Depositary Governments to the Governments of the signatory and acceding States.

Treaty on the Prohibition of the Emplacement of Nuclear Weapons and Other Weapons of Mass Destruction on the Seabed and the Ocean Floor and in the Subsoil Thereof

Signed at Washington, London, Moscow February 11, 1971
U.S. ratification deposited May 18, 1972
Entered into force May 18, 1972

The States Parties to this Treaty,

Recognizing the common interest of mankind in the progress of the exploration and use of the seabed and the ocean floor for peaceful purposes,

Considering that the prevention of a nuclear arms race on the seabed and the ocean floor serves the interests of maintaining world peace, reduces international tensions and strengthens friendly relations among States,

Convinced that this Treaty constitutes a step towards the exclusion of the seabed, the ocean floor and the subsoil thereof from the arms race,

Convinced that this Treaty constitutes a step towards a treaty on general and complete disarmament under strict and effective international control, and determined to continue negotiations to this end,

Convinced that this Treaty will further the purposes and principles of the Charter of the United Nations, in a manner consistent with the principles of international law and without infringing the freedoms of the high seas,

Have agreed as follows:

Article I

1. The States Parties to this Treaty undertake not to emplant or emplace on the seabed and the ocean floor and in the subsoil thereof beyond the outer limit of a seabed zone, as defined in article II, any nuclear weapons or any other types of weapons of mass destruction as well as structures, launching installations or any other facilities specifically designed for storing, testing or using such weapons.

2. The undertakings of paragraph 1 of this article shall also apply to the seabed zone referred to in the same paragraph, except that within such seabed zone, they shall not apply either to the coastal State or to the seabed beneath its territorial waters.

3. The States Parties to this Treaty undertake not to assist, encourage or induce any State to carry out activities referred to in paragraph 1 of this article and not to participate in any other way in such actions.

Article II

For the purpose of this Treaty, the outer limit of the seabed zone referred to in article I shall be coterminous with the twelve-mile outer limit of the zone referred to in part II of the Convention on the Territorial Sea and the Contiguous Zone, signed at Geneva on April 29, 1958, and shall be measured in accordance with the provisions of part I, section II, of that Convention and in accordance with international law.

Article III

1. In order to promote the objectives of and insure compliance with the provisions of this Treaty, each State Party to the Treaty shall have the right to verify through observation the activities of other States Parties to the Treaty on the seabed and the ocean floor and in the subsoil thereof beyond the zone referred to in article I, provided that observation does not interfere with such activities.

2. If after such observation reasonable doubts remain concerning the fulfillment of the obligations assumed under the Treaty, the State Party having such doubts and the State Party that is responsible for the activities giving rise to the doubts shall consult with a view to removing the doubts. If the doubts persist, the State Party having such doubts shall notify the other States Parties, and the Parties concerned shall cooperate on such further procedures for verification as may be agreed, including appropriate inspection of objects, structures, installations or other facilities that reasonably may be expected to be of a kind described in article I. The Parties in the region of the activities, including any coastal State, and any other Party so requesting, shall be entitled to participate in such consultation and cooperation. After completion of the further procedures for verification, an appropriate report shall be circulated to other Parties by the Party that initiated such procedures.

3. If the State responsible for the activities giving rise to the reasonable doubts is not identifiable by observation of the object, structure, installation or other facility, the State Party having such doubts shall notify and make appropriate inquiries of States Parties in the region of the activities and of any other State Party. If it is ascertained through these inquiries that a particular State Party is responsible for the activities, that State Party shall consult and cooperate with other Parties as provided in paragraph 2 of this article. If the identity of the State responsible for the activities cannot be ascertained through these inquiries, then further verification procedures, including inspection, may be undertaken by the inquiring State Party, which shall invite the participation of the Parties in the region of the activities, including any coastal State, and of any other Party desiring to cooperate.

4. If consultation and cooperation pursuant to paragraphs 2 and 3 of this article have not removed the doubts concerning the activities and there remains a serious question concerning fulfillment of the obligations assumed under this Treaty, a State Party may, in accordance with the provisions of the Charter of the United Nations, refer the matter to the Security Council, which may take action in accordance with the Charter.

5. Verification pursuant to this article may be undertaken by any State Party using its own means, or with the full or partial assistance of any other State Party, or through appropriate international procedures within the framework of the United Nations and in accordance with its Charter.

6. Verification activities pursuant to this Treaty shall not interfere with activities of other States Parties and shall be conducted with due regard for rights recognized under international law, including the freedoms of the high seas and the rights of coastal States with respect to the exploration and exploitation of their continental shelves.

Article IV

Nothing in this Treaty shall be interpreted as supporting or prejudicing the position of any State Party with respect to existing international conventions, including the 1958 Convention on the Territorial Sea and the Contiguous Zone, or with respect to rights or claims which such State Party may assert, or with respect to recognition or non-recognition of rights or claims asserted by any other State, related to waters off its coasts, including, inter alia, territorial seas and contiguous zones, or to the seabed and the ocean floor, including continental shelves.

Article V

The Parties to this Treaty undertake to continue negotiations in good faith concerning further measures in the field of disarmament for the prevention of an arms race on the seabed, the ocean floor and the subsoil thereof.

Article VI

Any State Party may propose amendments to this Treaty. Amendments shall enter into force for each State Party accepting the amendments upon their acceptance by a majority of the States Parties to the Treaty and, thereafter, for each remaining State Party on the date of acceptance by it.

Article VII

Five years after the entry into force of this Treaty, a conference of Parties to the Treaty shall be held at Geneva, Switzerland, in order to review the operation of this Treaty with a view to assuring that the purposes of the preamble and the provisions of the Treaty are being realized. Such review shall take into account any relevant technological developments. The review conference shall determine, in accordance with the views of a majority of those Parties attending, whether and when an additional review conference shall be convened.

Article VIII

Each State Party to this Treaty shall in exercising its national sovereignty have the right to withdraw from this Treaty if it decides that extraordinary events related to the subject matter of this Treaty have jeopardized the supreme interests of its country. It shall give notice of such withdrawal to all other States Parties to the Treaty and to the United Nations Security Council three months in advance. Such notice shall include a statement of the extraordinary events it considers to have jeopardized its supreme interests.

Article IX

The provisions of this Treaty shall in no way affect the obligations assumed by States Parties to the Treaty under international instruments establishing zones free from nuclear weapons.

Article X

1. This Treaty shall be open for signature to all States. Any State which does not sign the Treaty before its entry into force in accordance with paragraph 3 of this article may accede to it at any time.

2. This Treaty shall be subject to ratification by signatory States. Instruments of ratification and of accession shall be deposited with the Governments of the United States of America, the United Kingdom of Great Britain and Northern Ireland, and the Union of Soviet Socialist Republics, which are hereby designated the Depositary Governments.

3. This Treaty shall enter into force after the deposit of instruments of ratification by twenty-two Governments, including the Governments designated as Depositary Governments of this Treaty.

4. For states whose instruments of ratification or accession are deposited after the entry into force of this Treaty, it shall enter into force on the date of the deposit of their instruments of ratification or accession.

5. The Depositary Governments shall promptly inform the Governments of all signatory and acceding States of the date of each signature, of the date of deposit of each instrument of ratification or of accession, of the date of the entry into force of this Treaty, and of the receipt of other notices.

6. This Treaty shall be registered by the Depositary Governments pursuant to Article 102 of the Charter of the United Nations.

Article XI

This Treaty, the English, Russian, French, Spanish and Chinese texts of which are equally authentic, shall be deposited in the archives of the Depositary Governments. Duly certified copies of this Treaty shall be transmitted by the Depositary Governments to the Governments of the States signatory and acceding thereto.

IN WITNESS WHEREOF the undersigned, being duly authorized thereto, have signed this Treaty.

DONE in triplicate, at the cities of Washington, London and Moscow, this eleventh day of February, one thousand nine hundred seventy-one.

Treaty Banning Nuclear Weapon Tests in the Atmosphere, in Outer Space and Under Water

Done at Moscow August 5, 1963
U.S. ratification deposited October 10, 1963
Entered into force October 10, 1963

The Governments of the United States of America, the United Kingdom of Great Britain and Northern Ireland, and the Union of Soviet Socialist Republics, hereinafter referred to as the "Original Parties",

Proclaiming as their principal aim the speediest possible achievement of an agreement on general and complete disarmament under strict international control in accordance with the objectives of the United Nations which would put an end to the armaments race and eliminate the incentive to the production and testing of all kinds of weapons, including nuclear weapons,

Seeking to achieve the discontinuance of all test explosions of nuclear weapons for all time, determined to continue negotiations to this end, and desiring to put an end to the contamination of man's environment by radioactive substances,

Have agreed as follows :

Article I

1. Each of the Parties to this Treaty undertakes to prohibit, to prevent, and not to carry out any nuclear weapon test explosion, or any other nuclear explosion, at any place under its jurisdiction or control :

(a) in the atmosphere; beyond its limits, including outer space; or under water, including territorial waters or high seas ; or

(b) in any other environment if such explosion causes radioactive debris to be present outside the territorial limits of the State under whose jurisdiction or control such explosion is conducted. It is understood in this connection that the provisions of this subparagraph are without prejudice to the conclusion of a treaty resulting in the permanent banning of all nuclear test explosions, including all such explosions underground, the conclusion of which, as the Parties have stated in the Preamble to this Treaty, they seek to achieve.

2. Each of the parties to this Treaty undertakes furthermore to refrain from causing, encouraging, or in any way participating in, the carrying out of any nuclear weapon test explosion, or any other nuclear explosion, anywhere which would take place in any of the environments described, or have the effect referred to, in paragraph 1 of this Article.

Article II

1. Any Party may propose amendments to this Treaty. The text of any proposed amendment shall be submitted to the Depositary Governments which shall circulate it to all Parties to this Treaty. Thereafter, if requested to do so by one-third or more of the Parties, the Depositary Governments shall convene a conference, to which they shall invite all of the Parties, to consider such amendment.

2. Any amendment to this Treaty must be approved by a majority of the votes of all the Parties to this Treaty, including the votes of all of the Original Parties. The amendment shall enter into force for all Parties upon the deposit of instruments of ratification by a majority of all the Parties, including the instruments of ratification of all of the Original Parties.

Article III

1. This Treaty shall be open to all States for signature. Any State which does not sign this Treaty before its entry into force in accordance with paragraph 3 of this Article may accede to it at any time.

2. This Treaty shall be subject to ratification by signatory States. Instruments of ratification and instruments of accession shall be deposited with the Governments of the Original Parties—the United States of America, the United Kingdom of Great Britain and Northern Ireland, and the Union of Soviet Socialist Republics—which are hereby designated the Depositary Governments.

3. This Treaty shall enter into force after its ratification by all the Original Parties and the deposit of their instruments of ratification.

4. For States whose instruments of ratification or accession are deposited subsequent to the entry into force of this Treaty, it shall enter into force on the date of the deposit of their instruments of ratification or accession.

5. The Depositary Governments shall promptly inform all signatory and acceding States of the date of each signature, the date of deposit of each instrument of ratification of and accession to this Treaty, the date of its entry into force, and the date of receipt of any requests for conferences or other notices.

6. This Treaty shall be registered by the Depositary Governments pursuant to Article 102 of the Charter of the United Nations.

Article IV

This Treaty shall be of unlimited duration.

Each Party shall in exercising its national sovereignty have the right to withdraw from the Treaty if it decides that extraordinary events, related to the subject matter of this Treaty, have jeopardized the supreme interests of its country. It shall give notice of such withdrawal to all other Parties to the Treaty three months in advance.

Article V

This Treaty, of which the English and Russian texts are equally authentic, shall be deposited in the archives of the Depositary Governments. Duly certified copies of this Treaty shall be transmitted by the Depositary Governments to the Governments of the signatory and acceding States.

IN WITNESS WHEREOF the undersigned, duly authorized, have signed this Treaty.

DONE in triplicate at the city of Moscow the fifth day of August, one thousand nine hundred and sixty-three.

For the Government of the United States of America	For the Government of the United Kingdom of Great Britain and Northern Ireland	For the Government of the Union of Soviet Socialist Republics

Treaty Between the United States of America and the Union of Soviet Socialist Republics on the Limitation of Underground Nuclear Weapon Tests, July 3, 1974

The United States of America and the Union of Soviet Socialist Republics, hereinafter referred to as the Parties,

Declaring their intention to achieve at the earliest possible date the cessation of the nuclear arms race and to take effective measures toward reductions in strategic arms, nuclear disarmament, and general and complete disarmament under strict and effective international control,

Recalling the determination expressed by the Parties to the 1963 Treaty Banning Nuclear Weapon Tests in the Atmosphere, in Outer Space and Under Water in its Preamble to seek to achieve the discontinuance of all test explosions of nuclear weapons for all time, and to continue negotiations to this end,

Noting that the adoption of measures for the further limitation of underground nuclear weapon tests would contribute to the achievement of these objectives and would meet the interests of strengthening peace and the further relaxation of international tension,

Reaffirming their adherence to the objectives and principles of the Treaty Banning Nuclear Weapon Tests in the Atmosphere, in Outer Space and Under Water and of the Treaty on the Non-Proliferation of Nuclear Weapons,

Have agreed as follows:

Article I

1. Each Party undertakes to prohibit, to prevent, and not to carry out any underground nuclear weapon test having a yield exceeding 150 kilotons at any place under its jurisdiction or control, beginning March 31, 1976.

2. Each Party shall limit the number of its underground nuclear weapon tests to a minimum.

3. The Parties shall continue their negotiations with a view toward achieving a solution to the problem of the cessation of all underground nuclear weapon tests.

Article II

1. For the purpose of providing assurance of compliance with the provisions of this Treaty, each Party shall use national technical means of verification at its disposal in a manner consistent with the generally recognized principles of international law.

2. Each Party undertakes not to interfere with the national technical means of verification of the other Party operating in accordance with paragraph 1 of this Article.

3. To promote the objectives and implementation of the provisions of this Treaty the Parties shall, as necessary, consult with each other, make inquiries and furnish information in response to such inquiries.

Article III

The provisions of this Treaty do not extend to underground nuclear explosions carried out by the Parties for peaceful purposes. Underground nuclear explosions for peaceful purposes shall be governed by an agreement which is to be negotiated and concluded by the Parties at the earliest possible time.

Article IV

This Treaty shall be subject to ratification in accordance with the constitutional procedures of each Party. This Treaty shall enter into force on the day of the exchange of instruments of ratification.

Article V

1. This Treaty shall remain in force for a period of five years. Unless replaced earlier by an agreement in implementation of the objectives specified in paragraph 3 of Article I of this Treaty, it shall be extended for successive five-year periods unless either Party notifies the other of its termination no later than six months prior to the expiration of the Treaty. Before the expiration of this period the Parties may, as necessary, hold consultations to consider the situation relevant to the substance of this Treaty and to introduce possible amendments to the text of the Treaty.

2. Each Party shall, in exercising its national sovereignty, have the right to withdraw from this Treaty if it decides that extraordinary events related to the subject matter of this Treaty have jeopardized its supreme interests. It shall give notice of its decision to the other Party six months prior to withdrawal from this Treaty. Such notice shall include a statement of the extraordinary events the notifying Party regards as having jeopardized its supreme interests.

3. This Treaty shall be registered pursuant to Article 102 of the Charter of the United Nations.

Done at Moscow on July 3, 1974, in duplicate, in the English and Russian languages, both texts being equally authentic.

For the United States of America:
RICHARD NIXON
The President of the United States of America
For the Union of Soviet Socialist Republics:
L. I. BREZHNEV
General Secretary of the Central Committee of the CPSU

Protocol to the Treaty Between the United States of America and the Union of Soviet Socialist Republics on the Limitation of Underground Nuclear Weapon Tests

The United States of America and the Union of Soviet Socialist Republics, hereinafter referred to as the Parties,
Having agreed to limit underground nuclear weapon tests,
Have agreed as follows:

1. For the Purpose of ensuring verification of compliance with the obligations of the Parties under the Treaty by national technical means, the Parties shall on the basis of reciprocity, exchange the following data:

a. The geographic coordinates of the boundaries of each test site and of the boundaries of the geophysically distinct testing areas therein.

b. Information on the geology of the testing areas of the sites (the rock characteristics of geological formations and the basic physical properties of the rock, i.e., density, seismic velocity, water saturation, porosity and depth of water table).

c. The geographic coordinates of underground nuclear weapon tests, after they have been conducted.

d. Yield, date, time, depth and coordinates for two nuclear weapon tests for calibration purposes from each geophysically distinct testing area where underground nuclear weapon tests have been and are to be conducted. In this connection the yield of such explosions for calibration purposes should be as near as possible to the limit defined in Article I of the Treaty and not less than one-tenth of that limit. In the case of testing areas where data are not available on two tests for calibration purposes, the data pertaining to one such test shall be exchanged, if available, and the data pertaining to the second test shall be exchanged as soon as possible after the second test having a yield in the above-mentioned range. The provisions of this Protocol shall not require the Parties to conduct tests solely for calibration purposes.

2. The Parties agree that the exchange of data pursuant to subparagraphs a, b, and d of paragraph 1 shall be carried out simultaneously with the exchange of instruments of ratification of the Treaty, as provided in Article IV of the Treaty, having in mind that the Parties shall, on the basis of reciprocity, afford each other the opportunity to familiarize themselves with these data before the exchange of instruments of ratification.

3. Should a Party specify a new test site or testing area after the entry into force of the Treaty, the data called for by subparagraphs a and b of paragraph 1 shall be transmitted to the other Party in advance of use of that site or area. The data called for by subparagraph d of paragraph 1 shall also be transmitted in advance of use of that site or area if they are available; if they are not avail-

able, they shall be transmitted as soon as possible after they have been obtained by the transmitting Party.

4. The Parties agree that the test sites of each Party shall be located at places under its jurisdiction or control and that all nuclear weapon tests shall be conducted solely within the testing areas specified in accordance with paragraph 1.

5. For the purposes of the Treaty, all underground nuclear explosions at the specified test sites shall be considered nuclear weapon tests and shall be subject to all the provisions of the Treaty relating to nuclear weapon tests. The provisions of Article III of the Treaty apply to all underground nuclear explosions conducted outside of the specified test sites, and only to such explosions.

This Protocol shall be considered an integral part of the Treaty.

Done at Moscow on July 3, 1974.

For the United States of America :
RICHARD NIXON
The President of the United States of America
For the Union of Soviet Socialist Republics :
L. I. BREZHNEV
General Secretary of the Central Committee of the CPSU

NOTE.—The treaty and protocol were signed at a ceremony in St. Vladimir Hall of the Grand Kremlin Palace on Wednesday, July 3, 1974.

Protocol for the Prohibition of the Use in War of Asphyxiating, Poisonous or Other Gases, and of Bacteriological Methods of Warfare

Signed at Geneva June 17, 1925
Entered into force February 8, 1928

The undersigned plenipotentiaries, in the name of their respective Governments :

Whereas the use in war of asphyxiating, poisonous or other gases, and of all analogous liquids, materials or devices, has been justly condemned by the general opinion of the civilized world ;

Whereas the prohibition of such use has been declared in Treaties to which the majority of Powers of the world are Parties ; and

To the end that this prohibition shall be universally accepted as a part of International Law, binding alike the conscience and the practice of nations ;

Declare :

That the High Contracting Parties, so far as they are not already Parties to Treaties prohibiting such use, accept their prohibition, agree to extend this prohibition to the use of bacteriological methods of warfare and agree to be bound as between themselves according to the terms of this declaration.

The High Contracting Parties will exert every effort to induce other States to accede to the present Protocol. Such accession will be notified to the Government of the French Republic, and by the latter to all signatory and acceding Powers, and will take effect on the date of the notification by the Government of the French Republic.

The present Protocol, of which the French and English texts are both authentic, shall be ratified as soon as possible. It shall bear today's date.

The ratifications of the present Protocol shall be addressed to the Government of the French Republic, which will at once notify the deposit of such ratification to each of the signatory and acceding Powers.

The instruments of ratification of and accession to the present Protocol will remain deposited in the archives of the Government of the French Republic.

The present Protocol will come into force for each signatory Power as from the date of deposit of its ratification, and, from that moment, each Power will be bound as regards other powers which have already deposited their ratifications.

IN WITNESS WHEREOF the Plenipotentiaries have signed the present Protocol.

DONE at Geneva in a single copy, the seventeenth day of June, One Thousand Nine Hundred and Twenty-Five.

Convention on the Prohibition of the Development, Production and Stockpiling of Bacteriological (Biological) and Toxin Weapons and on Their Destruction

Signed at Washington, London, Moscow April 10, 1972

The States Parties to this Convention,

Determined to act with a view to achieving effective progress towards general and complete disarmament, including the prohibition and elimination of all types of weapons of mass destruction, and convinced that the prohibition of the development, production and stockpiling of chemical and bacteriological (biological) weapons and their elimination, through effective measures, will facilitate the achievement of general and complete disarmament under strict and effective international control,

Recognizing the important significance of the Protocol for the Prohibition of the Use in War of Asphyxiating, Poisonous or Other Gases, and of Bacteriological Methods of Warfare, signed at Geneva on June 17, 1925, and conscious also of the contribution which the said Protocol has already made, and continues to make, to mitigating the horrors of war,

Reaffirming their adherence to the principles and objectives of that Protocol and calling upon all States to comply strictly with them,

Recalling that the General Assembly of the United Nations has repeatedly condemned all actions contrary to the principles and objectives of the Geneva Protocol of June 17, 1925,

Desiring to contribute to the strengthening of confidence between peoples and the general improvement of the international atmosphere,

Desiring also to contribute to the realization of the purposes and principles of the Charter of the United Nations,

Convinced of the importance and urgency of eliminating from the arsenals of States, through effective measures, such dangerous weapons of mass destruction as those using chemical or bacteriological (biological) agents,

Recognizing that an agreement on the prohibition of bacteriological (biological) and toxin weapons represents a first possible step towards the achievement of agreement on effective measures also for the prohibition of the development, production and stockpiling of chemical weapons, and determined to continue negotiations to that end,

Determined, for the sake of all mankind, to exclude completely the possibility of bacteriological (biological) agents and toxins being used as weapons,

Convinced that such use would be repugnant to the conscience of mankind and that no effort should be spared to minimize this risk,

Have agreed as follows :

Article I

Each State Party to this Convention undertakes never in any circumstances to develop, produce, stockpile or otherwise acquire or retain :

(1) Microbial or other biological agents, or toxins whatever their origin or method of production, of types and in quantities that have no justification for prophylactic, protective or other peaceful purposes ;

(2) Weapons, equipment or means of delivery designed to use such agents or toxins for hostile purposes or in armed conflict.

Article II

Each State Party to this Convention undertakes to destroy, or to divert to peaceful purposes, as soon as possible but not later than nine months after the entry into force of the Convention, all agents, toxins, weapons, equipment and means of delivery specified in article I of the Convention, which are in its possession or under its jurisdiction or control. In implementing the provisions of this article all necessary safety precautions shall be observed to protect populations and the environment.

Article III

Each State Party to this Convention undertakes not to transfer to any recipient whatsoever, directly or indirectly, and not in any way to assist, encourage, or induce any State, group of States or international organizations to manufacture or otherwise acquire any of the agents, toxins, weapons, equipment or means of delivery specified in article I of the Convention.

Article IV

Each State Party to this Convention shall, in accordance with its constitutional processes, take any necessary measures to prohibit and prevent the development, production, stockpiling, acquisition or retention of the agents, toxins, weapons, equipment and means of delivery specified in article I of the Convention, within the territory of such State, under its jurisdiction or under its control anywhere.

Article V

The States Parties to this Convention undertake to consult one another and to cooperate in solving any problems which may arise in relation to the objective of, or in the application of the provisions of, the Convention. Consultation and cooperation pursuant to this article may also be undertaken through appropriate international procedures within the framework of the United Nations and in accordance with its Charter.

Article VI

(1) Any State Party to this Convention which finds that any other State Party is acting in breach of obligations deriving from the provisions of the Convention

may lodge a complaint with the Security Council of the United Nations. Such a complaint should include all possible evidence confirming its validity, as well as a request for its consideration by the Security Council.

(2) Each State Party to this Convention undertakes to cooperate in carrying out any investigation which the Security Council may initiate, in accordance with the provisions of the Charter of the United Nations, on the basis of the complaint received by the Council. The Security Council shall inform the States Parties to the Convention of the results of the investigation.

Article VII

Each State Party to this Convention undertakes to provide or support assistance, in accordance with the United Nations Charter, to any Party to the Convention which so requests, if the Security Council decides that such Party has been exposed to danger as a result of violation of the Convention.

Article VIII

Nothing in this Convention shall be interpreted as in any way limiting or detracting from the obligations assumed by any State under the Protocol for the Prohibition of the Use in War of Asphyxiating, Poisonous or Other Gases, and of Bacteriological Methods of Warfare, signed at Geneva on June 17, 1925.

Article IX

Each State Party to this Convention affirms the recognized objective of effective prohibition of chemical weapons and, to this end, undertakes to continue negotiations in good faith with a view to reaching early agreement on effective measures for the prohibition of their development, production and stockpiling and for their destruction, and on appropriate measures concerning equipment and means of delivery specifically designed for the production or use of chemical agents for weapons purposes.

Article X

(1) The States Parties to this Convention undertake to facilitate, and have the right to participate in, the fullest possible exchange of equipment, materials and scientific and technological information for the use of bacteriological (biological) agents and toxins for peaceful purposes. Parties to the Convention in a position to do so shall also cooperate in contributing individually or together with other States or international organizations to the further development and application of scientific discoveries in the field of bacteriology (biology) for prevention of disease, or for other peaceful purposes.

(2) This Convention shall be implemented in a manner designed to avoid hampering the economic or technological development of States Parties to the Convention or international cooperation in the field of peaceful bacteriological (biological) activities, including the international exchange of bacteriological (biological) agents and toxins and equipment for the processing, use or production of bacteriological (biological) agents and toxins for peaceful purposes in accordance with the provisions of the Convention.

Article XI

Any State Party may propose amendments to this Convention. Amendments shall enter into force for each State Party accepting the amendments upon their acceptance by a majority of the States Parties to the Convention and thereafter for each remaining State Party on the date of acceptance by it.

Article XII

Five years after the entry into force of this Convention, or earlier if it is requested by a majority of Parties to the Convention by submitting a proposal to this effect to the Depositary Governments, a conference of States Parties to the Convention shall be held at Geneva, Switzerland, to review the operation of the Convention, with a view to assuring that the purposes of the preamble and the provisions of the Convention, including the provisions concerning negotiations on chemical weapons, are being realized. Such review shall take into account any new scientific and technological developments relevant to the Convention.

Article XIII

(1) This Convention shall be of unlimited duration.

(2) Each State Party to this Convention shall in exercising its national sovereignty have the right to withdraw from the Convention if it decides that extraordinary events, related to the subject matter of the Convention, have jeopardized the supreme interests of its country. It shall give notice of such withdrawal to all other States Parties to the Convention and to the United Nations Security Council three months in advance. Such notice shall include a statement of the extraordinary events it regards as having jeopardized its supreme interests.

Article XIV

(1) This Convention shall be open to all States for signature. Any State which does not sign the Convention before its entry into force in accordance with paragraph (3) of this Article may accede to it at any time.

(2) This Convention shall be subject to ratification by Signatory States. Instruments of ratification and instruments of accession shall be deposited with the Governments of the United States of America, the United Kingdom of Great Britain and Northern Ireland and the Union of Soviet Socialist Republics, which are hereby designated the Depositary Governments.

(3) This Convention shall enter into force after the deposit of instruments of ratification by twenty-two Governments, including the Governments designated as Depositaries of the Convention.

(4) For States whose instruments of ratification or accession are deposited subsequent to the entry into force of this Convention, it shall enter into force on the date of the deposit of their instruments of ratification or accession.

(5) The Depositary Governments shall promptly inform all signatory and acceding States of the date of each signature, the date of deposit of each instru-

ment of ratification or of accession and the date of the entry into force of this Convention, and of the receipt of other notices.

(6) This Convention shall be registered by the Depositary Governments pursuant to Article 102 of the Charter of the United Nations.

Article XV

This Convention, the English, Russian, French, Spanish and Chinese texts of which are equally authentic, shall be deposited in the archives of the Depositary Governments. Duly certified copies of the Convention shall be transmitted by the Depositary Governments to the Governments of the signatory and acceding States.

Treaty Between the United States of America and the Union of Soviet Socialist Republics on the Limitation of Anti-Ballistic Missile Systems

Signed at Moscow May 26, 1972

The United States of America and the Union of Soviet Socialist Republics, hereinafter referred to as the Parties,

Proceeding from the premise that nuclear war would have devastating consequences for all mankind,

Considering that effective measures to limit anti-ballistic missile systems would be a substantial factor in curbing the race in strategic offensive arms and would lead to a decrease in the risk of outbreak of war involving nuclear weapons,

Proceeding from the premise that the limitation of anti-ballistic missile systems, as well as certain agreed measures with respect to the limitation of strategic offensive arms, would contribute to the creation of more favorable conditions for further negotiations on limiting strategic arms,

Mindful of their obligations under Article VI of the Treaty on the Non-Proliferation of Nuclear Weapons,

Declaring their intention to achieve at the earliest possible date the cessation of the nuclear arms race and to take effective measures toward reductions in strategic arms, nuclear disarmament, and general and complete disarmament,

Desiring to contribute to the relaxation of international tension and the strengthening of trust between States,

Have agreed as follows:

Article I

1. Each Party undertakes to limit anti-ballistic missile (ABM) systems and to adopt other measures in accordance with the provisions of this Treaty.

2. Each Party undertakes not to deploy ABM systems for a defense of the territory of its country and not to provide a base for such a defense, and not to deploy ABM systems for defense of an individual region except as provided for in Article III of this Treaty.

Article II

1. For the purpose of this Treaty an ABM system is a system to counter strategic ballistic missiles or their elements in flight trajectory, currently consisting of:

(a) ABM interceptor missiles, which are interceptor missiles constructed and deployed for an ABM role, or of a type tested in an ABM mode;

(b) ABM launchers, which are launchers constructed and deployed for launching ABM interceptor missiles; and

(c) ABM radars, which are radars constructed and deployed for an ABM role, or of a type tested in an ABM mode.

2. The ABM system components listed in paragraph 1 of this Article include those which are:

(a) operational;
(b) under construction;
(c) undergoing testing;
(d) undergoing overhaul, repair or conversion; or
(e) mothballed.

Article III

Each Party undertakes not to deploy ABM systems or their components except that:

(a) within one ABM system deployment area having a radius of one hundred and fifty kilometers and centered on the Party's national capital, a Party may deploy: (1) no more than one hundred ABM launchers and no more than one hundred ABM interceptor missiles at launch sites, and (2) ABM radars within no more than six ABM radar complexes, the area of each complex being circular and having a diameter of no more than three kilometers; and

(b) within one ABM system deployment area having a radius of one hundred and fifty kilometers and containing ICBM silo launchers, a Party may deploy: (1) no more than one hundred ABM launchers and no more than one hundred ABM interceptor missiles at launch sites, (2) two large phased-array ABM radars comparable in potential to corresponding ABM radars operational or under construction on the date of signature of the Treaty in an ABM system deployment area containing ICBM silo launchers, and (3) no more than eighteen ABM radars each having a potential less than the potential of the smaller of the above-mentioned two large phased-array ABM radars.

Article IV

The limitations provided for in Article III shall not apply to ABM systems or their components used for development or testing, and located within current or additionally agreed test ranges. Each Party may have no more than a total of fifteen ABM launchers at test ranges.

Article V

1. Each Party undertakes not to develop, test, or deploy ABM systems or components which are sea-based, air-based, space-based, or mobile land-based.

2. Each Party undertakes not to develop, test, or deploy ABM launchers for launching more than one ABM interceptor missile at a time from each launcher, nor to modify deployed launchers to provide them with such a capability, nor to

develop, test, or deploy automatic or semi-automatic or other similar systems for rapid reload of ABM launchers.

Article VI

To enhance assurance of the effectiveness of the limitations on ABM systems and their components provided by this Treaty, each Party undertakes:

(a) not to give missiles, launchers, or radars, other than ABM interceptor missiles, ABM launchers, or ABM radars, capabilities to counter strategic ballistic missiles or their elements in flight trajectory, and not to test them in an ABM mode; and

(b) not to deploy in the future radars for early warning of strategic ballistic missile attack except at locations along the periphery of its national territory and oriented outward.

Article VII

Subject to the provisions of this Treaty, modernization and replacement of ABM systems or their components may be carried out.

Article VIII

ABM systems or their components in excess of the numbers or outside the areas specified in this Treaty, as well as ABM systems or their components prohibited by this Treaty, shall be destroyed or dismantled under agreed procedures within the shortest possible agreed period of time.

Article IX

To assure the viability and effectiveness of this Treaty, each Party undertakes not to transfer to other States, and not to deploy outside its national territory, ABM systems or their components limited by this Treaty.

Article X

Each Party undertakes not to assume any international obligations which would conflict with this Treaty.

Article XI

The Parties undertake to continue active negotiations for limitations on strategic offensive arms.

Article XII

1. For the purpose of providing assurance of compliance with the provisions of this Treaty, each Party shall use national technical means of verification at its disposal in a manner consistent with generally recognized principles of international law.

2. Each Party undertakes not to interfere with the national technical means of verification of the other Party operating in accordance with paragraph 1 of this Article.

3. Each Party undertakes not to use deliberate concealment measures which

impede verification by national technical means of compliance with the provisions of this Treaty. This obligation shall not require changes in current construction, assembly, conversion, or overhaul practices.

Article XIII

1. To promote the objectives and implementation of the provisions of this Treaty, the Parties shall establish promptly a Standing Consultative Commission, within the framework of which they will:

(a) consider questions concerning compliance with the obligations assumed and related situations which may be considered ambiguous;

(b) provide on a voluntary basis such information as either Party considers necessary to assure confidence in compliance with the obligations assumed;

(c) consider questions involving unintended interference with national technical means of verification;

(d) consider possible changes in the strategic situation which have a bearing on the provisions of this Treaty;

(e) agree upon procedures and dates for destruction or dismantling of ABM systems or their components in cases provided for by the provisions of this Treaty;

(f) consider, as appropriate, possible proposals for further increasing the viability of this Treaty, including proposals for amendments in accordance with the provisions of this Treaty;

(g) consider, as appropriate, proposals for further measures aimed at limiting strategic arms.

2. The Parties through consultation shall establish, and may amend as appropriate, Regulations for the Standing Consultative Commission governing procedures, composition and other relevant matters.

Article XIV

1. Each Party may propose amendments to this Treaty. Agreed amendments shall enter into force in accordance with the procedures governing the entry into force of this Treaty.

2. Five years after entry into force of this Treaty, and at five-year intervals thereafter, the Parties shall together conduct a review of this Treaty.

Article XV

1. This Treaty shall be of unlimited duration.

2. Each Party shall, in exercising its national sovereignty, have the right to withdraw from this Treaty if it decides that extraordinary events related to the subject matter of this Treaty have jeopardized its supreme interests. It shall give notice of its decision to the other Party six months prior to withdrawal from the Treaty. Such notice shall include a statement of the extraordinary events the notifying Party regards as having jeopardized its supreme interests.

Article XVI

1. This Treaty shall be subject to ratification in accordance with the constitutional procedures of each Party. The Treaty shall enter into force on the day of the exchange of instruments of ratification.

2. This Treaty shall be registered pursuant to Article 102 of the Charter of the United Nations.

Done at Moscow on May 26, 1972, in two copies, each in the English and Russian languages, both texts being equally authentic.

FOR THE UNITED STATES   FOR THE UNION OF SOVIET
OF AMERICA   SOCIALIST REPUBLICS

President of the United   General Secretary of the Central
States of America   Committee of the CPSU

Interim Agreement Between the United States of America and the Union of Soviet Socialist Republics on Certain Measures With Respect to the Limitation of Strategic Offensive Arms

Signed at Moscow May 26, 1972

The United States of America and the Union of Soviet Socialist Republics, hereinafter referred to as the Parties,

Convinced that the Treaty on the Limitation of Anti-Ballistic Missile Systems and this Interim Agreement on Certain Measures with Respect to the Limitation of Strategic Offensive Arms will contribute to the creation of more favorable conditions for active negotiations on limiting strategic arms as well as to the relaxation of international tension and the strengthening of trust between States,

Taking into account the relationship between strategic offensive and defensive arms,

Mindful of their obligations under Article VI of the Treaty on the Non-Proliferation of Nuclear Weapons,

Have agreed as follows:

Article I

The Parties undertake not to start construction of additional fixed land-based intercontinental ballistic missile (ICBM) launchers after July 1, 1972.

Article II

The Parties undertake not to convert land-based launchers for light ICBMs, or for ICBMs of older types deployed prior to 1964, into land-based launchers for heavy ICBMs of types deployed after that time.

Article III

The Parties undertake to limit submarine-launched ballistic missile (SLBM) launchers and modern ballistic missile submarines to the numbers operational and under construction on the date of signature of this Interim Agreement, and in addition to launchers and submarines constructed under procedures established by the Parties as replacements for an equal number of ICBM launchers of older types deployed prior to 1964 or for launchers on older submarines.

Article IV

Subject to the provisions of this Interim Agreement, modernization and replacement of strategic offensive ballistic missiles and launchers covered by this Interim Agreement may be undertaken.

Article V

1. For the purpose of providing assurance of compliance with the provisions of this Interim Agreement, each Party shall use national technical means of verification at its disposal in a manner consistent with generally recognized principles of international law.

2. Each Party undertakes not to interfere with the national technical means of verification of the other Party operating in accordance with paragraph 1 of this Article.

3. Each Party undertakes not to use deliberate concealment measures which impede verification by national technical means of compliance with the provisions of this Interim Agreement. This obligation shall not require changes in current construction, assembly, conversion, or overhaul practices.

Article VI

To promote the objectives and implementation of the provisions of this Interim Agreement, the Parties shall use the Standing Consultative Commission established under Article XIII of the Treaty on the Limitation of Anti-Ballistic Missile Systems in accordance with the provisions of that Article.

Article VII

The Parties undertake to continue active negotiations for limitations on strategic offensive arms. The obligations provided for in this Interim Agreement shall not prejudice the scope or terms of the limitations on strategic offensive arms which may be worked out in the course of further negotiations.

Article VIII

1. This Interim Agreement shall enter into force upon exchange or written notices of acceptance by each Party, which exchange shall take place simultaneously with the exchange of instruments of ratification of the Treaty on the Limitation of Anti-Ballistic Missile Systems.

2. This Interim Agreement shall remain in force for a period of five years unless replaced earlier by an agreement on more complete measures limiting strategic offensive arms. It is the objective of the Parties to conduct active follow-on negotiations with the aim of concluding such an agreement as soon as possible.

3. Each Party shall, in exercising its national sovereignty, have the right to withdraw from this Interim Agreement if it decides that extraordinary events related to the subject matter of this Interim Agreement have jeopardized its supreme interests. It shall give notice of its decision to the other Party six months prior to withdrawal from this Interim Agreement. Such notice shall include a statement of the extraordinary events the notifying Party regards as having jeopardized its supreme interests.

Done at Moscow on May 26, 1972, in two copies, each in the English and Russian languages, both texts being equally authentic.

FOR THE UNITED STATES OF AMERICA

FOR THE UNION OF SOVIET SOCIALIST REPUBLICS

The President of the United States

General Secretary of the Central Committee of the CPSU

PROTOCOL

To the Interim Agreement Between the United States of America and the Union of Soviet Socialist Republics on Certain Measures With Respect to the Limitation of Strategic Offensive Arms

Signed at Moscow May 26, 1972

The United States of America and the Union of Soviet Socialist Republics, hereinafter referred to as the Parties,

Having agreed on certain limitations relating to submarine-launched ballistic missile launchers and modern ballistic missile submarines, and to replacement procedures, in the Interim Agreement,

Have agreed as follows:

The Parties understand that, under Article III of the Interim Agreement, for the period during which that Agreement remains in force:

The U.S. may have no more than 710 ballistic missile launchers on submarines (SLBMs) and no more than 44 modern ballistic missile submarines. The Soviet Union may have no more than 950 ballistic missile launchers on submarines and no more than 62 modern ballistic missile submarines.

Additional ballistic missile launchers on submarines up to the above-mentioned levels, in the U.S.—over 656 ballistic missile launchers on nuclear-powered submarines, and in the U.S.S.R.—over 740 ballistic missile launchers on nuclear-powered submarines, operational and under construction, may become operational as replacements for equal numbers of ballistic missile launchers of older types deployed prior to 1964 or of ballistic missile launchers on older submarines.

The deployment of modern SLBMs on any submarine, regardless of type, will be counted against the total level of SLBMs permitted for the U.S. and the U.S.S.R.

This Protocol shall be considered an integral part of the Interim Agreement.

Done at Moscow this 26th day of May, 1972.

FOR THE UNITED STATES OF AMERICA

The President of the
United States of America

FOR THE UNION OF SOVIET SOCIALIST REPUBLICS

The General Secretary of the
Central Committee of the CPSU

SALT: AGREED INTERPRETATIONS AND UNILATERAL STATEMENTS

1. AGREED INTERPRETATIONS

(*a*) *Initialed Statements.*—The texts of the statements set out below were agreed upon and initialed by the Heads of the Delegations on May 26, 1972.

ABM TREATY

[A]

The Parties understand that, in addition to the ABM radars which may be deployed in accordance with subparagraph (a) of Article III of the Treaty, those non-phased-array ABM radars operational on the date of signature of the Treaty within the ABM system deployment area for defense of the national capital may be retained.

[B]

The Parties understand that the potential (the product of mean emitted power in watts and antenna area in square meters) of the smaller of the two large phased-array ABM radars referred to in subparagraph (b) of Article III of the Treaty is considered for purposes of the Treaty to be three million.

[C]

The Parties understand that the center of the ABM system deployment area centered on the national capital and the center of the ABM system deployment area containing ICBM silo launchers for each Party shall be separated by no less than thirteen hundred kilometers.

[D]

The Parties agree not to deploy phased-array radars having a potential (the product of mean emitted power in watts and antenna area in square meters) exceeding three million, except as provided for in Articles III, IV and VI of the Treaty, or except for the purposes of tracking objects in outer space or for use as national technical means of verification.

[E]

In order to insure fulfillment of the obligation not to deploy ABM systems and their components except as provided in Article III of the Treaty, the Parties agree that in the event ABM systems based on other physical principles and including components capable of substituting for ABM interceptor missiles, ABM launchers, or ABM radars are created in the future, specific limitations on such systems and their components would be subject to discussion in accordance with Article XIII and agreement in accordance with Article XIV of the Treaty.

[F]

The Parties understand that Article V of the Treaty includes obligations not to develop, test or deploy ABM interceptor missiles for the delivery by each ABM interceptor missile of more than one independently guided warhead.

[G]

The Parties understand that Article IX of the Treaty includes the obligation of the US and the USSR not to provide to other States technical descriptions or blueprints specially worked out for the construction of ABM systems and their components limited by the Treaty.

INTERIM AGREEMENT

[H]

The parties understand that land-based ICBM launchers referred to in the Interim Agreement are understood to be launchers for strategic ballistic missiles capable of ranges in excess of the shortest distance between the northeastern border of the continental U.S. and the northwestern border of the continental USSR.

[I]

The Parties understand that fixed land-based ICBM launchers under active construction as of the date of signature of the Interim Agreement may be completed.

[J]

The Parties understand that in the process of modernization and replacement the dimensions of land-based ICBM silo launchers will not be significantly increased.

[K]

The Parties understand that dismantling or destruction of ICBM launchers of older types deployed prior to 1964 and ballistic missile launchers on older submarines being replaced by new SLBM launchers on modern submarines will be initiated at the time of the beginning of sea trials of a replacement submarine, and will be completed in the shortest possible agreed period of time. Such dismantling or destruction, and timely notification thereof, will be accomplished under procedures to be agreed in the Standing Consultative Commission.

[L]

The Parties understand that during the period of the Interim Agreement there shall be no significant increase in the number of ICBM or SLBM test and training launchers, or in the number of such launchers for modern land-based heavy ICBMs. The Parties further understand that construction or conversion of ICBM launchers at test ranges shall be undertaken only for purposes of testing and training.

(b) *Common Understandings.*—Common understanding of the Parties on the following matters was reached during the negotiations:

A. INCREASE IN ICBM SILO DIMENSIONS

Ambassador Smith made the following statement on May 26, 1972:

The Parties agree that the term "significantly increased" means that an increase will not be greater than 10–15 percent of the present dimensions of land-based ICBM silo launchers.

Minister Semenov replied that this statement corresponded to the Soviet understanding.

B. LOCATION OF ICBM DEFENSES

The U.S. Delegation made the following statement on May 26, 1972:

Article III of the ABM Treaty provides for each side one ABM system deployment area centered on its national capital and one ABM system deployment area containing ICBM silo launchers. The two sides have registered agreement on the following statement: "The Parties understand that the center of the ABM system deployment area centered on the national capital and the center of the ABM system deployment area containing ICBM silo launchers for each Party shall be separated by no less than thirteen hundred kilometers." In this connection, the U.S. side notes that its ABM system deployment area for defense of ICBM silo launchers, located west of the Mississippi River, will be centered in the Grand Forks ICBM silo launcher deployment area. (See Initialed Statement [C].)

C. ABM TEST RANGES

The U.S. Delegation made the following statement on April 26, 1972:

Article IV of the ABM Treaty provides that "the limitations provided for in Article III shall not apply to ABM systems or their components used for development or testing, and located within current or additionally agreed test ranges." We believe it would be useful to assure that there is no misunderstanding as to current ABM test ranges. It is our understanding that ABM test ranges encompass the area within which ABM components are located for test purposes. The current U.S. ABM test ranges are at White Sands, New Mexico, and at Kwajalein Atoll, and the current Soviet ABM test range is near Sary Shagan in Kazakhstan. We consider that non-phased array radars of types used for range safety or instrumentation purposes may be located outside of ABM test ranges. We interpret the reference in Article IV to "additionally agreed test ranges" to mean that ABM components will not be located at any other test ranges without prior agreement between our Governments that there will be such additional ABM test ranges.

On May 5, 1972, the Soviet Delegation stated that there was a common understanding on what ABM test ranges were, that the use of the types of non-ABM radars for range safety or instrumentation was not limited under the Treaty, that the reference in Article IV to "additionally agreed" test ranges was sufficiently clear, and that national means permitted identifying current test ranges.

D. MOBILE ABM SYSTEMS

On January 28, 1972, the U.S. Delegation made the following statement:

Article V(1) of the Joint Draft Text of the ABM Treaty includes an undertaking not to develop, test, or deploy mobile land-based ABM systems and their components. On May 5, 1971, the U.S. side indicated that, in its view, a prohibition on deployment of mobile ABM systems and components would rule out the deployment of ABM launchers and radars which were not permanent fixed types. At that time, we asked for the Soviet view of this interpretation. Does the Soviet side agree with the U.S. side's interpretation put forward on May 5, 1971?

On April 13, 1972, the Soviet Delegation said there is a general common understanding on this matter.

E. STANDING CONSULTATIVE COMMISSION

Ambassador Smith made the following statement on May 22, 1972:

> The United States proposes that the sides agree that, with regard to initial implementation of the ABM Treaty's Article XIII on the Standing Consultative Commission (SCC) and of the consultation Articles to the Interim Agreement on offensive arms and the Accidents Agreement,* agreement establishing the SCC will be worked out early in the follow-on SALT negotiations; until that is completed, the following arrangements will prevail: when SALT is in session, any consultation desired by either side under these Articles can be carried out by the two SALT Delegations; when SALT is not in session, *ad hoc* arrangements for any desired consultations under these Articles may be made through diplomatic channels.

Minister Semenov replied that, on an *ad referendum* basis, he could agree that the U.S. statement corresponded to the Soviet understanding.

F. STANDSTILL

On May 6, 1972, Minister Semenov made the following statement:

> In an effort to accommodate the wishes of the U.S. side, the Soviet Delegation is prepared to proceed on the basis that the two sides will in fact observe the obligations of both the Interim Agreement and the ABM Treaty beginning from the date of signature of these two documents.

In reply, the U.S. Delegation made the following statement on May 20, 1972:

> The U.S. agrees in principle with the Soviet statement made on May 6 concerning observance of obligations beginning from date of signature but we would like to make clear our understanding that this means that, pending ratification and acceptance, neither side would take any action prohibited by the agreements after they had entered into force. This understanding would continue to apply in the absence of notification by either signatory of its intention not to proceed with ratification or approval.

The Soviet Delegation indicated agreement with the U.S. statement.

2. UNILATERAL STATEMENTS

(a) The following noteworthy unilateral statements were made during the negotiations by the United States Delegation:

---

*See Article 7 of Agreement to Reduce the Risk of Outbreak of Nuclear War Between the United States of America and the Union of Soviet Socialist Republics, signed Sept. 30, 1971.

A. WITHDRAWAL FROM THE ABM TREATY

On May 9, 1972, Ambassador Smith made the following statement:

The U.S. Delegation has stressed the importance the U.S. Government attaches to achieving agreement on more complete limitations on strategic offensive arms, following agreement on an ABM Treaty and on an Interim Agreement on certain measures with respect to the limitation of strategic offensive arms. The U.S. Delegation believes that an objective of the follow-on negotiations should be to constrain and reduce on a long-term basis threats to the survivability of our respective strategic retaliatory forces. The USSR Delegation has also indicated that the objectives of SALT would remain unfulfilled without the achievement of an agreement providing for more complete limitations on strategic offensive arms. Both sides recognize that the initial agreements would be steps toward the achievement of more complete limitations on strategic arms. If an agreement providing for more complete strategic offensive arms limitations were not achieved within five years, U.S. supreme interests could be jeopardized. Should that occur, it would constitute a basis for withdrawal from the ABM Treaty. The U.S. does not wish to see such a situation occur, nor do we believe that the USSR does. It is because we wish to prevent such a situation that we emphasize the importance the U.S. Government attaches to achievement of more complete limitations on strategic offensive arms. The U.S. Executive will inform the Congress, in connection with Congressional consideration of the ABM Treaty and the Interim Agreement, of this statement of the U.S. position.

B. LAND-MOBILE ICBM LAUNCHERS

The U.S. Delegation made the following statement on May 20, 1972:

In connection with the important subject of land-mobile ICBM launchers, in the interest of concluding the Interim Agreement the U.S. Delegation now withdraws its proposal that Article I or an agreed statement explicitly prohibit the deployment of mobile land-based ICBM launchers. I have been instructed to inform you that, while agreeing to defer the question of limitation of operational land-mobile ICBM launchers to the subsequent negotiations on more complete limitations on strategic offensive arms, the U.S. would consider the deployment of operational land-mobile ICBM launchers during the period of the Interim Agreement as inconsistent with the objectives of that Agreement.

C. COVERED FACILITIES

The U.S. Delegation made the following statement on May 26, 1972:

I wish to emphasize the importance that the United States attaches to the provisions of Article V, including in particular their application to fitting out or berthing submarines.

D. "HEAVY" ICBM'S

The U.S. Delegation made the following statement on May 26, 1972:

The U.S. Delegation regrets that the Soviet Delegation has not been willing to agree on a common definition of a heavy missile. Under these circumstances, the U.S. Delegation believes it necessary to state the following: The United States would consider any ICBM having a volume significantly greater than that of the largest light ICBM now operational on either side to be a heavy ICBM. The U.S. proceeds on the premise that the Soviet side will give due account to this consideration.

E. TESTED IN ABM MODE

On April 7, 1972, the U.S. Delegation made the following statement:

Article II of the Joint Text Draft uses the term "tested in an ABM mode," in defining ABM components, and Article VI includes certain obligations concerning such testing. We believe that the sides should have a common understanding of this phrase. First, we would note that the testing provisions of the ABM Treaty are intended to apply to testing which occurs after the date of signature of the Treaty, and not to any testing which may have occurred in the past. Next, we would amplify the remarks we have made on this subject during the previous Helsinki phase by setting forth the objectives which govern the U.S. view on the subject, namely, while prohibiting testing of non-ABM components for ABM purposes: not to prevent testing of ABM components, and not to prevent testing of non-ABM components for non-ABM purposes. To clarify our interpretation of "tested in an ABM mode," we note that we would consider a launcher, missile or radar to be "tested in an ABM mode" if, for example, any of the following events occur: (1) a launcher is used to launch an ABM interceptor missile, (2) an interceptor missile is flight tested against a target vehicle which has a flight trajectory with characteristics of a strategic ballistic missile flight trajectory, or is flight tested in conjunction with the test of an ABM interceptor missile or an ABM radar at the same test range, or is flight tested to an altitude inconsistent with interception of targets against which air defenses are deployed, (3) a radar makes measurements on a cooperative target vehicle of the kind referred to in item (2) above during the reentry portion of its trajectory or makes measurements in conjunction with the test of an ABM interceptor missile or an ABM radar at the same test range. Radars used for purposes such as range safety or instrumentation would be exempt from application of these criteria.

F. NO-TRANSFER ARTICLE OF ABM TREATY

On April 18, 1972, the U.S. Delegation made the following statement:

In regard to this Article [IX], I have a brief and I believe self-explanatory statement to make. The U.S. side wishes to make clear that the provisions of this Article do not set a precedent for whatever provision may be considered for a Treaty on Limiting Strategic Offensive Arms. The question of transfer of strategic offensive arms is a far more complex issue, which may require a different solution.

G. NO INCREASE IN DEFENSE OF EARLY WARNING RADARS

On July 28, 1970, the U.S. Delegation made the following statement:

Since Hen House radars [Soviet ballistic missile early warning radars] can detect and track ballistic missile warheads at great distances, they have a significant ABM potential. Accordingly, the U.S. would regard any increase in the defenses of such radars by surface-to-air missiles as inconsistent with an agreement.

*   *   *   *   *   *   *

(b) The following noteworthy unilateral statement was made by the Delegation of the U.S.S.R. and is shown here with the U.S. reply:

On May 17, 1972, Minister Semenov made the following unilateral "Statement of the Soviet Side":

> Taking into account that modern ballistic missile submarines are presently in the possession of not only the U.S., but also of its NATO allies, the Soviet Union agrees that for the period of effectiveness of the Interim 'Freeze' Agreement the U.S. and its NATO allies have up to 50 such submarines with a total of up to 800 ballistic missile launchers thereon (including 41 U.S. submarines with 656 ballistic missile launchers). However, if during the period of effectiveness of the Agreement U.S. allies in NATO should increase the number of their modern submarines to exceed the numbers of submarines they would have operational or under construction on the date of signature of the Agreement, the Soviet Union will have the right to a corresponding increase in the number of its submarines. In the opinion of the Soviet side, the solution of the question of modern ballistic missile submarines provided for in the Interim Agreement only partially compensates for the strategic imbalance in the deployment of the nuclear-powered missile submarines of the USSR and the U.S. Therefore, the Soviet side believes that this whole question, and above all the question of liquidating the American missile submarine bases outside the U.S., will be appropriately resolved in the course of follow-on negotiations.

On May 24, Ambassador Smith made the following reply to Minister Semenov:

> The United States side has studied the statement made by the Soviet side" of May 17 concerning compensation for submarine basing and SLBM submarines belonging to third countries. The United States does not accept the validity of the considerations in that statement.

On May 26 Minister Semenov repeated the unilateral statement made on May 24. Ambassador Smith also repeated the U.S. rejection on May 26.

Text of Basic Principles, May 29

BASIC PRINCIPLES OF RELATIONS BETWEEN THE UNITED STATES OF AMERICA AND THE UNION OF SOVIET SOCIALIST REPUBLICS

The United States of America and the Union of Soviet Socialist Republics,

Guided by their obligations under the Charter of the United Nations and by a desire to strengthen peaceful relations with each other and to place these relations on the firmest possible basis,

Aware of the need to make every effort to remove the threat of war and to create conditions which promote the reduction of tensions in the world and the strengthening of universal security and international cooperation,

Believing that the improvement of US-Soviet relations and their mutually advantageous development in such areas as economics, science and culture, will meet these objectives and contribute to better mutual understanding and business-like cooperation, without in any way prejudicing the interests of third countries,

Conscious that these objectives reflect the interests of the peoples of both countries,

Have agreed as follows:

First. They will proceed from the common determination that in the nuclear age there is no alternative to conducting their mutual relations on the basis of peaceful coexistence. Differences in ideology and in the social systems of the USA and the USSR are not obstacles to the bilateral development of normal relations based on the principles of sovereignty, equality, non-interference in internal affairs and mutual advantage.

Second. The USA and the USSR attach major importance to preventing the development of situations capable of causing a dangerous exacerbation of their relations. Therefore, they will do their utmost to avoid military confrontations and to prevent the outbreak of nuclear war. They will always exercise restraint in their mutual relations, and will be prepared to negotiate and settle differences by peaceful means. Discussions and negotiations on outstanding issues will be conducted in a spirit of reciprocity, mutual accommodation and mutual benefit.

Both sides recognize that efforts to obtain unilateral advantage at the expense of the other, directly or indirectly, are inconsistent with these objectives. The prerequisites for maintaining and strengthening peaceful relations between the USA and the USSR are the recognition of the security interests of the Parties based on the principle of equality and the renunciation of the use or threat of force.

Third. The USA and the USSR have a special responsibility, as do other countries which are permanent members of the United Nations Security Council, to do everything in their power so that conflicts or situations will not arise which would serve to increase international tensions. Accordingly, they will seek to promote conditions in which all countries will live in peace and security and will not be subject to outside interference in their internal affairs.

Fourth. The USA and the USSR intend to widen the juridical basis of their mutual relations and to exert the necessary efforts so that bilateral agreements which they have concluded and multilateral treaties and agreements to which they are jointly parties are faithfully implemented.

Fifth. The USA and the USSR reaffirm their readiness to continue the practice of exchanging views on problems of mutual interest and, when necessary, to conduct such exchanges at the highest level, including meetings between leaders of the two countries.

The two governments welcome and will facilitate an increase in productive contacts between representatives of the legislative bodies of the two countries.

Sixth. The Parties will continue their efforts to limit armaments on a bilateral as well as on a multilateral basis. They will continue to make special efforts to limit strategic armaments. Whenever possible, they will conclude concrete agreements aimed at achieving these purposes.

The USA and the USSR regard as the ultimate objective of their efforts the achievement of general and complete disarmament and the establishment of an effective system of international security in accordance with the purposes and principles of the United Nations.

Seventh. The USA and the USSR regard commercial and economic ties as an important and necessary element in the strengthening of their bilateral relations and thus will actively promote the growth of such ties. They will facilitate cooperation between the relevant organizations and enterprises of the two countries and the conclusion of appropriate agreements and contracts, including long-term ones.

The two countries will contribute to the improvement of maritime and air communications between them.

Eighth. The two sides consider it timely and useful to develop mutual contacts and cooperation in the fields of science and technology. Where suitable, the USA and the USSR will conclude appropriate agreements dealing with concrete cooperation in these fields.

Ninth. The two sides reaffirm their intention to deepen cultural ties with one another and to encourage fuller familiarization with each other's cultural values. They will promote improved conditions for cultural exchanges and tourism.

Tenth. The USA and the USSR will seek to ensure that their ties and cooperation in all the above-mentioned fields and in any others in their mutual interest are built on a firm and long-term basis. To give a permanent character to these efforts, they will establish in all fields where this is feasible joint commissions or other joint bodies.

Eleventh. The USA and the USSR make no claim for themselves and would not recognize the claims of anyone else to any special rights or advantages in world affairs. They recognize the sovereign equality of all states.

The development of US-Soviet relations is not directed against third countries and their interests.

Twelfth. The basic principles set forth in this document do not affect any obligations with respect to other countries earlier assumed by the USA and the USSR.

Moscow, *May 29, 1972*

For the United States
of America

For the Union of Soviet
Socialist Republics

RICHARD NIXON

LEONID I. BREZHNEV

President of the
United States
of America

General Secretary of the
Central Committee,
CPSU

Standing Consultative Commission on Arms Limitation

Memorandum of Understanding signed at Geneva December 21, 1972;
Entered into force December 21, 1972

MEMORANDUM OF UNDERSTANDING BETWEEN THE GOVERNMENT OF THE UNITED STATES OF AMERICA AND THE GOVERNMENT OF THE UNION OF SOVIET SOCIALIST REPUBLICS REGARDING THE ESTABLISHMENT OF A STANDING CONSULTATIVE COMMISSION

I

The Government of the United States of America and the Government of the Union of Soviet Socialist Republics hereby establish a Standing Consultative Commission.

II

The Standing Consultative Commission shall promote the objectives and implementation of the provisions of the Treaty between the USA and the USSR on the Limitation of Anti-Ballistic Missile Systems of May 26, 1972, the Interim Agreement between the USA and the USSR on Certain Measures with Respect to the Limitation of Strategic Offensive Arms of May 26, 1972, and the Agreement on Measures to Reduce the Risk of Outbreak of Nuclear War between the USA and the USSR of September 30, 1971, and shall exercise its competence in accordance with the provisions of Article XIII of said Treaty, Article VI of said Interim Agreement, and Article 7 of said Agreement on Measures.

III

Each Government shall be represented on the Standing Consultative Commission by a Commissioner and a Deputy Commissioner, assisted by such staff as it deems necessary.

IV

The Standing Consultative Commission shall hold periodic sessions on dates mutually agreed by the Commissioners but no less than two times per year. Sessions shall also be convened as soon as possible, following reasonable notice, at the request of either Commissioner.

V

The Standing Consultative Commission shall establish and approve Regulations governing procedures and other relevant matters and may amend them as it deems appropriate.

VI

The Standing Consultative Commission will meet in Geneva. It may also meet at such other places as may be agreed.

DONE in Geneva, on December 21, 1972, in two copies, each in the English and Russian languages, both texts being equally authentic.

Standing Consultative Commission on Arms Limitation: Regulations

Protocol, with regulations, signed at Geneva May 30, 1973;
Entered into force May 30, 1973

STANDING CONSULTATIVE COMMISSION

PROTOCOL

Pursuant to the provisions of the Memorandum of Understanding between the Government of the United States of America and the Government of the Union of Soviet Socialist Republics Regarding the Establishment of a Standing Consultative Commission, dated December 21, 1972, the undersigned, having been duly appointed by their respective Governments as Commissioners of said Standing Consultative Commission, hereby establish and approve, in the form attached, Regulations governing procedures and other relevant matters of the Commission, which Regulations shall enter into force upon signature of this Protocol and remain in force until and unless amended by the undersigned or their successors.

DONE in Geneva on May 30, 1973, in two copies, each in the English and Russian languages, both texts being equally authentic.

ATTACHMENT

STANDING CONSULTATIVE COMMISSION

REGULATIONS

1. The Standing Consultative Commission, established by the Memorandum of Understanding between the Government of the United States of America and the Government of the Union of Soviet Socialist Republics Regarding the Establishment of a Standing Consultative Commission of December 21, 1972, shall consist of a U.S. component and Soviet component, each of which shall be headed by a Commissioner.

2. The Commissioners shall alternately preside over the meetings.

3. The Commissioners shall, when possible, inform each other in advance of the matters to be submitted for discussion, but may at a meeting submit for discussion any matter within the competence of the Commission.

4. During intervals between sessions of the Commission, each Commissioner may transmit written or oral communications to the other Commissioner concerning matters within the competence of the Commission.

5. Each component of the Commission may invite such advisers and experts as it deems necessary to participate in a meeting.

6. The Commission may establish working groups to consider and prepare specific matters.

7. The results of the discussion of questions at the meetings of the Commission may, if necessary, be entered into records which shall be in two copies, each in the English and the Russian languages, both texts being equally authentic.

8. The proceedings of the Standing Consultative Commission shall be conducted in private. The Standing Consultative Commission may not make its proceedings public except with the express consent of both Commissioners.

9. Each component of the Commission shall bear the expenses connected with its participation in the Commission.

Protocol to the Treaty Between the United States of America and the Union of Soviet Socialist Republics on the Limitation of Anti-Ballistic Missile Systems, July 3, 1974

The United States of America and the Union of Soviet Socialist Republics, hereinafter referred to as the Parties,

Proceeding from the Basic Principles of Relations between the United States of America and the Union of Soviet Socialist Republics signed on May 29, 1972,

Desiring to further the objectives of the Treaty between the United States of America and the Union of Soviet Socialist Republics on the Limitation of Anti-Ballistic Missile Systems signed on May 26, 1972, hereinafter referred to as the Treaty,

Reaffirming their conviction that the adoption of further measures for the limitation of strategic arms would contribute to strengthening international peace and security,

Proceeding from the premise that further limitation of anti-ballistic missile systems will create more favorable conditions for the completion of work on a permanent agreement on more complete measures for the limitation of strategic offensive arms,

Have agreed as follows:

Article I

1. Each Party shall be limited at any one time to a single area out of the two provided in Article III of the Treaty for deployment of anti-ballistic missile (ABM) systems or their components and accordingly shall not exercise its right to deploy an ABM system or its components in the second of the two ABM system deployment areas permitted by Article III of the Treaty, except as an exchange of one permitted area for the other in accordance with Article II of this Protocol.

2. Accordingly, except as permitted by Article II of this Protocol: the United States of America shall not deploy an ABM system or its components in the area centered on its capital, as permitted by Article III(a) of the Treaty, and the Soviet Union shall not deploy an ABM system or its components in the deployment area of intercontinental ballistic missile (ICBM) silo launchers permitted by Article III(b) of the Treaty.

Article II

1. Each Party shall have the right to dismantle or destroy its ABM system and the components thereof in the area where they are presently deployed and to deploy an ABM system or its components in the alternative area permitted by Article III of the Treaty, provided that prior to initiation of construction, notification is given in accord with the procedure agreed to by the Standing Consultative Commission, during the year beginning October 3, 1977, and ending October 2, 1978, or during any year which commences at five year intervals there-

after, those being the years for periodic review of the Treaty, as provided in Article XIV of the Treaty. This right may be exercised only once.

2. Accordingly, in the event of such notice, the United States would have the right to dismantle or destroy the ABM system and its components in the deployment area of ICBM silo launchers and to deploy an ABM system or its components in an area centered on its capital, as permitted by Article III(a) of the Treaty, and the Soviet Union would have the right to dismantle or destroy the ABM system and its components in the area centered on its capital and to deploy an ABM system or its components in an area containing ICBM silo launchers, as permitted by Article III(b) of the Treaty.

3. Dismantling or destruction and deployment of ABM systems or their components and the notification thereof shall be carried out in accordance with Article VIII of the ABM Treaty and procedures agreed to in the Standing Consultative Commission.

Article III

The rights and obligations established by the Treaty remain in force and shall be complied with by the Parties except to the extent modified by this Protocol. In particular, the deployment of an ABM system or its components within the area selected shall remain limited by the levels and other requirements established by the Treaty.

Article IV

This Protocol shall be subject to ratification in accordance with the constitutional procedures of each Party. It shall enter into force on the day of the exchange of instruments of ratification and shall thereafter be considered an integral part of the Treaty.

Done at Moscow on July 3, 1974, in duplicate, in the English and Russian languages, both texts being equally authentic.

For the United States of America:
RICHARD NIXON
President of the United States of America
For the Union of Soviet Socialist Republics:
L. I. BREZHNEV
General Secretary of the Central Committee of the CPSU

Joint Statement on Strategic Offensive Arms Issued at Vladivostok November 24

JOINT U.S.-SOVIET STATEMENT

During their working meeting in the area of Vladivostok on November 23–24, 1974, the President of the USA Gerald R. Ford and General Secretary of the Central Committee of the CPSU L. I. Brezhnev discussed in detail the question of further limitations of strategic offensive arms.

They reaffirmed the great significance that both the United States and the USSR attach to the limitation of strategic offensive arms. They are convinced that a long-term agreement on this question would be a significant contribution to improving relations between the US and the USSR, to reducing the danger of war and to enhancing world peace. Having noted the value of previous agreements on this question, including the Interim Agreement of May 26, 1972, they reaffirm the intention to conclude a new agreement on the limitation of strategic offensive arms, to last through 1985.

As a result of the exchange of views on the substance of such a new agreement, the President of the United States of America and the General Secretary of the Central Committee of the CPSU concluded that favorable prospects exist for completing the work on this agreement in 1975.

Agreement was reached that further negotiations will be based on the following provisions.

1. The new agreement will incorporate the relevant provisions of the Interim Agreement of May 26, 1972, which will remain in force until October 1977.

2. The new agreement will cover the period from October 1977 through December 31, 1985.

3. Based on the principle of equality and equal security, the new agreement will include the following limitations:

a. Both sides will be entitled to have a certain agreed aggregate number of strategic delivery vehicles;

b. Both sides will be entitled to have a certain agreed aggregate number of ICBMs and SLBMs [intercontinental ballistic missiles; submarine-launched ballistic missiles] equipped with multiple independently targetable warheads (MIRVs).

4. The new agreement will include a provision for further negotiations beginning no later than 1980–1981 on the question of further limitations and possible reductions of strategic arms in the period after 1985.

5. Negotiations between the delegations of the US and USSR to work out the new agreement incorporating the foregoing points will resume in Geneva in January 1975.

Conference on Security and Cooperation in Europe, Final Act

Document on confidence-building measures and certain aspects of security and disarmament

The participating States,

Desirous of eliminating the causes of tension that may exist among them and thus of contributing to the strengthening of peace and security in the world;

Determined to strengthen confidence among them and thus to contribute to increasing stability and security in Europe;

Determined further to refrain in their mutual relations, as well as in their international relations in general, from the threat or use of force against the territorial integrity or political independence of any State, or in any other manner inconsistent with the purposes of the United Nations and with the Declaration on Principles Guiding Relations between Participating States as adopted in this Final Act;

Recognizing the need to contribute to reducing the dangers of armed conflict and of misunderstanding or miscalculation of military activities which could give rise to apprehension, particularly in a situation where the participating States lack clear and timely information about the nature of such activities;

Taking into account considerations relevant to efforts aimed at lessening tension and promoting disarmament;

Recognizing that the exchange of observers by invitation at military manœuvres will help to promote contacts and mutual understanding;

Having studied the question of prior notification of major military movements in the context of confidence-building;

Recognizing that there are other ways in which individual States can contribute further to their common objectives;

Convinced of the political importance of prior notification of major military manœuvres for the promotion of mutual understanding and the strengthening of confidence, stability and security;

Accepting the responsibility of each of them to promote these objectives and to implement this measure, in accordance with the accepted criteria and modalities, as essentials for the realization of these objectives;

Recognizing that this measure deriving from political decision rests upon a voluntary basis;

Have adopted the following:

I

Prior notification of major military manœuvres

They will notify their major military manœuvres to all other participating States through usual diplomatic channels in accordance with the following provisions:

Notification will be given of major military manœuvres exceeding a total of 25,000 troops, independently or combined with any possible air or naval components (in this context the word "troops" includes amphibious and airborne troops). In the case of independent manœuvres of amphibious or airborne troops, or of combined manœuvres involving them, these troops will be included in this total. Furthermore, in the case of combined manœuvres which do not reach the above total but which involve land forces together with significant numbers of either amphibious or airborne troops, or both, notification can also be given.

Notification will be given of major military manœuvres which take place on the territory, in Europe, of any participating State as well as, if applicable, in the adjoining sea area and air space.

In the case of a participating State whose territory extends beyond Europe, prior notification need be given only of manœuvres which take place in an area within 250 kilometres from its frontier facing or shared with any other European participating State, the participating State need not, however, give notification in cases in which that area is also contiguous to the participating State's frontier facing or shared with a non-European non-participating State.

Notification will be given 21 days or more in advance of the start of the manœuvre or in the case of a manœuvre arranged at shorter notice at the earliest possible opportunity prior to its starting date.

Notification will contain information of the designation, if any, the general purpose of and the States involved in the manœuvre, the type or types and numerical strength of the forces engaged, the area and estimated time-frame of its conduct. The participating States will also, if possible, provide additional relevant information, particularly that related to the components of the forces engaged and the period of involvement of these forces.

Prior notification of other military manœuvres

The participating States recognize that they can contribute further to strengthening confidence and increasing security and stability, and to this end may also notify smaller-scale military manœuvres to other participating States, with special regard for those near the area of such manœuvres.

To the same end, the participating States also recognize that they may notify other military manœuvres conducted by them.

Exchange of observers

The participating States will invite other participating States, voluntarily and on a bilateral basis, in a spirit of reciprocity and goodwill towards all participating States, to send observers to attend military manœuvres.

The inviting State will determine in each case the number of observers, the procedures and conditions of their participation, and give other information which it may consider useful. It will provide appropriate facilities and hospitality.

The invitation will be given as far ahead as is conveniently possible through usual diplomatic channels.

Prior notification of major military movements

·In accordance with the Final Recommendations of the Helsinki Consultations the participating States studied the question of prior notification of major military movements as a measure to strengthen confidence.

Accordingly, the participating States recognize that they may, at their own discretion and with a view to contributing to confidence-building, notify their major military movements.

In the same spirit, further consideration will be given by the States participating in the Conference on Security and Co-operation in Europe to the question of prior notification of major military movements, bearing in mind, in particular, the experience gained by the implementation of the measures which are set forth in this document.

Other confidence-building measures

The participating States recognize that there are other means by which their common objectives can be promoted.

In particular, they will, with due regard to reciprocity and with a view to better mutual understanding, promote exchanges by invitation among their military personnel, including visits by military delegations.

* * *

In order to make a fuller contribution to their common objective of confidence-building, the participating States, when conducting their military activities in the area covered by the provisions for the prior notification of major military manœuvres, will duly take into account and respect this objective.

They also recognize that the experience gained by the implementation of the provisions set forth above, together with further efforts, could lead to developing and enlarging measures aimed at strengthening confidence.

II

Questions relating to disarmament

The participating States recognize the interest of all of them in efforts aimed at lessening military confrontation and promoting disarmament which are designed to complement political détente in Europe and to strengthen their security. They are convinced of the necessity to take effective measures in these fields which by their scope and by their nature constitute steps towards the ultimate achievement of general and complete disarmament under strict and effective international control, and which should result in strengthening peace and security throughout the world.

III

General considerations

Having considered the views expressed on various subjects related to the strengthening of security in Europe through joint efforts aimed at promoting détente and disarmament, the participating States, when engaged in such efforts, will, in this context, proceed, in particular, from the following essential considerations:

— The complementary nature of the political and military aspects of security;

— The interrelation between the security of each participating State and security in Europe as a whole and the relationship which exists, in the broader context of world security, between security in Europe and security in the Mediterranean area;

— Respect for the security interests of all States participating in the Conference on Security and Co-operation in Europe inherent in their sovereign equality;

— The importance that participants in negotiating fora see to it that information about relevant developments, progress and results is provided on an appropriate basis to other States participating in the Conference on Security and Co-operation in Europe and, in return, the justified interest of any of those States in having their views considered.

Treaty for the Prohibition of Nuclear Weapons in Latin America

Preamble

In the name of their peoples and faithfully interpreting their desires and aspirations, the Governments of the States which sign the Treaty for the Prohibition of Nuclear Weapons in Latin America,

Desiring to contribute, so far as lies in their power, towards ending the armaments race, especially in the field of nuclear weapons, and towards strengthening a world at peace, based on the sovereign equality of States, mutual respect and good neighbourliness.

Recalling that the United Nations General Assembly, in its Resolution 808 (IX), adopted unanimously as one of the three points of a coordinated programme of disarmament "the total prohibition of the use and manufacture of nuclear weapons and weapons of mass destruction of every type",

Recalling that militarily denuclearized zones are not an end in themselves but rather a means for achieving general and complete disarmament at a later stage,

Recalling United Nations General Assembly Resolution 1911 (XVIII), which established that the measures that should be agreed upon for the denuclearization of Latin America should be taken "in the light of the principles of the Charter of the United Nations and of regional agreements",

Recalling United Nations General Assembly Resolution 2028 (XX), which established the principle of an acceptable balance of mutual responsibilities and duties for the nuclear and non-nuclear powers, and

Recalling that the Charter of the Organization of American States proclaims that it is an essential purpose of the Organization to strengthen the peace and security of the hemisphere,

Convinced:

That the incalculable destructive power of nuclear weapons has made it imperative that the legal prohibition of war should be strictly observed in practice if the survival of civilization and of mankind itself is to be assured,

That nuclear weapons, whose terrible effects are suffered, indiscriminately and inexorably, by military forces and civilian population alike, constitute, through the persistence of the radioactivity they release, an attack on the integrity of the human species and ultimately may even render the whole earth uninhabitable,

That general and complete disarmament under effective international control is a vital matter which all the peoples of the world equally demand,

That the proliferation of nuclear weapons, which seems inevitable unless States, in the exercise of their sovereign rights, impose restrictions on themselves in order to prevent it, would make any agreement on disarmament enormously difficult and would increase the danger of the outbreak of a nuclear conflagration,

That the establishment of militarily denuclearized zones is closely linked with the maintenance of peace and security in the respective regions,

That the military denuclearization of vast geographical zones, adopted by the sovereign decision of the States comprised therein, will exercise a beneficial influence on other regions where similar conditions exist,

That the privileged situation of the signatory States, whose territories are wholly free from nuclear weapons, imposes upon them the inescapable duty of preserving that situation both in their own interests and for the good of mankind,

That the existence of nuclear weapons in any country of Latin America would make it a target for possible nuclear attacks and would inevitably set off, throughout the region, a ruinous race in nuclear weapons which would involve the unjustifiable diversion, for warlike purposes, of the limited resources required for economic and social development,

That the foregoing reasons, together with the traditional peace-loving outlook of Latin America, give rise to an inescapable necessity that nuclear energy should be used in that region exclusively for peaceful purposes, and that the Latin American countries should use their right to the greatest and most equitable possible access to this new source of energy in order to expedite the economic and social development of their peoples.

Convinced finally :

That the military denuclearization of Latin America—being understood to mean the undertaking entered into internationally in this Treaty to keep their territories forever free from nuclear weapons—will constitute a measure which will spare their peoples from the squandering of their limited resources on nuclear armaments and will protect them against possible nuclear attacks on their territories, and will also constitute a significant contribution towards preventing the proliferation of nuclear weapons and a powerful factor for general and complete disarmament, and

That Latin America, faithful to its tradition of universality, must not only endeavour to banish from its homelands the scourge of a nuclear war, but must also strive to promote the well-being and advancement of its peoples, at the same time co-operating in the fulfilment of the ideals of mankind, that is to say, in the consolidation of a permanent peace based on equal rights, economic fairness and social justice for all, in accordance with the principles and purposes set forth in the Charter of the United Nations and in the Charter of the Organization of American States,

Have agreed as follows :

Obligations

Article 1

1. The Contracting Parties hereby undertake to use exclusively for peaceful purposes the nuclear material and facilities which are under their jurisdiction, and to prohibit and prevent in their respective territories :

(a) The testing, use, manufacture, production or acquisition by any means whatsoever of any nuclear weapons, by the Parties themselves, directly or indirectly, on behalf of anyone else or in any other way, and

(b) The receipt, storage, installation, deployment and any form of possession of any nuclear weapons, directly or indirectly, by the Parties themselves, by anyone on their behalf or in any other way.

2. The Contracting Parties also undertake to refrain from engaging in, encouraging or authorizing, directly or indirectly, or in any way participating in the testing, use, manufacture, production, possession or control of any nuclear weapon.

Definition of the Contracting Parties

Article 2

For the purposes of this Treaty, the Contracting Parties are those for whom the Treaty is in force.

Definition of territory

Article 3

For the purposes of this Treaty, the term "territory" shall include the territorial sea, air space and any other space over which the State exercises sovereignty in accordance with its own legislation.

Zone of application

Article 4

1. The zone of application of this Treaty is the whole of the territories for which the Treaty is in force.

2. Upon fulfilment of the requirements of article 28, paragraph 1, the zone of application of this Treaty shall also be that which is situated in the western hemisphere within the following limits (except the continental part of the territory of the United States of America and its territorial waters) : starting at a point located at 35° north latitude, 75° west longitude ; from this point directly southward to a point at 30° north latitude, 75° west longitude ; from there, directly eastward to a point at 30° north latitude, 50° west longitude ; from there, along a loxodromic line to a point at 5° north latitude, 20° west longitude ; from there, directly southward to a point at 60° south latitude, 20° west longitude ; from there, directly westward to a point at 60° south latitude, 115° west longitude ; from there, directly northward to a point at 0 latitude, 115° west longitude ; from there, along a loxodromic line to a point at 35° north latitude, 150° west longitude ; from there, directly eastward to a point at 35° north latitude, 75° west longitude.

Definition of nuclear weapons

Article 5

For the purposes of this Treaty, a nuclear weapon is any device which is capable of releasing nuclear energy in an uncontrolled manner and which has a group of characteristics that are appropriate for use for warlike purposes. An instrument that may be used for the transport or propulsion of the devise is not included in this definition if it is separable from the device and not an indivisible part thereof.

Meeting of signatories

Article 6

At the request of any of the signatory States or if the Agency established by article 7 should so decide, a meeting of all the signatories may be convoked to consider in common questions which may affect the very essence of this instrument, including possible amendments to it. In either case, the meeting will be convoked by the General Secretary.

Organization

Article 7

1. In order to ensure compliance with the obligations of this Treaty, the Contracting Parties hereby establish an international organization to be known as the "Agency for the Prohibition of Nuclear Weapons in Latin America", hereinafter referred to as "the Agency". Only the Contracting Parties shall be affected by its decisions.

2. The Agency shall be responsible for the holding of periodic or extraordinary consultations among Member States on matters relating to the purposes, measures and procedures set forth in this Treaty and to the supervision of compliance with the obligations arising therefrom.

3. The Contracting Parties agree to extend to the Agency full and prompt co-operation in accordance with the provisions of this Treaty, of any agreements they may conclude with the Agency and of any agreements the Agency may conclude with any other international organization or body.

4. The headquarters of the Agency shall be in Mexico City.

Organs

Article 8

1. There are hereby established as principal organs of the Agency a General Conference, a Council and a Secretariat.

2. Such subsidiary organs as are considered necessary by the General Conference may be established within the purview of this Treaty.

The General Conference

Article 9

1. The General Conference, the supreme organ of the Agency, shall be composed of all the Contracting Parties; it shall hold regular sessions every two years, and may also hold special sessions whenever this Treaty so provides or, in the opinion of the Council, the circumstances so require.

2. The General Conference:

(a) May consider and decide on any matters or questions covered by this Treaty, within the limits thereof, including those referring to powers and functions of any organ provided for in this Treaty.

(b) Shall establish procedures for the control system to ensure observance of this Treaty in accordance with its provisions.

(c) Shall elect the Members of the Council and the General Secretary.

(d) May remove the General Secretary from office if the proper functioning of the Agency so requires.

(e) Shall receive and consider the biennial and special reports submitted by the Council and the General Secretary.

(f) Shall initiate and consider studies designed to facilitate the optimum fulfilment of the aims of this Treaty, without prejudice to the power of the General Secretary independently to carry out similar studies for submission to and consideration by the Conference.

(g) Shall be the organ competent to authorize the conclusion of agreements with Governments and other international organizations and bodies.

3. The General Conference shall adopt the Agency's budget and fix the scale of financial contributions to be paid by Member States, taking into account the systems and criteria used for the same purpose by the United Nations.

4. The General Conference shall elect its officers for each session and may establish such subsidiary organs as it deems necessary for the performance of its functions.

5. Each Member of the Agency shall have one vote. The decisions of the General Conference shall be taken by a two-thirds majority of the Members present and voting in the case of matters relating to the control system and measures referred to in article 20, the admission of new Members, the election or removal of the General Secretary, adoption of the budget and matters related thereto. Decisions on other matters, as well as procedural questions and also determination of which questions must be decided by a two-thirds majority, shall be taken by a simple majority of the Members present and voting.

6. The General Conference shall adopt its own rules of procedure.

The Council

Article 10

1. The Council shall be composed of five Members of the Agency elected by the General Conference from among the Contracting Parties, due account being taken of equitable geographic distribution.

2. The Members of the Council shall be elected for a term of four years. However, in the first election three will be elected for two years. Outgoing Members may not be re-elected for the following period unless the limited number of States for which the Treaty is in force so requires.

3. Each Member of the Council shall have one representative.

4. The Council shall be so organized as to be able to function continuously.

5. In addition to the functions conferred upon it by this Treaty and to those which may be assigned to it by the General Conference, the Council shall, through the General Secretary, ensure the proper operation of the control system in

accordance with the provisions of this Treaty and with the decisions adopted by the General Conference.

6. The Council shall submit an annual report on its work to the General Conference as well as such special reports as it deems necessary or which the General Conference requests of it.

7. The Council shall elect its officers for each session.

8. The decisions of the Council shall be taken by a simple majority of its Members present and voting.

9. The Council shall adopt its own rules of procedure.

The Secretariat

Article 11

1. The Secretariat shall consist of a General Secretary, who shall be the chief administrative officer of the Agency, and of such staff as the Agency may require. The term of office of the General Secretary shall be four years and he may be re-elected for a single additional term. The General Secretary may not be a national of the country in which the Agency has its headquarters. In case the office of General Secretary becomes vacant, a new election shall be held to fill the office for the remainder of the term.

2. The staff of the Secretariat shall be appointed by the General Secretary, in accordance with rules laid down by the General Conference.

3. In addition to the functions conferred upon him by this Treaty and to those which may be assigned to him by the General Conference,—the General Secretary shall ensure, as provided by article 10, paragraph 5, the proper operation of the control system established by this Treaty, in accordance with the provisions of the Treaty and the decisions taken by the General Conference.

4. The General Secretary shall act in that capacity in all meetings of the General Conference and of the Council and shall make an annual report to both bodies on the work of the Agency and any special reports requested by the General Conference or the Council or which the General Secretary may deem desirable.

5. The General Secretary shall establish the procedures for distributing to all Contracting Parties information received by the Agency from governmental sources and such information from non-governmental sources as may be of interest to the Agency.

6. In the performance of their duties the General Secretary and the staff shall not seek or receive instructions from any Government or from any other authority external to the Agency and shall refrain from any action which might reflect on their position as international officials responsible only to the Agency; subject to their responsibility to the Agency, they shall not disclose any industrial secrets or other confidential information coming to their knowledge by reason of their official duties in the Agency.

7. Each of the Contracting Parties undertakes to respect the exclusively inter-

national character of the responsibilities of the General Secretary and the staff and not to seek to influence them in the discharge of their responsibilities.

Control system

Article 12

1. For the purpose of verifying compliance with the obligations entered into by the Contracting Parties in accordance with article 1, a control system shall be established which shall be put into effect in accordance with the provisions of articles 13–18 of this Treaty.

2. The control system shall be used in particular for the purpose of verifying:

(a) That devices, services and facilities intended for peaceful uses of nuclear energy are not used in the testing or manufacture of nuclear weapons,

(b) That none of the activities prohibited in article 1 of this Treaty are carried out in the territory of the Contracting Parties with nuclear materials or weapons introduced from abroad, and

(c) That explosions for peaceful purposes are compatible with article 18 of this Treaty.

IAEA safeguards

Article 13

Each Contracting Party shall negotiate multilateral or bilateral agreements with the International Atomic Energy Agency for the application of its safeguards to its nuclear activities. Each Contracting Party shall initiate negotiations within a period of 180 days after the date of the deposit of its instrument of ratification of this Treaty. These agreements shall enter into force, for each Party, not later than eighteen months after the date of the initiation of such negotiations except in case of unforeseen circumstances or force majeure.

Reports of the Parties

Article 14

1. The Contracting Parties shall submit to the Agency and to the International Atomic Energy Agency, for their information, semi-annual reports stating that no activity prohibited under this Treaty has occurred in their respective territories.

2. The Contracting Parties shall simultaneously transmit to the Agency a copy of any report they may submit to the International Atomic Energy Agency which relates to matters that are the subject of this Treaty and to the application of safeguards.

3. The Contracting Parties shall also transmit to the Organization of American States, for its information, any reports that may be of interest to it, in accordance with the obligations established by the Inter-American System.

Special reports requested by the General Secretary

Article 15

1. With the authorization of the Council, the General Secretary may request any of the Contracting Parties to provide the Agency with complementary or

supplementary information regarding any event or circumstance connected with compliance with this Treaty, explaining his reasons. The Contracting Parties undertake to co-operate promptly and fully with the General Secretary.

2. The General Secretary shall inform the Council and the Contracting Parties forthwith of such requests and of the respective replies.

Special inspections

Article 16

1. The International Atomic Energy Agency and the Council established by this Treaty have the power of carrying out special inspections in the following cases :

    (a) In the case of the International Atomic Energy Agency, in accordance with the agreements referred to in article 13 of this Treaty ;

    (b) In the case of the Council :

        (i) When so requested, the reasons for the request being stated, by any Party which suspects that some activity prohibited by this Treaty has been carried out or is about to be carried out, either in the territory of any other Party or in any other place on such latter Party's behalf, the Council shall immediately arrange for such an inspection in accordance with article 10, paragraph 5.

        (ii) When requested by any Party which has been suspected of or charged with having violated this Treaty, the Council shall immediately arrange for the special inspection requested in accordance with article 10, paragraph 5.

The above requests will be made to the Council through the General Secretary.

2. The costs and expenses of any special inspection carried out under paragraph 1, sub-paragraph (b), sections (i) and (ii) of this article shall be borne by the requesting Party or Parties, except where the Council concludes on the basis of the report on the special inspection that, in view of the circumstances existing in the case, such costs and expenses should be borne by the Agency.

3. The General Conference shall formulate the procedures for the organization and execution of the special inspections carried out in accordance with paragraph 1, sub-paragraph (b), sections (i) and (ii) of this article.

4. The Contracting Parties undertake to grant the inspectors carrying out such special inspections full and free access to all places and all information which may be necessary for the performance of their duties and which are directly and intimately connected with the suspicion of violation of this Treaty. If so requested by the authorities of the Contracting Party in whose territory the inspection is carried out, the inspectors designated by the General Conference shall be accompanied by representatives of said authorities, provided that this does not in any way delay or hinder the work of the inspectors.

5. The Council shall immediately transmit to all the Parties, through the General Secretary, a copy of any report resulting from special inspections.

6. Similarly, the Council shall send through the General Secretary to the Secretary-General of the United Nations, for transmission to the United Nations

Security Council and General Assembly, and to the Council of the Organization of American States, for its information, a copy of any report resulting from any special inspection carried out in accordance with paragraph 1, sub-paragraph (b), sections (i) and (ii) of this article.

7. The Council may decide, or any Contracting Party may request, the convening of a special session of the General Conference for the purpose of considering the reports resulting from any special inspection. In such a case, the General Secretary shall take immediate steps to convene the special session requested.

8. The General Conference, convened in special session under this article, may make recommendations to the Contracting Parties and submit reports to the Secretary-General of the United Nations to be transmitted to the United Nations Security Council and the General Assembly.

Use of nuclear energy for peaceful purposes

Article 17

Nothing in the provisions of this Treaty shall prejudice the rights of the Contracting Parties, in conformity with this Treaty, to use nuclear energy for peaceful purposes, in particular for their economic development and social progress.

Explosions for peaceful purposes

Article 18

1. The Contracting Parties may carry out explosions of nuclear devices for peaceful purposes—including explosions which involve devices similar to those used in nuclear weapons—or collaborate with third parties for the same purpose, provided that they do so in accordance with the provisions of this article and the other articles of the Treaty, particularly articles 1 and 5.

2. Contracting Parties intending to carry out, or to cooperate in carrying out, such an explosion shall notify the Agency and the International Atomic Energy Agency, as far in advance as the circumstances require, of the date of the explosion and shall at the same time provide the following information:

(a) The nature of the nuclear device and the source from which it was obtained,
(b) The place and purpose of the planned explosion,
(c) The procedures which will be followed in order to comply with paragraph 3 of this article,
(d) The expected force of the device, and
(e) The fullest possible information on any possible radioactive fall-out that may result from the explosion or explosions, and measures which will be taken to avoid danger to the population, flora, fauna and territories of any other Party or Parties.

3. The General Secretary and the technical personnel designated by the Council and the International Atomic Energy Agency may observe all the preparations,

including the explosion of the device, and shall have unrestricted access to any area in the vicinity of the site of the explosion in order to ascertain whether the device and the procedures followed during the explosion are in conformity with the information supplied under paragraph 2 of this article and the other provisions of this Treaty.

4. The Contracting Parties may accept the collaboration of third parties for the purpose set forth in paragraph 1 of the present article, in accordance with paragraphs 2 and 3 thereof.

Relations with other international organizations

Article 19

1. The Agency may conclude such agreements with the International Atomic Energy Agency as are authorized by the General Conference and as it considers likely to facilitate the efficient operation of the control system established by this Treaty.

2. The Agency may also enter into relations with any international organization or body, especially any which may be established in the future to supervise disarmament or measures for the control of armaments in any part of the world.

3. The Contracting Parties may, if they see fit, request the advice of the Inter-American Nuclear Energy Commission on all technical matters connected with the application of this Treaty with which the Commission is competent to deal under its Statute.

Measures in the event of violation of the Treaty

Article 20

1. The General Conference shall take note of all cases in which, in its opinion, any Contracting Party is not complying fully with its obligations under this Treaty and shall draw the matter to the attention of the Party concerned, making such recommendations as it deems appropriate.

2. If, in its opinion, such non-compliance constitutes a violation of this Treaty which might endanger peace and security, the General Conference shall report thereon simultaneously to the United Nations Security Council and the General Assembly through the Secretary-General of the United Nations, and to the Council of the Organization of American States. The General Conference shall likewise report to the International Atomic Energy Agency for such purposes as are relevant in accordance with its Statute.

United Nations and Organization of American States

Article 21

None of the provisions of this Treaty shall be construed as impairing the rights and obligations of the Parties under the Charter of the United Nations or, in the case of States Members of the Organization of American States, under existing regional treaties.

Privileges and immunities

Article 22

1. The Agency shall enjoy in the territory of each of the Contracting Parties such legal capacity and such privileges and immunities as may be necessary for the exercise of its functions and the fulfilment of its purposes.

2. Representatives of the Contracting Parties accredited to the Agency and officials of the Agency shall similarly enjoy such privileges and immunities as are necessary for the performance of their functions.

3. The Agency may conclude agreements with the Contracting Parties with a view to determining the details of the application of paragraphs 1 and 2 of this article.

Notification of other agreements

Article 23

Once this Treaty has entered into force, the Secretariat shall be notified immediately of any international agreement concluded by any of the Contracting Parties on matters with which this Treaty is concerned; the Secretariat shall register it and notify the other Contracting Parties.

Settlement of disputes

Article 24

Unless the Parties concerned agree on another mode of peaceful settlement, any question or dispute concerning the interpretation or application of this Treaty which is not settled shall be referred to the International Court of Justice with the prior consent of the Parties to the controversy.

Signature

Article 25

1. This Treaty shall be open indefinitely for signature by :

(a) All the Latin American Republics, and
(b) All other sovereign States situated in their entirety south of latitude 35° north in the western hemisphere; and, except as provided in paragraph 2 of this article, all such States which become sovereign, when they have been admitted by the General Conference.

2. The General Conference shall not take any decision regarding the admission of a political entity part or all of whose territory is the subject, prior to the date when this Treaty is opened for signature, of a dispute or claim between an extra-continental country and one or more Latin American States, so long as the dispute has not been settled by peaceful means.

Ratification and deposit

Article 26

1. This Treaty shall be subject to ratification by signatory States in accordance with their respective constitutional procedures.

2. This Treaty and the instruments of ratification shall be deposited with the

Government of the Mexican United States, which is hereby designated the Depositary Government.

3. The Depositary Government shall send certified copies of this Treaty to the Governments of signatory States and shall notify them of the deposit of each instrument of ratification.

Reservations

Article 27

This Treaty shall not be subject to reservations.

Entry into force

Article 28

1. Subject to the provisions of paragraph 2 of this article, this Treaty shall enter into force among the States that have ratified it as soon as the following requirements have been met:

(a) Deposit of the instruments of ratification of this Treaty with the Depositary Government by the Governments of the States mentioned in article 25 which are in existence on the date when this Treaty is opened for signature and which are not affected by the provisions of article 25, paragraph 2;

(b) Signature and ratification of Additional Protocol I annexed to this Treaty by all extra-continental or continental States having de jure or de facto international responsibility for territories situated in the zone of application of the Treaty;

(c) Signature and ratification of the Additional Protocol II annexed to this Treaty by all powers possessing nuclear weapons;

(d) Conclusion of bilateral or multilateral agreements on the application of the Safeguards System of the International Atomic Energy Agency in accordance with article 13 of this Treaty.

2. All signatory States shall have the imprescriptible right to waive, wholly or in part, the requirements laid down in the preceding paragraph. They may do so by means of a declaration which shall be annexed to their respective instrument of ratification and which may be formulated at the time of deposit of the instrument or subsequently. For those States which exercise this right, this Treaty shall enter into force upon deposit of the declaration, or as soon as those requirements have been met which have not been expressly waived.

3. As soon as this Treaty has entered into force in accordance with the provisions of paragraph 2 for eleven States, the Depositary Government shall convene a preliminary meeting of those States in order that the Agency may be set up and commence its work.

4. After the entry into force of this Treaty for all the countries of the zone, the rise of a new power possessing nuclear weapons shall have the effect of suspending the execution of this Treaty for those countries which have ratified it without waiving requirements of paragraph 1, sub-paragraph (c) of this article, and which request such suspension; the Treaty shall remain suspended until the new power, on its own initiative or upon request by the General Conference, ratifies the annexed Additional Protocol II.

Amendments

Article 29

1. Any Contracting Party may propose amendments to this Treaty and shall submit its proposals to the Council through the General Secretary, who shall transmit them to all the other Contracting Parties and, in addition, to all other signatories in accordance with article 6. The Council, through the General Secretary, shall immediately following the meeting of signatories convene a special session of the General Conference to examine the proposals made, for the adoption of which a two-thirds majority of the Contracting Parties present and voting shall be required.

2. Amendments adopted shall enter into force as soon as the requirements set forth in article 28 of this Treaty have been complied with.

Duration and denunciation

Article 30

1. This Treaty shall be of a permanent nature and shall remain in force indefinitely, but any Party may denounce it by notifying the General Secretary of the Agency if, in the opinion of the denouncing State, there have arisen or may arise circumstances connected with the content of this Treaty or of the annexed Additional Protocols I and II which affect its supreme interests or the peace and security of one or more Contracting Parties.

2. The denunciation shall take effect three months after the delivery to the General Secretary of the Agency of the notification by the Government of the signatory State concerned. The General Secretary shall immediately communicate such notification to the other Contracting Parties and to the Secretary-General of the Untied Nations for the information of the United Nations Security Council and the General Assembly. He shall also communicate it to the Secretary-General of the Organization of American States.

Authentic texts and registration

Article 31

This Treaty, of which the Spanish, Chinese, English, French, Portuguese and Russian texts are equally authentic, shall be registered by the Depositary Government in accordance with article 102 of the United Nations Charter. The Depositary Government shall notify the Secretary-General of the United Nations of the signatures, ratifications and amendments relating to this Treaty and shall communicate them to the Secretary-General of the Organization of American States for its information.

Transitional Article

Denunication of the declaration referred to in article 28, paragraph 2, shall be subject to the same procedures as the denunciation of this Treaty, except that it will take effect on the date of delivery of the respective notification.

In witness whereof the undersigned Plenipotentiaries, having deposited their full powers, found in good and due form, sign this Treaty on behalf of their respective Governments.

Done at Mexico, Distrito Federal, on the Fourteenth day of February, one thousand nine hundred and sixty-seven.

ADDITIONAL PROTOCOL I [a]

The undersigned Plenipotentiaries, furnished with full powers by their respective Governments,

Convinced that the Treaty for the Prohibition of Nuclear Weapons in Latin America, negotiated and signed in accordance with the recommendations of the General Assembly of the United Nations in Resolution 1911 (XVIII) of 27 November 1963, represents an important step towards ensuring the non-proliferation of nuclear weapons,

Aware that the non-proliferation of nuclear weapons is not an end in itself but, rather, a means of achieving general and complete disarmament at a later stage, and

Desiring to contribute, so far as lies in their power, towards ending the armaments race, especially in the field of nuclear weapons, and towards strengthening a world at peace, based on mutual respect and sovereign equality of States,

Have agreed as follows:

Article 1. To undertake to apply the statute of denuclearization in respect of warlike purposes as defined in articles 1, 3, 5 and 13 of the Treaty for the Prohibition of Nuclear Weapons in Latin America in territories for which, de jure or de facto, they are internationally responsible and which lie within the limits of the geographical zone established in that Treaty.

Artcle 2. The duration of this Protocol shall be the same as that of the Treaty for the Prohibition of Nuclear Weapons in Latin America of which this Protocol is an annex, and the provisions regarding ratification and denunciation contained in the Treaty shall be applicable to it.

Article 3. This Protocol shall enter into force, for the States which have ratified it, on the date of the deposit of their respective instruments of ratification.

In witness whereof the undersigned Plenipotentiaries, having deposited their full powers, found in good and due form, sign this Protocol on behalf of their respective Governments.

---

[a] The United Kingdom and the Netherlands are parties to this Protocol.

Additional Protocol II to the Treaty for the Prohibition of Nuclear Weapons in Latin America

Signed by the United States at Mexico April 1, 1968
Underlying Treaty signed by others at Mexico February 14, 1967
U.S. ratification with understandings and declarations deposited
  May 12, 1971
Entered into force for the United States May 12, 1971 [a]

BY THE PRESIDENT OF THE UNITED STATES OF AMERICA

A PROCLAMATION

CONSIDERING THAT:
Additional Protocol II to the Treaty for the Prohibition of Nuclear Weapons in Latin America, done at the City of Mexico on February 14, 1967, was signed on behalf of the United States of America on April 1, 1968, the text of which Protocol is word for word as follows:

ADDITIONAL PROTOCOL II

The undersigned Plenipotentiaries, furnished with full powers by their respective Governments,
Convinced that the Treaty for the Prohibition of Nuclear Weapons in Latin America, negotiated and signed in accordance with the recommendations of the General Assembly of the United Nations in Resolution 1911 (XVIII) of 27 November 1963, represents an important step towards ensuring the non-proliferation of nuclear weapons,
Aware that the non-proliferation of nuclear weapons is not an end in itself but, rather, a means of achieving general and complete disarmament at a later stage, and
Desiring to contribute, so far as lies in their power, towards ending the armaments race, especially in the field of nuclear weapons, and towards promoting and strengthening a world at peace, based on mutual respect and sovereign equality of States,
Have agreed as follows:

Article 1. The statute of denuclearization of Latin America in respect of warlike purposes, as defined, delimited and set forth in the Treaty for the Prohibition of Nuclear Weapons in Latin America of which this instrument is an annex, shall be fully respected by the Parties to this Protocol in all its express aims and provisions.

---

[a] The United Kingdom is also a party to Protocol II.

Article 2. The Governments represented by the undersigned Plenipotentiaries undertake, therefore, not to contribute in any way to the performance of acts involving a violation of the obligations of article 1 of the Treaty in the territories to which the Treaty applies in accordance with article 4 thereof.

Article 3. The Governments represented by the undersigned Plentipotentiaries also undertake not to use or threaten to use nuclear weapons against the Contracting Parties of the Treaty for the Prohibition of Nuclear Weapons in Latin America.

Article 4. The duration of this Protocol shall be the same as that of the Treaty for the Prohibition of Nuclear Weapons in Latin America of which this protocol is an annex, and the definitions of territory and nuclear weapons set forth in articles 3 and 5 of the Treaty shall be applicable to this Protocol, as well as the provisions regarding ratification, reservations, denunciation, authentic texts and registration contained in articles 26, 27, 30 and 31 of the Treaty.

Article 5. This Protocol shall enter into force, for the States which have ratified it, on the date of the deposit of their respective instruments of ratification.

IN WITNESS WHEREOF the undersigned Plenipotentiaries, having deposited their full powers, found in good and due form, sign this Additional Protocol on behalf of their respective Governments.

The Senate of the United States of America by its resolution of April 19, 1971, two-thirds of the Senators present concurring, gave its advice and consent to the ratification of Additional Protocol II, with the following understandings and declarations:

I

That the United States Government understands the reference in Article 3 of the treaty to "its own legislation" to relate only to such legislation as is compatible with the rules of international law and as involves an exercise of sovereignty consistent with those rules, and accordingly that ratification of Additional Protocol II by the United States Government could not be regarded as implying recognition, for the purposes of this treaty and its protocols or for any other purpose, of any legislation which did not, in the view of the United States, comply with the relevant rules of international law.

That the United States Government takes note of the Preparatory Commission's interpretation of the treaty, as set forth in the Final Act, that, governed by the principles and rules of international law, each of the Contracting Parties retains exclusive power and legal competence, unaffected by the terms of the treaty, to grant or deny non-Contracting Parties transit and transport privileges.

That as regards the undertaking in Article 3 of Protocol II not to use or threaten to use nuclear weapons against the Contracting Parties, the United States Government would have to consider that an armed attack by a Contracting Party, in which it was assisted by a nuclear-weapon state, would be incompatible with the Contracting Party's corresponding obligations under Article I of the treaty.

II

That the United States Government considers that the technology of making nuclear explosive devices for peaceful purposes is indistinguishable from the technology of making nuclear weapons, and that nuclear weapons and nuclear explosive devices for peaceful purposes are both capable of releasing nuclear energy in an uncontrolled manner and have the common group of characteristics of large amounts of energy generated instantaneously from a compact source. Therefore, the United States Government understands the definition contained in Article 5 of the treaty as necessarily encompassing all nuclear explosive devices. It is also understood that Articles 1 and 5 restrict accordingly the activities of the Contracting Parties under paragraph 1 of Article 18.

That the United States Government understands that paragraph 4 of Article 18 of the treaty permits, and that United States adherence to Protocol II will not prevent, collaboration by the United States with Contracting Parties for the purpose of carrying out explosions of nuclear devices for peaceful purposes in a manner consistent with a policy of not contributing to the proliferation of nuclear weapons capabilities. In this connection, the United States Government notes Article V of the Treaty on the Non-Proliferation of Nuclear Weapons, under which it joined in an undertaking to take appropriate measures to ensure that potential benefits of peaceful applications of nuclear explosions would be made available to non-nuclear-weapon states party to that treaty, and reaffirms its willingness to extend such undertaking, on the same basis, to states precluded by the present treaty from manufacturing or acquiring any nuclear explosive device.

III

That the United States Government also declares that, although not required by Protocol II, it will act with respect to such territories of Protocol I adherents as are within the geographical area defined in paragraph 2 of Article 4 of the treaty in the same manner as Protocol II requires it to act with respect to the territories of Contracting Parties.

The President ratified Additional Protocol II on May 8, 1971, with the above-recited understandings and declarations, in pursuance of the advice and consent of the Senate.

It is provided in Article 5 of Additional Protocol II that the Protocol shall enter into force, for the States which have ratified it, on the date of the deposit of their respective instruments of ratification.

The instrument of ratification of the United Kingdom of Great Britain and Northern Ireland was deposited on December 11, 1969 with understandings and a declaration, and the instrument of ratification of the United States of America was deposited on May 12, 1971 with the above-recited understandings and declarations.

In accordance with Article 5 of Additional Protocol II, the Protocol entered into force for the United States of America on May 12, 1971, subject to the above recited understandings and declarations.

NOW, THEREFORE, I, Richard Nixon, President of the United States of America, proclaim and make public Additional Protocol II to the Treaty for the Prohibition of Nuclear Weapons in Latin America to the end that it shall be observed and fulfilled with good faith, subject to the above-recited understandings and declarations, on and after May 12, 1971 by the United States of America and by the citizens of the United States of America and all other persons subject to the jurisdiction thereof.

IN TESTIMONY WHEREOF, I have signed this proclamation and caused the Seal of the United States of America to be affixed.

DONE   at the city of Washington this eleventh day of June in the year of our Lord one thousand nine hundred seventy-one and of the Independence of the United States of America the one hundred ninety-fifth.

(SEAL)

Treaty on the Non-Proliferation of Nuclear Weapons

Signed at Washington, London, Moscow July 1, 1968
U.S. ratification deposited March 5, 1970
Entered into force March 5, 1970

The States concluding this Treaty, hereinafter referred to as the "Parties to the Treaty",

Considering the devastation that would be visited upon all mankind by a nuclear war and the consequent need to make every effort to avert the danger of such a war and to take measures to safeguard the security of peoples,

Believing that the proliferation of nuclear weapons would seriously enhance the danger of nuclear war,

In conformity with resolutions of the United Nations General Assembly calling for the conclusion of an agreement on the prevention of wider dissemination of nuclear weapons,

Undertaking to cooperate in facilitating the application of International Atomic Energy Agency safeguards on peaceful nuclear activities,

Expressing their support for research, development and other efforts to further the application, within the framework of the International Atomic Energy Agency safeguards system, of the principle of safeguarding effectively the flow of source and special fissionable materials by use of instruments and other techniques at certain strategic points,

Affirming the principle that the benefits of peaceful applications of nuclear technology, including any technological by-products which may be derived by nuclear-weapon States from the development of nuclear explosive devices, should be available for peaceful purposes to all Parties to the Treaty, whether nuclear-weapon or non-nuclear-weapon States,

Convinced that, in furtherance of this principle, all Parties to the Treaty are entitled to participate in the fullest possible exchange of scientific information for, and to contribute alone or in cooperation with other States to, the further development of the applications of atomic energy for peaceful purposes,

Declaring their intention to achieve at the earliest possible date the cessation of the nuclear arms race and to undertake effective measures in the direction of nuclear disarmament,

Urging the cooperation of all States in the attainment of this objective,

Recalling the determination expressed by the Parties to the 1963 Treaty banning nuclear weapon tests in the atmosphere in outer space and under water in its Preamble to seek to achieve the discontinuance of all test explosions of nuclear weapons for all time and to continue negotiations to this end,

Desiring to further the easing of international tension and the strengthening of trust between States in order to facilitate the cessation of the manufacture of nuclear weapons, the liquidation of all their existing stockpiles, and the elimination from national arsenals of nuclear weapons and the means of their delivery pursuant to a treaty on general and complete disarmament under strict and effective international control,

Recalling that, in accordance with the Charter of the United Nations, States must refrain in their international relations from the threat or use of force against the territorial integrity or political independence of any State, or in any other manner inconsistent with the Purposes of the United Nations, and that the establishment and maintenance of international peace and security are to be promoted with the least diversion for armaments of the world's human and economic resources,

Have agreed as follows :

Article I

Each nuclear-weapon State Party to the Treaty undertakes not to transfer to any recipient whatsoever nuclear weapons or other nuclear explosive devices or control over such weapons or explosive devices directly, or indirectly; and not in any way to assist, encourage, or induce any non-nuclear-weapon State to manufacture or otherwise acquire nuclear weapons or other nuclear explosive devices, or control over such weapons or explosive devices.

Article II

Each non-nuclear-weapon State Party to the Treaty undertakes not to receive the transfer from any transferor whatsoever of nuclear weapons or other nuclear explosive devices or of control over such weapons or explosive devices directly, or indirectly; not to manufacture or otherwise acquire nuclear weapons or other nuclear explosive devices; and not to seek or receive any assistance in the manufacture of nuclear weapons or other nuclear explosive devices.

Article III

1. Each non-nuclear-weapon State Party to the Treaty undertakes to accept safeguards, as set forth in an agreement to be negotiated and concluded with the International Atomic Energy Agency in accordance with the Statute of the International Atomic Energy Agency and the Agency's safeguards system, for the exclusive purpose of verification of the fulfillment of its obligations assumed under this Treaty with a view to preventing diversion of nuclear energy from peaceful uses to nuclear weapons or other nuclear explosive devices. Procedures for the safeguards required by this article shall be followed with respect to source or special fissionable material whether it is being produced, processed or used in any principal nuclear facility or is outside any such facility. The safeguards required by this article shall be applied on all source or special fissionable material in all peaceful nuclear activities within the territory of such State, under its jurisdiction, or carried out under its control anywhere.

2. Each State Party to the Treaty undertakes not to provide: (a) source or special fissionable material, or (b) equipment or material especially designed or prepared for the processing, use or production of special fissionable material, to any non-nuclear-weapon State for peaceful purposes, unless the source or special fissionable material shall be subject to the safeguards required by this article.

3. The safeguards required by this article shall be implemented in a manner designed to comply with article IV of this Treaty, and to avoid hampering the economic or technological development of the Parties or international coopera- tion in the field of peaceful nuclear activities, including the international exchange of nuclear material and equipment for the processing, use or production of nuclear material for peaceful purposes in accordance with the provisions of this article and the principle of safeguarding set forth in the Preamble of the Treaty.

4. Non-nuclear-weapon States Party to the Treaty shall conclude agreements with the International Atomic Energy Agency to meet the requirements of this article either individually or together with other States in accordance with the Statute of the International Atomic Energy Agency. Negotiation of such agree- ments shall commence within 180 days from the original entry into force of this Treaty. For States depositing their instruments of ratification or accession after the 180-day period, negotiation of such agreements shall commence not later than the date of such deposit. Such agreements shall enter into force not later than eighteen months after the date of initiation of negotiations.

Article IV

1. Nothing in this Treaty shall be interpreted as affecting the inalienable right of all the Parties to the Treaty to develop research, production and use of nuclear energy for peaceful purposes without discrimination and in conformity with articles I and II of this Treaty.

2. All the Parties to the Treaty undertake to facilitate, and have the right to participate in, the fullest possible exchange of equipment, materials and scientific and technological information for the peaceful uses of nuclear energy. Parties to the Treaty in a position to do so shall also cooperate in contributing alone or together with other States or international organizations to the further develop- ment of the applications of nuclear energy for peaceful purposes, especially in the territories of non-nuclear-weapon States Party to the Treaty, with due considera- tion for the needs of the developing areas of the world.

Article V

Each Party to the Treaty undertakes to take appropriate measures to ensure that, in accordance with this Treaty, under appropriate international observation and through appropriate international procedures, potential benefits from any peaceful applications of nuclear explosions will be made available to non-nuclear- weapon States Party to the Treaty on a non-discriminatory basis and that the charge to such Parties for the explosive devices used will be as low as possible and exclude any charge for research and development. Non-nuclear-weapon States Party to the Treaty shall be able to obtain such benefits, pursuant to a special international agreement or agreements, through an appropriate international body with adequate representation of non-nuclear-weapon States. Negotiations on this subject shall commence as soon as possible after the Treaty enters into force. Non-nuclear-weapon States Party to the Treaty so desiring may also obtain such benefits pursuant to bilateral agreements.

Article VI

Each of the Parties to the Treaty undertakes to pursue negotiations in good faith on effective measures relating to cessation of the nuclear arms race at an early date and to nuclear disarmament, and on a treaty on general and complete disarmament under strict and effective international control.

Article VII

Nothing in this Treaty affects the right of any group of States to conclude regional treaties in order to assure the total absence of nuclear weapons in their respective territories.

Article VIII

1. Any Party to the Treaty may propose amendments to this Treaty. The text of any proposed amendment shall be submitted to the Depositary Governments which shall circulate it to all Parties to the Treaty. Thereupon, if requested to do so by one-third or more of the Parties to the Treaty, the Depositary Governments shall convene a conference, to which they shall invite all the Parties to the Treaty, to consider such an amendment.

2. Any amendment to this Treaty must be approved by a majority of the votes of all the Parties to the Treaty, including the votes of all nuclear-weapon States Party to the Treaty and all other Parties which, on the date the amendment is circulated, are members of the Board of Governors of the International Atomic Energy Agency. The amendment shall enter into force for each Party that deposits its instrument of ratification of the amendment upon the deposit of such instruments of ratification by a majority of all the Parties, including the instruments of ratification of all nuclear-weapon States Party to the Treaty and all other Parties which, on the date the amendment is circulated, are members of the Board of Governors of the International Atomic Energy Agency. Thereafter, it shall enter into force for any other Party upon the deposit of its instrument of ratification of the amendment.

3. Five years after the entry into force of this Treaty, a conference of Parties to the Treaty shall be held in Geneva, Switzerland, in order to review the operation of this Treaty with a view to assuring that the purposes of the Preamble and the provisions of the Treaty are being realized. At intervals of five years thereafter, a majority of the Parties to the Treaty may obtain, by submitting a proposal to this effect to the Depositary Governments, the convening of further conferences with the same objective of reviewing the operation of the Treaty.

Article IX

1. This Treaty shall be open to all States for signature. Any State which does not sign the Treaty before its entry into force in accordance with paragraph 3 of this article may accede to it at any time.

2. This Treaty shall be subject to ratification by signatory States. Instruments of ratification and instruments of accession shall be deposited with the Governments of the United States of America, the United Kingdom of Great Britain and Northern Ireland and the Union of Soviet Socialist Republics, which are hereby designated the Depositary Governments.

3. This Treaty shall enter into force after its ratification by the States, the Governments of which are designated Depositaries of the Treaty, and forty other States signatory to this Treaty and the deposit of their instruments of ratification. For the purposes of this Treaty, a nuclear-weapon State is one which has manufactured and exploded a nuclear weapon or other nuclear explosive device prior to January 1, 1967.

4. For States whose instruments of ratification or accession are deposited subsequent to the entry into force of this Treaty, it shall enter into force on the date of the deposit of their instruments of ratification or accession.

5. The Depositary Governments shall promptly inform all signatory and acceding States of the date of each signature, the date of deposit of each instrument of ratification or of accession, the date of the entry into force of this Treaty, and the date of receipt of any requests for convening a conference or other notices.

6. This Treaty shall be registered by the Depositary Governments pursuant to article 102 of the Charter of the United Nations.

Article X

1. Each Party shall in exercising its national sovereignty have the right to withdraw from the Treaty if it decides that extraordinary events, related to the subject matter of this Treaty, have jeopardized the supreme interests of its country. It shall give notice of such withdrawal to all other Parties to the Treaty and to the United Nations Security Council three months in advance. Such notice shall include a statement of the extraordinary events it regards as having jeopardized its supreme interests.

2. Twenty-five years after the entry into force of the Treaty, a conference shall be convened to decide whether the Treaty shall continue in force indefinitely, or shall be extended for an additional fixed period or periods. This decision shall be taken by a majority of the Parties to the Treaty.

Article XI

This Treaty, the English, Russian, French, Spanish and Chinese texts of which are equally authentic, shall be deposited in the archives of the Depositary Governments. Duly certified copies of this Treaty shall be transmitted by the Depositary Governments to the Governments of the signatory and acceding States.

Discussion Questions

CHAPTER 2

1. The chapter outlines four institutions for the control of war: ethical principles, international law, international organization, and arms control. Under what circumstances do you think each of these would be the most effective?

2. Under what circumstances, e.g. different experiences of war or different forms of government, do you think nations would be most likely to emphasize each of the different institutions for control of war?

3. When will the practical requirements of diplomacy be as effective a restraint on war as those more formal restraints discussed in this chapter?

4. If you were a legislator voting on an arms procurement bill, what questions would you like to have answered before deciding how to vote?

5. Suppose you were the same legislator but were voting on an arms control agreement?

6. Which of the motivations for arms control discussed in this chapter do you believe are the most important?

CHAPTER 3

1. What do you think would happen if a major leader made a public proposal as far-reaching as that of Secretary Hughes's at one of today's negotiations?

2. If, with the benefit of hindsight, you had been advising at the 1922 Washington Conference, what suggestions would you have made?

3. Same question, but you were advising at Versailles?

4. When would it be possible for a powerful nation and a weak nation to reach an effective arms control agreement?

5. (Review question.) What are the similarities between deterrence theory and the naval theories that shaped the Anglo-German naval arms race and the 1922 agreement? What are the implications of this similarity?

CHAPTER 4

1. If you were the President, what information would you like to have about the technical aspects of advanced weapons?

2. Same question, but you were a member of the public?

3. If you had been a decision-maker in the 1950's, would you have recommended development of ICBMs?

4. What would the world be like after a nuclear war?

5. When might initiation of a nuclear war be justified?

6. What would the world be like after a "very small" nuclear war, e.g. perhaps ten cities destroyed altogether?

7. What is meant by a "military-industrial complex" and how would you tell whether the United States has one?

8. How might you improve the military budget review process within the Executive branch or within Congress?

CHAPTER 5

1. Among the key U.S. decisions affecting the course of arms control negotiations were (*a*) the inclusion in the 1946 Baruch plan of a requirement for U.N. sanctions, (*b*) the 1955 decision to reserve all earlier arms control proposals, and (*c*) the decision slipped into between 1957 and 1959 to begin negotiations toward a separable test ban treaty. Why were these decisions important? What other decisions were important? Had you been deciding, what factors would have been important to you in each decision, and how would you have made it?

2. Do you think that the tensions of the cold war necessarily doomed negotiations during the mid-1950's?

3. Do you think that asymmetries necessarily doomed negotiations on strategic arms until the late 1960's?

4. What is the difference between use of hard bargaining positions to avoid agreement and their use to improve the outcome of a negotiation? How would you tell which was happening in the real world?

5. What are some examples of "linkage" of arms control proposals? Why is linkage used?

6. What are the lessons of the chapter for the design of negotiating institutions and of arms control study groups within governments?

7. Why are broad proposals like those of 1955 little discussed in the 1970's?

CHAPTER 6

1. How might the "Hot Line" be helpful in avoiding nuclear war? How might it be used for deception? Should it be extended to other nations?

2. What is the value of the "regime-oriented" treaties? Do they deserve the negotiating effort they have received? Are there other regions suitable for such treaties? Is the concept of nuclear-free regimes politically expandable to cover the entire world?

3. If you were the President, would you accept a comprehensive test ban? If so, how would you decide what, if any, on-site verification to require? What are the real issues involved in the CTB question?

4. Although completely nonlethal use of chemicals is impossible, because lethal doses differ from person to person and are typically lower for children and for the aged, proponents of chemical warfare have often pointed to the possible use of nonlethal chemical weapons as a more humane way to conduct warfare. What effect does this argument have on your attitude toward a CW agreement?

5. How much do you think the environmental movement affected the nuclear test ban and the BW negotiations? How might it affect CW negotiations?

CHAPTER 7

1. Is strategic deterrence a theory or a fact?
2. What alternative ways to live with nuclear weapons can you imagine?
3. Are the ethical arguments discussed in this section relevant to the President? To the strategic force designer? To the strategic targeter? To anyone?
4. Could strategic deterrence ever be negotiated away?
5. What would be the effect on strategic relationships if long-range delivery vehicles were to become so accurate that they could destroy silos with a conventional (non-nuclear) warhead?
6. If you were President, would you prefer to react if U.S.S.R. force advances seemed likely to place Minuteman survival in serious danger?
7. According to deterrence theory, what would be the conditions for stability if China had strategic force comparable to that of the United States and the Soviet Union?
8. Why does the United States maintain the "triad"—three separate strategic systems (submarines, aircraft, and ICBMs)?
9. What are the advantages and disadvantages of the "no-first-use" agreement proposed by China and (in the past) by the Soviet Union?
10. Should the President have the authority to use nuclear weapons without Congressional approval?

CHAPTER 8

1. Are the United States and the Soviet Union engaged in an arms race? What do you mean by an arms race?
2. How might arms control negotiations tend to increase arms procurements? To decrease arms procurements?
3. When would tacit arms control agreements be better than explicit ones?
4. Why are arms control negotiations given so little independent authority?
5. If you were a senator seeking to encourage or discourage a particular arms control agreement, what would you do?
6. Are the 1975 critiques of the intelligence community likely to encourage or discourage arms control?
7. Is secrecy in arms control negotiations desirable?
8. How important is Presidential leadership in controlling arms competitions?

CHAPTER 9

1. Do you agree or disagree with the text's argument that SALT could not have begun until the two sides were in rough strategic parity?
2. Should President Johnson have broken off discussions after the Soviet invasion of Czechoslovakia?
3. What were the role and effect of the initial proposals made at the second session of SALT?
4. Was the U.S. decision against serious MIRV negotiations wise?
5. Was the U.S. decision to link an ABM treaty with an agreement on offensive forces wise?

6. What are the advantages and disadvantages of using a separate "back channel" negotiation?

7. What are the advantages and disadvantages of using a summit meeting as a deadline for negotiation?

8. Do the final agreements show that the Soviet Union has accepted the theory of deterrence?

9. As a leader in China, how would you evaluate the SALT agreements? In Japan? In Western Europe? In Eastern Europe? In Latin America?

10. What are the long-term implications of the two superpowers' explicit acceptance of "defenselessness" in the ABM treaty?

CHAPTER 10

1. How would you advise the U.S. government on the issues at dispute in the negotiations following Vladivostok (verification, cruise missiles, Soviet long-range aircraft)?

2. How would you evaluate the Vladivostok accord?

3. What agenda for SALT III would you seek if you were the U.S. President? His U.S.S.R. counterpart? A private citizen?

4. What is your overall evaluation of the role Congress has played in strategic arms control?

5. How could China and France be brought into strategic arms control negotiations?

6. Should SALT be continued?

CHAPTER 11

1. Why are defense budgets (as a share of world GNP) higher since World War II than in earlier times?

2. Why have world defense expenditures (as a share of world GNP) fallen since the mid-1960's? Do you expect this trend to continue? Why or why not?

3. Are you troubled by present military budgets? Why or why not?

4. If you were Secretary of Defense, how would you respond to the trends in defense costs?

5. Is the politics of defense expenditure still different from that of human resources expenditures? If so, why?

6. If you were the President and hoped to reach an arms control agreement that significantly affected the defense budget, how would you proceed domestically to encourage military, Congressional, and public acceptance?

CHAPTER 12

1. If you had been in the French government at the time, would you have supported French development of nuclear weapons? Why? Did this decision ultimately help or hurt France?

2. If you had been in the West German government at the time, would you have supported *Ostpolitik*?

3. Why might all parties concerned have accepted a basically symbolic CSCE agreement, separate from an MFR agreement?

4. Proposals have been made for an integrated West European army. Would development of such a force be wise? What if the integrated force included the French and British nuclear weapons?

5. If you were in Congress during the mid-1970's, would you vote to withdraw a substantial portion of the U.S. forces in Europe? Of the U.S. tactical nuclear weapons there?

6. Would a nuclear free zone in Central Europe be wise?

7. What arms control future might you propose for other areas of which you have knowledge (Mideast, Northeast Asia, Indian Ocean, Latin America)? How would the issues and problems in these areas differ from those in Europe?

CHAPTER 13

1. What sort of verification system would be necessary to enforce limitations on weapons such as supersonic aircraft or tanks which are already spread widely through the world?

2. If you were chairperson of a study group to consider the feasibility and desirability of international controls on precision-guided munitions, how would you proceed?

3. If you were in Congress, what sort of legislation might you propose to govern military assistance programs? What hearings would you hold?

4. Why has arms control attention in the conventional arms area focused on the arms trade rather than on the large developed-world conventional forces?

5. Would an agreement among developed-world arms suppliers to make no further arms sales to the developing world be desirable? Feasible?

6. What are the most far-reaching provisions that you might reasonably expect to emerge from the Latin American talks discussed in this chapter?

7. Is much control of conventional arms possible unless the U.N. collective security and peacekeeping structures are strengthened? At what stage would such strengthening be required?

CHAPTER 14

1. How serious are the dangers of widespread proliferation?

2. Did the Non-Proliferation Treaty and its negotiation help or hurt the cause of non-proliferation?

3. How would you evaluate the Latin American Nuclear Free Zone Treaty? Should the United States sign Protocol I?

4. Would you recommend that nuclear free zones be considered in other areas? If so, with what modifications?

5. Should the United States continue to export nuclear reactors?

6. How might the Chinese proposal for a no-first-use agreement help with proliferation? Would you recommend its acceptance? What conditions might you put on such an agreement?

7. In the developed world, there are some indications of a citizens' revolt against nuclear power, based on safety and environmental grounds. If this revolt continues to be strong, what effect would you expect it to have on nuclear proliferation?

8. What might the United States or the Soviet Union do now to slow proliferation?

9. How does nuclear proliferation complicate the achievement of arms control agreements outside the proliferation area?

CHAPTER 15

1. Has the arms control effort pursued since World War II been worthwhile?

2. Do you agree with the text's pessimism about the step-by-step "building block" approach? Is an alternative approach practical?

3. How might U.S.-U.S.S.R. relations evolve over the next decade or two? What about developed world–developing world relations?

4. What individual items might reasonably be combined in a large arms control package? Would such a package negotiation be desirable? What political conditions would be necessary for it to happen?

5. In what ways could greater arms control and more significant international organization work together? How might such changes occur politically? Would a world incorporating such changes be more or less desirable than today's world?

6. Of all the issues discussed in this book, which ones are best left to experts? Which ones to citizens? Realistically, what can citizens do about those issues that should not be left to experts?

7. What do you expect international politics to be like in fifty years?

Suggested Further Readings

CHAPTER 1

G. Allison. Essence of Decision. Boston, 1971.
G. Alperovitz. Atomic Diplomacy: Hiroshima and Potsdam. New York, 1965.
Daedalus. "Arms, Defense Policy, and Arms Control." Special issue, Summer, 1975.
H. Feis. Between War and Peace: The Potsdam Conference. Princeton, N.J., 1960.
———. From Trust to Terror: The Outset of the Cold War, 1945–1950. New York, 1970.
———. Japan Subdued: The Atomic Bomb and the End of the War in the Pacific. Princeton, N.J., 1961.
A. Fontaine. History of the Cold War. New York, 1968–69.
R. Hewlett and O. Anderson. A History of the United States Atomic Energy Commission. Vol. I, The New World, 1939–1946. University Park, Pa., 1962.
G. Quester. Nuclear Diplomacy: The First Twenty-Five Years. New York, 1970.
C. Roberts. The Nuclear Years. New York, 1970.
H. York. Race to Oblivion. New York, 1970.

CHAPTER 2

R. Aron. The Industrial Society. New York, 1967.
———. Peace and War, A Theory of International Relations. Garden City, N.Y., 1966.
R. Bainton. Christian Attitudes Toward War and Peace. New York, 1960.
R. Barnet and R. Falk, eds. Security in Disarmament. Princeton, N.J., 1965.
K. Boulding. Conflict and Defense: A General Theory. New York, 1962.
A. Bozeman. The Future of Law in a Multicultural World. Princeton, N.J., 1971.
J. Brierly. The Law of Nations. 6th ed. Oxford, 1963.
R. Falk. Law, Morality, and War in the Contemporary World. New York, 1963.
B. Feld. "Human Values and the Technology of Weapons," *Zygon*, 8 (1973), 48.

426   *Suggested Further Readings*

L. Gross. "The Peace of Westphalia, 1648–1949," *American Journal of International Law*, 42 (1948), 20.

John XXIII. Pacem in Terris. Rome, 1963.

K. Lorenz. On Aggression. New York, 1966.

S. de Madariaga. Disarmament. New York, 1929.

R. North and N. Choucri. "Population, Technology, and Resources in the Future International System," *Journal of International Affairs*, 25 (1971), 224.

R. Osgood and R. Tucker. Force, Order and Justice. Baltimore, 1967.

M. Rakove, ed. Arms and Foreign Policy in the Nuclear Age. New York, 1972.

P. Ramsey. The Just War. New York, 1968.

T. Taylor. Nuremberg and Vietnam. Chicago, 1970.

Vatican II. Gaudium et Spes. Rome, 1965.

K. Waltz. Man, The State, and War: A Theoretical Analysis. New York, 1959.

R. Wasserstrom, ed. War and Morality. Belmont, Calif., 1970.

Q. Wright. A Study of War. Chicago, 1942 and 1964.

A. Zimmern. The League of Nations and the Rule of Law, 1918–1935. London, 1939.

CHAPTER 3

R. Art. The Influence of Foreign Policy on Seapower: New Weapons and Weltpolitik in Wilhelmian Germany. Beverly Hills, Calif., 1973.

T. Buckley. The United States and the Washington Conference, 1921–1922. Knoxville, Tenn., 1970.

R. Chaput. Disarmament in British Foreign Policy. London, 1935.

G. Craig and P. Paret. "The Control of International Violence: Some Historical Notes," *Stanford Journal of International Studies*, 7 (1972), 1.

P. Halpern. The Mediterranean Naval Situation, 1908–1914. Cambridge, Mass., 1971.

A. Marder. From the Dreadnought to Scapa Flow. London, 1961–70.

H. Sprout and M. Sprout. Toward a New Order of Sea Power; American Naval Policy and the World Scene, 1918–1922. Princeton, N.J., 1940.

J. Steinberg. Yesterday's Deterrent. London, 1965.

A. Taylor. The Struggle for Mastery in Europe 1848–1918. Oxford, 1954.

S. Williamson. The Politics of Grand Strategy: Britain and France Prepare for War, 1904–14. Cambridge, Mass., 1969.

E. Woodward. Great Britain and the German Navy. Oxford, 1935.

CHAPTER 4

W. Biddle. Weapons Technology and Arms Control. New York, 1972.

B. Brodie and F. Brodie. From Crossbow to H-Bomb. New York, 1962.

N. Calder, ed. Unless Peace Comes. London, 1968.

S. Glasstone, ed. The Effects of Nuclear Weapons. U.S. Department of Defense and Atomic Energy Commission, Washington, D.C., 1962.

B. Feld et al. Impact of New Technologies on the Arms Race. Cambridge, Mass., 1971.

T. Greenwood. Qualitative Improvements in Offensive Strategic Arms: The Case of MIRV. Cambridge, Mass., 1973.

R. Hewlett and O. Anderson. A History of the United States Atomic Energy

Commission. Vol. I, The New World, 1939–1946. University Park, Pa., 1962.

C. Hitch and R. McKean. The Economics of Defense in the Nuclear Age. Cambridge, Mass., 1960.

M. Peck and F. Scherer. The Weapons Acquisition Process. Boston, 1962 and 1964.

W. Shilling. "The H-Bomb Decision: How to Decide Without Actually Choosing," *Political Science Quarterly*, 76 (1961), 24.

Stockholm International Peace Research Institute (SIPRI). Yearbook of World Armaments and Disarmament. Cambridge, Mass., 1968/69, 1969/70, 1972, 1973, 1974, 1975.

A. Wohlstetter. "Is There a Strategic Arms Race?" *Foreign Policy*, 15 (Summer, 1974), 3.

H. York. Arms Control, Readings from Scientific American. San Francisco, 1973.

————. Race to Oblivion. New York, 1970.

CHAPTER 5

B. Beckhoefer. Postwar Negotiations for Arms Control. Washington, D.C., 1961.

B. Bernstein. "The Quest for Security: American Foreign Policy and International Control of Atomic Energy, 1942–1946," *Journal of American History*, 60 (March 1974), 1003.

H. Bull. The Control of the Arms Race. New York, 1961.

A. Dean. Test Ban and Disarmament: The Path of Negotiations. New York, 1966.

H. Jacobson and E. Stein. Diplomats, Scientists, and Politicians: The United States and the Nuclear Test Ban Negotiations. Ann Arbor, Mich., 1966.

P. Noel-Baker. The Arms Race, A Programme for World Disarmament. New York, 1958.

C. Roberts. The Nuclear Years. New York, 1970.

Royal Institute of International Affairs. Summary of International Affairs. London, approximately annually.

SIPRI. Yearbooks.

L. Weiler and A. Simons. The United States and the United Nations. New York, 1967.

E. Young. A Farewell to Arms Control? Harmondsworth, 1972.

CHAPTER 6

R. Gillette. "Test Ban: Arms Control Groups Denounce Summit Treaty," *Science*, 185 (Aug. 2, 1974), 420.

H. Jacobson and E. Stein. Diplomats, Scientists and Politicians: The United States and the Nuclear Test Ban Negotiations. Ann Arbor, Mich., 1966.

R. Lawrence. Arms Control and Disarmament: Practice and Promise. Minneapolis, 1973.

M. Lepper. Foreign Policy Formulation: A Case Study of the Nuclear Test Ban Treaty of 1963. Columbus, O., 1971.

SIPRI. Yearbook, 1969/70.

Stanford Journal of International Studies. Vol. VIII, Arms Control. Spring, 1972.

E. Stein. "Impact of New Weapons Technology on International Law: Selected Aspects," in *Recueil des Cours*, Vol. II. Leyden, 1971.
P. Taubenfeld. Controls for Outer Space and the Antarctic Analogy. New York, 1959.
H. York. Arms Control: Readings from Scientific American. San Francisco, 1973.

CHAPTER 7

R. Aron. The Great Debate: Theories of Nuclear Strategy. Garden City, N.Y., 1965.
D. Brennan. "The Case for Missile Defense," *Foreign Affairs*, 47 (April 1969), 433.
Z. Brzezinski. "How the Cold War Was Played," *Foreign Affairs*, 51 (Oct. 1972), 181.
M. Bundy. "To Cap the Volcano," *Foreign Affairs*, 48 (Oct. 1969), 1.
J. Coffey. Strategic Power and National Security. Pittsburgh, 1971.
A. Dallin. The Soviet Union and Disarmament: An Appraisal of Soviet Attitudes and Intentions. New York, 1964.
A. George and R. Smoke. Deterrence in American Foreign Policy: Theory and Practice. New York, 1974.
T. Greenwood and M. Nacht. "The New Nuclear Debate: Sense or Nonsense?" *Foreign Affairs*, 52 (July 1974), 761.
M. Halperin. China and the Bomb. New York, 1965.
———. Defense Strategies for the Seventies. Boston, 1971.
A. Horelick and M. Rush. Strategic Power and Soviet Foreign Policy. Chicago, 1966.
F. Ikle. "Can Nuclear Deterrence Last Out the Century?" *Foreign Affairs*, 51 (Jan. 1973), 267.
H. Kahn. On Thermonuclear War. Princeton, N.J., 1960.
M. Kaplan. Strategic Thinking and Its Moral Implications. Chicago, 1973.
H. Kissinger. Nuclear Weapons and Foreign Policy. New York, 1957.
R. Kolkowicz. The Soviet Union and Arms Control. Baltimore, 1970.
C. Murphy. "Mainland China's Evolving Nuclear Deterrent," *Bulletin of Atomic Scientists*, 28 (Jan. 1972), 29.
W. Panofsky. "The Mutual-Hostage Relationship Between America and Russia," *Foreign Affairs*, 52 (Oct. 1973), 109.
Senate Committee on Foreign Relations. Hearings on U.S.-U.S.S.R. Strategic Policies, March-April, 1974.
T. Schelling. Arms and Influence. New Haven, 1966.
———. The Strategy of Conflict. Cambridge, Mass., 1960.
K. Tsipis, A. Cahn, and B. Feld, eds. The Future of the Sea-Based Deterrent. Cambridge, Mass., 1973.
A. Wohlstetter. "The Delicate Balance of Terror," *Foreign Affairs*, 37 (Jan. 1959), 211.

CHAPTER 8

G. Allison. Essence of Decision. Boston, 1971.
R. Barnet and R. Falk. Security in Disarmament. Princeton, N.J., 1965.
J. Bingham. "Can Military Spending Be Controlled?" *Foreign Affairs*, 48 (Oct. 1969), 51.

G. Bunn. "Missile Limitation: By Treaty or Otherwise?" *Columbia Law Review*, 70 (1970), 1.

A. Chayes. "An Inquiry into the Workings of Arms Control Agreements," *Harvard Law Review*, 85 (1972), 905.

K. Clark and L. Legere. The President and the Management of National Security. New York, 1969.

L. Finkelstein. "Arms Inspection," *International Conciliation*, No. 540 (Nov. 1962).

R. Gillette. "Nuclear Testing Violation: Keeping It All in the Family," *Science*, 185 (Aug. 9, 1974), 506.

S. Gorove. "The First Multinational Atomic Inspection and Control System at Work: Euratom's Experience," *Stanford Law Review*, 18 (1965), 160.

T. Greenwood. Reconnaissance, Surveillance, and Arms Control. Adelphi Paper No. 88. London, 1972.

S. Huntington. Changing Patterns of Military Politics. New York, 1962.

F. Ikle. How Nations Negotiate. New York, 1964.

Institute for Defense Analysis. Verification and Response in Disarmament Agreements. Woods Hole Summer Study, Mass., 1962.

A. Myrdal. "The International Control of Disarmament," *Scientific American*, 23 (Oct. 1974), 28.

R. Neustadt. Alliance Politics. New York, 1970.

G. Rathjens, A. Chayes, and J. Ruina. Nuclear Arms Control Agreements: Process and Input. Washington, D.C., 1974.

L. Scheinman. "Nuclear Safeguards, the Peaceful Atom, and the IAEA," *International Conciliation*, No. 572 (March 1969).

J. Stevenson. "Constitutional Aspects of the Executive Agreement Procedure," *Department of State Bulletin*, 66 (June 19, 1972), 840.

Subcommittee on National Security Policy and Scientific Developments of the House Committee on Foreign Affairs. Review of Arms Control Legislation and Organization. Farley Report. Sept. 1974.

L. Weiler. The Arms Race, Secret Negotiations and the Congress. Muscatine, Ia., 1976.

CHAPTER 9

M. Kaplan, ed. SALT: Problems and Prospects. Morristown, N.J., 1973.

W. Kintner and R. Pfaltzgraff, Jr., eds. SALT: Implications for Arms Control in the 1970s. Pittsburgh, 1973.

M. Mackintosh. "Moscow's View of the Balance of Power," *The World Today*, 29 (March 1973), 108.

J. Newhouse. Cold Dawn: The Story of SALT. New York, 1973.

M. Willrich and J. Rhinelander, eds. SALT: The Moscow Agreements and Beyond. New York, 1974.

CHAPTER 10

E. Bates. "The SALT Standing Consultative Commission—An American Analysis," *Millennium*, 4 (1975), 132.

L. Carter. "Strategic Arms Limitation" (a series of articles under varying separate titles), *Science*, 187 (Jan. 31, Feb. 21, March 14, 1975), 327, 627, 936; *Science*, 188 (April 11, 1975), 130.

L. Korb. "The Issues and Costs of the New United States Nuclear Policy," *Naval War College Review*, Nov./Dec. 1974, p. 28.
P. Nitze. "Assuring Strategic Stability in an Era of Détente," *Foreign Affairs*, 54 (Jan. 1976), 207.
A. Quanbeck and B. Blechman. Strategic Forces: Issues for the Mid-Seventies. Washington, D.C., 1973.
D. Shapley. "Cruise Missiles: Air Force, Navy Weapons Pose New Arms Issues," *Science*, 184 (Feb. 7, 1975), 416.
K. Tsipis, A. Cahn, and B. Feld, eds. The Future of the Sea-Based Deterrent. Cambridge, Mass., 1973.
L. Weiler. "The Status of SALT: A Perspective," *Arms Control Today*, Dec. 1974.

CHAPTER 11

E. Benoit. Defense and Economic Growth in Developing Countries. Lexington, Mass., 1973.
C. Hitch and R. McKean. The Economics of Defense in the Nuclear Age. Cambridge, Mass., 1960.
Joint Economic Committee, 93d Congress, 1st Sess. Soviet Economic Prospects for the Seventies. Compendium of Papers. Washington, D.C., 1973.
Joint Economic Committee, Subcommittee on Foreign Economic Policy, 91st Congress, 2d Sess. Economic Performance and the Military Burden in the Soviet Union. Compendium of Papers. Washington, D.C., 1970.
M. Kaldor. European Defense Industries—National and International Implications. Sussex, 1972.
R. Kaufman. The War Profiteers. Indianapolis, 1972.
S. Melman, ed. The War Economy of the United States. New York, 1971.
C. Schultze et al. Setting National Priorities: The 1971 Budget. Washington, D.C., 1970 (and successor volumes).
SIPRI. Yearbook, 1974, pp. 123–286.
R. Sivard. World Military and Social Expenditures, 1974. New York, 1974.
United Nations. Disarmament and Development, Report of the Group of Experts on the Economic and Social Consequences of Disarmament. ST/ECA/174, New York, 1972.
———. Reduction of the Military Budgets of States Permanent Members of the Security Council by 10 Per Cent and Utilization of Part of the Funds Thus Saved to Provide Assistance to Developing Countries. A/9770. New York, Oct. 19, 1974.
U.S. Arms Control and Disarmament Agency. World Military Expenditures and Arms Trade, 1963–1973. Washington, D.C., 1975.
M. Weidenbaum. The Economics of Peacetime Defense. New York, 1974.
A. Yarmolinsky. The Military Establishment. New York, 1971.

CHAPTER 12

C. Bertram. Mutual Force Reductions in Europe: The Political Aspects. Adelphi Paper No. 84. London, 1972.
———. "The Politics of MBFR," *The World Today*, 29 (Jan. 1973), 1.
S. Canby. NATO Military Policy: Obtaining Conventional Comparability with the Warsaw Pact. RAND R-1088-ARPA, June 1973.

A. Enthoven. "U.S. Forces in Europe: How Many? Doing What?" *Foreign Affairs*, 53 (April 1975), 513.
A. Enthoven and K. Smith. How Much Is Enough? Shaping the Defense Program, 1961–1969. New York, 1971.
A. Fontaine. History of the Cold War. New York, 1968–69.
R. Foster. Strategy for the West. New York, 1974.
R. Hunter. "Mutual and Balanced Force Reduction: The Next Step in Détente," *International Conciliation*, No. 587 (March 1972), p. 39.
————. Security in Europe. Bloomington, Ind., 1972.
R. King and R. Dean, eds. East European Perspectives on European Security and Cooperation. New York, 1974.
H. Kissinger. The Troubled Partnership: A Reappraisal of the Atlantic Alliance. New York, 1965.
W. Klaiber. Era of Negotiation. Lexington, Mass., 1973.
W. Kohl. French Nuclear Diplomacy. Princeton, N.J., 1971.
R. Lawrence and J. Record. U.S. Force Structure in NATO; An Alternative. Washington, D.C., 1974.
J. Newhouse. "Stuck Fast," *Foreign Affairs*, 51 (Jan. 1973), 353.
————. U.S. Troops in Europe. Washington, D.C., 1971.
R. Neustadt. Alliance Politics. New York, 1970.
R. Pfaltzgraff, Jr. "The U.S. and Europe: Partners in a Multipolar World," *Orbis*, 17 (Spring, 1973), 31.
A. Pierre. "Nuclear Diplomacy: Britain, France and America," *Foreign Affairs*, 49 (Jan. 1971), 283.
————. Nuclear Politics. London, 1972.
R. Ranger. "MBFR: Political or Technical Arms Control?" *The World Today*, 30 (Oct. 1974), 411.
J. Record. U.S. Nuclear Weapons in Europe; Issues and Alternatives. Washington, D.C., 1974.
T. Stanley and D. White. Détente Diplomacy: The United States and European Security in the 1970s. Cambridge, Mass., 1970.
J. Yochelson. "MBFR: The Search for an American Approach," *Orbis*, 17 (Spring, 1973), 155.

CHAPTER 13

J. Barton. "The Developing Nations and Arms Control," *Studies in Comparative International Development*, 10 (1975), 67.
B. Blechman. The Control of Naval Armaments: Prospects and Possibilities. Washington, D.C., 1975.
Center for Defense Information. "U.S. Military Assistance and Sales" (first in a series), *The Defense Monitor* (May 1974).
L. Einaudi et al. Arms Transfers to Latin America: Toward a Policy of Mutual Respect. RAND R-1173-DOS, June 1973.
R. Gillette. "Military R & D: Hard Lessons of an Electronic War," *Science*, 182 (Nov. 9, 1973), 559.
G. Pauker et al. In Search of Self-Reliance: U.S. Security Assistance to the Third World Under the Nixon Doctrine. RAND R-1092-ARPA, June 1973.
A. Pierre. "Limiting Soviet and American Conventional Forces," *Survival*, 15 (Mar. Apr. 1973).

SIPRI. The Arms Trade with the Third World. Stockholm, 1971.
SIPRI. Yearbook, 1974.
R. Sivard. World Military and Social Expenditures, 1974. New York, 1974.
G. Thayer. The War Business: The International Trade in Armaments. New York, 1969.
U.S. ACDA. The International Transfer of Conventional Arms. A Report to the Congress Pursuant to Section 302 of The Foreign Relations Authorization Act of 1972. P.L. 92-352, Sept. 1975.
T. Wintringham and J. Blashford-Snell. Weapons and Tactics. Harmondsworth, 1973.

CHAPTER 14

W. Bader. The United States and the Spread of Nuclear Weapons. New York, 1968.
B. Bechhoefer. "Negotiating the Statute of the International Atomic Energy Agency," *International Organization*, 13 (1959), 38.
L. Bloomfield. "Nuclear Spread and World Order," *Foreign Affairs*, 53 (July 1975), 743.
W. Doub and J. Dukert. "Making Nuclear Energy Safe and Secure," *Foreign Affairs*, 53 (July 1975), 756.
M. Gowing. Independence and Deterrence: Britain and Atomic Energy, 1945–52. New York, 1974.
R. Lawrence and J. Larus. Nuclear Proliferation: Phase II. Lawrence, Kan., 1974.
A. Marks, ed. NPT: Paradoxes and Problems. Washington, D.C., 1975.
W. Mendl. Deterrence and Persuasion. New York, 1970.
H. Nau. National Politics and International Technology: Nuclear Reactor Development in Western Europe. Baltimore, 1974.
A. Pierre. Nuclear Politics. London, 1972.
G. Quester. The Politics of Nuclear Proliferation. Baltimore, 1973.
J. Redick. "Regional Nuclear Arms Control in Latin America," *International Organization*, 29 (1975), 415.
L. Scheinman. "Nuclear Safeguards, the Peaceful Atom, and the IAEA," *International Conciliation*, No. 572 (March 1969).
SIPRI. Nuclear Proliferation Problems. Stockholm, 1974.
United Nations. Comprehensive Study of the Question of Nuclear-Weapons-Free Zones in All Its Aspects. A/10027/Add. 1, New York, 1975.
M. Willrich. International Safeguards and Nuclear Industry. Baltimore, 1973.
————. Non-Proliferation Treaty, Framework for Nuclear Arms Control. Charlottesville, Va., 1969.
M. Willrich and T. Taylor. Nuclear Theft: Risks and Safeguards. Cambridge, Mass., 1974.

CHAPTER 15

R. Aron. The Industrial Society. New York, 1967.
————. Peace and War, A Theory of International Relations. Garden City, N.Y., 1966.
R. Art and K. Waltz. The Use of Force. Boston, 1971.
R. Barnet and R. Falk, eds. Security in Disarmament. Princeton, N.J., 1965.

L. Beaton. The Reform of Power, A Proposal for an International Security System. New York, 1972.

K. Boulding. Conflict and Defense: A General Theory. New York, 1962.

H. Bull. The Control of the Arms Race. New York, 1965.

R. Falk, R. Tucker, and O. Young. On Minimizing the Use of Nuclear Weapons. Princeton, N.J., 1966.

R. Goldman. "A Transactional Theory of Political Integration and Arms Control," *American Political Science Review*, 63 (1969), 719.

S. Huntington. "Arms Races: Prerequisites and Results," *Public Policy*, 8 (1958), 41.

K. Knorr. On the Uses of Military Power in the Nuclear Age. Princeton, N.J., 1966.

R. Levine. The Arms Debate. Cambridge, Mass., 1963.

K. Lorenz. On Aggression. New York, 1966.

S. de Madariaga. Disarmament. New York, 1929.

W. Millis. An End to Arms. New York, 1965.

R. North and N. Choucri. "Population, Technology, and Resources in the Future International System," *Journal of International Affairs*, 25 (1971), 224.

L. Richardson. Arms and Insecurity. Pittsburgh, 1960.

K. Waltz. Man, the State, and War: A Theoretical Analysis. New York, 1959.

Q. Wright. A Study of War. Chicago, 1942 and 1964.

Index

ABMs, *see* Anti-ballistic missile (ABM) systems; Anti-Ballistic Missile (ABM) Treaty
Accident Measures Agreement (SALT I) (1971), 193, 197
Acheson, Dean, 70–71
Acheson-Lilienthal Report, 70, 93, 291
Adams, John Quincy, 32
Adenauer, Konrad, 251, 253f, 262
Africa, nuclear-free zone in, 249
Aircraft, conventional, 272, 277. *See also* Bombers, strategic long-range
Air defense systems, 137–38. *See also* Anti-ballistic missile systems
Alamogordo, New Mexico, 1f
Alexander I, Tsar, 32
Amchitka Island, 115
American University, 107–8
Amoral (Realpolitik) tradition of international relations, 12–15
Anglo-French disarmament memorandum (1954), 75
Anglo-Japanese alliance (1902), 35, 43
Antarctic Treaty (1959), 82–83, 96–97, 98
Anti-ballistic missile (ABM) systems, 58–61, 137–38, 204–5; U.S., 59, 89, 175–79 *passim*, 226; Soviet, 89, 172–74; function and effect on strategic doctrine, 132–36; in SALT I negotiations, 177–97 *passim*; NCA (National Command Authority) option, 184–85, 187, 191, 195; Zero-ABM option, 184–85; in SALT II negotiations, 218–19, 226; economic consequences of nondeployment, 244
Anti-Ballistic Missile (ABM) Treaty

(SALT I) (1972), 59–60, 61, 89, 92, 197–200, 208f; verification measures, 199–200; effects, 202, 204–5
Anti-submarine warfare (ASW), 215–16, 223
Aquinas, St. Thomas, 11
Arab-Israeli interim resolution, 250
Arbitration, 18–20
Argentina, 277 table, 279, 286, 293ff, 302
Arms control, 92–93, 147–50; background of study, 1–6; definition, 3n; cultural context, 9–30; motivation, 22–30; naval, in interwar period, 40–44, 45; negotiations since World War II, 66–93; institutions of, 151–71; economics of, 228–48; through budget limitation, 247–48; regional European, 249–70; of conventional arms, 271–87; of nuclear proliferation, 288–309; evaluation of, 310–21
Arms Control and Disarmament Agency (ACDA), 82, 84, 120, 164, 210, 245, 296; role in arms control negotiations, 155–58, 177, 180
Arms procurement process, 24–26, 229–40
Arms race, 24, 34–37, 44
Arms sales, 5, 274 fig., 275–79, 281–86
Asia, Southeast, 222, 276, 282
ASW, 215–16, 223
Aswan High Dam, 305
Atlas missiles, 54
Atomic bomb, *see* Nuclear weapons
Atomic Energy Act, 290
Atomic Energy Commission (AEC), 68, 76, 289–90
Attlee, Clement, 69–70

Augustine, St., 11
Australia, 96, 291, 298, 302
Ayacucho, Declaration of (1974), 286

Balkan Wars, 311
Bangladesh, 284
Bargaining counters ("chips"), 178, 226, 270
Bargaining deadlines, 194–97, 226
Baruch, Bernard, 2, 70–71
Baruch Plan, 74, 289–90
Battleships, 35–36
Beaufre, André, 256
Beersheba, Israel, 305
Belgium, 18, 37, 96, 250, 265, 291
Berlin crises, 72, 259
Bermuda Conference (1962), 258
Bethmann Hollweg, Theobald von, 36
Bevin, Ernest, 70
Bikini atoll, 101
Biological Warfare Convention (1972), 91, 116–22
Biological weapons, 39, 90–91
Bismarck, Prince Otto von, 33
Blockades, 34
Bodin, Jean, 16
Bolivia, 293
Bombers, strategic long-range, 17, 179 table; B-52, 54, 57, 64, 87, 208n; B-1, 64, 203, 208, 217, 226; B-47, 87; TU-16, 87; in SALT II negotiations, 211–12, 214–16, 220f; Mirage-IV, 257
Borah, Sen. William, 41
Brandt, Willy, 259, 260–62
Brazil, 114, 293ff, 307; and NPT, 92, 302; and arms trade, 275, 277 table, 279, 286
Brezhnev, Leonid, 91, 194, 197, 217–18, 223, 262, 264; budget limitation proposals, 247–48; Brezhnev doctrine, 261, 263
Briand, Aristide, 20f
Brooke, Sen. Edward, 178
Brussels Treaty (1948), 250f
Budget limitation, arms control through, 87, 247–48. *See also* Military expenditures
Bulganin, Nikolai, 77f, 97, 102
Bulgaria, 38, 265
Bülow, Bernhard von, 36
Bundy, McGeorge, 156
Bureaucratic pressures in negotiation, 152–57, 167, 208, 226–27
Byrnes, James F., 70

Calley, Lieut. William, 17
Canada, 250, 275, 303; arms control efforts, 69–70, 74, 263, 265, 291, 302
Cannikin test, 115
Castlereagh, Lord, 32
Castro, Fidel, 279
Catholicism, just-war position of, 10–12
Caucasus Mountains, 38
CCD, *see* Conference of the Committee on Disarmament
Central American Disarmament Convention (1923), 38–39
Cesium 137, 50–51
Champlain, Lake, 32
Chemical Warfare Convention, 116–22
Chemical weapons, 39, 90–91, 121–22, 219
Ch'en Yi, 145
Ch'iao Kuan-hua, 149
Ch'ien Hsüeh-sen, 145
Chile, 96, 286, 293, 295
China, People's Republic of, 1, 20, 160, 224–25, 258, 304, 306–7; U.S. policy toward, 6, 114, 147, 193–94, 206; as nuclear power, 14, 145–46, 292, 304; attitude toward disarmament negotiations and treaties, 92f, 108, 147–50, 248, 294, 302; strategic doctrines, 144–50; Soviet policy toward, 186–87; military expenditures, 231f; arms sales, 275, 284
Chou En-lai, 207
Christianity, just-war position of, 10–12
Churchill, Winston S., 36
Clarendon, Lord, 33
COCOM (NATO Coordinating Committee), 285
Cold War, 2, 72–74
Collateral agreements, arms control through, 81–86
Collective security, 20–21, 123–24
Colombia, 286
Common Market, 260
Conference of the Committee on Disarmament (CCD), 90–91, 100, 118f, 161–63, 285
Conference on Security and Cooperation in Europe (CSCE), 91, 262–64
Congo (Zaire), 21
Conrad, Montana, 245
Conscientious objection, 13
Conventional arms, control of, 271–87
Copenhagen, Denmark, 95

Costa Rica, 39, 286
Crisis communication agreements, 94–96. *See also* "Hot Line" agreements
Cruise missiles, 63, 221–23
CSCE, 91, 262–64
Cuba, 279, 293, 295
Cuban missile crisis (1962), 24, 86, 128ff, 259, 293; and "Hot Line" agreement, 94; and arms control discussions, 107, 169–70, 249–50
Cyprus, 21
Czechoslovakia, 261, 265, 267, 275; Communist coup (1948), 72, 250; Soviet intervention (1968), 89, 177, 261

Damage limitation, strategic doctrine of, 141–44
Deadlines, bargaining, 194–97, 226
Defensive systems, 58–61. *See also* Antiballistic missile systems
Defoliants, 118
De Gaulle, Charles, 254, 255–56, 260f
Delivery systems, 54–58, 87, 125, 177–79, 181, 188, 189. *See also* Bombers, strategic long-range; Intercontinental ballistic missiles; Strategic weapons; Submarine-launched ballistic missiles
Denmark, 250, 265, 283
Descartes, René, 12
Détente, 222, 249, 315
Deterrence theory, *see* Nuclear deterrence
Developing world, military expenditures of, 231–32, 276
Dien Bien Phu, 126
Disarmament, 21–22, 31–45, 67–68, 83f; general background, 1–6; defined, 3n; Chinese position on, 147–50. *See also* General and Complete Disarmament
Dobrynin, Anatoly, 179, 188–89
Doctrine, strategic, 6–7, 123–50. *See also individual doctrines*
Dresden, Germany, 14
Dubna, U.S.S.R., 145
Dulles, John Foster, 76, 80, 102, 156, 255, 262; and control of nuclear proliferation, 2, 290f; and doctrine of massive retaliation, 124–25
Dumdum bullets, 13, 17

Echeverría, Luís, 294
Economic motivation for arms control, 28–29, 243–47

Ecuador, 293
EDC, 251, 254
Eden, Anthony, 15, 252
Edward VII, King, 36
Egypt, 118, 279, 284, 302
Eighteen-Nation Disarmament Committee (ENDC), 84–90, 94, 99, 172, 262; and NPT, 296–300 *passim*
Eisenhower, Pres. Dwight D., 3, 29–30, 81, 83, 97; disarmament policy, 74, 76, 102–6, 155f; "Open Skies" proposal, 77f, 127; "Atoms for Peace" speech, 82, 290
Electronic battlefield, 272
El Salvador, 39
ENDC, *see* Eighteen-Nation Disarmament Committee
Environmental issues, arms control and, 29, 219
Erfurt, East Germany, 261
Ethics of war, 9–15, 130–31
Ethiopia, 20, 117
Europe, arms control in, 249–70
European Atomic Energy Community (EURATOM), 164–65, 299–300, 302, 307
European Defense Community (EDC), 251, 254
Exports of arms, *see* Arms sales

Fallout, nuclear, 78, 86, 101–2; effects, 50–51, 53–54, 109, 111, 134; U.S. shelter campaign, 128
Faure, Edgar, 247
FBS, *see* Forward-Based System
Finland, 38
Fisher, Adrian, 84, 297
Fission weapons, *see* Nuclear weapons
Five-Power Treaty (1921), 42–43
Fléchettes, 13, 17, 281
Flexible targeting, strategic doctrine of, 141–44
FOBS, 99
Ford, Pres. Gerald, 92, 219–23
Forward-Based System (FBS), 180–81, 185, 189, 206; Soviet position, 183–84, 187; in SALT II negotiations, 211, 219–20
Foster, Dr. John, 138
Foster, William, 84
Fractional orbital bombardment system (FOBS), 99
France, 15, 83; as nuclear power, 4, 126, 224, 255–56, 292, 304; and interwar

disarmament, 19, 38–40, 42ff; attitude toward disarmament negotiations and treaties, 73ff, 79, 85f, 92, 96, 108, 224f, 247, 291, 294; refusal to sign LTB Treaty, 108, 302, 307f; arms sales, 243, 247 fig., 275, 278, 282, 284, 286; and European security, 247, 250f, 254–64 *passim*, 269

Frederick the Great, 31

French-German alliance (1963), 254

Fulbright, Sen. J. William, 120, 210

Fusion weapons, *see* Nuclear weapons

Galosh system (Soviet ABM), 173, 191, 195, 199

Gandhi, Mohandas, 10

Gas, asphyxiating, 33, 39, 116–17, 118f

General and Complete Disarmament (GCD), 83–86, 106, 247, 281

Geneva, Switzerland, 43, 77, 86, 180, 216–23; Geneva Protocol (1925), 19, 39, 117–21 *passim*; Geneva Conference (1958–63), 83, 255

Germany, 14, 18ff, 34–37, 39–40, 44, 117, 311; reunification, 253, 260–61

Germany, Democratic Republic of, 261, 265, 267

Germany, Federal Republic of, 67–68, 72, 124, 265, 275; rearmament, 78, 102, 250–54; Soviet fear of, 88, 173, 295–301 *passim*; strategic policies, 259–60; *Ostpolitik*, 260–61; and NPT, 298, 302

Glassboro, N.J., 175

Gomulka, Wladislaw, 252

Grand Forks, N.D. (ABM site), 191, 194f, 199

Great Britain, 260, 289; pre-World War II disarmament agreements, 17ff, 32, 34–37, 38, 40f, 311, 315; cooperation with U.S., 54, 250, 255; arms control and disarmament efforts, 69–70, 73ff, 97, 101, 108, 265, 291, 294, 301f; domestic politics and arms control, 102, 154, 161, 258–59, 266; strategic policies, 258–59; arms sales, 274 fig., 275, 284f

Great Lakes, 32

Greece, 250, 265

Gromyko, Andrei, 30, 87, 97, 261, 298

Gross national product (GNP), military expenditure measured by, 230, 232–33, 236

Grotius, Hugo, 16

Guantánamo base, Cuba, 294

Guatemala, 39

Guerrilla warfare, 17, 280

Guyana, 293

Hague, The, Peace Conferences (1899, 1907), 16–17, 33–34, 36, 116, 247

Hague Conventions for the Pacific Settlement of International Disputes, 19

Haldane, Lord, 36

Harding, Pres. Warren G., 41f

Helsinki, Finland, 95, 179–81, 187, 189–97 *passim*, 263f

Hibbs, A. R., 146

Hiroshima, Japan, 1, 47, 49–51, 53

Hitler, Adolf, 39–40, 164

Hobbes, Thomas, 12, 16

Ho Chi Minh, 126

Holy Loch, Scotland, 183

"Holy wars," 12

Honan, China, 1

Honduras, 39

"Hot Line" agreements, 89, 95; of 1963, 27, 86, 94–96; of 1967, 94–96; of 1971, 95–96, 193, 197–98

Hughes, Charles Evans, 42

Humphrey, Sen. Hubert H., 84

Hungary, 38, 255, 265, 267

Huntsville, Ala., 245

Hydrogen bomb, *see* Nuclear weapons

ICBMs, *see* Intercontinental ballistic missiles

Iceland, 250, 283, 285

Ideology, arms control and, 6–7

IGY, 82–83, 96

Ikle, Fred, 210

India, 10, 108, 114, 160–61, 282, 284; as nuclear power, 4, 160–61, 303, 309; and NPT, 92, 298, 302, 303–5; Indo-Pakistan War (1965), 279, 282, 284

Indian Ocean Zone of Peace, 91, 249

Indonesia, 279

Industry, defense, 44, 239–40, 242

Inflation, 238, 240–41

Infrared sensors, detection by, 174

Inspection arrangements, 71, 74, 77, 79f, 291f; on-site, 87, 90, 97, 172; distinguished from verification, 164; in SALT negotiations, 183f, 185–86

Intelligence service, problems of use for verification, 169–70

Intercontinental ballistic missiles

(ICBMs), 54–57; Soviet, 54, 56–57, 87, 126, 172f, 176, 179 table; U.S., 54–55, 60, 172f, 176, 179 table, 186; and deterrence doctrine, 126, 128; limitation of, 182–83, 185, 194, 196–97, 200–204 *passim*, 211–12, 219–23; mobile, 194, 196–97. *See also* Delivery systems; Multiple independently targetable reentry vehicles; *names of specific missiles*
Interim Offensive Agreement and Protocol (1972), 200–204, 218
Intermediate-range ballistic missiles (IRBMs), 54, 56, 64, 125, 128, 181–83, 185
International Atomic Development Authority, 70
International Atomic Energy Agency (IAEA), 72, 82, 90, 205, 260, 290–92, 307; verification procedures, 168, 299–300, 302–3; and Latin American Nuclear Free Zone, 294f
International Court of Justice, 19
International Geophysical Year (IGY), 82–83, 96
International law, 15–18
International order, arms control and change of, 318–21
International organizations, law against war and, 18–22
Iran, 243, 277 table, 279, 302
IRBMs, *see* Intermediate-range ballistic missiles
Ireland, 295–96
Israel, 15, 255, 260, 302, 304–5
Italy, 20, 42, 117, 124, 275; and European security, 54, 250, 265

Jackson, Sen. Henry, 208–10, 220–21, 315; Jackson amendment, 157, 208–11, 220
Japan, 10, 20, 72, 96, 117, 124, 285; postwar disarmament, 15, 67–68, 102, 161, 240; prewar disarmament, 40–44, 315; and NPT, 298, 302, 306–7
Johnson, Pres. Lyndon B., 15, 88–89, 155, 285, 296–97; and ABM deployment, 60, 173; proposes freeze on delivery systems, 87, 171; summit meetings, 175, 177; and SALT negotiations, 176ff
Johnson, U. Alexis, 210
Joint Chiefs of Staff, 62, 111, 153, 155
Joint Statement of Agreed Principles for

Disarmament Negotiations (U.S.-Soviet Union, 1961), 84–85
Joseph II (Austria), 31
Jupiter missiles, 54
Just-war tradition of international relations, 10–12, 130–31

Kant, Immanuel, 12–13
Kashmir, 282
Kassel, West Germany, 261
Kaunitz, Prince, 31
Kellogg-Briand Pact (1928), 20f
Kellogg, Frank, 20f
Kennedy, Pres. John F., 84, 86f, 129, 155f, 169–70, 173; and LTB, 106–7, 109, 111, 157
Khrushchev, Nikita, 29–30, 83f, 87, 104, 107f, 254, 316
King, William, 69–70
Kissinger, Henry, 6, 193, 208, 218, 221, 262; and SALT proposals, 156–57, 178, 182, 218f; and "back-channel" negotiations, 188–89, 195
Korea, Republic of, 307
Korean war, 20–21, 72, 118, 124, 145, 173
Kosygin, Aleksei, 136, 173ff, 177
Kwajalein Island, 59

Laird, Melvin, 138, 178, 208
Lanchow, China, 145
LANFZ, *see* Latin American Nuclear Free Zone Treaty
Laos, 170, 285–86
Lasers, 193
Lasswell, Harold D., 316
Latin America, arms trade in, 277 table, 278–79, 280, 282, 286. *See also specific countries*
Latin American Nuclear Free Zone (LANFZ) Treaty (1967), 25, 88, 149, 249, 292–95
Lausanne, Treaty of (1923), 38
Law, international, and law of war, 15–22, 33–34
Lead time, ABM development and, 134
League of Nations, 19f, 37–40, 67
Leningrad, U.S.S.R., 172
Leninism, just-war doctrine and, 10
Leonard, James, 101
Lieber, Francis, 16
Lilienthal, David, 70, 93, 291
Limited Nuclear Test Ban (LTB) Treaty (1963), 3, 9, 28f, 81, 83, 86,

89, 148, 314; effects, 63, 109, 111;
discussion and negotiation of, 101–16;
verification procedures, 111–13, 168–
69
Lloyd George, David, 41
Locarno, Treaties of (1925), 19, 39
London, 14, 95
London Naval Conference (1935), 44
London Subcommittee (Subcommittee
for Disarmament), 74–81, 83, 281
London Treaty (1954), 251
LTB Treaty, *see* Limited Nuclear Test
Ban Treaty
Lucky Dragon, 101
Luxembourg, 250, 265

McCloy, James, 84
Machiavelli, Niccolò, 12
Macmillan, Harold, 258–59
McNamara, Robert, 62, 109, 142,
155, 174f
Mahan, Alfred T., 34
Malmstrom Air Force Base, Montana,
ABM site at, 195, 199
Malta, 282f
Manchuria, 20
Maneuverable reentry vehicles
(MARVs), 213
Manhattan District Project, 61, 288
Manpower, U.S. military expenditure
for, 230–31, 234–35, 238
Mansfield amendment, 262
Mao Tse-tung, 148
MARVs, 213
Massive retaliation, strategic doctrine of,
124–26
Matsu, 126
Mediterranean Sea, 180, 249
Medium-range ballistic missiles
(MRBMs), 129, 181, 185
Medvedev, Roy, 318
Metternich, Prince Clemens von, 32
Mexico, 155, 248, 285, 293, 302
Mexico City, Mexico, 88, 293
MFR, 91, 262–69
Middle Ages, arms control in, 31
Mideast, 21, 249f, 260, 273; wars, 38,
95, 273, 279, 284; arms trade, 276,
282, 284, 311–12
Military expenditures, 229 fig., 229–32,
240–43, 286; worldwide, 229 fig.,
229–32; measures of, 230–32; of
Soviet Union, 231, 233 fig., 235–36;
of U.S., 232–35, 233 fig., 237–40

Military-industrial complex, 44, 242
Mines, 17
Minuteman missiles, 55, 64, 129, 133,
136, 177
"Mirror-imaging," ABM development
and, 134–35
MIRVs, *see* Multiple independently
targetable reentry vehicles
MLF, 258f, 296–99
Montgomery, Field Marshal Bernard,
254
Moscow, U.S.S.R., 108, 194, 217–18;
ABM site, 59, 184–85, 187, 199
MRBMs, 129, 181, 185
MRVs, 55f
Multilateral Nuclear Force (MLF),
258f, 296–99
Multiple independently targetable re-
entry vehicles (MIRVs), 27, 136–41;
U.S., 56, 63, 172, 177–78, 186; Soviet,
57, 63, 172, 177–78, 186; limitation
of, 178–79, 181–87 *passim*, 204, 214–
16, 217, 219, 223
Multiple reentry vehicles (MRVs), 55f
Muslim culture, war and, 15–16
Mussolini, Benito, 117
Mustard gas, 117f
Mutual Force Reduction (MFR) talks,
91, 262–69
Myrdal, Alva, 297

Nagasaki, Japan, 1, 47, 53
Napalm, 13, 17, 281
Napoleon III, 33
National Academy of Sciences, 52
NATO, *see* North Atlantic Treaty
Organization
Naval Appropriations Act of 1916, 40
Naval strategy and weaponry, 34–35,
272f, 276
NCA option, *see* under Anti-ballistic
missile systems
Negotiating techniques, 92–93, 183,
298–99; linkages, 102–3, 195; do-
mestic political pressure and, 152–59;
informal and "back-channel" negotia-
tions, 162–63, 188–89; "bargaining
chips," 178, 226, 270
Nehru, Jawaharlal, 101
Nerve gas, 116, 118f
Netherlands, 250, 265, 294
Neutrality, law of, 17f
New Zealand, 97
Nicaragua, 39, 294

Nicholas II, Tsar, 33–34
Nike-Zeus system, 59
Nixon, Pres. Richard M., 26, 92, 142–43, 156, 193, 306–7; and SALT negotiations, 6, 29, 91, 115, 156, 160, 178–79, 182, 185–86, 194, 208, 216–19, 315; ABM policy, 59f, 184–85, 197; ban on biological and lethal chemical weapons, 90, 118–19; arms sales policy, 278, 285
Non-Proliferation Treaty (NPT) (1968), 27, 72, 81, 88, 163, 173, 176, 295–304, 307; Chinese refusal to sign, 147; German acceptance, 259–60; asymmetry of, 302–3
North Atlantic Treaty Organization (NATO), 231, 265, 285; creation, 72, 174, 250–57; role in disarmament negotiations, 80–81, 83–84, 262, 264–69 *passim*, 295–98 *passim*
Norway, 97, 250, 265
NPT, *see* Non-Proliferation Treaty (NPT)
Nuclear deterrence, strategic doctrine of, 126–32, 141–44, 160, 203, 256–58, 312
Nuclear free zones, 249, 252, 292–95
Nuclear proliferation, control of, 288–309
Nuclear weapons, 1, 46–48, 66–72, 124–26; effect, 48–54, 134; technology, 64–65
Nuremberg trials, 18

Oder-Neisse line, 251, 260f
Oman, 272
Organization of American States (OAS), 286
Ostpolitik, 259–63 *passim*, 270
Outer Space Treaty (1967), 81, 87f, 97–99

Pacifist tradition, 10, 13, 23
Pakistan, 279, 282, 284, 302–4, 302
Palmerston, Lord, 33
Pardo, Arvid, 99
Paris peace talks (1968–73), 174, 285
Paris Treaty (1954), 251
Pastore, Sen. John, 115
Pastore Resolution, 297
"Peaceful nuclear explosives" (PNEs), 113–16, 293f, 298, 300, 303, 309
Peru, 286
Poland, 38, 251, 261, 265, 267

Polaris missiles, 55, 129, 258
Politics, domestic, arms control and, 6, 152–63, 222–23, 214–18
Politics, international, arms control and, 5–6
Pompidou, Georges, 260
Portugal, 250, 291
Poseidon missiles, 56f, 64, 136, 177
Precision-guided munition (PGM), 272f, 280
Preventive arms control, 28
Prisoners of war, 17
Puerto Rico, 294
Pugwash conferences, 317
Punte del Este Summit Declaration (1967), 286

Quakers, 10
Quemoy, 126

Radar systems, 60, 127, 198
Radiation damage, 49–50, 53–54, 134
Ramsey, Dr. Paul, 130–31
Rand Corporation, 103
Rapacki Plan, 252
Reactors, nuclear, sale of, 307
Realpolitik tradition of international relations, 12–15
Regime-oriented treaties, 96–101
Regional arms control, 249–70, 292–95
Religion, international law and, 15–16
Research and development (R&D), military, 231, 235f, 238, 239–40
Response, verification distinguished from, 164
Revised "Hot Line" Agreement (1971) (SALT I), 193, 197–98
Rhodesia, 284
Robles, García, 293
Rota, Spain, 183
Rumania, 263, 265, 298, 301
Rush-Bagot Agreement, 232
Rusk, Dean, 29–30, 297f
Russia, 33–34, 38, 347. *See also* Soviet Union

Safeguard ABM system, 59f, 64, 133, 178, 191f, 245; proposed sites, 185, 191, 194
Saint-Germain, Treaty of, 38
Sakharov, Andrei, 316ff
SALT, *see* Strategic Arms Limitation Talks

San Clemente declaration (1973), 260, 306
San Francisco, Calif., 67, 142, 175
Satellites, 95, 128–29, 146, 174–75, 200
Saudi Arabia, 243, 302
SCC, 200, 205, 219
Scheel, Walter, 261
Schlesinger, Arthur M., Jr., 106
Schlesinger, James, 6, 143, 147, 155, 213, 218, 221f
Schröder, Gerhard, 259
Seabed Arms Control Treaty (1971), 89–90, 99–101
Seismic detection, 103–5, 112–13, 115
Sentinel ABM system, 59–60, 175, 178
Sino-Soviet relations, 86, 108, 186–87
Skybolt program, 258, 260
SLBMs, *see* Submarine-launched ballistic missiles
Smith, Gerald, 180, 192, 210
Solzhenitsyn, Aleksandr, 317
South Africa, Republic of, 97, 284, 291, 298, 302, 307
Soviet Union, 2, 20–21, 28, 39–40, 51–52, 154, 249–50, 305, 314–18; strategic doctrines, 2–3, 125–29, 142, 174; and arms control negotiations in 1950's and 1960's, 3–4, 73–82 *passim*, 84–85, 87–88, 92–93, 161–63, 171; and SALT I negotiations, 6, 88–89, 173–74, 176, 178, 180–97 *passim*, 202–7; weapons systems, 7, 56–59, 89, 125f, 136, 141, 172, 179 table, 181, 273; military expenditures, 25–26, 231, 233 fig., 235–36, 242–43, 247–48; and ABM system, 58–59, 89, 132–33, 136, 172–74, 184, 187–89, 191–93; and international control of atomic energy, 70f, 82; China and, 86, 108, 145–47, 186–87, 193–94; and chemical-biological warfare, 91, 116, 120; and regime-oriented treaties, 94–101; and LTB negotiations, 102–8, 113–16; and PNEs, 113–14, 309; and SALT II negotiations, 217, 219, 222; and European security, 251–53, 264f, 267f, 270, 273; arms sales, 274 fig., 275–79 *passim*, 283f; and NPT, 290f, 295–303
Spartan missiles, 60
Sprint missiles, 60
Sputnik, 81–82, 127
SS-9s (Soviet missiles), 56, 138, 182f, 189, 194, 200
SS-11s, 56, 196, 200

SS-18s, 57, 217
Stalin, Joseph, 71
"Stand-off" missiles, 57
Standing Consultation Commission (SCC), 200, 205, 219
Stassen, Harold, 76f, 80f, 92, 156
Stevenson, Adlai, 78
Stimson, Henry, 68–69, 289
Stockholm, Sweden, 74, 95
Stoph, Willi, 261
Strategic Arms Limitation Talks, 3, 4, 6, 26, 60, 63, 132, 223–27; motivation for, 26–29
—SALT I, 56, 138, 141, 156, 158, 170–79; origin, 88–89; agreements, 89, 95, 167, 193, 197–98, 207, 312, 314f; and U.S. elections, 159–60; session-by-session negotiations, 179–97; third-party reactions, 205–7; U.S. ratification, 208–10; economic consequences, 244
—SALT II: issues, 210–16; Nixon phase, 216–19; agreements, 218–19; Ford phase and Vladivostok, 219–23
—SALT III, 223
Strategic bombing, *see* Bombers, strategic long-range
Strategic doctrines, 123–50. *See also specific doctrines*
Strategic forces and weapons, 46–65; Soviet Union, 172f, 179 table; U.S., 172f, 173, 178, 179 table; defined, 180–81, 183; arms control limits on, 182–83, 200–202, 211–12, 219–23; French, 256–58
Strontium 90, 50–51, 102
Subcommittee for Disarmament (London Subcommittee), 74–81, 83, 102, 281
Submarine-launched ballistic missiles (SLBMs), 55ff, 64, 128; U.S., 55f, 172f, 176, 179 table, 186; Soviet, 56f, 87, 172f, 176, 179 table, 195–96, 197; MIRVed, 186; in SALT I, 189–90, 194–97, 201, 203–4; in SALT II, 211–12, 214–16, 219–23
Submarines, 14, 17; missile-launching, 55f, 101, 183f, 189–90, 196, 203, 208, 257, 259, 278; limitation of, 201, 214–16
Suez war (1956), 15, 255
Sukarno, 279
Sweden, 90, 155, 285, 300, 302
Switzerland, 301

Taiwan, 307
Tanaka, Kakuei, 306
Tangiers, Morocco, 95
Tanks, 272, 276
Taunton, Mass., 245
Tear gas, 118
Technology, arms control and, 7, 34–36, 64–65, 272–75
Ten-Nation Disarmament Committee, 83–84
Territorial waters, defined, 101
Test ban discussions, 78f, 86, 91, 101–8, 115–16; test moratorium, 61, 103. *See also* Limited Nuclear Test Ban Treaty
Thor missiles, 54
Threshold Test Ban Treaty (1974), 91, 115–16, 218–19
Throw weight, 56–57, 213
Tirpitz, Alfred von, 34, 35–36
Titan missiles, 54f, 129
Tlatelolco, Treaty of (1967), 88, 293
Tokyo, 14, 18
Trident submarines, 64, 203, 208, 217, 226
Trinidad and Tobago, 293, 295
Truman Doctrine, 72, 124
Truman, Pres. Harry S, 68–71, 250
Turkey, 38, 54, 250, 265, 282

Underground testing, 86, 89f, 111
United Nations, 101, 120, 261; Atomic Energy Commission, 2, 70f, 73; General Assembly, 2, 20–21, 78, 82, 87, 98f; principles, 15, 20f, 67, 123–24; Security Council, 20, 71f, 119f; and disarmament, 67, 73–81, 91–92, 102, 120, 161–63, 248, 282–83, 290–91, 293, 295–96, 300–301, 318–19, 321; arms embargo, 284
United States of America, 6, 10, 20–21, 51–52, 52 fig., 62, 101–2, 138, 155, 247, 249–50, 306–7, 314–19; strategic doctrines, 2ff, 124–29, 137–38, 142–44; and arms control negotiations in 1950's and 1960's, 3–4, 20–21, 68–87 *passim*, 92–93, 161–71; China policy, 6, 114, 147, 193–94, 206; and SALT I negotiations, 6, 165–66, 177, 178–97 *passim*, 202–7, 208–10; weapons systems, 7, 54–64, 127, 132–33, 136–41, 172, 175, 177, 179, 203, 208, 213; Congress, role of, in arms control and military policy, 15, 61, 108–9, 111, 120, 153, 157–61, 170, 173, 176, 178,

185, 208–10, 222, 226, 281–82, 289–91, 296–97; and pre–World War II arms control, 17f, 32, 39–41; military procurement, 25–26, 61–64, 151, 231–35, 237–43; and ABM system, 58–60, 132–33, 135–38, 173, 175ff, 178, 182–85, 187–88, 191–93, 195–97, 200, 208, 218–19; Dept. of Defense role in military procurement and arms control, 61f, 137, 155–57, 231, 234; Presidency, and arms control, 61f, 153–61 *passim*; Joint Chiefs of Staff, role in military procurement and arms control, 62, 111, 153, 155; and NPT, 88, 295–302; and chemical-biological warfare, 90, 116–18, 120; and regime-oriented treaties, 94–101; and LTB Treaty, 101–8, 113–14; and PNEs, 113–14, 309; and European security, 124, 250–69 *passim*, 296–97; MIRVs, 136–41, 177, 213, 217; domestic pressure and arms control negotiations, 151–71, 314–19; and FBSs, 180–81, 183, 201; and SALT II, 216–19, 222–23; arms sales, 274 fig., 275–85 *passim*. *See also specific presidents by name*
Uranium, 291
U-2 reconnaissance flights, 106, 169–70

V-2 attacks, 14
Vandenberg Air Force Base, 59
Vatican II, 130
Venezuela, 286
Verification Panel, 156–57, 178
Verification procedures, 100–101, 121–22, 139–40, 141, 163–71, 202, 221, 268; distinguished from inspection and response, 164; by satellite, 174–75, 200; in SALT II negotiations, 221, 223; for NPT, 299–300, 302–3
Versailles, Treaty of, 38, 45, 117
Vienna, Austria, 179, 181–87, 187–89, 193–94
Vietnam war, 29, 118, 232ff, 272, 285; effect on arms control negotiations, 88, 159, 174
Virgin Islands, 294
Vladivostok summit (1974), 4, 89, 141, 219–21, 224

War: ethics of, 9–15; law of, 15–18; in U.N. Charter, 21; type of, and arms

sales, 280–81; prevented by arms
    control, 311–14
War of 1812, 17, 32
Warheads, 57 table, 58
Warsaw Pact, 83–84, 231, 251–52, 262–
    63, 265, 267–68
Washington, D.C., ABM site for, 184–
    85, 187, 199
Washington Disarmament Conference
    (1922), 44, 117, 154, 314f
Watergate crisis, effect on SALT II, 89,
    92–93, 217–19
Weisner, Jerome, 152, 156
Westphalia, Treaty of (1648), 16, 31

Wheeler, Gen. Earle, 175
Wilhelm II, Emperor, 35f
Wilson, Harold, 259
Wilson, Woodrow, 40
Woods Hole, Mass., 115
World Conference of Non-Nuclear
    Nations, 298
World Disarmament Conference (1932),
    38, 39–40, 44, 91–92, 248
World War I, 5, 14, 116–17, 311
World War II, 5–6, 117–18, 311

Yellow River, 146
Yemen, 118